SOUTH CAROLINA IN THE CIVIL WAR AND RECONSTRUCTION ERAS

SOUTH CAROLINA IN THE CIVIL WAR AND RECONSTRUCTION ERAS

Essays from the *Proceedings of the South Carolina Historical Association*

Edited by
Michael Brem Bonner and Fritz Hamer

The University of South Carolina Press

© 2016 University of South Carolina

Published by the University of South Carolina Press
Columbia, South Carolina 29208

www.sc.edu/uscpress

Manufactured in the United States of America

24 23 22 21 20 19 18 17 16
10 9 8 7 6 5 4 3 2 1

Library of Congress Cataloging-in-Publication Data
can be found at http://catalog.loc.gov/.

ISBN: 978-61117-664-3 (cloth)
ISBN: 978-61117-665-0 (paperback)
ISBN: 978-1-61117-666-7 (ebook)

CONTENTS

Editors' Note vii
Acknowledgments ix

Introduction 1

The Politics of Secession and Civil War

The Age of Lincoln: Then and Now (2010) 11
Orville Vernon Burton

Francis W. Pickens and the War Begins (1970) 27
John B. Edmunds Jr.

Attorney General Isaac W. Hayne and the
South Carolina Executive Council of 1862 (1952) 36
Lowry P. Ware

William L. Yancey and the League of United Southerners (1946) 43
Austin L. Venable

William W. Boyce: A Leader of the Southern Peace Movement (1978) 53
Roger P. Leemhuis

On the Battlefront

The Bombardment of Charleston, 1863–1864:
Union General Quincy Gillmore, the Targeting
of Civilians, and the Ethics of Modern War (2004) 67
Christopher A. Mekow

Dalton and the Rebirth of the Army of Tennessee (2002) 79
Louis B. Towles

On the Home Front

The South Carolina Ordnance Board, 1860–1861 (1945) 95
Frank Vandiver

The Work of Soldiers' Aid Societies in
South Carolina during the Civil War (1938) 104
James Welch Patton

Dissatisfaction and Desertion in
Greenville District, South Carolina, 1860–1865 (2001) 114
Aaron W. Marrs

The Problem of Relief for the Families of
   Confederate Soldiers in South Carolina (1994). 126
   Patricia Dora Bonnin

Emancipation, Race, and Society

Fateful Legacy: White Southerners
   and the Dilemma of Emancipation (1977) 137
   Dan T. Carter

The Freedmen's Bureau and Its Carolina Critics (1962) 152
   Martin Abbott

Edgefield Reconstruction: Political Black Leaders (1988) 161
   Orville Vernon Burton

The New Regime: Race, Politics, and Police in
   Reconstruction Charleston, 1865–1875 (1994) 173
   Laylon Wayne Jordan

A Reconsideration: The University of
   South Carolina during Reconstruction (1974) 184
   John Herbert Roper

The Politics of Reconstruction

Wade Hampton and the Rise of One-Party
   Racial Orthodoxy in South Carolina (1977) 197
   Richard Mark Gergel

The South Carolina Constitution of
   1865 as a Democratic Document (1942) 209
   John Harold Wolfe

Andrew Johnson: The Second Swing 'Round the Circle (1966) 221
   Robert J. Moore

Righteous Lives: A Comparative Study of the
   South Carolina Scalawag Leadership during Reconstruction (2003) . . . 230
   Lewie Reece

Wade Hampton: Conflicted Leader of the
   Conservative Democracy? (2007) 240
   Fritz Hamer

Governor Chamberlain and the End of Reconstruction (1977) 254
   Robert J. Moore

No Tears of Penitence: Religion, Gender, and the
   Aesthetic of the Lost Cause in the 1876 Hampton Campaign (2001) . . . 265
   W. Scott Poole

Contributors 273
Index 277

EDITORS' NOTE

Throughout the process of preparing this collection of outstanding articles, we have learned a great deal about editing and the technology used to assist in this endeavor. We do not consider ourselves to be experts at editing procedures and confess to have been completely unaware of the optical character recognition (OCR) process before we embarked upon this project. We worked hard to improve antiquated usages in the articles like a variety of formatting styles and different citation methods by updating then into a more uniform and up-to-date format. This was no easy task. There was a widespread problem with partial notations in the original articles. We attempted to track down all the original source materials and were successful in many cases, but some of the full citations remained elusive, despite our best efforts. For this we apologize, but the problem demonstrates the importance of consistent editing in the historical profession and the vital role of source citation in providing future generations with the ability to dig deeper into individual works of scholarship. The articles contained mistakes which we tried to correct, but we also attempted not to impose any further errors into the material. We made our best effort to rehabilitate these articles, but we also take full responsibility for any remaining errors. We hope that the benefits of bringing this impressive collection of previously little-known scholarship to a wider audience will outweigh any detractive errors in the text.

Fritz Hamer
Michael Brem Bonner

ACKNOWLEDGMENTS

On the surface, editing projects such as this would seem straightforward. The reality is that many people are involved. As the editors we needed a way to transcribe these twenty-four articles from over eighty years of the *Proceedings* without having to retype each one. Today's technology is wonderful, but it required the skills and assistance of several people for us to find our way through the maze. Without cooperation from these individuals, this project would have been much harder, if not impossible. First we want to acknowledge the assistance of two colleagues at Thomas Cooper Library at the University of South Carolina. Elvin Boone, manager of Cooper Technology Lounge, led us to Bill Boland, of the Interlibrary Loan Department, who scanned all the articles. Next we are particularly indebted to William Schmidt, Jr., for converting all these scanned files to OCR text in order for us to format each article to standards that conformed to the University of South Carolina Press requirements. This step was crucial to the project, and each article took one to two hours to convert. Bill, as always, was very gracious in volunteering so much of his time in this process. We also want to thank University of South Carolina Press editor Alex Moore for his help throughout, providing guidance on press standards and reviewing each article for compatibility and consistency. Finally we also want to thank our colleagues at the South Carolina Historical Association for their enthusiastic support for the project. We trust that it will meet their expectations and that this volume will increase the visibility and readership of the organization in for the future.

INTRODUCTION

Events in South Carolina serve as historical bookends to the era between 1860 and 1877. Historians recognize South Carolina's centrality to the Civil War's beginning in 1861 and to the end of Reconstruction in 1877. The secession crisis of 1860–61 centered on fire-eating secessionists, many either in, or with direct links to, South Carolina. After Lincoln's election in 1860, national attention turned to South Carolina's secession on December 20 and then to the Fort Sumter crisis. Americans on both sides of the Mason-Dixon line anxiously watched the events that culminated in the bombardment of April 12, 1861. After this dramatic episode, Civil War events in South Carolina were overshadowed by the bloody battles and campaigns in the Eastern and Western theaters. To be sure, South Carolina witnessed its share of fighting at Port Royal, Charleston, and eventually the final reckoning with Sherman's March through the state in 1865, but most wartime attention was rightly focused elsewhere from 1862 to 1864.

Reconstruction in South Carolina also garnered national attention for several reasons. As Eric Foner points out, "only in South Carolina did blacks come to dominate the legislative process." African American political leaders "throughout Reconstruction . . . comprised a majority of the House of Representatives, controlled its key committees, and, beginning in 1872, elected black speakers. . . . [In 1874] blacks gained a majority in the state senate as well."[1] In addition to famous African American national political figures like congressmen Joseph H. Rainey and Robert Smalls, Reconstruction South Carolina secured public service from two lieutenant governors, a state treasurer, and two secretaries of state, among others—all of whom were African Americans.

The backlash against African American political control was widespread across the South but particularly extensive in regions of South Carolina. In 1870–71, South Carolina witnessed determined Ku Klux Klan activity, particularly in the northwestern counties of the state, which required President Grant to intervene. Ku Klux Klan trials were conducted by federal prosecutors, and the writ of habeas corpus was temporarily suspended in select counties. The Klan's mixture of political targeting and paramilitary tactics boded ill for the Republican state government and set the stage for the dramatic events of 1876–77.

Introduction

The nation's attention again turned to the Palmetto State in 1876 with regard to both the gubernatorial and presidential elections. Governor Daniel Chamberlain tried in vain to keep the Republican state government in control but could not overcome the personal popularity and threatening tactics of Wade Hampton and the Democratic Party. Many historians view this election as a watershed moment for South Carolina. The 1876 election portended the resumption of "home rule" by the state's whites and the demise of serious biracial political participation in South Carolina as well as the end of Reconstruction as a national policy objective of the Republican Party.

South Carolina history in the decades leading up to the Civil War has been much examined by late-twentieth-century scholars. To understand why the Palmetto State became a hotbed of political radicalism and secession, scholars have delved deeply into the social, economic, and political history of the state. Excellent book-length scholarly works like *Prelude to Civil War: The Nullification Controversy in South Carolina, 1816–1836* (1965) by William Freehling, *The Origins of Southern Radicalism: The South Carolina Upcountry, 1800–1860* (1988) by Lacy Ford, and *The Counterrevolution of Slavery: Politics and Ideology in Antebellum South Carolina* (2000) by Manisha Sinha are just a few examples of the attempts to satisfy the fascination that antebellum South Carolina holds for professional historians and general audiences alike.

Curiously enough, however, the amount of book-length scholarship devoted to South Carolina's wartime experience and Reconstruction has not generated a corresponding amount of synthetic scholarship over the past half-century. The dawn of a more objective approach to Reconstruction arrived with the still quotable *South Carolina during Reconstruction* (1932) by Francis Butler Simkins and Robert Henley Woody. And one of the most frequently cited books about the Civil War in the Palmetto State is still *South Carolina Goes to War, 1860–1865* (1950) by Charles Edward Cauthen. Both books represented the historiographical and ideological dogmas of their respective eras. Cauthen's book devoted over half of its pages to the secession crisis years of 1860 and 1861. Simkins and Woody's work exhibited a sharp break with the implicit racism and portrayal of white southerners as victims of Radical Republicans previously found in the William E. Dunning school of Reconstruction history. As noted by historian Peter Novick in *That Noble Dream: The "Objectivity Question" in the American Historical Profession* (1988), the work of Simkins and Woody "did not gloss over the intimidation and brutalizing of Negroes," and they argued that Reconstruction's "failure was a consequence of accepting the continuation of white domination."[2] Both works are fine pieces of scholarship and have stood the test of time in many respects, but they were written prior to the entry of social history into the academy and lack the contemporaneous influence of the twentieth-century civil rights movement.

Introduction

The history of South Carolina's Reconstruction has been comprehensively covered in a number of books, but rarely in a work solely devoted to the Palmetto State. For example, Eric Foner's masterpiece, *Reconstruction: America's Unfinished Revolution* (1988), effectively describes the major events and leaders in South Carolina, but only in the larger context of the period. A fine study that focused solely on the state is Richard Zuczek's *State of Rebellion: Reconstruction in South Carolina* (1996). Other state-specific studies tend to focus on specific topics. Among these contributions are *Black Over White* (1977) by Thomas Holt, *The Great South Carolina Ku Klux Klan Trials, 1871–1872* (1996) by Lou Falkner Williams, and *The Work of Reconstruction: From Slave to Wage Laborer in South Carolina, 1860–1870* (1996) by Julie Saville. In short, there remains a need for up-to-date monographic scholarship on the history of South Carolina in the Civil War and Reconstruction eras.

Despite the relative lack of monographs, scholars have utilized scholarly periodicals to copious and innovative ends. They have written numerous valuable articles about South Carolina's experience in the Civil War and Reconstruction in the *Proceedings of the South Carolina Historical Association*. Since 1931 the South Carolina Historical Association (SCHA) has sponsored an annual conference and published a select group of papers in the association's journal, the *Proceedings*. Over the course of eight decades, the SCHA has accumulated a great amount of scholarly material on a wide variety of topics, and naturally many of these articles were about these eras. Preeminent scholars such as Frank Vandiver, Dan Carter, and Orville Burton are among the authors who have contributed article-length studies. The number and breadth of topics suggest that a new synthesis of South Carolina history from 1861 to 1877 is indeed possible, and this anthology of the best essays of the SCHA serves as an excellent starting point. All articles published after 2002 from the *Proceedings* are available on the SCHA website, but this volume offers, for the first time, easy access to the journal's best articles on the Civil War and Reconstruction up through 2001. This anthology, written by well-respected historians over the past seventy-five years, should reinvigorate interest in a new historical synthesis of these periods.

Given that the SCHA began publishing the *Proceedings* in 1931, three years before the founding of the Southern Historical Association, one might expect to find a great deal of Lost Cause interpretations of the Civil War and Dunning-school views of Reconstruction, but this is not the case. Readers might be pleasantly surprised by the objectivity and professionalism in the articles from the 1930s and 1940s. This welcome situation corresponded with the larger theme of "consensus" in the American historical profession throughout World War II and the early years of the Cold War.[3] The advent of the civil rights movement in the 1950s precipitated a shift toward varieties of social history which dealt primarily with issues of race, gender, and class conflict. As a result, articles in the

Proceedings began to approach Civil War and Reconstruction topics using more viewpoints and new methodologies to analyze the volatile nature of the eras. The pages of the *Proceedings* were certainly not filled with radical new approaches, but the SCHA and its journal began to symbolize the collapse of consensus in the 1960s and 1970s. Historian Peter Novick described the new professional historical landscape, noting that "most historians, to be sure, were not found at the extremes, but the center had lost its vitality."[4] Readers will find that the articles presented here have closely mirrored larger trends in the American historical profession from 1931 to 2016.

This compilation of historical articles is a treasure trove of accessible scholarship for students, professors, and general audiences. The variety of topics covered is impressive. Here one can find an essay about almost any aspect of Civil War and Reconstruction history. Since most of the articles are made readily available for the first time, this book is a must-have for serious historians of these eras. And a wide range of writing styles delivers the information. In many cases, historians—even the ones who manage to write well for general audiences—occasionally become long-winded and pummel their readers with hundreds of pages replete with mind-numbing amounts of anecdotal evidence. Even the most talented writers eventually tend to bore their audiences. These essays, however, have the benefit of brevity and alternating writing styles—some better than others, but definite varieties of style from one author to the next. Each contribution is also refreshingly brief. Over the decades, the SCHA has typically maintained the eight-to-ten-page maximum length for each article, although a few run over by several pages. This traditional restriction is a good way to deliver scholarly information succinctly and in formats that comport with the reading habits of twenty-first-century students. Due to its range of content and styles, this collection makes an excellent text for graduate and advanced undergraduate courses in historiography or historical methodology.

The book is divided by topic into several subsections. In the "The Politics of Secession and Civil War," several pieces stimulate thought on many of the era's leading political figures and their respective policies. Orville Vernon Burton embarks upon a complete rethinking of Lincoln's presidency and its importance in popular memory. Burton implements five major themes to delve into controversial topics about Lincoln's central role in American history. This thought-provoking foray into the history of America's sixteenth president forces readers to reconsider many long-held beliefs about our nation's most beloved leader and was the genesis of Burton's book-length study, *The Age of Lincoln* (2007). John Edmunds Jr. tells the fascinating story of South Carolina's secession governor, Francis W. Pickens. Absent from the state during his diplomatic mission to Russia in the late antebellum period, Pickens deftly adjusted to the

Introduction

pulse of secession in 1860 and guided the state through tense negotiations with the federal government. Pickens's decisions precipitated the showdown over Fort Sumter that eventually sparked the war. Lowry P. Ware describes the political career of Isaac W. Hayne and his leadership in the Executive Council that governed South Carolina in 1862. Hayne was one of five members who assumed power to prosecute the war, presumably in a more efficient manner than the governor and state assembly. Hayne and the Executive Council symbolize the willingness of devoted secessionists to bend their states' rights principles and to centralize authority in an attempt to win the war. Austin L. Venable provides a revisionist view of the famous fire-eater William Lowndes Yancey and his role in the League of United Southerners during the 1860 election cycle. Yancey was one of the most outspoken secessionists, and his rhetoric and actions are carefully scrutinized with respect to his constitutional beliefs. Roger P. Leemhuis highlights the political career of conservative William W. Boyce, who navigated the complicated political eras of the 1850s and 1860s in South Carolina politics. As a Confederate congressman, Boyce became a leading voice in the Confederate peace movement, and he eventually advocated steps toward equality in the postwar South.

In the section devoted to Civil War military experiences, "On the Battlefront," two authors describe the effects of war on soldiers and civilians. Christopher A. Mekow indicts the Union's General Gillmore for breaching accepted ethical standards of war by bombarding civilians in Charleston from August 1863 to February 1865. Gillmore's reason for targeting civilians forces historians to reassess the Union's policy of total war. Louis B. Towles explores the methods used to rehabilitate the demoralized Army of Tennessee after its disastrous collapse at Missionary Ridge in November 1863. In addition to finding a new leader, the main Rebel army in the Western Theater required improved policies and more material resources. Towles gets to the heart of the Confederacy's capability of fielding an army in early 1864, and thus highlights the incapability only one year later.

Several historians investigate the people and institutions of southern society at war. In "On the Home Front," Frank Vandiver discusses the extensive war preparations in the Palmetto State between December 1860 and April 1861. The South Carolina Ordnance Board hurriedly scraped together a solid foundation of war materiel eventually used by the Confederacy. James Welch Patton details the collective efforts of southern women to support the war effort. The widespread creation of Soldier's Aid Societies was important not only for the supply and comfort of troops, but also as the symbol of increased participation by women in Confederate society. Aaron W. Marrs investigates war weariness in the northwest corner of South Carolina. In this detailed local study, four categories of complaint are analyzed as the cause of anti-Confederate sentiment and rampant desertion in the Greenville area. Patricia D. Bonin analyzes the motivations and elucidates the distribution of government relief in Edgefield District. The author then extrapolates the gendered nature and social significance of the relief system as a statewide policy.

In the section "Emancipation, Race, and Society," Dan T. Carter addresses the impact of Emancipation on the South in the early stages of Reconstruction. Carter poses core questions about the nature of southern history, such as: "Why did southerners make such a horrendous miscalculation for the second time in five years?" and "What drove them to their own political self-destruction?" Martin Abbott reexamines the complaints against the Freedmen's Bureau by opponents of the Republican Reconstruction governments. In a detailed analysis of land redistribution, labor relations, and education, Abbott points out a major paradox in the nature of this widespread criticism. Orville Vernon Burton profiles the lives and political careers of black political leaders from Edgefield District. Common elements of military experience, literacy, business experience, and pride provided a solid foundation for rising black politicians. Laylon Wayne Jordan analyzes the integration of Charleston's police force and its ramifications on crime, party politics, and urban society during Reconstruction. John Herbert Roper tells the fascinating story of an institution of higher education in transition from the Old South into Reconstruction. Roper focuses on African American professors and leaders like Richard Greener, who trained a small, but influential, cadre of young black students who eventually assumed important positions in the New South.

In "The Politics of Reconstruction," several essays investigate the contentious end of Reconstruction in South Carolina. Richard M. Gergel discusses the pivotal role Wade Hampton played in the dual strategy of winning statewide elections in 1876. Hampton successfully deflected northern criticism of statewide Democratic tactics on the path to one-party rule. John Harold Wolfe looks at the relatively democratic features of South Carolina's 1865 constitution when compared to the antebellum document. Often overshadowed by the 1868 constitution, the postwar constitution took significant steps away from the Old South political order in the Palmetto State. Robert J. Moore provides a detailed historiography of Andrew Johnson, looking back on one hundred years of scholarship and interpretations of the controversial Reconstruction president. Lewie Reece profiles the lives and political careers of four influential but little-known "scalawags" in South Carolina. Alexander Wallace, Simeon Corley, Edmund Mackey, and Samuel Melton each played important roles in South Carolina's Republican state government during Reconstruction and maintained their advocacy for African American equality after 1877. Fritz Hamer details the political career of Wade Hampton to determine whether his rhetoric of racial inclusion in 1876 was genuine or merely an expedient deception. Hampton's motives form the basis of a fascinating study of party politics at the state and national levels. Hamer tests whether the personality and prestige of political leaders can overcome the negative aspects of electoral culture. In his second contribution, Robert J. Moore tells the tragic story of Republican Governor Daniel Chamberlain, who was ousted from office after the 1876 elections. Chamberlain hoped for support from the national party but waited in vain as disputed President-elect Rutherford B. Hayes distanced the Republican Party from southern conflicts. W. Scott Poole examines the social culture of "Hampton Days" during the 1876 election. Symbols of race, gender, and the "Lost Cause" played prominent roles in defining the meaning of the 1876 election for South Carolinians.

The articles in this anthology should contribute to a new synthesis about the Palmetto State's experience during Civil War and Reconstruction. In addition, this collection offers a brief study of professional history in South Carolina from 1931 to 2014. Preparing these excellent essays, some of them long-forgotten or inaccessible, for a wider reading audience has been both tedious and joyous. This book is dedicated to all the members—past and present—of the South Carolina Historical Association who have contributed to the organization's eighty-five years of continual existence. Let us strive to pass this legacy on to future generations of historians in hopes that we can extend the life of our organization for another eighty-five years!

NOTES

1. Eric Foner, *Reconstruction: America's Unfinished Revolution* (New York: Harper & Row, 1988), 354.

2. Peter Novick, *That Noble Dream: The "Objectivity Question" and the American Historical Profession* (Cambridge, U.K.: Cambridge University Press, 1988), 232–33.

3. For a more detailed look at the idea of consensus history, see Novick, *That Noble Dream*, chapters 10, "The Defense of the West," and 11, "A Convergent Culture," 281–360.

4. Novick, *That Noble Dream*, 417.

THE POLITICS OF SECESSION AND CIVIL WAR

THE AGE OF LINCOLN
Then and Now
(2010)

Orville Vernon Burton

You are forewarned that you are listening to the interpretation of an academic whose judgment led him to study the American South and teach at the University of Illinois for thirty-four years, became a Lincoln scholar, and now teaches at Coastal Carolina University in South Carolina.

Before talking about my book, *The Age of Lincoln,* I would like to suggest you take a look at a website (TheAgeofLincoln.com) where I have tried marrying the Internet with the book, providing more extensive notes and discussions. The website also has Internet links to many of the sources in the notes. I was inspired to include the primary documents upon which *The Age of Lincoln*'s interpretation is based when Dr. James McPherson, my thesis advisor (who was, as usual, gracious enough to read the manuscript), questioned me on my interpretation of Jefferson Davis's response to the assassination of Abraham Lincoln. I argue very differently than most historians who make the case that Jefferson Davis expressed regret about Lincoln's assassination. In my response to Jim McPherson, I photocopied the testimony of Lewis F. Bates, at whose home in Charlotte, North Carolina, Davis was staying on April 19 when he learned of Booth's success. Bates testified in May 1865 at the trial of the Lincoln murder conspirators that Davis loosely quoted from Shakespeare's *Macbeth,* "if it were to be done at all, it were better that it were well done"—meaning that the conspirators should have completed their goal of also killing Vice-President Andrew Johnson, Secretary of State William Seward, and War Secretary Edwin Stanton. Since Jim had not seen this testimony, I decided to put all sources that were available in the public domain on the website. TheAgeofLincoln.com contains excerpts from the book, extensive documentation, historiographical discussions, explorations of where I agree and disagree with other historians, sources, a discussion board, instruction regarding how to email me, and the assurance that I will respond! I want the website to be useful to teachers so that they can help students learn historical thinking, particularly how historians, or at least one historian, frames historical problems, how historians use evidence, and how historians produce a historical narrative. I hope the website makes this process as transparent as possible. I also have hopes that the website will engage an expanding generation of younger folks at home on the Internet. Perhaps it will stimulate interest in learning the joys of reading a book.

Already Lincoln is the most written-about American and, on the world scene, is behind only Jesus and Shakespeare; if the number of books I have been asked to review on Lincoln in the last two years is an indication, Shakespeare has concern for his second-place ranking. Thus, I am often asked, what is different about my book? *The Age of Lincoln* is comprehensive and interpretive, and I cannot cover everything. But I thought you might enjoy hearing about five topics where I have made what are either new arguments or done something different than most scholars of the Civil War era. Thus, while I will not be able to develop these areas in any detail, I hope it will give you something to think about. And I would like to conclude with some remarks relevant to race and today.

First, I was interested in Lincoln's legacy, and in an answer to a question, I will rephrase from one of President Bill Clinton's more infamous lines. Rather than worrying what the meaning of "is" is, I am interested in what the meaning of "us" is. Lincoln is about us, who we are. In the April 13, 2009, edition of *Newsweek,* editor Jon Meacham argued that Americans "value individual freedom and free (or largely free) enterprise. . . . The foundational documents are the Declaration of Independence and the Constitution." Without acknowledging it, Meacham was explaining why Americans will always be interested in Lincoln.

Lincoln proclaimed early in 1865 that the Emancipation Proclamation was "the central act of my administration and the great event of the nineteenth century." But I disagree. Instead it was Lincoln's understanding of liberty that became the greatest legacy of the age. He revolutionized personal freedom in the United States. He assured that the principle of personal liberty was protected by law, even incorporated into the Constitution. Thus Lincoln elevated the Founding Fathers' (and Andrew Jackson's) more restricted vision to a universal one. Basically, Lincoln inserted our mission statement, the Declaration of Independence, into our rule book, the Constitution of the United States.

Liberty and freedom are the interpretative centerpiece, the theses of *The Age of Lincoln*. Told as a story of freedoms and liberty rather than of the enslaved's emancipation, the nineteenth century makes greater sense. If we place Emancipation as one point on a long continuum of freedoms and unfreedom, we can see where Emancipation fits without the right to a meaningful vote. A meaningful vote helps define citizenship and belonging in a democracy, and it did in the young republic in 1793, 1865 and 1867, 1895, 1965, and today.

In *Liberty and Freedom,* David Hackett Fischer found five hundred ideas (not definitions, but ideas) of liberty and freedom. His book includes a section of nearly two hundred pages on many different ideas of liberty and freedom in the era of the Civil War—differences by region, ethnicity, religion, race, class, gender, age, and generation. Thus, both Union and Confederate soldiers understood the war as a war about freedom and liberty, but they defined those terms differently. What freedom meant to an enslaved person on a plantation in South Carolina was, of course, quite different from what freedom meant for the slaveholder, or for an overseer. But freedom was also different for a young woman or twelve-year-old boy working in a shoe factory sewing the soles on shoes in the Northeast or for a yeoman farmer in Mississippi or Indiana. Lincoln often spoke about the differences between two antagonistic groups who "declare for liberty." Some, he said, used the word "liberty" to mean that each man could "do as he pleases with himself, and the product of his labor." Others held the word liberty to mean "some men to do as they please with other men, and the product of other men's labor." He proffered a parable to nail the point. "The shepherd drives the wolf from the sheep's throat," he said, "for which the sheep thanks the shepherd as a liberator, while the wolf denounces him for the same act as a destroyer of liberty, especially as the sheep is a black one."

Second, the development of liberty and democracy has to be understood in the context of the growth of capitalism and what unrestrained capitalism and extremes of wealth meant for tenuous democracy in the emerging republic. I had taught Harriet Beecher Stowe's *Uncle Tom's Cabin* for nearly thirty years, and when I reread it while writing *The Age of Lincoln,* I realized that *Uncle Tom's Cabin* was not just an indictment of slavery, but was also an indictment of greed within a growing system of American capitalism. (Stowe was not an abolitionist, but, like Lincoln, was a colonizationist.) Intellectuals expressed great anxiety over unbridled capitalism, especially over the resultant increasing wealth of a few. The growing disparity in wealth made some wonder if the young republic founded on principles of equality and liberty, however imperfectly implemented, could survive. Increased immigration of different sorts of people, many not evangelical Protestants, most of whom worked for wages and were not property owners, was another concern. The pursuit of mammon at the expense of all else became a major theme of the literature and a concern of intellectuals. They worried that pursuit of wealth would come at the expense of a virtuous citizenship and concern for country. In 1852 Wendell Phillips addressed a Massachusetts antislavery society: "Eternal vigilance is the price of liberty—power is ever stealing from the many to the few. . . . only by unintermitted agitation can a people be kept sufficiently awake to principle not to let liberty be smothered in material prosperity." Would the expansion of the electorate to include the propertyless and those beholden to others for their income destroy the republic? Certainly major world powers, all monarchies, wanted the United States to fail.

Third, I center religion in *The Age of Lincoln*. I argue that Lincoln was not only the greatest president, but also the greatest theologian of the nineteenth century. In order to understand secession, and to understand how men thought about dying in the Civil War, and women thought about sending their men off to die, as well as to understand the nineteenth century, one has to understand how religion was interwoven into the culture and thinking.

The Age of Lincoln opens with the Gettysburg Address, Lincoln's benediction. The first chapter begins with Baptist minister William Miller on October 22, 1844. The Millerites fully expected the return of Jesus Christ to earth that day. But when Jesus did not come, they went back into society and with a different kind of faith tried to make the United States into God's Kingdom to help bring on the millennium. Evangelist, abolitionist, and president of Oberlin College, Charles Grandison Finney argued that the "great business of the church is to reform the world—to put away every kind of sin." Christians, he believed, were "bound to exert their influence to secure a legislation that is in accordance with the law of God." The Age of Lincoln was a time of millennialism: the radical belief that Americans, God's chosen people, could expedite the reign of Christ on earth by living piously and remaking society according to God's will.

Just as today, in the nineteenth century religious fanaticism in both North and South strongly influenced events. In order to perfect the society of the United States, reformers attacked various evils that they saw: temperance societies attacked alcohol consumption, women demanded rights, prison and school reforms. Utopian societies endorsing no sex, or lots of sex, or simply eating Graham crackers splattered across the United States like a shotgun pattern as reformers strove to eradicate evil. But eventually, most reform efforts in the North lined up to declare slavery as the single greatest evil in the country. Abolitionism, while still a small minority position in the North, rose to prominence in the late 1850s. Many northerners believed if the United States was to be a society ordained by God, and was to become the utopia that would bring on the millennium, the evil of slavery had to be eradicated.

Reform movements, except for abolitionism, were also active, though much less so, in the South. And many slave owners believed that patriarchal plantation society, such as they imagined ("imagined" is the key word) the South to be, based on slavery with its ordered hierarchy, was the utopia and ordained by God. They argued that slavery was fit not just for the South, not just for African Americans, but for all societies and all workers. And thus slavery would help bring on the millennium.

Religious fanatics, both North and South, were sure they understood God's will, and all thought they were obeying it. If you think you are doing God's will, you are unwilling to compromise.

Lincoln had a very different understanding of God than most of his contemporaries. While everyone else knew God's will, Lincoln knew that we cannot understand God's will. Although he came to see himself as a part of God's plan for human history, he could not be certain what God's will was. Even with the outcome determined, Lincoln would still qualify, "If God now wills. . . ." Lincoln never proclaimed something God's will; it is always in the subjunctive, "If. . . ." This is even reflected in the great Second Inaugural Address about slavery and God's will. A similar sentence in the April 4, 1864, letter from Lincoln to Albert Hodges is one of the epigraphs for *The Age of Lincoln*: "If God now wills the removal of a great wrong, and wills also that we of the North as well as you of the South, shall pay fairly for our complicity in that wrong, impartial history will find therein new cause to attest and revere the justice and goodness of God."

Lincoln read the Bible in the Jewish tradition of reading the Old Testament, understanding God and people in a corporate sense, not the individual salvation of the dominant Protestant evangelicals grown out of the Second Great Awakening. Interestingly, this corporate understanding of God using his people to work out his will in history is also the African American theological perspective.

Thus while the Civil War caused a theological crisis for both white northerners and southerners, it did not for African Americans. The Civil War and the early developments of Reconstruction were the fulfilling of God's plan to free his people from slavery in the United States and to punish those pharaohs of the South. It all made sense from this theological perspective.

Fourth, I emphasize the importance of seeing Abraham Lincoln as the southerner he was, and how that influenced history and particularly the Civil War and then America itself. This is perhaps one of the most controversial arguments in the book. But I do feel good about one thing: this argument has helped reconcile northerners and Confederates. Yankees did not like that I said Lincoln was a southerner, and now I discover, neither do many white southerners! At last they have united to direct their anger toward me!

I have ready an hour's talk on Lincoln as a southerner, but very quickly let me cut to why this is important. Lincoln's southern habits went beyond turns of speech, food favorites, storytelling, literary references, preference for plump southern belles, or indulgent child-rearing practices. Critical to his life's decisions and to his handling of the crisis to come were Lincoln's understanding of and respect for southern honor. This projection of Lincoln as a southerner is more than a simple mind game; Lincoln's very yeoman southernness contributed to his defense of the Union against a cabal of slaveholding oligarchs. For Lincoln it was more than just the preservation of the Union. It was also a matter of honor. As he told a committee of the Young Men's Christian Association (April 22, 1861) from Baltimore trying to persuade him to let the South go, "You would have me break my oath and surrender the Government without a blow. There is no Washington in that—no Jackson in that—no manhood nor honor in that."

Although scholars have argued that Lincoln did not understand the South, he thought he knew the white South. He believed the South was very much more than just plantations, that there were many yeomen and non–slave-owning southerners like himself. He did not think non-slaveholding white southerners would fight for slavery. He has been criticized for this as historians point to the Civil War and say that Lincoln was wrong. But Lincoln defined the war as preserving the union, not about slavery. If he had defined the issue as one of slavery, he might very well have been right about white non-slaveholding southerners not fighting. But he also would not have been able to raise a corporal's guard from the North to fight to end slavery.

Finally, I have never accepted the separation of Reconstruction from the Civil War, or the traditional dating for the end of Reconstruction. We have bookended American history so that the Civil War closes out one era of our history and Reconstruction begins the next period or second half of American history. And yet, Reconstruction is part and parcel of the Civil War. I also disagree with the traditional timing of the end of Reconstruction. Historians usually argue that Reconstruction ends with the withdrawal of federal troops from the former Confederate states in 1877, but that is not how the people saw it or lived their lives at the time. Moreover, the gains of freedom during Reconstruction were not legally undone till sanctioned by the Supreme Court in *Plessy v. Ferguson* in 1896 and by the former Confederate state constitutions of the 1890s and early twentieth century. The Age of Lincoln coincides with a millennialist impulse in politics, one I see ending with the 1896 presidential third-party campaign of the Populists, the last political party to advocate for African American rights and equality based on Lincoln's rule of law until the modern civil rights movement.

At stake during the Civil War was the very existence of the United States. The bloodiest war in our history, the Civil War also posed in a crucial way what clearly became persistent themes in American history, the character of the nation, and the fate of African Americans (read large, the place of minorities and different sorts of people in a democracy, the very meaning of pluralism). Consequently, scholars have been vitally interested in the Civil War, searching out clues therein for the identity of America. But we may have been looking in the wrong place. If the identity of America is in the Civil War, the meaning of America and what we become and how we do things is found in Reconstruction.

It matters profoundly when a period of history is said to begin and end, a professional historian's truism particularly evident when discussing America's nineteenth century. To blend all the strands of nineteenth-century history and present it as a piece, *The Age of Lincoln* uses Abraham Lincoln as a fulcrum to put together the story of sectional conflict, Civil War, and Reconstruction. The formation of Lincoln's ideas before the Civil War, his leadership, and the development of his thinking during the Civil War and how those *ideas played out,* for good and bad in the years following the Civil War into our own modern America, sets the organization of this story.

The Civil War itself inspired both intense hatred and extraordinary idealism, especially in race relations. Nowhere is our lack of understanding of the importance of chronology so evident as in the four years of the Civil War itself. We have flattened out and compressed the Civil War, so that we distort the actual war and what happened, and how that influenced the postwar years. The very nature of the war itself changes in those dramatic four years. Our Civil War was anything but civil; it became a war of hatred. Initially few understood what the war would really become. Southerners were fond of boasting that they would drink all the blood spilled or mop it up with their handkerchief. The South talks a lot about blood, but not the North. Lincoln does refer to blood, but much more in religious terms of communion, and, of course, he is a southerner. Young men wanted to get in on the glory before the fighting was over. But as the war continued, with more deadly and horrible weaponry that made the Civil War the first modern war, and as more and more people died, became disfigured and psychologically scarred, the very nature of the war changed.

Especially from the South and from the Midwest, companies were composed from neighborhoods, communities, towns, and counties where brothers, uncles, cousins, best friends, fathers and sons fought side by side, making for great unit cohesion. But after the first years of the war, Confederate and Union soldiers write about how a brother or friend is killed by the enemy and their lust for revenge: "They killed my best friend and I can't wait to kill some of them!" The war becomes, as all wars are inevitably destined, a war of hatred.

Perhaps the most celebrated Civil War image is of "Happy Appomattox," where federal troops salute the immaculate Virginian Robert E. Lee or the Union forces under Little Roundtop hero and Maine's General Joshua Chamberlain salute Georgia's John B. Gordon and his men at the surrender of arms. While this is true, it is also true that other Union troops jeered and spit at Lee. And, of course, Lee had countermanded Jefferson Davis's orders to keep on fighting, to have the troops become guerrillas, and thus some Confederate leaders refused to surrender with Lee and led their troops out of Appomattox to continue the fight, which they did for more than a decade after the war ended. It was indeed a Civil War in the South where neighbor fought neighbor, whites against black and some white Republicans. The North called not only for the hanging of Jefferson Davis, but of Robert E. Lee as well. The war had become one of hatred, the only result of a sustained war with so much killing. Edmund Wilson in *Patriotic Gore* (1962) explained that we have a very thin veneer on civil societies and that war strips that veneer away.

Reconstruction has to be understood as part of the long Civil War. During Reconstruction, some former Confederate generals led terrorist groups manned with many former Confederate soldiers. But I also found men who were too young to fight in the Civil War, but who fought in these terrorist paramilitary groups even as late as 1876 and 1878 and even applied for their state's Confederate Civil War pensions. They understood their actions and Reconstruction to be part of the Civil War.

Yet it is important to remember that most whites in the South were not part of these counterrevolutionary terrorist organizations like the Ku Klux Klan, the most familiar. The tragedy was that most good people just did nothing and did not stand up for a bedrock of Lincoln's philosophy, that is, the rule of law. But that should not obscure just how many white southerners actually fought for the Union in the Civil War. One of my favorite illustrations in the book (you can view at the website) is titled "White Southerners Who Commanded Union Troops," with Lincoln in the center. The most radical of the generals is John C. Fremont, "The Pathfinder" who was the first Republican candidate for president. Fremont was born in Savannah, Georgia, reared in Charleston, South Carolina, graduated the College of Charleston. When you consider the number of white southerners who fought for the Union, every Confederate state except South Carolina had a regiment that fought for the Union; South Carolina Unionists joined North Carolina, Tennessee, and Georgia Union regiments. Together with the number of southern African Americans who fought for the Union, the numbers add up. And if one includes those cultural southerners from Kentucky, Missouri, southern Ohio, Indiana, and Illinois, one sees that there was a southern Civil War as the numbers begin to reach parity.

Although we are finally moving away from the *Gone with the Wind* and *Birth of a Nation* mythology about the antebellum period and slavery, in the popular culture the view of an overreaching and doomed Reconstruction still predominates. When in 1969 I studied the Civil War with Jim McPherson at Princeton, historians were not talking about contingency in the Civil War, and somehow the Confederacy was made more noble by having struggled against overwhelming odds in a war it could not have won. With Vietnam, that view has changed. Historians now grant contingency to the Civil War, arguing that there were moments and times that the Confederacy could have won.

For example, I open chapter 7, "A Giant Holocaust of Death," with Jefferson Davis's 1864 replacement of General Joe Johnston with John Bell Hood. Hood was incredibly brave, like Monty Python's knight in the *Holy Grail* who keeps getting cut to pieces, but keeps advancing. As Lee said, Hood was too much the lion and not enough the fox. I argue that Lincoln believed that he would have lost the 1864 election except for Sherman's taking Atlanta and subsequent March to the Sea, and we would have a different outcome on slavery and a different America. Johnston, like Longstreet, understood that one made the enemy come to them. When Sherman faced Johnston after a disastrous frontal attack, he began flanking movements. As one Illinois soldier wrote, "Sherman will never go to hell, he will outflank the devil yet." But Hood, for his part, took the offense, and Atlanta was lost.

I am often asked what would have happened if Lincoln had not been killed. My personal favorite example of contingency is Civil War hero Robert Smalls (one of many persons whose stories I follow throughout the book). In 1862 Lincoln met for over an hour with Smalls, and he asked Smalls why he risked his life to steal the vessel *The Planter* from the Confederacy in Charleston Harbor and deliver it to the Union. Small's one-word answer was "freedom," which dovetailed with Lincoln's own new birth of freedom as he would express it the next year in his Gettysburg Address. Robert Smalls campaigned for Lincoln's reelection in 1864 and greatly admired and respected the president. Smalls was one of several African Americans whom Lincoln had met while he was president and who helped Lincoln advance in his thinking regarding race.

When Abraham Lincoln was invited to participate in raising the United States flag over Fort Sumter, April 14, 1865, four years to the day the flag had been struck, he was advised and convinced that it would be too dangerous for him to travel to South Carolina. Ironically, Lincoln would have been on *The Planter* with Robert Smalls. I am convinced that because Smalls and bodyguards would have been protective of the president in South Carolina, Lincoln would not have been killed on April 14 if he had been at Fort Sumter instead of at Ford's Theater. When Robert Smalls heard the news of Booth's assassination of Lincoln, the former slave exclaimed, "Lord have mercy on us all."

Historians have not been willing to grant contingency to the story of Reconstruction. My interpretation of Reconstruction highlights its successes as an interracial democracy on the local level, where new grassroots alliances flourished. I document a number of southern whites who went against the grain and actually supported interracial democracy during Reconstruction. These include a number of former Confederate heroes and prominent white southerners who supported black rights, including South Carolina–born James Longstreet, General P. G. T. Beauregard (who remained a Democrat), John Mosby (the Gray Ghost of TV fame when I was a boy), and Virginia Governor Henry Wise (who had hanged John Brown). Wise's son, also a former Confederate officer, became one of the great civil rights attorneys of the late-nineteenth and early twentieth centuries. I have tried to reframe Reconstruction, and ask why, if Reconstruction was such a failure, did southern whites have to use terrorism, fraud, and violence to overthrow an interracial legal government?

We have not studied Reconstruction in the North as we should have. Many northern states also rewrote their constitutions during Reconstruction. The Civil War and Lincoln in particular inspired idealism in the North, just as they did in the South, and this is nowhere more evident than in the Midwest, which had been extraordinarily racist before the Civil War. There were two kinds of southern immigrants into southern Illinois, Ohio, Indiana, and Missouri: those like Thomas Lincoln who hated slavery and left the South to get away from slavery, and an even larger number who hated African Americans and were trying to get away from black people. Illinois almost voted to be a slave state; and while there was no slavery there, a person could be indentured for ninety-nine years. Free blacks could not settle in Illinois, and of course could not vote or serve on juries, for example. Lincoln was embarrassed during the Civil War by some of the racist legislation from his home state. His legacy challenges and changes this racism. Not all of the idealism dies out. When the civil rights cases of 1883 struck down the Civil Rights Act of 1875, and the Supreme Court ruled in *Hurtado v. California* in 1881 that the Fourteenth Amendment did not guarantee enforcement of the Bill of Rights, states led by the Midwest passed their own state civil rights statutes: Iowa and Ohio in 1884; Illinois, Indiana, Michigan, and Nebraska in 1885, and Pennsylvania in 1889. We have always explained the Great Migration of African Americans because of economics, but I believe it was also because of Illinois's and other midwestern and northeastern state civil rights statutes that guaranteed equal rights and the vote, even if they often were not actually practiced. Black leaders could use Lincoln's rule of law to advance that goal of equal treatment.

I am often asked about the great interest the reading public has in the Civil War. And there will always be an interest, but I have noticed that the general public now seems much more interested in early American history. It is easier to deal with the Founding Fathers and concepts of revolution and independence than with the Age of Lincoln.

The Age of Lincoln has left us with troublesome questions that we do not want to face. Questions of race tear at the fabric of our supposedly egalitarian society, at our system of justice and law and order. As Attorney General Eric Holder reminded us in what became a controversial statement, "In things racial we have always been, and I believe continue to be, in too many ways essentially a nation of cowards."

Just as the Civil War cannot be separated from Reconstruction any more than the sectional conflict and events that resulted in conflict can be separated from Lincoln and the war, I will step out on a limb and argue that the election of President Barack Obama cannot be separated from the Civil War, Lincoln, and Reconstruction.

Some see Obama's election, or more correctly, they argue that the election of a black man, is the fulfillment of Lincoln, the completion of Reconstruction and the Thirteenth, Fourteenth, and Fifteenth amendments. Some argue that race as a distinct problem in American life has been resolved by Obama. I was asked by National Public Radio to comment on this for the North Carolina Voting Rights case, *Bartlett v. Strickland,* that came down March 9, 2009, from the Supreme Court with its standard five-to-four decision.

The Chicago Tribune also asked on March 15, "Does the election of a black president mean racism is no longer a factor in American politics? And are civil rights laws outdated in the age of Obama?" The article, discussing legal briefs filed in the North Carolina and Texas Supreme Court cases, reported that "Obama's election heralds the emergence of a colorblind society in which special legal safeguards for minorities are no longer required." Plaintiffs in the important Texas case would undo the important Section Five preclearance of the Voting Rights Act. The *Tribune* erroneously reported that the Georgia governor filed another suit challenging the Voting Rights Act, but actually the governor filed an amicus brief to the Texas case.

On the other side, civil rights advocates have presented state-by-state data that shows persistent racial polarization in the Deep South and elsewhere. We need to remember that, when the former Confederate states undermined the Fourteenth and Fifteenth amendments after Reconstruction, the too-brief experiment in interracial democracy ended; it took the Civil Rights Act and the Voting Rights Act of 1964 and 1965 to reestablish those rights.

Steven Colbert, in the *Colbert Report* television show broadcast on March 16, 2009, said that rewriting history is a good thing because we can make it better. He facetiously recommends that now that an African American is president, we can say that slavery never existed. Although done in humor, there are indications that in the court of popular opinion, as well as with some justices on the Supreme Court, this is to some degree happening.

Writing and rewriting history reminds me of an interesting playwright. Pulitzer Prize winner, Tony Award winner, and recipient of a MacArthur Genius Grant, African American Suzan-Lori Parks is fascinated by the story of Lincoln, or to be more specific, by the death of Lincoln. While some in the African American community do not care for her work because of her use of stereotypes, two of her plays have stunned me. In her 1993 *The America Play,* Parks offers us a story about "the passage of time" and "the crossing of space." She writes about a gravedigger, the son of gravediggers, digging the huge "Hole of History." History summoned this digger like a memory, and in his big hole, he made a theme park where he reconstructed history.

The digger's favorite reconstruction was of Abraham Lincoln. Tall and thin, he resembles Lincoln, and when he puts on a fake wart, people pronounce him and Lincoln to be "in virtual twinship." Someone told him that he "played Lincoln so well that he ought to be shot," and after that his money-making endeavor was to sit still while a paying customer chose a blank/toy pistol and shot him in the back of the head. They would then shout "Thus to the tyrants!" or "The South is avenged!" Or other assorted remarks such as Robert E. Lee's last words, "Strike the tents!"

One of Parks's insights into Lincoln was the idea of uncertainty amid a grander, millennial, almost mystical, vision of freedom, when Lincoln "didn't know if the war was right, when it could be said he didn't always know which side he was on, not because he was a stupid man but because it was sometimes not two different sides at all but one great side surging toward something beyond either Northern or Southern."

In *Topdog/Underdog* (2002), for which she received the Pulitzer, Parks again wrote about the death of Lincoln. She says, "In the play's first act we watch a black man who has fashioned a career for himself: he sits in an arcade impersonating Abraham Lincoln and letting people come and play at shooting him dead—like John Wilkes Booth shot our sixteenth president in 1865 during a performance at Ford's Theatre." This man is not the entrepreneur of the earlier work; he works for a white man, and he has to wear whiteface on the job, echoing the minstrel shows where whites wore blackface. While this character takes pride in doing a good job, there remains a pull toward an earlier time in his life when he was a con man throwing cards in three-card monte. This character's father had named him Lincoln. As a joke, the father named the younger brother Booth. I will not tell you how the play ends.

Parks reminds us of how Americans identify with Lincoln in different ways, how so many of us, and especially historians, write ourselves into whom we make Lincoln to be. (Is it any coincidence that I portray Lincoln as a southerner and not only as the greatest president, but the greatest theologian of the nineteenth century?) Often it is our better angels, and sometimes our greatest fears and fantasies. Parks's plays also suggest the changing image of Lincoln among African Americans, from the Great Emancipator to the white honky. At a session last fall on my book, *The Age of Lincoln*, at a meeting of the Association for the Study of African American Life and History, every African American scholar younger than I am could not say anything good about Lincoln. An attempt to get right with Lincoln by African Americans was dramatically personalized in Henry Louis Gates Jr.'s documentary on PBS, *Looking for Lincoln*. The shift in views of Lincoln came about with the modern civil rights movement, correctly labeled the Second Reconstruction. In the public sphere, Stokely Carmichael attacked Lincoln as a racist, and Lerone Bennet, longtime editor of *Ebony*, publicized the view in an important essay in 1969, and has written about it again in *Forced Into Glory* (2000). With the civil rights movement, when historians' interests shifted from slavery to race and racism, Lincoln's more gradualist policy was seen as inadequate. So much so that Mark Neely found the Great Emancipator characterized as "the perfect embodiment of Northern racism" in the pathbreaking book *North of Slavery* by white scholar Leon Litwack in 1961.

I am part of that generation of scholars who came of age with the Vietnam war and who for various reasons rejected the idea of heroes. Partly because so many of us were social historians, we were not as interested in the great white men that had dominated American history. In my own field of southern history, I was fond of mentioning how those Confederate heroes like Robert E. Lee and Jefferson Davis had turned the South prematurely gray. We were eager to show that our national monuments were too often constructed of clay. On reflection, it is good to understand that heroes are people just like us with their good and bad qualities, and often their own personal demons. We need to understand that leaders like Lincoln were flawed, but we also have to judge them by their own time and place.

Like most people in the nineteenth century, Lincoln used the "n" word and told racist jokes. That does not mean we should not value his heroic characteristics and efforts. In 1864 a delegation of African American men came to see Lincoln to request equal pay for laborers. Henry Samuels remembered the event and how Lincoln listened quietly. Then, according to Samuels, Lincoln said in a jocular manner, "Well, gentlemen, you wish the pay of 'Cuffie' raised." The story does not end with that patronizing tone of Lincoln. When Samuels boldly confronted the president that they did not make use of the word "Cuffie" in their "vernacular," but they were there to request "the wages of the American Colored Laborer be equalized with those of the American White Laborer," Lincoln apologized. He told Samuels, "I stand corrected, young man, but you know I am by birth a Southerner and in our section that term is applied without any idea of an offensive nature." But, unlike so many others, Lincoln got the idea. Lincoln went on to say that he would "at the earliest possible moment, do all in my power to accede to your request." Wages were equalized only a month later. This and other corroborating evidence have shown that Lincoln's incredible, flexible mind allowed him to grow so that by the end of the Civil War he was leading the nation to a better place on race. To appreciate this change in Lincoln is a good thing in a democracy. We can grow better on issues when we are open-minded and willing to learn more about them.

One way to put Lincoln's racism into a historical context is a comparison between Lincoln and the other major political figure of the day, Stephen A. Douglas. I realized that in my generation's inability to believe in heroes, we also did away with villains. And that has led to our not understanding those less noble parts of American history, like those individuals who supported slavery and racism. We may not need villains to make heroes, but it is easier not to have them because we do not like dealing with the ugly parts of American history.

Douglas was much more in line with the rest of white America, North and South. It is important to compare Lincoln to Douglas because it offers quite a different perspective, and only by talking about Stephen Douglas's avocation for white supremacy and his use of the race card to mobilize voters can we appreciate where Lincoln was on race.

I am amazed that, when I ask students what they know about the Lincoln-Douglas debates, they will say that Lincoln was this tall dude, six-feet-four-inches tall, and Douglas was this squat short guy. Who cares! What is important is that Lincoln and Douglas were debating two visions of America. Stephen Douglas, the most dynamic politician of his age, the leading light of the Democratic Party, stood blatantly for white supremacy.

When Douglas learned that Lincoln would be his opponent for the Senate in 1858, he turned his considerable talents into discrediting him. On July 9, 1858, in Chicago, Douglas cited Lincoln's "House Divided" speech and accused Lincoln of advocating civil war. The following evening, from the same Chicago balcony, Lincoln responded. After clarifying his "House Divided" statement, he became more animated when refuting Douglas's assertion that the United States government was "made by the white man, for the benefit of the white man, to be administered by white men." Lincoln threw caution to the wind; he claimed remarkable privilege for the Declaration of Independence and its implications about race and equality. "I have only to say, let us discard all this quibbling about this man and the other man—this race and that race and the other race being inferior, and therefore they must be placed in an inferior position. . . . Let us discard all these things, and unite as one people throughout this land, until we shall once more stand up declaring that all men are created equal."

Douglas promptly turned his back on Lincoln, indignantly proclaiming "this Chicago doctrine of Lincoln's—declaring that the negro and the white man are made equal by the Declaration of Independence and by Divine Providence—is a monstrous heresy." Douglas denounced Lincoln's extraordinary suggestion to "discard all this quibbling" about race and to declare "that all men are created equal." He found a ready audience; only ten years earlier, in 1848, more than two-thirds of Illinois voters approved a constitutional amendment to exclude even free African Americans from the state. The old Whig territory in the middle of the state was very much opposed to the abolition of slavery, and both Douglas and Lincoln understood that no man who declared equality for blacks could be elected to a statewide office in Illinois. Republicans advised Lincoln to back away from his call for equality, and Lincoln did.

In his fourth debate at Charleston, near where his father had moved and his widowed stepmother still lived, Lincoln made statements that still haunt today. Southern Illinois was especially racist. Even in 1850, after the large migration of New Yorkers into the state, Kentucky ranked second as the birthplace for Illinois household heads, and 37.5 percent of all household heads were born in slave states. The southern influence was so great on Illinois that Springfield, Lincoln's eventual home and the eventual state capital, was initially named Calhoun after the South Carolina politician most associated with the proslavery argument.

This was the context in which Lincoln spoke and said some things we wish he had not. In his meanest pronouncement on race, he denied that he favored civil rights for African Americans. Yet he kept his ground in declaring that the Declaration of Independence included all men in its claim for natural rights. Douglas's plan of attack was to make certain that voters understood that those natural rights inevitably led to civil rights. In the last three debates, Lincoln went on the offense and became bolder on African American rights. In Alton, the second most southern location of the debates, Lincoln eloquently cast slavery as a moral issue.

Just like with the Lincoln-Douglas debates, anyone studying Lincoln can use historical context to evaluate other accusations used against him. This includes his views on colonization and his supposedly "slow" movement toward the Emancipation Proclamation. Within the context of the time, evidence used to condemn Lincoln as a racist can be used for just the opposite conclusion.

As Lincoln grew in his presidency, he came to see Emancipation as a war issue and a justice issue. And yet, Abraham Lincoln was killed not for the Emancipation Proclamation, but for advocating African American voting, as limited as that was. On April 11, 1865, when Lincoln gave his last speech, one man in the audience understood perfectly what Lincoln was speaking about. John Wilkes Booth told his companion, "That means n—— citizenship. Now, by God, I'll put him through. That is the last speech he will ever make." Hence, Lincoln is part of a long list of martyrs who died for black voting rights.

Thus Lincoln's legacy continues to reverberate in strange and interesting ways. Perhaps with President Barack Obama's identification with Lincoln as a leader, or at least the parallels created by the campaign and the media, we will see more willingness from Lincoln's critics to accept the good with the bad, to understand the context of the nineteenth century, the ambiguity of individuals and of humanity itself.

In our time, when the Democratic primary came down to Barack Obama and Hillary Clinton, the debates eerily reflected themes of race and gender from the Age of Lincoln. Before the Civil War, reformers who had worked for women's suffrage put women's rights on the back burner to focus on eradicating the larger evil of slavery. But when former male slaves received the franchise in

1867 and women did not, the women's movement split; while some women like Lucy Stone and Julia Ward Howe continued to support Reconstruction and the rights of African Americans, others such as Elizabeth Cady Stanton and Susan B. Anthony turned against interracial democracy in the South and joined the racist chorus against African Americans that helped to undermine the gains for African Americans during Reconstruction. Feminism and race were at odds.

Other comparisons to the nation's greatest president and his era reveal interesting parallels with our own times. Then, as now, a fearful America faced war, postwar occupation, and nation building. Terrorism did not begin with 9/11; African Americans in the United States lived in a terrorist society in the former Confederacy at least from 1865 till well after the Voting Rights Act of 1965. Then, as now, religious fanaticism strongly influenced events. People who believe they know and do God's will are not likely to compromise, whether on slavery, immigration, *jihads,* or conquest. Our own cultural wars parallel those of the nineteenth century in intensity—let's hope not in result. Both Lincoln and Obama had to finance a war. One of the reasons for our own terrible economic situation is our involvement in wars and our not having paid for them. The Confederacy believed that the United States could not possibly maintain a Civil War because without the South's cotton, they could not pay for the war. But Lincoln did pay for the war, imposed the first supposedly "temporary" income tax, and while he personally did not benefit financially from the war, the United States actually made money off the Civil War.

In both the Age of Lincoln and in our own day there is great anxiety about a changing economy, in the Age of Lincoln from independent yeoman or craftsman to market forces and manufacturing; in our own times we are changing from manufacturing to a knowledge-based economy. Both eras brought an intense fear of being left behind. At the same time there were more opportunities, and some entrepreneurs made great fortunes. In both periods we have our most extreme income distribution gap. Prior to our current financial meltdown, our own era was often compared with the period Mark Twain named the Gilded Age. And in both eras, unbridled capitalism led to recessions and depressions, from the Panic of 1857 and the Great Depression that began in 1873 and ran into the 1890s, and, of course, to our own economic crisis. And it needs to be a warning to us that, during those historically difficult economic times, revolutions can and do go backward, as in the Great Depression of 1873 into the 1890s; racial idealism and minority rights are often sacrificed when the economic pie shrinks.

Let me conclude with the conclusion of my book, *The Age of Lincoln*. Now, as two hundred years ago, Lincoln's words ring true: "Determine that the thing can and shall be done, and then we shall find the way."

FRANCIS W. PICKENS AND THE WAR BEGINS

(1970)

―――――・⚭・―――――

John B. Edmunds Jr.

By the middle of November 1860, South Carolina was seething with emotion. Already several members of her congressional delegation had resigned, and an election for delegates to a state convention to meet on December 17 had been approved by the state legislature. It was in the midst of this furor that Francis Pickens, who had been serving as a minister to Russia, returned home. His ship docked in New York. On his way home, Pickens stopped in Washington and had a lengthy interview with President James Buchanan, who asked him to use his influence on behalf of moderation.[1]

One prominent New Yorker wrote that Pickens's object in coming home was to tell his fellow Carolinians that they were making themselves a laughingstock.[2] At first he did advocate moderation, urging his state to work in concert with other southern states and to postpone any radical move until Buchanan left office, but this suggestion was ridiculed by the disunionists, whose sentiments were mounting in epidemic proportions. It was at this point that Pickens changed, becoming infected by secession fever. Instead of urging cooperation, he modified his views and urged disunion, provided no way could be found to resolve sectional differences. On November 30, in a Columbia speech, which obviously appealed to the hot-blooded Carolinians, he stated that he would be willing to "appeal to the god of battles . . . cover the state with ruin, conflagration and blood rather than submit."[3] Pickens was not only telling the attentive masses what they wanted to hear, but also paving his way to the governor's office, where he would assist in leading the state down the road to "ruin, conflagration and blood."

The keenly observant Mary Boykin Chesnut, whose husband had recently resigned his seat in the U.S. Senate, commented on Pickens's reversal. "Wigfall," she wrote, "says that before he left Washington, . . . Pickens and Trescot were openly against secession. Trescot does not pretend to like it now, but Pickens is a fire-eater down to the ground."[4]

It was widely predicted that Robert Barnwell Rhett, the so-called "father of secession," would be elected governor, but there were many people in the state who opposed his election, feeling that his views were even too radical for radical South Carolina. One contemporary wrote: "For God's sake and the sake of our beloved state, don't let Rhett be elected governor."[5]

In early December the Palmetto State seemed to have turned back toward conservatism of the South Carolina variety. On December 16, many candidates were put forward in the governor's race. When the Rhett forces were not able to gain votes, Rhett dropped out of the contest on the fifth ballot, and Pickens won the race by a slight majority on the seventh.[6] It is doubtful if anyone knew what beliefs the new governor espoused. He had in the past preached moderation, but now he seemed to have shifted his position after sensing the mood of the Carolinians. It is possible that the legislature in electing Pickens felt that his past reputation as a South Carolina moderate and his closeness to Buchanan would place the state in an ideal position to negotiate for the forts and resolve the problem before Lincoln was inaugurated. Since he was labeled a moderate, many hoped that he would be able to bring the diverse elements together and create harmony out of chaos. M. L. Bonham probably best expressed the situation when he wrote: "We see that Pickens is elected but do not know what it indicates."[7]

The state was readying itself for action, but no one, including the new governor, knew what lay ahead. One thing is certain. He was to encounter problems such as no past or future chief executive of the state would experience. Many of his difficulties were caused by misunderstandings; others by outside influences. Unfortunately, the new governor lacked the magnetism and personal popularity that was so essential at that crucial period. "He was a man of ideas, an acute observer, but not a man of positive action."[8] He said of himself, "I believe it my destiny to be disliked by all who know me well."[9]

In the early days of his administration the new governor was given extraordinary powers. An executive council was set up which was designed to function like a cabinet. It consisted of the lieutenant governor and five other members who were to represent the convention within the administration.[10] Pickens was authorized by the convention to levy war, negotiate treaties, send and receive ambassadors. Also his appointive powers were greatly increased. He was given the responsibility of negotiating with Buchanan and sending commissioners to the other southern states to urge secession. In reality he had been transformed from the position of state governor to the head of the sovereign Palmetto republic. Pickens was confronted by problems that he could have hardly foreseen. The state needed coastal defenses and troops to man these installations. The militia was inadequate and had to be armed, trained, and provided with leadership. Before the state joined the Confederacy, all actions dealing with military and logistical problems were the responsibility of the governor. All intelligence and engineering reports had to be reviewed by Pickens, and it was his decision as to how these reports would be handled ultimately.[11]

On December 20, 1860, four days after the gubernatorial contest, the secession convention declared South Carolina to be out of the Union. The state embarked on the new and dangerous experiment of secession with no plans having been formulated to provide the state with a government adequate to her needs. The problems that the government faced would have been immense if secession had occurred under the most favorable circumstances, but with war clouds on the horizon and a frenzied populace, the pressures were immeasurable.

"South Carolinians had exasperated and heated themselves into a fever that only bloodletting could cure," reported Mrs. Chesnut.[12] The state was sailing an uncharted course, and her new governor was faced with a problem that was irritating to the Carolinians. The forts in Charleston Harbor were regarded by many people as both a threat and an insult. Unfortunately, the governor's first efforts at diplomacy proved to be unsuccessful; instead of solving the problem, he made it worse. The day after taking office Pickens wrote Buchanan informing the president that the forts in the harbor were being readied to turn their guns upon the city and that the federal arsenal in Charleston had been turned over to the state.[13] The governor requested that Buchanan allow him to send a small force to take possession of unoccupied Fort Sumter. The president became alarmed and called in William Trescot, who was functioning unofficially as South Carolina's representative in Washington. Actually, the arsenal had not been turned over to South Carolina, and the governor had raised an issue over the forts in the harbor. Trescot hoped that the crucial situation could rest in abeyance until South Carolina sent commissioners to bargain for the forts, but in this instance the governor showed that his zeal was stronger than his discretion.[14] The governor had made the first of many blunders.

Pickens later explained that he corresponded with the president for the purpose of gaining a better understanding regarding the forts in order to chart his (Pickens's) own course.[15] The tense situation demanded that the president take action to prevent the South Carolinians from unleashing the war dogs. A frantic Buchanan, who had already sacrificed much personal prestige, sent his friend, Caleb Cushing, to South Carolina in hopes that some way might be found to maintain the *status quo*, at least until Lincoln took office.[16] When Cushing arrived he found that he was too late. South Carolina had embarked on an irreversible course. Excitement was high, and the secession convention was in full progress. Pickens realized there was to be no turning back. He candidly informed Cushing "that there was no hope for the Union."[17]

After secession had been inaugurated, the convention resolved that any attempt by the United States to build up the fortifications would be regarded "as an overt act of war."[18] The "overt act of hostility" that many thought would come occurred during the evening of December 26, 1860. This was the first of many events that were to cause the governor great embarrassment and unpopularity. Pickens, at the request of the convention, ordered the harbor to be constantly patrolled in order to stop any movement from Fort Moultrie to Fort Sumter by the Union force under its new commander, Major Robert Anderson. It was at this time that the governor began to reap much verbal abuse. Many felt that, instead of keeping Anderson from abandoning Fort Moultrie, the governor should have ordered the forts seized. Pickens had been assured by Trescot, who was still in Washington, that no attempt would be made by the Union to occupy Sumter.[19] But Trescot's letter and Pickens's constant vigil did not prevent Anderson from moving his command from untenable Fort Moultrie to Sumter right under the governor's nose. Many blamed the governor for what had happened. Mrs. Chesnut referred to him as a "dead head."[20]

Instead of waiting for action by the commissioners who had been sent to Washington to negotiate for the forts, the governor took immediate steps, asking Anderson to return his forces to Moultrie, but the federal commander refused.[21] The governor then made a serious blunder, ordering his military commanders to take the abandoned forts and to occupy a position off the Charleston bar.[22] The forts were federal property. Thus the order to seize the installations constituted an act of aggression against the United States. It is conceivable that, if the governor had bided his time and complained to Buchanan, Anderson would have been ordered to leave his island.[23] Such might have been the case, but in this instance it appears that the clamor of public opinion left the governor no choice but to take the federal properties in and around Charleston.

Great energy was being expended on both sides to ready the forts for the conflicts that everyone knew were eminent. Buchanan decided that Anderson should be supplied, but took a long time in implementing his decision. Instead of sending a warship, the president sent a merchant vessel, the *Star of the West*, which set sail on January 5, 1861. Though the ship was officially bound for New Orleans, Pickens was warned that the vessel should be expected in South Carolina waters.[24] On January 9, action took place that ordinarily would have precipitated war. On that morning the *Star of the West* entered Charleston Harbor. The guns on Morris Island and Fort Moultrie fired on the ship, scoring several hits, but Anderson did not permit his guns to retaliate. However, he warned the governor that, if the act was not disclaimed, he would "regard it as an act of war" and that he would not permit any vessel to pass within range of Sumter.[25] Pickens claimed that any effort to reinforce the fort would be regarded as an act of hostility.[26] On the same day that the *Star of the West* was fired upon, Pickens called together his officers to "consider . . . the most favorable plan . . . to reduce the fortress."[27] The fortifications in the harbor were feverishly strengthened. The governor planned to take the fort if necessary, but unlike Rhett and the *Mercury*, he desired to see bloodshed prevented if possible. He decided to ask Anderson to give up the fort. He must have realized before he sent his request to the major that it would be rejected. Obviously he was hoping that Anderson, who was painfully aware of the increased activity, would see that resistance was futile and abandon the fortress.[28] Anderson replied that he could not comply with the governor's demand.[29]

Major Anderson suggested that the governor send a representative to Washington in order to ascertain how the president intended to handle the inflamed situation. Isaac W. Hayne, South Carolina's attorney general, was dispatched with an ominous message in which the governor once again asked Buchanan to give up the fort, claiming Fort Sumter to be a threat to the state which could inevitably lead "to a bloody issue."[30] Hayne arrived in Washington on January 12 and had an unofficial interview with the president two days later. The senators of other southern states agreed that the occupation of Sumter by the Union was just cause for irritation, but they urged forbearance and requested Hayne to defer from delivering Pickens's letter until they made suggestions to both the governor and the president. If hostilities were to come, the southern leaders wanted to avoid them until after the meeting of the Montgomery Convention of February 15, that was to form the Confederate States of America.[31] Buchanan made it clear that he was willing to maintain the status quo provided no hostile action was commenced against the fort. He explained that he had no more right to cede federal property to South Carolina than to "sell the capitol of the United States to Maryland."[32] It was becoming more difficult for the governor to refrain from taking action. While the Edgefield paper and other upstate papers defended his lack of action, Rhett's *Mercury* asked: "Will South Carolina sit quietly with folded arms, and see a fort garrisoned by our enemies?"[33] Cooler heads were still advising delay as the governor's policy. Governor J. E. Brown of Georgia, Robert Toombs, the future Confederate secretary of state, and Jefferson Davis all advised against precipitate action.[34] In South Carolina, however, the overwhelming sentiment seemed to be for an immediate storming of the fortress.[35] Pickens was accused of sacrificing the honor of the state. One Carolinian wrote: "Pickens counts delay and to obtain this he sends and keeps sending men . . . to talk with Old Buck. . . . the state . . . is being disgraced everyday . . . and there is much dissatisfaction with Pickens."[36] William Henry Ravenel, a prominent South Carolina botanist and planter, wrote that "there is great dissatisfaction prevailing at the course of Governor Pickens. . . . He is overbearing, haughty and rude."[37]

The governor was in a dilemma, caught between the desires of the Carolinians and those of the southern leaders. But by February 6, Hayne, South

Carolina's negotiator in Washington, reported that conferences between himself and Buchanan had broken down. Hayne came home urging Pickens to stage an immediate attack on the fort.[38] The governor continued to stall. While Hayne was in Washington, Pickens had an excuse for remaining inactive, but with Hayne at home preaching instant war, the fire eaters were becoming even more vociferous. The governor longed for the problem of Sumter to be lifted from his shoulders. He suggested to a friend that Maryland and Virginia secede and seize Washington before it was adequately fortified.[39]

Matters continued to drag on while tempers remained feverish. The South Carolina delegates at the Montgomery Convention presented that assembly with a clear ultimatum either to unite and accept the Sumter problem as a common obligation, or let the Carolinas attack the fort. For the first time, Pickens saw an opportunity to wash his hands of the matter and at the same time save face. The governor wrote Robert Toombs that if the Confederate Congress would "indicate jurisdiction . . . then I would not hesitate to abide most cheerfully by your control."[40] Much to the delight of the Governor, the Confederate Congress decided to shoulder the burden of Sumter. Immediately the governor's tone and attitude changed. A dauntless governor replaced an ordinarily cautious one. Pickens now urged that the fort be taken, informing the Confederate government that he was prepared for action. The new government was slow to act, and many South Carolinians were fearful that a war of independence would never come. A bold Pickens promised in the last days of February that the fort would be taken. In a letter to his beautiful and flirtatious wife, who had gone to Texas, Pickens reported that he had five hundred men ready to storm Anderson's little island.[41] He made a fiery speech while "about half drunk" to the Citadel cadets in which he reiterated his promise.[42] On March 6, Brigadier General P. G. T. Beauregard arrived on the scene, resulting in the further fortification of Charleston Harbor.[43] Pickens urged that the popular Beauregard's command be expanded to include the entire coast, thus relieving the governor of this responsibility.[44]

Meanwhile, on March 4, Lincoln was inaugurated. He vowed that the power confided to him would be used to "hold, occupy, and possess the property and places belonging to the government."[45] Negotiations were attempted by the Confederate government with the new president, but they were to no avail. When Lincoln ultimately determined to provision the fort, the inevitable occurred. Firing commenced on April 12, 1861. The governor was jubilant. Instead of being cursed, he was applauded. Actually he had little to do with the situation, but he took as much credit as possible.[46] Pickens, who had never been known for his humility, was puffed with pride when he spoke to the masses in the street from the balcony of the Charleston Hotel. In a speech full of "I's" he stated that the victorious results were not attributable solely to his skill. Nevertheless, he did not fail to remind the populace that "I was determined to maintain our separate independence and freedom at any and every hazard. . . . when I knew we were prepared, I was ready to strike. . . . we have rallied; we have met them. . . . let it lead to what it might, even if it leads to blood and ruin. . . . we have defeated their twenty millions, we have met them and conquered them."[47] The *New York Times* soberly editorialized: "The curtain has fallen upon the first act of the great tragedy of the age."[48] The war that the fire eaters had hungered for was now the prospect. The gay times of the Carolinians were numbered, but in the closing days of April excitement and joy ruled the Palmetto State, although the once reluctant Pickens's new popularity was to prove to be ephemeral.

NOTES

1. Samuel W. Crawford, *The History of the Fall of Fort Sumter* (New York: S. L. McLean and Co., 1889), 79–81.
2. George T. Strong, *Diary of the Civil War, 1860–1865*, ed. Allan Nevins (New York: Macmillan Co., 1962), 76.
3. Charleston *Courier*, December 3, 1860.
4. Mary Boykin Chesnut, Diary, December, 1860, Williams-Manning-Chesnut Papers, South Caroliniana Library, University of South Carolina.
5. D. L. Wardlaw to Samuel McGowan, December 3, 1860, McGowan Papers, South Caroliniana Library, University of South Carolina.
6. Pickens defeated Benjamin J. Johnson by a vote of 83 to 64. *Edgefield Advertiser,* December 19, 1860; *Journal of the House of Representatives of the State of South Carolina, 1861,* 164, 167, 176, 180, 198.
7. M. L. Bonham to W. H. Gist, December 16, 1860, Bonham Papers, South Caroliniana Library, University of South Carolina; Charles E. Cauthen, *South Carolina Goes to War, 1860–1865* (Chapel Hill: University of North Carolina Press, 1950), 80; F. W. P. to M. L. Bonham, December 5, 1860, Bonham Papers.
8. Cauthen, *South Carolina Goes to War*, 80.
9. F. W. Pickens to Lucy Pickens, February 23, 1861, in the possession of A. T. Graydon, Columbia, S.C.
10. Lowry P. Ware, "South Carolina, Executive Councils of 1861 and 1862," master's thesis, University of South Carolina, 1952.
11. E. M. Law Papers, Southern Historical Collection, University of North Carolina; Pickens Papers, South Carolina Archives, Columbia; Pickens-Bonham Papers, Library of Congress; Cauthen, *South Carolina Goes to War*, 8–209.
12. Chesnut, Diary, December 1860.
13. Francis Pickens to James Buchanan, December 17, 1860, in W. A. Harris, ed., *The Record of Fort Sumter* (Columbia: South Carolina Steam Press, 1862), 7–8.
14. William Trescot to Francis Pickens, December 21, 1860, ibid., 80.
15. *Message Number 1, of his Excellency Francis W. Pickens to the Legislature Meeting in Extra Session, November 5, 1861* (Columbia, S.C., 1861); W. A. Swanberg, *First Blood: The Story of Fort Sumter* (New York: Scribner & Sons, 1957), 89–95.
16. W. H. Trescot to F. W. P., December 21, 1860. Harris, ed., *The Record of Fort Sumter*: "He had removed Colonel Gardiner from command of Fort Moultrie, for carrying ammunition from the arsenal at Charleston. He refused to send reinforcements to the garrison;

he had accepted the resignation of the oldest, most eminent and highest member of his cabinet, rather than consent to additional force, and the night before your letter arrived, upon a telegraphic communication that arms had been removed from the arsenal to Fort Moultrie, the Department of War issued prompt orders, by telegraph, to the officer removing them, to restore them immediately."

17. Claude M. Fuess, *The Life of Caleb Cushing* (New York: Harcourt-Brace & Co., 1923), vol. 2: 273; Diary of Edmund Ruffin, December 18, 1860, Edmund Ruffin Papers, Library of Congress.

18. Journal of the South Carolina Convention, December 27, 1860, South Carolina Archives.

19. W. H. Trescot to Francis Pickens, December 21, 1860, in Harris, ed., *The Record of Fort Sumter*.

20. Chesnut Diary, December 27, 1860; Wade Hampton to Fisher Hampton, December 17, 1861, Hampton Papers, Southern Historical Collections, University of North Carolina.

21. Diary of Samuel W. Crawford, December 28, 1860, Samuel W. Crawford Papers, Library of Congress.

22. Francis Pickens to Col. J. J. Pettigrew, December 27, 1860; Francis Pickens to General Schnierle, December 27, 1860, in Harris, ed., *The Record of Fort Sumter*. Francis Pickens to Capt. J. Carrington, January 1, 1861, and Francis Pickens to Military Commanders, December 27, 1860, Samuel W. Crawford Papers. Mayor Charles MacBeth to Francis Pickens, December 30, 1860, Pickens Papers, Duke University Library.

23. Diary of Samuel W. Crawford, December 28, 1860; Swanberg, *First Blood*, 123.

24. Louis Wigfall to Francis Pickens, telegram, January 8, 1861, Pickens Papers, South Carolina Archives.

25. Major Robert Anderson to Francis Pickens, January 9, 1861, in *Edgefield Advertiser*, January 16, 1861; *Charleston Courier*, January 10, 1861; *Charleston Mercury*, January 10–16, 1861.

26. *Charleston Mercury*, January 10–16, 1861.

27. Francis Pickens to Cols. Gwynn, White, and Trapier, Jauuary 9, in Harris, ed., The Record of Fort Sumter.

28. Francis Pickens to Robert Anderson, January 11, 1861, Crawford Papers.

29. Ibid.

30. Francis Pickens to Buchanan, January 11, 1861, in *Edgefield Advertiser*, February 13, 1861; Crawford, *The History of the Fall of Fort Sumter*, 195–96.

31. Francis Pickens to Robert Toombs, February 12, 1861, Crawford Papers; I. W. Hayne to Francis Pickens, Jauuary 16, 1861, Pickens-Bonham Papers.

32. I. W. Hayne to Francis Pickens, Jauuary 16, 1861, Pickens-Bonham Papers; Crawford, *The History of the Fall of Fort Sumter*, 226–34.

33. *Edgefield Advertiser*, January 30, 1861; *Charleston Mercury*, January 19, 1861.

34. Crawford, *The History of the Fall of Fort Sumter*, 266; Francis Pickens to Robert Toombs, February 12, 1861, Crawford Papers; Francis Pickens to Jefferson Davis, January 28, 1861, in *Jefferson Davis, Constitutionalist: His Letters, Papers and Speeches*, ed. Dunbar Rowland (Jackson: Mississippi Department of Archives and History, 1923), vol. 5: 39–40.

35. Columbia Southern Guardian quoted in the *Edgefield Advertiser*, January 30, 1861.

36. S. W. B. [not identifiable] to a Mrs. Coleman, January 27, 1861, William Dunlap Simpson Papers, Duke University Library.

37. *The Private Journal of Henry William Ravenel, 1859–1887*, ed. Arney Robinson Childs (Columbia: University of South Carolina Press, 1947), 51.
38. Ware, "South Carolina, Executive Councils of 1861 and 1862," 20.
39. Swanberg, *First Blood*, 193.
40. Francis Pickens to Toombs, February 12, 1861, Crawford Papers.
41. Francis Pickens to Lucy Pickens, February 23, 1861, property of A. T. Graydon, Columbia, S.C.
42. Robert L. Cooper to Thomas B. Fraser, February 23, 1861, T. B. Fraser Papers, South Caroliniana Library, University of South Carolina.
43. *Edgefield Advertiser*, March 13, 1861.
44. Francis Pickens to Jefferson Davis, March 17, 1861, Crawford Papers.
45. Inaugural Speech of Abraham Lincoln in Charleston, *Daily Courier*, March 13, 1861.
46. T. Harry Williams, *P. G. T. Beauregard, Napoleon in Gray* (Baton Rouge: Louisiana State University Press, 1954), 56.
47. *Charleston Mercury*, April 16, 1861. In the fort there were nine officers, seventy-four noncommissioned officers, and forty-three laborers.
48. *New York Times* as quoted in *Charleston Mercury*, April 18, 1861.

ATTORNEY GENERAL ISAAC W. HAYNE AND THE SOUTH CAROLINA EXECUTIVE COUNCIL OF 1862

(1952)

Lowry P. Ware

With the surrender of Fort Sumter in April 1861, the emphasis of the Civil War shifted quickly from Charleston harbor to Northern Virginia and the West. South Carolina stripped the leaders, materials, and men from its hurriedly erected coastal defenses and contributed them to the Confederate forces in the North and West. Paradoxically the state which had been most conscious of its interests and rights in the Union now became the least conscious of its self-interest in the Confederacy. Despite repeated warnings during the summer a Union force invaded Port Royal in November, found only slight resistance, and quickly overran most of the sea islands along the southeastern coast. The Confederacy could promise little aid, and the ineffectual efforts of Governor Francis W. Pickens and the legislature failed to arouse the people to their own defense. The invaders pillaged the rich cotton plantations, spread disaffection among the slaves, and posed a threat to the Charleston-Savannah railroad and even Charleston itself.[1]

At the very height of this crisis, in late December, the Secession Convention was called into an emergency session. It possessed unlimited authority, it alone retained the confidence of the people, and by common consent it included the state's most trusted and able patriots.[2] Many of its earlier leaders, such as Robert W. Barnwell, James L. Orr, and Christopher G. Memminger, were absent in the services of the Confederacy, but other and lesser-known leaders rose to the challenge for a new and bold leadership. One member, Attorney General Isaac W. Hayne, seemed to see the situation more clearly than the others, and he virtually assumed the direction of the convention and state in this crisis.[3]

Isaac Hayne had neither been active in the early secession movement nor prominent in the first sessions of the Secession Convention. In fact he had carefully avoided political controversy during most of his public life. In 1831 he had left the South Carolina College and the study of law to succeed James H. Hammond as editor of the states' rights journal, the *Southern Times* of Columbia. The next year he served as clerk of the state's famous Nullification Convention and later became private secretary to his cousin, Governor Robert Y. Hayne.[4] The demands of his family soon cut short his political apprenticeship, and in 1836 he left South Carolina politics for the lush cotton lands of Alabama. There, after a short venture at planting, he joined the Montgomery bar. Within a few years he returned to South Carolina to practice law in Charleston and was elected attorney general.[5]

Attorney General Hayne had remained aloof from the party factionalism which characterized antebellum state politics. Even in the Secession Convention, which climaxed the long movement for southern independence, he played an unspectacular, though important, role. He became Governor Pickens's personal messenger in the post-secession months and was chosen to deliver to President Buchanan South Carolina's final demand for Fort Sumter.[6] Yet he remained always in the background during those days of emotionalism and oratory. It was not until the crisis of late 1861 that his qualities—great energy, character, and courage—brought him to the fore. Then, while others deliberated, he proposed a bold plan of action which the convention adopted in early January 1862 with the creation of a commission to remove the displaced slaves from the coast, a naval commission, and, most important, an Executive Council.[7]

This new Executive Council was strongly opposed by Governor Pickens and his supporters in the convention. It was a radical departure from the Executive Council of early 1861 which the same convention had given Pickens just after secession. Whereas the governor had appointed the members and retained the power of final decision on the first council, the ordinance creating the new body provided equal votes for the five members—the governor, Lieutenant Governor W. W. Harlee, and three members selected by the convention.[8] The convention's choices, ex-Senator James Chesnut, Isaac Hayne, and former Governor William H. Gist, insured that body's control of its new creation. It conferred unlimited police, impressment, and conscription powers on the council and then adjourned on January 8, subject to recall by the petition of twenty members.[9]

In the council organization Chesnut became chief of the military, Hayne the chief of justice and police, and Gist the chief of treasury and finance.[10] Chief of the Military Chesnut's specified duties seemed to overshadow those of Hayne and Gist, but his ambitions lay in Richmond. He had not been active in either the creation or defense of the council, and, indeed, his forceful wife, Mrs. Mary Boykin Chesnut, constantly besought him to abandon it.[11] Hayne, on the other hand, by his devotion to every phase of its activity, became the council's undisputed leader and defender.

His own task as chief of justice and police was the development of an effective internal security program. Despite Governor Pickens's recent praise for the loyalty of "all classes of our people" there were potent threats to continued loyalty.[12] There had been rumored unrest among the free Negroes of Charleston, and in Columbia many of the merchants were northern-born.[13] Hayne moved quickly and forcefully. He alerted the cadets of the Arsenal Academy in Columbia and the Citadel in Charleston to serve as a special night police.[14] And, though much of the critical defense area already lay under martial law, he added a passport system for "strangers" in Columbia and a special police court in Charleston.[15]

Hayne received many charges of individual disloyalty, but most of the accusations proved more indicative of popular hysteria than of actual misconduct. He and his agents investigated cases in Marion, Newberry, Laurens, York, Columbia, and Charleston without making a single arrest or detention.[16] Only one case, that of John Caldwell, president and director of the South Carolina Railroad and a director of the Exchange Bank of Columbia, proved lengthy or unusual. Caldwell was charged with acts and sentiments incompatible with support of the Confederate cause.[17] Hayne reported, after a careful inquiry, that Caldwell, a former Unionist, had shown no sympathy for the North, though he had often and openly despaired of the success of the Confederacy. He had rejected Confederate bonds and currency as worthless. Immediately following this report in mid-May the council unanimously petitioned the directors of the South Carolina Railroad, in view of the strategic value of their road to the Confederacy, to replace Caldwell with a more patriotic executive.[18] The directors refused, and the council, though disavowing any charge of disloyalty, was impelled by a sense of "imperative duty to the state" to renew its request. It voted against airing the incident in the press, and the only public notice which appeared was that of the actual resignation of John Caldwell in late October.[19]

Both the Union invasion and the council's own program of impressing and assembling slave labor along the vital coastal defense line caused slave disturbances. There were servile insurrections in Chesterfield and Darlington which forced the council to suspend troop calls from those communities.[20] Even wider disorder may have followed but for the work of Hayne. He removed displaced slaves from the coast, levied fines on absentee slave owners, and secured the exemption from Confederate service of essential slave overseers.[21]

Other problems proved more difficult for Hayne than those of disloyalty. Among his first moves he had authorized the Confederate commanders "to close all grog shops and prohibit the sale of all intoxicating drinks."[22] This prohibition was extended to Columbia in March and a statewide ban clamped on the distillation of scarce grains.[23] He licensed distillation for medical purposes, purchased copper distilleries and lead pipes for war use, and closely regulated transportation of alcoholic beverages.[24] But whatever early value these controls may have had, Hayne soon found them so difficult to enforce that he was forced to abandon them.[25]

Efforts to relieve the serious shortages caused by the prolonged blockade were somewhat more successful. An experiment conducted by Lieutenant C. W. Geddes to manufacture artificial ice for the hospitals failed.[26] However in the case of the more critical salt shortage the council decided that the very "health of the Community" itself was at stake, and it gave Hayne a special fund and force of agents to encourage salt production.[27] He conducted and published a salt census, surveyed the salt springs of the interior, and financed the efforts of numerous small producers along the coast.[28]

Such piecemeal efforts promised no relief to the popular distress caused by the ravages of speculation and inflation. Hayne was one of the few who sensed this and sought vainly for a solution. He indignantly branded the profiteers as guilty of "unrighteous and unconscientious extortion" and of a monopoly against "the necessitous and the poor" and threatened them with prosecution as traitors.[29] He appealed to the cotton planters to turn four-fifths of their lands to the production of food.[30] In addition he surveyed various Confederate states and cities, and found that, though distress was universal, only North Carolina was willing to cooperate in a system of price controls.[31] In the end he did nothing but set up a state embargo on the export of such essentials as grain, cattle, and meat.[32]

The complexity of Hayne's own problems did not prevent him from constantly aiding other councilors in their work. He joined with Chief of Military Chesnut in studying and reorganizing the militia system.[33] He initiated the transfer of the facilities of the South Carolina College to the Confederacy for use as a hospital.[34] It was at his suggestion that the council adjourned to Charleston to supervise directly the defense program during a crisis in May.[35] Perhaps his greatest single contribution was his work in the impressment of slave labor for the coastal fortifications.

He secured the first permission from the council in early February for the Confederate commanders to initiate the impressment of the able-bodied slaves of the coastal districts.[36] Through the spring and summer he and Chesnut gradually extended the program until by mid-July it covered the entire state.[37] The labor calls, administered by Professor Francis S. Holmes and a force of agents, never reached the demands of the Confederate commanders, but they were extensive enough to elicit a storm of protest from both the planters and the more conservative councilors, Gist and Harlee.[38] The disgruntled planters protested that impressment was undermining the very institution of slavery, and they began to seek the abolition of the council.[39] By late summer their movement had forced Hayne to leave his work almost completely to defend the council itself.

He had always considered himself its father and defender. In his capacity as attorney general he declared the council's creation and work both legal and proper. It derived its authority directly from the accepted Calhoun doctrine of the unlimited sovereignty of a "convention of the people."[40] He even resented attempts by the council to limit its own authority. He well illustrated his attitude when, following the adoption of a new militia conscription plan, he moved that "all ordinances, acts, resolutions and regulations from any authorities in this state, conflicting with the above provisions, are hereby suspended in their operation for and during the existing war."[41]

The conflict hinged more clearly upon personalities than upon political theory. The personal supporters of Governor Pickens had denounced the creation of the council as a "slur."[42] Despite his own opposition Pickens himself cooperated warmly with the council during its early months and even proposed that it embark upon a more radical mobilization program.[43] Hayne apparently became afraid that Pickens might come to dominate the Council, and in April he succeeded in replacing the first secretary of the Council, F. J. Moses, Jr. who was also Pickens' private secretary, with B. F. Arthur, the clerk of the Convention.[44] Other conflicts followed, and in July Hayne and Pickens exchanged sharp notes over the council in a controversy which leaked out into the public press. Most of the state's newspapers, led by Richard Yeadon's *Charleston Courier,* enlisted on the side of Pickens under the banner of "constitutional government."[45] When the Pickens defenders united with the planters the anti-council forces became the most powerful and articulate political movement in the state.

Hayne continued to defend the council, and with powerful logic he contended in a published letter to Pickens in August that: "If the political Horn Book in which I was taught is not all wrong, the Constitution itself was the creature of a Convention, no more authoritative, and of no broader powers, than that against which you protest. You then the creature of a creature, itself created by a Convention, assume to question the authority of a body in all respects the same with that which established your office, and gave being to the body which elected you."[46] Only a few newspaper correspondents, however, rallied to the defense of the council, and on September 9 the Secession Convention assembled in its fourth session amid a distinctly anticouncil atmosphere.[47]

The convention delegated the examination of the records of the Executive Council to a Committee of Twenty-one, and the consideration of the future of the council to a Committee of Seven. The former committee agreed with Hayne that the council, in creation and operation, had been both necessary and proper; the latter suggested that the disposition of the council be left to the incoming legislature. These reports were adopted despite a number of proposals for more definite action, including a motion by Hayne to preserve the council by making it responsible to the legislature. The legislature, which had come to consider the council as its archenemy, not only eagerly abolished it but also recorded its disapproval of the whole experiment.[48]

The passing of the Executive Council of 1862 ended Isaac Hayne's career as an important political leader. It would, indeed, be difficult to consider him apart from the council. If it were due to Hayne that the council was often autocratic and its program austere, it was equally his achievement that the council accomplished something of the miracle which had been desired of it. Under its guidance South Carolina had clearly increased its strength and confidence. Whereas at the beginning of 1862 Isaac Hayne had headed a committee which considered the burning of threatened Charleston, by the end of 1862 his fellow Charlestonian, the poet laureate of the Confederacy, wrote that now the city stood calm, as "all untroubled in her faith, she waits the triumph or the tomb."[49]

NOTES

1. For a general picture of South Carolina in November and December 1861, see Laura White, "The Fate of Calhoun's Sovereign Convention in South Carolina," *American Historical Review* 34 (1929): 757–58, and Charles Edward Cauthen, *South Carolina Goes to War, 1860–1865* (Chapel Hill: University of North Carolina Press, 1950), 137–38.

2. *Journal of the Convention of the People of South Carolina, Held in 1860, 1861, and 1862* (Columbia: 1862), 301; Cauthen, *South Carolina Goes to War*, 139–42.

3. Cauthen, *South Carolina Goes to War*, 139–42.

4. For biographical sketches of Isaac W. Hayne, see *Biographical Sketches of Eminent American Lawyers,* ed. John Livingston (New York, 1852), 233–36; Theodore D. Jervey, "The Hayne Family," *South Carolina Historical and Genealogical Magazine* 5 (1904): 168–88; and Elizabeth Merritt, *James Henry Hammond, 1807–1864* (Baltimore: Johns Hopkins University Press, 1923), 20.

5. *Biographical Sketches of American Lawyers* (April–May 1852), 235–36.

6. Harold S. Schultz, *Nationalism and Sectionalism in South Carolina, 1852–1860: A Study of the Movement for Southern Independence* (Durham, N.C.: Duke University Press, 1950), 154, 170, 198, 218. See also "Journal of the Executive Council of 1861," January 30, February 9, MS volume in the possession of the S.C. Department of Archives and History, Columbia, S.C. (cited here after as SCDAH).

7. *Journal of the Convention of the People of South Carolina*, 55, 118, 273–74.

8. Ibid., 306–8, 330, 336–38, 367, 370–71, 375.

9. Ibid., 376, 378–79, 758, 793–96.

10. Ibid., 395, 587, 688, 793–96.

11. Mary Boykin Chesnut, *A Diary from Dixie*, ed. Ben Ames Williams (Boston: Houghton-Mifflin, 1949), 179, 213, 278; *Journal of the Convention of the People of South Carolina*, 588.

12. *Journal of the Convention of the People of South Carolina*, 674–76; *Journal of the Senate of the State of South Carolina* (Columbia, 1861), 18.

13. J.E.C.—1861, February 25; James L. Orr to Nelson L. Hill, "Letterbook of Governor Orr, No. 3" (1867), 178, MS volume, SCDAH.

14. "Journal of the Executive Council of 1862," February 19, April 16, MS volume in possession of the Historical Commission of South Carolina (hereafter cited as J.E.C.—1862).

15. J.E.C.—1862, March 4, 6; May 1, 17.
16. *Journal of the Convention of the People of South Carolina,* 676. J.E.C.—1862, March 12, 15; May 14; June 21; July 15, 21; September 12.
17. J.E.C.—1862, May 14.
18. Ibid., May 15, 17, 19.
19. *Charleston Courier,* October 23, 1862. J.E.C.—1862, May 24; June 2.
20. J.E.C.—1862, September 16, 25.
21. Ibid., February 7; June 9, 24.
22. Ibid., February 7; March 1.
23. Even the distillation of fruits was prohibited after May 15. J.E.C.—1862, February 20; March 11; May 15.
24. J.E.C.—1862, February 20; April 3; May 15; October 31.
25. Ibid., November 3.
26. Ibid., April 17.
27. Ibid., May 15.
28. Ibid., February 5; March 12, 24; April 25; May 20, 26, 30; August 5; October 21, 30.
29. Ibid., April 4, 9.
30. Ibid., March 10.
31. Ibid., April 14, 15.
32. Ibid., April 21.
33. Ibid., February 7, 12; March 7.
34. Ibid., June 16.
35. Ibid., March 4; May 3, 7.
36. Ibid., February 5.
37. Ibid., March 11, 19; April 13; June 9, 12, 21, 26; July 11.
38. *Charleston Mercury,* August 22, 1862. J.E.C.—1862, July 28; August 7.
39. *Tri-Weekly Southern Guardian* (Columbia), July 9, 1862.
40. *Journal of the Convention of the People of South Carolina,* 649, 653.
41. J.E.C.—1862, March 3, 5.
42. *Edgefield Advertiser* as quoted in the *Charleston Courier,* January 23, 1862.
43. J.E.C.—1862, February 2.
44. Ibid., April 9.
45. *Charleston Courier,* May 1, 5, 8, 15; July 16, 24, 25, 31; August 1. *Charleston Mercury,* May 3, 1862.
46. *Charleston Courier,* August 1, 1862.
47. Ibid., July 9 (One of the People), July 25, August 6 (Civis); *Charleston Mercury,* March 12, 1862; *Journal of the Convention of the People of South Carolina,* 399, 656.
48. *Journal of the Convention of the People of South Carolina,* 417, 425–26, 429–30, 433–34, 438, 734–36.
49. *Journal of the Convention of the People of South Carolina,* 370–71; Henry Timrod's poem "Charleston," which appeared in the *Charleston Mercury* on December 13, 1862.

WILLIAM L. YANCEY AND THE LEAGUE OF UNITED SOUTHERNERS

(1946)

Austin L. Venable

An interesting episode in the campaign of 1860 was the controversy over the constitution of the League of United Southerners. This dispute grew out of an effort by the Douglas and Bell forces to prove that William L. Yancey was a disunionist, and thereby discredit the Breckenridge Democracy, with which he was actively affiliated, as a party of secession and disunion.

During the bitter campaign the opposition asserted that Yancey had originated the League of United Southerners, that it was a secret organization, and that his motive was the disruption of the Union. Glaring headlines and earnest editorials warned the electorate against the terrible "fire-eater" and his subversive organization.

As proof of their charges, the superpatriots circulated copies of a document purporting to be the constitution of the League of United Southerners. Article I read as follows: "The members of this organization shall be known as the Leaguers of the South, and our motto shall be, 'A Southern republic is our only safety.'"[1]

A superficial consideration of the evidence affords a substantial basis for the charges against Yancey. Although he did not originate the idea of a League of United Southerners, he did play an active role in promoting the movement. On June 15, 1858, in a letter to James S. Slaughter, Yancey recommended the formation of such leagues. A few weeks later, on July 10, he spoke at Bethel Church in favor of the movement, and again at Benton on July 17. Furthermore, he organized a league at Montgomery and helped draft a constitution for it.

Further evidence indicating that Yancey was working for the disruption of the Union is the fact that he was cooperating with the secessionists, Edmund Ruffin, who had originated the movement for the league, and Robert Barnwell Rhett, in promoting it. Moreover, leading southern papers of both parties, such as the Know-Nothing Mobile *Adviser* and the Atlanta *National American*, and conservative Democratic papers like the Montgomery *Confederation*, Richmond *Enquirer*, and Marion (Alabama) *Commonwealth*, attacked the movement as endangering the safety of the Union.

Finally, Yancey was quoted as saying at Bethel Church that "he had little hope of justice for the South in the Union" and that "*he bided the time* when they [the southern people] would throw off the shackles both of parties and of the government, and assert their independence in a Southern Confederacy."[2] Also, he had written Slaughter that "if we could do as our fathers did, organize 'Committees of Safety' all over the Cotton States, . . . we shall fire the Southern heart, instruct the Southern mind, give courage to each other, and, at the proper moment, by one organized concerted action, we can precipitate the Cotton States into a revolution."

Yancey's remarks seem to establish a prima facie case for those who charged that he was promoting the league for the purpose of disrupting the Union, and historians have accepted their version.[3] Such a conclusion, however, can be supported only by isolating these few radical remarks and rejecting other available evidence.

Yancey's opponents naturally seized upon his more extreme remarks, made in the heat of passion and sometimes under the stimulation of drink, isolated them from their context, and cited them as proof that he was promoting the movement in order to bring about secession. Tactics such as these were to be expected from politicians.

A good illustration of these tactics is the case of the Slaughter letter. Slaughter, a radical southerner, had written Yancey asking for his help in breaking up the Democratic Party as a means of promoting secession. Yancey declined to participate in the movement, advised against it, and recommended instead the formation of the League of United Southerners as a better means of promoting the rights of the South.

As has been seen, the loquacious southerner, in his exuberance, stated that such an organization as the League of United Southerners would "fire the Southern heart" and "precipitate a revolution." These phrases afforded splendid ammunition for Yancey's critics. They were seized upon and widely circulated as proof that he was trying to "precipitate a revolution" for the overthrow of the Union. The *Washington States*, a Douglas journal, circulated the Slaughter letter during the campaign of 1860 under the caption, "The Scarlet Letter," and Horace Greeley printed it in his *Political Textbook for 1860*[4] as documentary proof of Yancey's sinister design against the Union.

A dispassionate appraisal of Yancey's letter to Slaughter in its proper setting indicates that the answer is not so simple. The letter was written in response to a request for help in breaking up the Democratic Party. Yancey declined to participate in the scheme, although it was apparent that such a step was necessary in any plan to bring about secession. A casual reading of the letter in its entirety also reveals that Yancey called for "resistance to the next aggression" and not a revolution against the federal Union. Furthermore, secession to a member of the states' rights school was not revolution, and Yancey, being a student of that school, believed in the constitutional right of secession. Consequently, he could not have had the disruption of the Union in mind when he advised that the movement for the League of United Southerners would "precipitate a revolution."

The answer to Yancey's meaning is found in his background, his philosophy, and his course of action. He was a disciple of Calhoun, and, like that great spokesman of southern rights, he believed that a firm, united resistance to aggression on the part of the southern people was the best means of preserving the constitutional rights of the South within the Union. Thus, he believed that such an organization as the League of United Southerners would "fire the Southern heart" and "precipitate a revolution" in the minds of the southern people for unity, and would put an end to the petty bickering and squabbling for the spoils of office which had brought dissension within the ranks of the southerners for so long.

Over against the radical remarks of Yancey at Bethel Church, which seem to indicate that he was working to disrupt the Union, are the bulk of his speeches in behalf of the League at Bethel, Benton, and Montgomery and the constitution of the league, which discloses that he was working to preserve the constitutional rights of the South within the framework of the federal Union until it should be clearly demonstrated that such a course was futile.

In his Bethel speech Yancey advised against the disruption of the Democratic Party. But he frankly faced the fact that even this party had not always been able to protect the interest of the South. He said the reason for this was that the people of the South had no organized means of expressing their opinions on the issues of the day. In order to meet that need, he recommended the formation of the League of United Southerners "to diffuse and maintain pure constitutional views of the rights of the South within the Union; or, as a last resort, [as a means] of aiding the South to resume her delegated powers and to become a Southern Confederacy."[5]

Yancey's speech at Benton clearly indicates that he was promoting the movement as a means of fighting the battles of the South within the Union. He declared there "that the league was not a disunion movement, but [that it] proposed to fight the battle of the South in the Union through all political parties." Continuing, he declared that the purpose of the league was "to elevate and purify all these great parties—and cause them, if possible, to abandon the law of Compromise, and adopt the law of the Constitution in dealing with the Southern question."[6]

In spite of these declarations, the ultra-Unionists and professional politicians were apprehensive. They hastened to attack the movement. Two charges were directed against it. One asserted that the league was aimed at disunion, and the other that it was a movement for a new party, and that as such, it was directed at the old parties. Yancey, in his speech at Montgomery on July 20, answered each of these allegations. In response to the first charge against the movement, he said:

> It has been said to be a *disunion* move.—The Constitution reported puts an emphatic denial upon that charge. It expresses its aims to be to uphold and enforce the Federal Constitution in lieu of the fundamental law of National parties—'Compromise.' It expresses its aims to be to maintain a Constitutional Union. Its great design is to create a public opinion that shall force all parties to a strict observance of all our Constitutional guarantees, by holding the Constitutional Rights of the South to be paramount to the political necessities of National Administrations or National Parties. These constitute a sure basis of a Constitutional Union. The attainment of these ends will perpetuate a Constitutional Union, and therefore a league which devotes itself to their attainment can never be truly branded as a disunion movement.

In answer to the second charge against the league, Yancey stated:

> It has been denounced as a new party, and therefore as designed to subvert the Democratic and American parties. The charge is entirely without foundation. A party means an organization of individuals, upon agreed principles, whose design is to control the Government by electing its members to its office. A party therefore nominates some of its members for office, and all its members are pledged to support the nominations. Now this Constitution expressly ignores this leading and necessary element of party—it declares that the League shall never nominate a candidate for any office.

Continuing, Yancey compared the organization and function of the league with that of the American Bible Society and of the American Tract Society, both of which were composed of members of different religious sects "not for purpose of forming a new sect and opposing all others, but for the purpose of distributing widely amongst their fellowmen a knowledge of that great fundamental rule, the Word of God—upon which all evangelical sects base their faith." "So of this League," he said, "it is formed to create a stronger and healthier tone of public sentiment in favor of the Constitution."[7]

The constitution adopted supported Yancey's interpretation and afforded further evidence that the League of United Southerners was designed to protect the constitutional rights of the South within the Union. "The object of this League is, by the use of proper means, to create a sound public opinion in the South on the subject of enforcing the rights of the South in the Union."[8] The "proper means," according to the constitution, was to support candidates in both of the national parties who were committed to a program of uncompromisingly upholding the rights of the South in national legislation.[9]

Despite the constitution and Yancey's explanations, his task was a difficult one. Personal antagonism and party politics soon became involved. Roger Pryor, editor of the Richmond *South,* who had been worsted in an acrimonious debate with Yancey in the meeting of the Southern Commercial Convention at Montgomery the preceding May, led the assault. Pryor asserted that the league was composed of defunct Know-Nothings and disaffected Democrats and that its objects were the overthrow of the Democratic Party and the disruption of the Union.[10]

Although affording dynamite for the bombastic politicians, Pryor's charges were ridiculous in view of his very recent past. Some eighteen months before, he had launched the *South* as a radical southern-rights paper with the acknowledged support of such ultra-southerners as Edmund Ruffin and Lawrence Keitt. This paper, while professing a general concurrence with the Democratic Party, had been unsparing in its denunciation of the Buchanan administration and untiring in warning people of the South against relying on national parties for the protection of their rights. It had scorned and ridiculed the federal Union. In fact, it was believed by its contemporaries to have been launched, for ulterior purposes, against the Union.[11]

Furthermore, the *South's* charge that the league was composed of defunct Know-Nothings is not supported by the evidence. The Know-Nothing press was practically unanimous in condemning the movement, with the notable exception of the Montgomery *Mail,* which also joined in the chorus of denunciation as soon as it learned that the league was not designed for disrupting the Union.[12]

The motives behind the policy of the *South* are further revealed by the fact that the league, which had been originated by Ruffin for the purpose of promoting secession, was first announced in its columns.[13] Moreover, it was only when his antagonist began sponsoring the league with its moderate constitution that Pryor began to see in it a menace to the Democratic Party and the federal Union.

At the other extreme of the Democratic press was the Montgomery *Confederation,* which, illustrating the old adage that politics make strange bedfellows, joined in an uncompromising attack on Yancey and the League of United Southerners. Although the course of the *Confederation* was more consistent than that of the *South,* its policy was determined by practical political considerations.

The *Confederation* was ultra-Unionist in sentiment, and it was supporting the conservative Democrat, Benjamin Fitzpatrick, for reelection to the United States Senate. Another prominent Montgomery paper, the *Advertiser,* a pronounced states' rights organ, was supporting Yancey for Fitzpatrick's place in the Senate. Thus it was only natural that the *Confederation* would join in a movement to discredit Yancey.

Despite the fact that the southern people were apprehensive over recent developments such as the Kansas question and Douglas's defection, the majority were sincerely attached to the Union and were endeavoring to secure the constitutional guarantees for minorities through the instrumentality of the national democracy. Many feared the league would bring dissension within the Democratic Party. Still others were afraid of it because of Yancey's radical tendencies.

The question was thoroughly debated in the press during the summer and fall of 1858. One of the serious charges against the league was that it was the counterpart of the southern rights party, which had been revived as the Great Southern Party for the purpose of promoting secession. Those who opposed the league claimed that its constitution and that of the Great Southern Party were one and the same thing. The conservative Democratic Marion *Commonwealth* had been one of the leaders in assiduously propagating this charge.

The battered leaguers, in a lengthy newspaper controversy, finally convinced the *Commonwealth* that the League of United Southerners and the Great Southern Party were two different organizations. They pointed out that "one purposes, in open, absolute terms, to form a party—the other is based upon the fact that it will be no party and invites members in good and regular standing in the various parties to join them." Furthermore, they pointed out that "one purposes [the] immediate dissolution of the Union—the other is opposed, and relies upon organizing so true and pure a public opinion that our rights will be secured 'in the Union.'"

In support of their thesis, one of the league's spokesmen stated that he knew "all the gentlemen who formed the 'constitution of the Great Southern Party,' and who adopted it at Prattville." He stated that "they are generally opposed to the League, because it will not advocate disunion." Moreover, he stated that the constitution was submitted to him for his individual judgment, in manuscript, and that it met his disapproval. Continuing, he said that "the two bodies are as different in name, in organization, in aim, and in principles, as were the old Whig and Democratic parties." By way of further explanation, he stated that the leaguers were "almost exclusively Democrats of the Calhoun school—intermixed with a few Whigs of the State Rights school, and that they proposed to work for the South, and to assail no parties."

The editor of the *Commonwealth* was convinced by this lengthy explanation that the league and the southern rights party were two separate and distinct organizations. He declared editorially:

> We are truly glad that the disclaimer has been entered upon by our correspondent, and as such, we make the *amende honorable,* by stating that at the time we thought the two organizations were one and the same thing. But as our correspondent assures us that the manuscript of that constitution was submitted to him for his individual judgment, and that he disapproved it, we are convinced that it is a different organization. This very fact, taken in connection with the constitution of the League, which we also published, shows that the Leaguers are opposed to the movement set on foot by the Prattville Gentlemen.

The editor vouched for the league spokesman and declared that he was a "gentleman of highly patriotic motives." Continuing, he stated: "we are truly glad that he and those who are associated with him, look upon the movement at Prattville, like ourself, as treasonable. Such being the case, we hope that the democracy may not be misled in supposing that the constitution of the Great Southern party is a part of the organization instituted by [our] talented fellow citizen, the Hon. Wm. L. [Yancey of] Montgomery."[14]

Further evidence that the League of United Southerners and Yancey were not associated with the southern rights party is afforded by an article in the *Dallas Gazette,* whose editor was one of the leaders in reviving that party. This organ declared: "Yancey is a member of the State Rights Democratic party, and in as good standing as any other member could be, *unless he has left it privately,* and his known courage and frankness forbid such a conjecture. It would be an insult to his character to think of such a thing."[15]

Despite the charges of the more partisan papers against the league and Yancey, the more conservative members of the press, such as the *Commonwealth* and the Richmond *Enquirer,* were convinced that the movement was not aimed at secession. Nevertheless, they preferred to rely on the national democracy for the protection of their constitutional rights, and they were apprehensive of the effect of the league on the democracy. The *Enquirer* expressed their point of view when its editor wrote concerning Yancey and the league:

> We believe him to be an honest man, and we are gratified to discover that we were mistaken in deducing from his letter the conclusion that he has aided in the formation of a league for the purpose of precipitating disunion. But taking his own ground that this league is intended only for the perpetuation of a Constitutional Union, we cannot coincide in the apprehension of impending aggression which has induced the step, nor endorse the movement which this apprehension has inaugurated. We see no

danger which threatens to render a resort to sectional organization necessary for the protection of Southern rights—and we rely confidently on the Democratic party, North and South, to afford, not only a defense against further invasion of the doctrine of state equality, but to obtain for them additional guarantees by means of Federal legislation.[16]

Under these conditions Yancey was compelled to abandon the league. It was to rise and plague him again, however, during the campaign of 1860. Evidence was produced early in the campaign showing that the purported constitution of the league was fictitious. On August 20, 1860, the official constitution of the League of United Southerners was produced under oath and supported by the following document:

> We hereby certify that, on the 20th of July, 1858, the following constitution of the Montgomery League of United Southerners was reported by a committee on a constitution, viz.; J. C. B. Mitchell, W. L. Yancey, and C. G. Gunter, and was adopted—that it is the only constitution ever adopted by the League, and has never been changed in any particular—and further, that all its meetings were public, and that there was no secrecy nor oath connected with the League.
>
> Sam L. L. Arrington,
> President William A. Gunter, Secretary

The disputed point was covered by the following article: "The object of this League is, by the use of proper means, to create a sound public opinion in the South on the subject of enforcing the rights of the South in the Union."[17]

A comparison of this text of the constitution with the one appearing in the Montgomery *Mail* the day after the constitution was adopted in Montgomery on July 20, 1858, reveals that they are identical. In other words, the comparison of the two documents substantiates the affidavit cited above.[18]

In view of the fact that this was the constitution of the Montgomery League, the question naturally arises as to whether it was the constitution of a local league and one which differed from that of the general league. An examination of the accompanying affidavit reveals that it was "the only constitution ever adopted by the League and that it has never been changed in any particular."

The origin of the bogus constitution, which was circulated during the campaign of 1860, as well as further evidence that Yancey was not promoting the league for the purpose of disrupting the Union, is found in the Montgomery

Mail, the radical Know-Nothing paper. For several days prior to the meeting at Bethel, the *Mail* carried a series of articles concerning the proposed league. The refrain of these articles was "a Southern Republic is our only safety." Moreover, the *Mail* proposed a constitution for the embryonic organization, article one of which stated: "The members of this organization shall be known as *The Leaguers of the South*; and our motto shall be, *A Southern Republic is our only Safety.*"

It will be observed that this is the exact wording of article I of the document which was circulated in the campaign of 1860 as the constitution of the League of United Southerners. But there is no evidence that it was ever adopted even by the local league at Bethel. Furthermore, the *Mail* was significantly silent on the question from the time of the meeting at Bethel on July 10 until the meeting at Montgomery on July 20 when "the only constitution ever adopted by the League" was drawn up and ratified. Then the *Mail* came out with the following editorial: "We publish today the remarks of Hon. W. L. Yancey, explaining the aims and objects of the 'Leaguers of the South,' and trust that the organs and leaders of the National Democracy—who have had the figets for several weeks—will now be able to 'sleep o' nights.' . . . They can now banish their fears. . . . the new organization is not for the purpose of destroying the existing parties."[19]

In the light of such evidence, and despite the few radical remarks of Yancey, the charges that he promoted the League of United Southerners in order to disrupt the Union lose their force. Yancey's intemperate remarks indicating that he was promoting the movement for the purpose of secession can be neither dismissed nor accepted at their face value. They must be fitted into the mosaic. This can be done only in terms of his personality and the stress of the times. The old crusader was not averse to an occasional drink before making a speech. He was a man of deep convictions and strong passions. Furthermore, he, and southerners in general, believed that powerful influences in the North threatened the federal Union and the agrarian way of life. Thus in the heat of passion and under the excitement of the turbulent period, he doubtless felt at times that secession was inevitable. But the assertion that he was plotting secession is not supported by the evidence.

The preponderance of evidence indicates that Yancey was working in good faith to organize the League of United Southerners as a means of preserving the constitutional rights of the South within the Union and that he anticipated using it for secession only as a last resort after all other efforts had failed. This is shown by his refusal to support Slaughter in his movement to disrupt the Democratic Party, by his advice against the dissolution of the national parties, and by his repudiation of the southern rights party.

NOTES

1. Nashville *Patriot,* August 24, 1860; speech of William L. Yancey delivered at Memphis, Tennessee, August 14, 1860 (typewritten copy from stenographic report of the Memphis *Daily Avalanche,* August 17, 1860), 64, in William L. Yancey Papers (Alabama State Department of Archives and History, Montgomery).
2. Montgomery *Advertiser and State Gazette,* July 21, 1858.
3. Laura A. White, *Robert Barnwell Rhett: Father of Secession* (New York: Century Co., 1931), 146–47; Emerson David Fite, *The Presidential Campaign* of 1860 (New York: Macmillan Co., 1911), 176–77; Daniel Wait Howe, *Political History of Secession* (New York: G. P. Putnam's Sons, 1914), 182–83.
4. Horace Greeley, *Political Textbook for 1860* (New York, 1860), 173.
5. Montgomery *Advertiser and State Gazette,* July 21, 1858; Montgomery *Weekly Advertiser,* December 14, 1859.
6. Montgomery *Weekly Advertiser,* December 14, 1859.
7. Montgomery *Mail,* July 22, 1858.
8. Ibid., July 21, 1858.
9. Ibid.
10. Richmond *South,* quoted in Richmond *Daily Enquirer,* August [date missing], 1858; Richmond *South,* July 21, 1858.
11. Richmond *Daily Enquirer,* August [date missing]. 1858.
12. Montgomery *Mail,* July 22, 1858.
13. Richmond *Daily Enquirer,* August [date missing], 1858; Avery Craven, *Edmund Ruffin, Southerner* (New York: Appleton and Co., 1932), 162–63.
14. Marion *Commonwealth,* October 6, 1858.
15. Cahawba *Dallas Gazette,* July 8, 1859.
16. Richmond *Daily Enquirer,* August [date missing], 1858.
17. Montgomery *Weekly Advertiser,* August 29, 1860. This bit of evidence has been neglected by historians.
18. Montgomery *Mail,* July 21, 1858; Montgomery *Weekly Advertiser,* August 29, 1860.
19. Montgomery *Mail,* July 22, 1858.

WILLIAM W. BOYCE

A Leader of the Southern Peace Movement

(1978)

―――――•―――――

Roger P. Leemhuis

William Waters Boyce (1818–1890) was a prominent South Carolina Democrat, known mainly for his efforts, as a Confederate congressman, to promote a negotiated peace. Born in Charleston, he attended South Carolina College and the University of Virginia, opened a law practice in Winnsboro, Fairfield District, in 1841, was a farmer, and served for one term (1846–47) in the state legislature. On the eve of the Civil War he owned twenty-seven slaves and an estate valued at over fifty-eight thousand dollars.[1]

He is historically interesting, because he was typical of South Carolina politicians during the 1850s, and because he became controversial during the Civil War. Boyce was a wealthy planter and man of stature, a conservative who wanted to maintain unity and stability in a slaveholding society.

In response to the Compromise of 1850, South Carolina was favorable to disunion. Opinion divided mainly between cooperationists and proponents of separate state secession. The small minority of unionists sided with the cooperationists. Boyce was a cooperationist who desired a southern confederacy, although he did not regard the compromise as particularly offensive. He did believe that there existed signs of northern antagonism which warranted the South's departure from the Union.[2]

Campaigning against separate action, he warned that a lone withdrawal would bring isolation and economic ruin. His arguments revealed anxiety about the racial equilibrium. In his words, separate secession would accelerate white emigration to the West. The slaves would be cut off from the western market, and the racial balance would be upset.[3]

The drive against separate secession succeeded, and when Boyce won his first election to the United States Congress in 1853, the disunionist agitation had subsided. His constituency, which had a slave majority, embraced the election districts of York, Chester, Fairfield, Kershaw, Richland, and Sumter, in the central part of the state. Regularly reelected without opposition, he served in Washington until December 1860.[4]

During the antebellum years his position on most issues reflected a large segment of public opinion in the state. The Winnsboro legislator supported the Kansas Nebraska Act of 1854, and for two years after its passage he urged a vigorous southern offensive in Kansas. Boyce evidently did not think that the South's posture towards Kansas was belligerent and provocative. In 1855 he declared that his section was asserting its "rights in the Union." He also hoped that conservative northerners would support the South's claim to "equality" in the territories.[5]

Except for his call for a forceful southern stand in Kansas, he was, during his years in Washington, temperate on sectional questions. Deprecating extremism, he speculated in 1854 that disunion would bring long and bloody wars. Like most South Carolina politicians, he was a conditioned unionist, and like the late John C. Calhoun, he was a "Marx of the Master Class." In an 1854 speech Boyce warned that the abolitionists' pursuit of the higher law and natural rights ideas would provoke a race war. Blacks would perish, southern whites would suffer, and the convulsions would spread to the North. Should the higher law theory become popular among northern laborers, all property interests would be imperiled. "It is surprising that the property-holders of the North do not see the dangerous consequences involved in the higher-law principle of the slavery agitation."[6]

He wanted conservatives to rule everywhere and protect slavery. In an 1855 speech he interpreted the slavery question as chiefly a social issue, affecting poor and rich alike. "It involves the question; shall we remain as we are, the advanced guard of civilization, enjoying the greatest amount of its blessings, and the least of its evils, or shall we run the hazards of another St. Domingo?"[7] The congressman argued that the prosperity of the civilized world was tied to slavery. Moreover, he occasionally taunted the North for its apparent social fragility, commenting that workers' strikes and disturbances occurred only under a free labor system.[8]

In his desire for social concord, Boyce wanted the country's population to remain stationary. Wishing to avoid any increase in the black population, he attacked the movement to legalize the foreign slave trade. He spoke against homestead legislation, stating that it would invite increased immigration, "too soon to bring upon us all the evils of a vast population."[9]

The same outlook led him to resist the Democratic Party's expansionist foreign policy. He believed that the acquisition of new lands would place an intolerable strain upon the country. When Cuban annexation was debated, the Winnsboro representative declared that "we do not need any more space." He also used the racist argument that the Cuban blacks, whites, and mulattoes were unfit for assimilation into the American society.[10]

Boyce complained that the South was subsidizing the North's prosperity through the protective tariff, and he adhered strongly to laissez-faire economics. Yet he regarded the defense of slavery as the South's main concern, and he wanted his section to be united as it faced the antislavery threat.[11]

In South Carolina, a one-party Democratic state, he did not affiliate with either of the two major factions—the National Democrats or the Southern Rights Democrats. The former, led by Congressman James L. Orr of Anderson, favored close ties with the national party as the most effective means to insure continued union under Democratic Party rule. The latter, led by Robert Barnwell Rhett, Maxcy Gregg, and congressmen Lawrence Keitt and John McQueen, regarded disunion as inevitable and would put no faith in national parties. Holding the balance between these two wings were many uncommitted Democrats, who were generally conditional unionists. Among them were Boyce, James H. Hammond, and James Chesnut Jr.[12]

The Winnsboro legislator contended that more intimate bonds with the national organization would restrict the state's freedom of action. Besides, he maintained, South Carolina was not obligated to the national party. Many Northern Democrats, he noted, had failed to stand by the Kansas-Nebraska Act after voting for it. Except in those northwestern states where Stephen A. Douglas's influence was great, the Northern Democrats "dodged" the issue. The congressman apparently had friendly relations with Douglas. When the Illinois senator formed a syndicate for a real estate venture in northern Wisconsin in the early 1850s, Boyce was one of the purchasers of shares.[13]

He opposed the National Democrats' campaign to secure South Carolina's presence at the 1856 Democratic National Convention in Cincinnati. His position did not prevail, and the state sent delegations to the 1856 and 1860 national gatherings.[14] Although Boyce shared the Southern Rights faction's conviction that the Northern Democrats were undependable friends of the South, he did, as a conditional unionist, wish to see the Democrats retain power in Washington. He suggested that a state convention endorse President Franklin Pierce for a second term in 1856, contending that such action would preserve "our political individuality."[15]

Desire for social stability influenced his opposition to the National Democrats in South Carolina. He frankly feared a leveling democracy, which would supposedly be stimulated by a rivalry between national parties in the state. Boyce declared: "if we wish to cherish the conservatism of the State, preserve existing forms and checks and compromises, we should above all things avoid fusion with a great national party, because in the fierce struggle for power between the different national parties—for as I have said, we will have more than one—it will soon become necessary to appeal to the fierce democratic spirit, and seek to govern from below, upwards."[16]

By the middle 1850s the congressman became pessimistic about the future of the Union. The country's growth had been so great, he remarked, that a weakening of the Union's cohesive force was unavoidable. Heightening his gloom was a fear that the Republican Party, which he viewed as anti-southern, would eventually gain power. He wanted the South to curb the Republican appeal by convincing the North that the slave states were peaceful and nonaggressive. However, should the North turn to the Republicans even while the South was moderate, then the southern people "will be satisfied that they have nothing further to hope from the North." The sensitive issues that Boyce wanted his section to avoid were demands for a legalized foreign slave trade and a slave code for the territories. He was satisfied to leave the slavery question "where the Constitution and the Dred Scott decision now place it."[17]

As the 1860 election approached he became uneasy. Early in the year he wrote of a general drift towards disunion, yet he doubted that "the Southern mind" was prepared for drastic measures. Before Christopher G. Memminger traveled to Virginia in January, with instructions from the South Carolina legislature to promote a cooperationist program, Boyce cautioned him not to be overbearing. He advised Memminger to give the impression that South Carolina would follow Virginia's lead, by remaining in or leaving the Union.[18]

While anticipating secession, he clung to his hope that the Union would be preserved. Pleading that the South "give no pretext" for the election of a Republican, he also warned that the Republicans, by expounding their "theory of irrepressible conflict" between the free and slave labor systems, were driving the South to desperation. Insisting that Republican victory in 1860 would justify immediate secession, Boyce was confident that the slave section would react affirmatively to South Carolina's initiative. A cooperationist in the past, he joined such disunionists as Keitt, McQueen, and Governor William Gist in demanding separate state secession. After Lincoln's election he called for immediate and decisive steps.[19]

In his social and political conservatism, in his militant defense of slavery and uncompromising racism, in his opposition to expansion of protective tariffs, in his stance on the Democratic Party, in his conditional unionism, in his resolve that the South should not tolerate Republican rule, Boyce was a typical and highly articulate South Carolina politician of the 1850s.[20]

In 1860 the Winnsboro representative had been a reluctant secessionist, wishing to avoid disunion but regarding it as the necessary response to Lincoln's election. Cautious and conservative, he had been hesitant in the prewar years to pursue radical measures which might disturb the social peace. He regretted the circumstances that led to the Civil War. Yet when war came he wanted to wage it effectively. If the South could not secure its independence on the battlefield, he finally reasoned, it should use diplomatic means to achieve the same goal. Boyce had the mind of a guerrilla fighter.

He sat in the Provisional, First, and Second congresses of the Confederacy. Frequently critical of Jefferson Davis, he did support some major administration measures, among them revenue legislation and the 1865 decision to arm the slaves. He usually opposed suspension of *habeas corpus,* and he voted against the early conscription laws, preferring instead a system of state quotas, but he voted for the 1864 draft law.[21]

In early 1862 he spoke out for more aggressive southern fighting, while privately he lamented that Confederate failure to advance boldly had jeopardized chances of winning the border states; for this failure he blamed Davis. As the war progressed the Carolinian came to doubt the wisdom of continued fighting. In the spring of 1862 he privately expressed misgivings about Confederate military prospects.[22]

He favored diplomatic initiatives that might distract the enemy, and he voted for various proposals for negotiations, with southern independence as a condition. In early 1863 he joined fellow South Carolinian William Porcher Miles and others in suggesting an alliance with the northwestern states of the Union. On February 6, 1863, Boyce introduced a resolution asking Davis to send a secret agent to Canada to promote such a connection.[23]

He was prominent in the congressional peace party. Among the others were Tennessee Representative Henry S. Foote and senators John Watson of Mississippi, William A. Graham of North Carolina, James L. Orr of South Carolina, and Herschel V. Johnson of Georgia. Many southerners viewed the Winnsboro legislator as the head of the peace movement. However, the congressional peace party had no recognized single leader and was casually organized.[24]

By the late summer of 1864 Boyce concluded that prolonged hostilities would ruin the South. In his words, Davis's "intermeddling with the armies is usually disastrous, and he has no diplomacy." The Union president he considered an unrelenting foe, and he believed that Lincoln's defeat in the November 1864 election would offer the South's only hope. The Carolinian reckoned that the South could undercut Lincoln by proposing an armistice and a congress of all northern and southern states. If Lincoln accepted the offer, "we might have peace as the fruit. If he declined it absolutely, or accepted it with impossible conditions, a reaction might set in against him strong enough to sweep him overboard in the Presidential election."[25]

Boyce doubted that Davis would make such an overture unless public opinion forced him. In October 1864 the congressman publicized his scheme in an open letter to Davis. He urged the Confederate president to aid the Northern Democrats by proposing an armistice and a convention of all states. The letter pictured a military despotism emerging in the South, and it warned that "a peace without reconciliation" would fasten upon both sides permanent war machines.[26]

The idea of a convention of Union and Confederate states was not new. It had been discussed throughout the war, and several politicians, among them Vice-President Alexander Stephens and Governor Joseph E. Brown, both of Georgia, were sympathetic. It was Boyce who openly approached Davis with the convention concept. The result of his boldness was a more earnest public consideration of the question.[27]

His action was courageous, and he became controversial. The letter writer encountered a largely negative response; his suggestion actually provoked declarations of support for Davis. In South Carolina the controlling political group, which represented the planter aristocracy, feared that the plan might promote reconstruction of the old Union. On October 17, a mass meeting in Columbia approved a resolution demanding the congressman's resignation. Facing the unfriendly crowd, Boyce maintained that his plan was "best calculated to defeat the North, by building up a peace party in that section." Writing the open letter to Davis subjected him to personal risk. "I am told there is a man in this crowd who has said he would kill me tonight."[28]

The plan's sponsor denied charges that he was encouraging defeatism and reunion. Shortly after the Columbia meeting he stated that southern delegates to his proposed convention should be committed against reconstruction. In Winnsboro on November 7, he visualized the opportunities open to the Confederacy should the Northern Democrats win the election. While Lincoln's successor sought an armistice, as the Democratic platform obliged him, the South could reopen its closed ports; sympathetic foreign nations would be able to intervene. Noting the numerical superiority of the Union, Boyce wanted to divide the enemy by strengthening the Northern Democrats.[29]

The allusion to the North's numerical edge aroused anger. Several days later the representative stated, "I by no means desired or intended to express the opinion that we could no longer continue the contest." By citing the enemy's numerical advantage, he replied, he was trying to foster a policy that would disintegrate the enemy. However, in the previous month he had privately written, "If the war goes on we are ruined. We lose both slavery and freedom."[30]

In spite of the denunciations that he faced in Columbia, there were signs of support for Boyce. One gathering passed a resolution rejecting reconstruction but urging the full use of diplomacy to end the conflict.[31]

On November 21, the Winnsboro legislator voted for a House resolution, unanimously passed, that the Confederacy would accept no peace short of independence. On December 2, he backed a call for a southern convention or, as an alternative, a council of state commissioners who would advise the Richmond government on matters of war and peace. This proposal, presented by Foote, was overwhelmingly defeated.[32]

Davis outmaneuvered the peace party by agreeing to the Hampton Roads conference of early February 1865. As he expected, this meeting of Union and Confederate leaders was abortive, and Davis gained support for his view that peace talks offered no hope. Boyce the peace advocate was now silenced. When the Confederacy collapsed he advised his constituents to acquiesce in the war's outcome.[33]

The former congressman, like most southern politicians, became anxious to see civil governments restored in his section. In June 1865 he spoke out for a conciliatory attitude towards the conqueror, acceptance of the end of slavery, and kind treatment of the blacks. Before President Andrew Johnson appointed Benjamin F. Perry provisional governor in June, Boyce was prominently mentioned for the position, and he received a presidential pardon.[34]

There were elements of opportunism and wisdom in his positions on postwar issues. His opinion of the democratic reform movement, which he had opposed in the past, changed drastically. Johnson, a longtime antagonist of the southern aristocracy, now sat in the White House, and Boyce was courting the president's favor. In letters to Johnson he proposed the creation of "a people's State." Before Perry's appointment was announced, Boyce urged the president to rely upon James L. Orr and himself to establish a loyal government and guide the reform process. "He and I acting together could answer for this State, and be of more service to you than any number of other people could be." The Winnsboro politician was disappointed by his failure to obtain a leadership role. In the fall he ran unsuccessfully for the United States Senate.[35]

Skeptical about the future of southern race relations, Boyce called for friendship between southern and northern whites. The blacks he considered indolent and improvident, unlikely to succeed as free laborers. In his mind, the region's prosperity required black colonization and white immigration. "Receive immigrants from Europe and the United States with open arms." In late 1865 he predicted a reduction in the plantation work forces, with much black unemployment resulting. He wanted the United States to establish agencies at every southern courthouse to ascertain what blacks were idle. He proposed that federal officials then relocate them on plantations "in the extreme South."[36]

On issues of civil and political rights for blacks, Boyce was more liberal than most white South Carolinians in 1865. He wanted the freedom to enjoy "perfect equality and justice before the law," but he opposed a universal black suffrage as a condition for southern representation in Congress. Privately he favored for both races a qualified suffrage, with the vote granted to all literate persons who owned real estate valued at one hundred and fifty dollars. Because many blacks and whites could not have met this requirement, the proposal was conservative, not a likely suggestion from an advocate of democratic reform. There was an incongruity between Boyce's suffrage position and his desire that South Carolina become "a people's State."[37]

His wealth destroyed by war, the former Confederate moved to Washington in 1866 with his wife. There he practiced law and watched public affairs. In a public letter of July 1867 he advised the white South Carolinians to comply with the recently passed Reconstruction Acts and befriend the blacks. Thereby, he maintained, the whites could preserve racial harmony and keep political power "in safe hands." He also cautioned his readers against antagonizing the Republicans, who were now dominant.[38]

Most whites ignored this advice, while the newly franchised blacks spurned the overtures of a conservative white minority to form a coalition. The freedmen provided the voting base for Republican rule, which came to South Carolina in 1868. The turn of events saddened Boyce, who commented in 1872 that the new regime was plundering his native state shamelessly. Three years later he remarked that universal black suffrage had proven a failure, and he wondered if the North might "profit by the lesson."[39] Successful in his law practice, he spent his last years in retirement in Fairfax County, Virginia. He died in 1890.[40]

NOTES

1. William Edrington, *History of Fairfield County, South Carolina* (Tuscaloosa, Ala., no date), 35; United States Census manuscript returns, Fairfield District, South Carolina, 1860. His grandfather was John Boyce, an Irish Protestant who came to South Carolina in 1765. His father, Robert Boyce, married Lydia Waters, of the Waters family which migrated from England in the seventeenth century. In 1838 Boyce married Mary E. Pearson.

2. Boyce to Benjamin F. Perry, March 17, 1851, Perry Papers, Alabama Department of Archives and History; *Southern Patriot* (Greenville), July 11, 1851. California's admission as a free state did not disturb him. And while many southerners would have accepted an extension of the Missouri Compromise line to the Pacific Ocean, Boyce disliked the proposal. Such an arrangement, he argued, would have divided California into two free states. Another controversial part of the compromise, the banning of the slave trade in the District of Columbia, he considered inconsequential except for the expression of "a hostile spirit."

3. Letter from Boyce to Hon. John R. Richardson, 1851, Boyce Pamphlets, South Caroliniana Library, University of South Carolina.

4. Harold V. Schultz, *Nationalism and Sectionalism in South Carolina, 1852-1860* (Durham, NC: Duke University Press, 1950), 52–53; *Sumter Banner*, March 8, 1853. In 1860 the population of his congressional district was 130,082, of which 62 percent were slaves. John B. Robbins, "Confederate Nationalism: Politics and Government in the Confederate South," PhD diss., Rice University, 1964, 264.

5. *Congressional Globe*, 33 Cong., 1 Sess., Appendix, 723; *Sumter Watchman,* August 15, 1855. In the summer of 1857 Boyce noted that Kansas was "slipping from our grasp," and in the following summer he conceded that Kansas would eventually become a free state. With

the Kansas issue settled, he hoped that there would no longer be any sectional quarrel. *Charleston Mercury,* July 1, 1857; August 23, 1858.

6. *Congressional Globe,* 33 Cong., 1 Sess., Appendix, 723–26. Richard Hofstadter interpreted John C. Calhoun as a "Marx of the Master Class" in *The American Political Tradition and the Men Who Made It* (New York: Knopf & Co., 1948), 68–92.

7. *Sumter Watchman,* November 14, 1855. Boyce scoffed at the contention that emancipation would benefit the blacks. He argued that emancipation had worsened the condition of the West Indian slaves. *Congressional Globe,* 35 Cong., 1 Sess., 1361.

8. *Congressional Globe,* 33 Cong., 1 Sess., 100; 35 Cong., 1 Sess., 1361.

9. Ibid., 33 Cong., 1 Sess., 536. Boyce to James J. Pettigrew, May 14, 1858, Pettigrew Papers, North Carolina Department of Archives and History. *Sumter Watchman,* August 15, 1855; September 20, 1859. Also, Boyce observed, most immigrants settled in the North, thereby augmenting the free section's political strength.

10. *Sumter Watchman,* November 14, 1855. *Congressional Globe,* 33 Cong., 2 Sess., Appendix, 91–94; 34 Cong., 1 Sess., Appendix, 337–39. He rejected the notion that possession of Cuba was necessary to safeguard American commerce, and he warned that ownership of Cuba might draw the United States into unnecessary foreign conflicts.

11. *Congressional Globe,* 33 Cong., 1 Sess., Appendix, 209–14; 34 Cong., 3 Sess., Appendix, 215–18. *Sumter Watchman,* August 15, November 14, 1855; October 28, November 11, 1857. Urging regional harmony, he sharply assailed the Know-Nothing movement, which he viewed as divisive.

12. Schultz, *Nationalism and Sectionalism in South Carolina,* 92–101, 147–49, 175–77. Hammond and Chesnut were elected to the United States Senate in the late 1850s.

13. *Sumter Watchman,* November 14, 1855; Robert W. Johannsen, *Stephen A. Douglas* (New York: Oxford University Press, 1973), 435–36. During a Congressional debate in 1856 Boyce declared that he would not subject himself to the "dictation" of the Democratic Party. *Congressional Globe,* 34 Cong., 1 Sess., 143–44.

14. *Sumter Watchman,* November 14, 1855. As the 1860 election approached, Boyce suggested that the Democratic presidential nominee should be a southerner, while his choice, if a southerner were not named, was Oregon Senator Joseph Lane. He opposed Douglas's bid for southern support, and he was annoyed by the Illinois senator's position that a territory could ban slavery by unfriendly legislation. However, he also opposed the effort, made by some southerners, to demand a federal slave code. *Sumter Watchman,* July 12, September 20, 1859; *Edgefield Advertiser,* May 25, 1859; *Charleston Mercury,* October 14, 1859.

15. *Sumter Watchman,* April 16, 1856.

16. Ibid., November 14, 1855. Many of the National Democrats wanted to democratize the state's political system, one of the most oligarchic in the country.

17. Ibid., November 14, 1855; September 20, 1859. *Congressional Globe,* 34 Cong., 1 Sess., 143–44; 35 Cong., 1 Sess., 1358–61.

18. Boyce to Christopher G. Memminger, January 4, 1860, Memminger Papers, Southern Historical Collection, University of North Carolina.

19. *Yorkville Enquirer,* August 16; November 15, 1860. *Congressional Globe,* 36 Cong., 1 Sess., 308–9. *Charleston Mercury,* November 7, 1860. Laura White, *Robert Barnwell Rhett: Father of Secession* (New York: Century Co., 1931), 171–72n.

20. On politics and public opinion in the state during the 1850s, see Schultz, *Nationalism and Sectionalism in South Carolina,* and Steven Channing, *Crisis of Fear: Secession in South Carolina* (New York: Simon & Schuster, 1970).

21. *Journal of the Confederate Congress of the Confederate States of America, 1861–1865* (7 vols., Washington, D.C., 1904–5), vol. 5: 517–18; vol. 6: 107, 382, 764, 843, 846; vol. 7: 54, 350, 379, 673. "Proceedings of the Confederate Congress," *Southern Historical Society Papers* 44: 102; 46: 110. Boyce to James H. Hammond, April 4, 1862, "Boyce-Hammond Correspondence," ed. Rosser Taylor, *Journal of Southern History* 3 (1937): 352.

22. Boyce to Hammond, March 17, April 4, 1862, "Boyce-Hammond Correspondence," ed. Taylor, 349–52. "Proceedings of the Confederate Congress," *Southern Historical Society Papers* 44: 32; 46: 110.

23. *Journal of the Confederate Congress* 5: 385–86; 6: 80–81. Boyce to Hammond, April 15, 1863, "Boyce-Hammond Correspondence," ed. Taylor, 353. When the first formal peace proposal was submitted in Congress in September 1862, by Tennessee's Henry S. Foote and Georgia's Hines Holt, Boyce backed it.

24. Mary B. Chesnut, *A Diary from Dixie,* ed. Ben Ames Williams (New York: Houghton-Mifflin, 1949), 448; Thomas B. Alexander and Richard Beringer, *The Anatomy of the Confederate Congress* (Nashville: Vanderbilt University Press, 1972), 294; Wilfred B. Yearns, *The Confederate Congress* (Athens: University of Georgia Press, 1960), 178; *Journal of the Confederate Congress* 7: 150–51; Reminiscences of Jehu A. Orr, typescript (no date, no pagination), Mississippi Department of Archives and History.

25. Boyce to Hammond, October 5, 1864, "Boyce-Hammond Correspondence," ed. Taylor, 354; Boyce to Lawrence M. Keitt, November 4, 1864, Keitt Papers, Duke University Library; Boyce to Alexander Stephens, August 24, 1864, Stephens Papers, Emory University Library.

26. Boyce to Stephens, August 24, 1864, Stephens Papers; *Charleston Daily Courier,* October 13, 1864.

27. John R. Brumgardt, "Alexander H. Stephens and the Peace Issue in the Confederacy" (PhD diss., University of California at Riverside, 1974) 297–313.

28. Yearns, *Confederate Congress,* 177; R. Nicholas Olsberg, "A Government of Class and Race: William Henry Trescot and the South Carolina Chivalry, 1860–1865" (PhD diss., University of South Carolina, 1972) 407–8; *The South Carolinian* (Columbia), October 19, 1864.

29. *Charleston Mercury,* October 24, 1864; *Charleston Daily Courier,* November 16, 1864.

30. *Charleston Daily Courier,* November 28, 1864; Boyce to Hammond, October 5, 1864, "Boyce-Hammond Correspondence," ed. Taylor, 354.

31. Charles E. Cauthen, *South Carolina Goes to War, 1860–1865* (Chapel Hill: University of North Carolina Press, 1950), 218–20; White, *Robert Barnwell Rhett,* 237–38.

32. "Proceedings of the Confederate Congress," *Southern Historical Society Papers* 51: 342–43, 409–10.

33. Yearns, *Confederate Congress,* 181; *Winnsboro Tri-Weekly News,* July 4, 1865.

34. *Winnsboro Tri-Weekly News,* July 4, 1865; Lillian A. Kibler, *Benjamin F. Perry: South Carolina Unionist* (Durham, N.C.: Duke University Press, 1946), 377–78; Boyce to Johnson, July 12, 1865, Andrew Johnson Papers, Library of Congress. Perry, a Greenville editor and lawyer, had been a prewar unionist. He was a Confederate judge during the war.

35. Boyce to Johnson, June 23, July 5, July 9, 1865; Boyce to F. P. Blair, Sr., October 7, 1865, Andrew Johnson Papers. *Yorkville Enquirer,* November 9, 1865.

36. Boyce, "President Johnson's Policy of Reconstruction," *DeBow's Review* 1 (January 1866): 22–24; *Winnsboro Tri-Weekly News,* December 9, 1865.

37. *Winnsboro Tri-Weekly News,* July 4, December 9, 1865; Boyce, "President Johnson's Policy of Reconstruction," 25; Boyce to F. P. Blair Sr., October 7, 1865, Johnson Papers,

Library of Congress. Boyce proposed that his suffrage plan should take effect after a four-year period.

38. William Edrington, *History of Fairfield County,* 36–37, originally in *News & Herald* (Winnsboro), 1901. Boyce to J. D. B. DeBow, June 13, October 1, 1866; January 17, January 20, 1867, DeBow Papers, Duke University Library. *Yorkville Enquirer,* July 25, 1867.

39. Boyce to Clement C. Clay, January 10, 1872, Clay Papers, Duke University Library; Boyce to William Porcher Miles, September 22, 1875, Miles Papers, Southern Historical Collection.

40. Edrington, *History of Fairfield County,* 36–37.

ON THE BATTLEFRONT

THE BOMBARDMENT OF CHARLESTON, 1863–1865

Union General Quincy Gillmore, the Targeting of Civilians, and the Ethics of Modern War

(2004)

Christopher A. Mekow

During the early morning hours of August 22, 1863, an artillery shell fired from a 200-pounder Parrot rifle crashed into the city of Charleston, South Carolina. This shot, fired by Union forces on Morris Island located five miles southeast of town, opened a 587-day-long intermittent bombardment campaign. The initial cannonade caused little damage and produced only a few fires, which were quickly extinguished by the local fire companies. As the bombardment dragged on and gained in intensity, however, damage and casualties mounted from the hundreds of shells fired on select days. The first civilian resident of Charleston killed during the so-called "siege," as reported three months later in *The Charleston Mercury* newspaper, proved to be "an old negro woman belonging to a Mr. Lindsay."[1] This event indicated that no one in the city would be safe from the Union Army's seemingly indiscriminate shelling. Taken as a whole, the bombardment campaign in the greater Charleston area would reach an intensity hitherto inconceivable by Confederate defenders and local residents. But was there any military legitimacy for firing on this city, the "Cradle of Secession"? By exploring the basic philosophy of eighteenth- and nineteenth-century warfare, and by then comparing the bombardment of Charleston to the sieges of Vicksburg and Petersburg, this study will assess a policy that arguably ran counter to contemporary military doctrine, namely the shelling of civilians in the absence of clear military objectives.

To better appreciate the practice of firing shells into a civilian population in 1863, we must first examine the accepted military conventions of the day. A siege by definition involves an assault against a city or fortress with the purpose of capturing it. Christopher Duffy defines a bombardment as a "general cannonade by which the besieger intended to open a fortress by striking directly at the morale of the garrison and townspeople rather than destroying the works."[2] His argument, however, presumes that the town in question was itself the fortress, in essence, a walled fortification or castle. According to this perspective, Charleston was not a "fortified" city by seventeenth- and eighteenth-century models, although its harbor was protected by forts and batteries.

Two influential eighteenth-century works codified the "laws" regarding the use of military force against civilian populations. The first was *The Law of Nations* published first in 1758 by the Swiss legal philosopher Emmerich de Vattel. The author examined extensively the rules of war as they related to an enemy or materials belonging to an enemy. To Vattel, the bombardment of a city such as Charleston, though full of "enemies" who did not bear arms, would run counter to the accepted rules of war. He wrote: "Women, children, feeble old men and sick persons, come under the description of enemies; and we have certain rights over them. . . . but these [are] enemies who make no resistance; and consequently we have no right to maltreat their persons, or use any violence against them, much less take away their lives. . . . to destroy a town with bombs and red-hot balls is an extremity to which we do not proceed without cogent reasons."[3]

The second work was written by G. F. von Martens, a German philosopher of international law, and published in 1789. In the *Summary of the Law of Nations* Martens addresses the siege of a town and observes that "the besiegers ought to direct their artillery against the fortifications only, and not, intentionally, against the public edifices, or any other buildings."[4] When the bombardment of Charleston was first reported in the *New York Herald* for northern readers, the account noted that the first shell "hit the spire of St. Michael's church at the corner of Meeting and Broad streets; one burst in the store and warehouses of John Fraser and Co., on East Bay; another at the corner of Broad and Church streets, near the telegraph office; and the fourth struck the bath house."[5]

One could perhaps make a case that the telegraph office could be used for military purposes. None of the other targets mentioned, however, had a military character. According to Vattel's analysis one could certainly inquire whether there had been a cogent pretext for the bombing of a church or a bathhouse. In addition, Martens's maxim of directing fire against "fortifications only" was not followed on this and on other occasions. The question could have been formulated thus: Would the destruction of a target like a bathhouse or church have brought the conflict to a quicker conclusion? Vattel's and Martens's rules would seem to condemn the Union Army's tactic of bombarding a civilian target unless this bombardment could have brought an end to the war or even just the fighting around Charleston.

Edward Hagerman observes that military doctrine after the French revolution was influenced by a "cautious and conservative" strategy, which was "more concerned with codification than with change."[6] He notes that Antoine Jomini, a former French officer on Napoleon's staff, was most responsible for the conservative idea of warfare. Dennis Hart Mahan later taught this doctrine to West Pointers. Cadets like Gillmore, Grant, Sherman, and others heard continuously that maneuver was the key to warfare. More importantly, Jomini preached—through intermediaries such as Mahan—the preferred tactics of attacking vulnerable points with massed assaults or cutting an enemy's lines of communication and supply. In siege operations, the latter stratagem would be crucial. Nonetheless, Jomini's doctrine of cutting "an opponent's line of communication" was missing from Union strategy during the siege of Charleston.[7]

Charleston was not the only southern town during the American Civil War to come under attack. On May 18, 1863, the bluff city of Vicksburg, Mississippi, first came under sustained Federal artillery fire and would endure subsequently a forty-seven-day siege. Ulysses S. Grant had pushed the Confederate troops commanded by General John C. Pemberton into entrenchments before this important Mississippi River town. Vicksburg was an important target not just on account of the Confederate forces bottled up there, but because seizing control of Vicksburg was part of a much larger Union "grand strategy." As Kenneth Urquhart concludes, the "conquest of the Mississippi River was an essential facet of Union strategy."[8] If the Federals were successful in controlling the entire watercourse, the Confederacy would be cut in two. Vital materials and reinforcements from Louisiana, Texas, and Arkansas would be cut off from the Confederate armies in the Western and Eastern theaters. Grant had been pushing the Confederates hard in this region for months, forcing them westward from Jackson to the trenches before Vicksburg. In the meantime, Admiral David Dixon Porter's Union gunboats had also passed from south to north under Vicksburg's river guns. Once Pemberton withdrew into the defenses of the city, Grant could assault the Confederates from the east as Union gunboats bombarded the defenders from the west. The Confederates were then caught in a true siege, as escape for them was now very unlikely.

William Foster, a Confederate soldier trapped in Vicksburg, confessed that "here we are shut in by a powerful foe—prisoners."[9] In addition, Foster asked himself, "how long will our rations last. . . . all hope now is from without."[10] Soldiers and civilians in Vicksburg would suffer from lack of food and supplies during the bombardment. Grant had surrounded Vicksburg from the landside and was determined, as he wrote in his *Memoirs,* to "out-camp the enemy."[11] The besieged inhabitants had little chance for reinforcements, supplies, or escape.

Nineteenth-century siege operations normally consisted of targeting the enemy's war-making capability to bring the combat to conclusion. Grant at

Vicksburg had the enemy surrounded to the east, while Porter's Union gunboats began "targeting fortifications and gun emplacements from the west."[12] The soldiers and civilians inside besieged Vicksburg now had to compete for the same resources, mainly food, and both slowly starved. The reader should remember that, according to Vattel, the bombardment of civilians is "an extremity to which we do not proceed without cogent reasons."[13] Therefore Grant, who was targeting the Confederate gun emplacements while preventing resupply or escape for the enemy garrison, carried out the siege of Vicksburg within the accepted military philosophy of the era.

On June 18, 1864, following the bloody battles of the Wilderness, Spotsylvania Court House, North Anna, and Cold Harbor, the same General Grant pushed the Confederates under General Robert E. Lee into the trenches before Petersburg, Virginia. This, one could argue, opened the most important stage of the war. After suffering terrible losses during the campaign, Grant's forces again settled down into siege operations, as had been the case at Vicksburg. The Federal commander recorded plainly in his memoirs that at that juncture, "driving the enemy from Petersburg and Richmond and terminating the contest" had been his goal.[14]

Michael Haskew notes that the horrific Union casualties already suffered during Grant's campaign had "changed the character of war in the East."[15] Joseph Cullen agrees, observing that the campaign after Cold Harbor changed "from a war of maneuver to a war of siege."[16] Now, however, with Lee's army entrenched before Petersburg, Grant somewhat altered his strategy of driving enemy troops out of entrenched positions to defeat them in the open field.[17] He also focused on two very important targets within the town, neither of which directly involved the civilians of Petersburg.

Petersburg contained a vital military target other than its Confederate defenders. The town rested just about twenty miles south of Richmond and served as a critical rail hub that supplied both Lee's army and the Confederate capital. "Five railroads converged there and through it passed a current stream of war materials."[18] If these rail lines could be cut and held by Federal troops, Lee's supply lines would vanish. Therefore, by laying siege to Petersburg, Grant's army could defeat the Army of Northern Virginia in two ways, either by direct assault or by depriving the enemy of the necessary supplies. Even Lee himself recognized that the severing of his supply lines would soon lead to defeat and the end of the war.[19] By autumn 1864, because of the siege, both Lee's army and the civilians of Petersburg began to suffer from "starvation, disease, bitter cold and desertion."[20] Although it has been portrayed as a "city under siege," the town itself was not the actual target. Lee's army and its supply lines were.

By the time Lee finally pulled his seriously reduced forces out of the Petersburg trenches and fell back across the Appomattox River on April 3, 1865, Grant had succeeded in eliminating the enemy's supply lines. The latter's ultimate goal was realized six days later when Lee surrendered the Army of Northern Virginia. Moreover, because the siege of Petersburg brought the conflict in this theater to a successful conclusion for the besieger, Vattel's requirement, namely that Grant had "cogent" reasons or a clear purpose for laying siege to this civilian population, had been met.

In April 1863, Federal military forces began "knocking on the door" of the "Cradle of Secession," Charleston, South Carolina. Throughout the war Union strategy in the Charleston military theater included the capture or reduction of Fort Sumter, which was perceived as the keystone to the city. In its first attempt to take the harbor on the afternoon of April 7, 1863, the Federal Navy tried to silence the fort. This purely naval attack was, however, a complete disaster for Union forces, and therefore a new strategy would have to be devised.

Brigadier General Quincy Adams Gillmore commanded the Federal Army's Department of the South. He was an engineer who had graduated first in his class at the United States Military Academy at West Point in 1849, had served as chief engineer during the siege and capture of Fort Pulaski in April 1862, and was promoted for his service during that operation. By May 1863, Gillmore found himself in Washington discussing military options for the Charleston arena.[21] He and the War Department resolved first and foremost to continue operations against Fort Sumter. But the larger strategy for the Charleston Harbor consisted of four parts: "First, to make a descent upon and obtain possession of the South end of Morris Island. Second, to lay siege and reduce Fort Wagner . . . situated at the North end of Morris Island. Third, from the position now secured to demolish Fort Sumter and afterwards cooperate with the fleet, when it was ready to move in, by heavy artillery fire. Fourth, the monitors and iron-clads enter . . . run the batteries on James and Sullivan's Islands, and reach the city."[22]

Gillmore understood that in the fourth phase the navy had the responsibility for reaching the city first and without the aid of land forces. His infantry was to make no attempt to take the city of Charleston itself. He would later write that "a land attack on Charleston was not even discussed at any of the interviews to which I was invited."[23] Accordingly, if Gillmore were successful in the first three stages of the overall plan, the navy would be solely responsible for the fourth.

Gillmore launched his first assault against Morris Island on July 10, 1863. Although Union forces gained a foothold on the southern part of the island, Confederates at Battery Wagner thwarted the attempt for complete capture of the island. Gillmore then laid siege to Wagner and attempted another assault on July 18. This second assault, known today as the "Grand Assault" led by the 54th Massachusetts Colored Infantry, was driven back with heavy casualties suffered by the Union attackers. As the *New York Herald* reported, "a storming party of eleven regiments had a bloody fight around and in the fort, which resulted in our repulse, with heavy loss."[24] Gillmore's army forces and Admiral John Dahlgren's Union naval vessels then opened a siege against Battery Wagner and Fort Sumter.

As early as July 21, 1863, Gillmore had decided to construct a long-range battery in the saltwater marsh and pluff mud west of Morris Island to throw shells into the city of Charleston. Gillmore first selected an engineer, Colonel Edward Serrell, to oversee what he called the "marsh battery" project. Initially, when Gillmore asked what would be required to build his marsh battery, Serrell replied, "one hundred men, eighteen feet high, to wade through mud sixteen feet deep."[25] Even though Gillmore soon replaced Serrell, a gun platform capable of housing a 200-pounder Parrot rifle was completed in the marshes. On July 22, men from the Eleventh Maine Infantry under the command of Lieutenant Charles Sellmer volunteered to man the battery and departed for Charleston from their base in Fernandina, Florida. These two dates (July 21 and 22, 1863) are significant in this study, as they suggest that Gillmore apparently contemplated shelling civilians immediately after his July 18 defeat at Battery Wagner.

As the "marsh battery" project continued, Federal rifled guns on Morris Island reduced Sumter to rubble during what is characterized today as the "first great Bombardment of Sumter," Confederate engineer John Johnson reported that "for seven days the breaching batteries of General Gillmore were served vigorously against the fort. Their ponderous missiles, thrown with great precision of aim . . . had well-nigh done their work of destroying the strong artillery post."[26]

According to Gillmore's own report, Federal guns fired an amazing 5,009 total shells at the Confederate fort during the seven-day shelling of Fort Sumter.[27] The Confederates responded to this massive bombardment by moving the heavier caliber guns out of harm's way and remounting them in other batteries around the harbor. Gillmore noticed this activity and later complained bitterly that "the weakness of the enemy's interior defences was most palpably apparent. . . . success could have easily been achieved by the fleet."[28] Gillmore's growing frustration with the Union naval forces and their commander, John Dahlgren, was becoming steadily more apparent.

Gillmore subsequently complained often of the navy's refusal to fulfill its role in the overall Union strategy in seizing the city and its harbor. As noted earlier, the navy was to "run the batteries of James and Sullivan's Islands and reach the city."[29] By August 1863, he had effectively removed Fort Sumter as an artillery post, but, although he continued to besiege Battery Wagner, he was no closer to capturing the rest of Morris Island than he had been in July. Gillmore had come to believe that the navy, by refusing to enter the harbor and begin operations to capture the city, was not holding up its end of the bargain.

Gillmore's frustration with the Confederates and his own ineffective navy was exacerbated by the losses he had suffered during the two failed assaults on Battery Wagner and by mounting casualties from sickness on Morris Island. Gillmore later recalled that he had reported to the War Department that "the unexpected reduction of my effective force by sickness, was, at the time I wrote, quite alarming."[30] The combination of these factors resulted in the issuance of a letter, or rather an ultimatum, to General P. G. T. Beauregard, the Confederate commander in Charleston.

At 6:45 p.m. on August 21, 1863, a letter from the Union lines made its way under a flag of truce to the Confederates stationed at Battery Wagner. This communication from Gillmore demanded that General Beauregard remove his Confederate forces from Fort Sumter and Battery Wagner within four hours, or else Federal artillery would begin bombarding the city of Charleston itself. Beauregard was absent inspecting fortifications when Gillmore's note arrived at his headquarters in Charleston at around 10:45 p.m. Once in possession of this unprecedented note, however, the Confederate general questioned its authenticity, as Gillmore had sent the message unsigned. As Beauregard recounted three days later in *The Charleston Mercury*, "this communication, to my address, without signature, was of course returned" immediately.[31] By the time the note had made its way back to Gillmore for a signature, however, the Union general decided that he had given the enemy ample warning and began firing shells into the town.

Thus, the bombardment of Charleston began that morning of August 22, 1863. Yet the circumstances surrounding this event differed greatly from the sieges of Vicksburg and Petersburg. Unlike the two siege operations discussed earlier, Charleston was not a city besieged, but rather a city suffering an indiscriminate bombardment. British journalist Frank Vizetelli was in Charleston as the bombardment began and wrote the following for the *London Illustrated News*: "It was now that, foiled at all points, and smarting under his many failures, the Federal general was guilty of that barbarity which has disgraced him as a soldier. Unable to capture the forts in his immediate front, he intimated that unless they were surrendered, he would turn the most powerful guns upon the city."[32]

Gillmore directed fire not at a military target but rather at the civilian population. The soldiers of the Eleventh Maine Infantry manning the siege gun, now called the "Swamp Angel," were ordered to take the bearings of the steeple of St. Michael's Church to aim their weapon at the city. Even at Vicksburg, a city that had come under siege because of the Union strategic goal to control the entire Mississippi River, the Union guns had aimed solely at military targets. During the siege of Petersburg, Grant would target Lee's Army of Northern Virginia, not civilians. In Charleston, however, Gillmore's bombardment strategy seemed to have contravened a recognized restraint on war conduct.

Beauregard immediately sent a message to Gillmore requesting the cessation of the indiscriminate shelling of civilians: "It would appear, sir, that, despairing of reducing these works, you now resort to the novel measure of turning your guns against old men, the women and children, and the hospitals of a sleeping city; an act of inexcusable barbarity . . . [that] will give you a bad eminence in history."[33]

The shelling of Charleston had begun after Gillmore's unsuccessful demand for the immediate surrender of Fort Sumter and Battery Wagner. As the local papers reported, Beauregard now asked why the Union general had not demanded more: "why did you not also include the works on Sullivan's and James Islands—nay, even the city of Charleston?"[34] In effect, Beauregard insinuated that Gillmore had demanded the evacuation of a military post that was not even physically connected with the target subsequently shelled. This charge was echoed by the local Charleston press, as *The Charleston Mercury* asked, "can a city be shelled when a fort not contiguous to it, will not surrender?"[35] In addition, arguably legitimate military targets within the city itself were not threatened in the least.

Not only were Gillmore's actions questionable on these grounds, but the general himself left documented evidence of his motives for the bombardment. Just days after the shelling began, Fort Sumter ceased to be a viable defensive artillery position for the Confederates due to the pounding it had received from Gillmore's rifled guns. Furthermore, by September 7, 1863, the Confederate defenders of Battery Wagner abandoned their position and Morris Island altogether, leaving the Federals in control there. Even with these military successes, however, Gillmore continued to bombard the city. In a congratulatory letter to his troops Gillmore observed: "You now hold in undisputed possession of the whole of Morris Island and the city and harbor of Charleston lie at the mercy of your artillery from the very spot where the first shot was fired at your country's flag and the rebellion itself was inaugurated."[36]

Gillmore's words reveal a man intent on retribution. Could there have been any other reason for the continued bombardment? In other words, was Charleston's importance as a manufacturing town—with iron works, munitions plants, and wharves—enough to make it a legitimate target? Did the presence of Confederate troops and the scattered locations of military-industrial sites in the city warrant indiscriminate shelling? One could argue that the indiscriminate nature of the bombardment made such questions irrelevant; its true purpose was not the destruction of the limited war-making capabilities of Charleston's industries, but the need to secure the surrender of Fort Sumter and Battery Wagner. In any event, since these fortifications that protected the harbor were not "contiguous" to the city itself, Charleston was not a true "fortified city." Thus, the nature of Gillmore's bombardment strategy ran contrary to Martens's philosophy of directing "artillery against fortifications only."[37] The general had ordered the shelling of other targets to achieve success against fortifications.

With the exception of September, Gillmore ordered continuous bombardment of Charleston throughout the fall of 1863. As Confederate Major Henry Brown's report stated, the destruction from the shelling was minimal with regard to military targets: "The general result has been the injury of a large number of dwellings and stores, and many banks, public halls, churches &c. The casualties have been remarkably few and fallen almost entirely upon civilians."[38]

In fact, five civilians were killed in the bombardment from August 23 to December 31, 1863. Included in this number was a Mr. Knighton on Christmas Day, "A man eighty-three years old, right leg shot off, below the knee."[39] He certainly was not a legitimate target for the bombardment of a city allegedly undertaken for "cogent" reasons. Such results are proof enough that civilians were definitely Gillmore's targets. Ironically, it was the Union general who had initially notified Beauregard early in the bombardment that the Confederate leader would be responsible "if the life a single non-combatant is exposed to peril" especially as the Confederates "held all its approaches."[40]

Needless to say, in the end, Gillmore's operations against Charleston had no effect on the outcome of the war or even the local theater. Union forces had captured Morris Island by September 7, 1863, but they were never able to advance any farther into the harbor or closer to Charleston. The Confederate defenses in the harbor and on the islands kept Union forces at bay almost until the end of the war. The bombardment of the city continued until the Confederate forces evacuated Charleston on February 17, 1865. The only reason for this abandonment was the capture of Columbia, South Carolina, by General William T. Sherman, which effectively cut the supply lines for Charleston's defenders. Sherman knew he did not have to go to Charleston to seize it; he needed only to isolate the enemy garrison there. The only military benefit Gillmore's operations had for the Union's war effort was that they forced the Confederacy to keep a garrison in Charleston to man its defenses. That being said, we now know that Charleston's Confederate forces were stretched alarmingly thin, so much so that the local militia, made up of boys and old men, was patrolling the streets of the city.

So what was the purpose of Gillmore's bombardment? The Union Army had not surrounded the citizens of Charleston to prevent their escape or to interdict reinforcements and supplies, as was the case in Vicksburg. The bombardment of Charleston was unlike that of Petersburg, where Federals under Grant were targeting not civilians, but the Confederate military machine and its resupply capabilities. By contrast, Charleston was cannonaded for a different reason. Even though he had reduced Fort Sumter to rubble, Gillmore's high casualty rates on Morris Island and his frustration with the inaction of Dahlgren and Union naval forces led him to introduce a new type of "modern" warfare on

Charleston. Nevertheless, Gillmore's warfare style differed fundamentally from Sherman's subsequent destructive campaign through Georgia and South Carolina. It is generally accepted that the latter "took the war" to the Confederate civilian population in a manner that earned him fame or infamy as a pioneer of "total war." But during the "March to the Sea" Sherman always operated, as far as his issued orders were concerned, within accepted contemporary rules of war."[41] Gillmore, on the other hand, deliberately targeted civilians without a "cogent" or clear military objective and thus appeared to act contrary to the accepted military practices of the day.

These conclusions both indicate a larger context and suggest further lines of inquiry regarding the "total war" aspects of the Union's military campaigns in Georgia and the Carolinas during the final years of this conflict. Was there an explicit, conscious, and shared understanding among leading and lesser Union commanders—like Sherman and Gillmore—to implement new strategies and tactics within or beyond the traditional "rules" of war-making that would inflict suffering, intentional or not, on the civilian population? How, if at all, did the Lincoln administration participate in the formulation of these new strategies and tactics? Seen from this perspective, the bombardment of Charleston's civilians is but a single aspect—albeit a not unimportant one—in the larger development of "total war" doctrine in the modern age.

NOTES

1. "The Siege-One Hundred and Thirty-Fourth Day," *Charleston Mercury,* November 23, 1863, www.accessiblearchives.com (Malvern, PA: Accessible Archives).

2. Christopher Duffy, *Fire and Stone: The Science of Fortress Warfare, 1660–1860* (London: David and Charles, 1975), 98.

3. Emmerich de Vattel, *The Law of Nations; or Principles of the Law of Nature Applied to the Conduct and Affairs of Nations and Sovereigns* (Philadelphia: P. H. Nicklen, 1835), 351, 369.

4. G. F. von Martens, *Summary of the Law of Nations: Being the Science of Natural Law, Covenants, Power &c. Founded upon the Treaties and Customs of Modern Nations in Europe,* 4th ed. (London: William Corbett. 1829), 302.

5. "Charleston and Its Vicinity," *New York Herald,* September 21, 1863, www.accessiblearchives.com (accessed November 2002).

6. Edward Hagerman, *The American Civil War and the Origins of Modern Warfare: Ideas, Organization, and Field Command* (Bloomington: Indiana University Press, 1988), 3.

7. Ibid., 4. Another work on the close connection between Vattel and American military doctrine during the American Civil War is Mark Grimsley, *The Hard Hand of War: Union Military Policy Toward Southern Civilians, 1861–1865* (New York: Cambridge University Press, 1995), 214, who states, "The laws, and usages of war, under which Civil War commanders operated were redolent in Vattel's *Law of Nations.*" For discussions of Jomini's influence on military doctrine at West Point and during the Civil War see Russell F. Weigley, *The American Way of War: A History of United States Military Strategy and Policy* (Bloomington: University of Indiana Press, 1973), 82; Gary Gallagher, "Upon Their Success Hang

Momentous Interests: Generals," in Gabor S. Borit, ed., *Why the Confederacy Lost* (New York: Oxford University Press, 1992), 86; and T. Harry Williams, "The Military Leadership of North and South," in David Donald, ed., *Why the North Won the Civil War* (New York: Simon and Schuster, 1996), 42.

8. Kenneth T. Urquhart, ed., *Vicksburg: Southern City Under Siege* (New Orleans: Historic New Orleans Collection, 1980), xiv.

9. Ibid., 20.

10. Ibid., 41.

11. Ulysses S. Grant, *Personal Memoirs of U. S. Grant* (New York: Dover, 1995), 210.

12. Phillip A. B. Leonard, "Forty-seven Days," *Civil War Times Illustrated* 39 (2000): 43.

13. Vattel, *The Law of Nations*, 369.

14. Grant, *Personal Memoirs*, 410.

15. Michael E. Haskew, "The Siege of Petersburg," *Military History* 12, no. 10 (1995): 46.

16. Joseph P. Cullen, "The Siege of Petersburg," *Civil War Times Illustrated* 9, no. 5 (1970): 5. It is estimated today that Union forces suffered almost fifty thousand dead, wounded, and captured by the time the Confederates entrenched themselves before Petersburg. Consequently, Grant began to receive severe criticism in northern newspapers for his deadly tactics.

17. Regarding Grant's former approach see Noah Andre Trudeau, *The Last Citadel: Petersburg, Virginia June 1864–April 1865* (Boston: Little Brown & Co., 1991), 30.

18. Cullen, "The Siege of Petersburg," 7.

19. Cullen, "The Siege of Petersburg."

20. Haskew, "The Siege of Petersburg," 52.

21. Mark Mayo Boatner, *The Civil War Dictionary* (New York: Vintage Books, 1988), 343.

22. Ibid., 16–17.

23. Ibid., 13.

24. "Important from Charleston," *New York Herald*, July 27, 1863, www.accessible archives.com (accessed November 2002).

25. *The Story of One Regiment: The Eleventh Maine Infantry Volunteers in the War of the Rebellion* (New York: J. J. Little & Co., 1896), 138.

26. John Johnson, *The Defense of Charleston Harbor; Including Fort Sumter and the Adjacent Islands, 1863–1865* (Freeport, N.Y.: Books for Libraries Press, 1970), 133.

27. Quincy Adams Gillmore, *Engineer and Artillery Operations against the Defenses of Charleston Harbor in 1863* (New York: D. Van Nostrand, 1865), 64.

28. Ibid., 64. According to engineer John Johnson, Confederate forces began removing Fort Sumter's guns after Union forces landed on Morris Island. He also notes that Beauregard ordered the removal of the remaining guns after the first "great bombardment" and that this task was accomplished by engineer John F. Matthews. John Johnson, *The Defense of Charleston Harbor*, 108, 139. For a report on Matthews's work see *The War of the Rebellion: A Compilation of the Official Records of the Union and Confederate Armies* (Washington, D.C.: Government Printing Office, 1895), vol. 28, part 1: 617–18. Although there is a myth that the guns in Sumter were buried under the rubble and not uncovered until the 1950s by the National Park Service, only three guns from the Confederate defense of the fort were actually found during excavations; see William Luckett, "Completion Report of Construction Project Excavation," *Fort Sumter Excavations, 1951–1959* (Washington, D.C.: Government Printing Office, 1959), no page numbers.

29. Gillmore, *Engineer and Artillery Operations against the Defenses of Charleston Harbor in 1863*, 17.

30. Ibid., 55.
31. "General Gillmore's Demand for the Evacuation of Morris Island and Fort Sumter," *The Charleston Mercury*, August 24, 1863, www.accessiblearchives.com (accessed November 2002).
32. Frank Vizetelli, "When Charleston Was under Fire," *New Age Magazine* 15, no. 3 (1911): 344.
33. *The Charleston Mercury*, August 24, 1863, www.accessiblearchives.com (accessed November 2002).
34. Ibid.
35. Ibid., August 28, 1863, www.acccssiblcarchives.com (accessed November 2002).
36. Quincy A. Gillmore, "General Orders" in *The War of the Rebellion* 28, part 2: 94.
37. Martens, *Summary of the Law of Nations*, 302.
38. Henry Bryan, "Report of Major Henry Bryan, Assistant Inspector-General, C.S. Army," January 6, 1864, in *The War of the Rebellion* 28, part 1: 682–83.
39. Alfred Rhett, "Reports of Colonel Alfred Rhett, 1 January 1864," in *The War of the Rebellion* 28, part 1: 684–85.
40. Quincy A. Gillmore, "Generals' Papers and Books," National Archives and Records Administration, Washington. D.C., Record Group 94, Entry 159, August 22, 1863. Today it is difficult to ascertain the total number of civilian casualties resulting from the bombardment. The *Charleston Daily Courier* did report periodically on Charleston civilians killed or wounded by shelling; see the front pages of the following issues: December 28, 1863; January 21, February 3, February 4, March 5, June 2, June 4, and June 16, 1864; and p. 2 of January 12, 1865.
41. John Bennett Walters, "General William T. Sherman and Total War," *Journal of Southern History* 14, no. 4 (November 1948): 475.

DALTON AND THE REBIRTH OF THE ARMY OF TENNESSEE

(2002)

Louis P. Towles

It was the afternoon of November 25, 1863, and the Confederate Army of Tennessee was in disorderly retreat into northern Georgia. The force that had previously contested the fields of Perryville, Stones River, and Chickamauga so stubbornly had collapsed now on the slopes of Missionary Ridge. The army's losses, 75 percent of whom were prisoners, numbered nearly 7,000 men. This exceeded the 6,000 casualties suffered by the assaulting Union columns. Likewise devastating was the loss of more than a third of the army's artillery and the bulk of its caissons, wagons, equipment, and supplies. Even more shattering was the realization that the army's commander, General Braxton Bragg, was at fault.[1]

Earlier that fall of 1863, while in the midst of a campaign to capture Chattanooga, Bragg unwittingly had initiated the sequence of events that would lead to this defeat. A quarrelsome commander by nature and never inclined to forget a slight, he had implemented changes he felt would have reduced conflict within the army. He had transferred senior and popular commanders who disliked him, had reshuffled the composition of many of his brigades and divisions to undercut his chief detractors, and had sought to intimidate those opponents who remained with the army. Thus engrossed in a personal war he had failed to keep his men adequately fed and sheltered. Even worse, with morale dropping, desertions increasing, and units in disarray, he had divided his command and sent a part against Knoxville. As a result he had retained fewer than 35,000 soldiers to defend a seven-mile front against as many as 100,000 Federals. He had also overlooked the most obvious signs of impending conflict—military actions on October 27 and 29, increased enemy movements, and frequent shelling. Instead of recognizing the obvious, on November 19 he had signaled the end of campaigning by ordering the construction of winter huts and camps.[2]

"No one apprehends any danger of [the Union forces] attempting to advance," wrote Captain John S. Palmer of the Tenth South Carolina. "General Bragg has begun to furlough pretty freely. I think it a capital idea." And when the battle came five days later no one was more surprised than Braxton Bragg. If being taken unaware was not serious enough, he compounded his errors by failing to lay out adequate defensive works, to give proper direction to his subordinates, and to coordinate the defense. As a result Union soldiers easily broke through hastily constructed works. "Gray clad men," wrote one Union combatant, "rushed wildly down the hill and into the woods, tossing away knapsacks, muskets, and blankets as they ran. . . . in ten minutes all that remained of the defiant rebel army that has so long besieged Chattanooga was captured guns, disarmed prisoners, moaning wounded, ghastly dead, and scattered, demoralized fugitives." Only a stubborn defense by Patrick Cleburne's division at Tunnel Hill and Ringgold Gap saved the army from complete destruction.[3]

It now remained to be seen how many "demoralized fugitives" would make it to Rocky Face, a hastily selected natural abutment in front of Dalton, Georgia. For the soldiers who arrived at the destination, it was then a matter of what leader could keep them together, restore their faith in the "Just & right cause," and rekindle the confidence of the army in itself. Would this reconstituted force be capable of defending Georgia and the all-important rail junction at Atlanta? And would the Army of Tennessee also be able to resume the offensive, drive Union forces hack, and reassert control over Tennessee's grain fields and recruiting grounds, as Confederate President Jefferson Davis required?[4]

To examine the effectiveness of reconstructing the shattered army, the only such effort ever attempted by Confederate authorities, it would be necessary to analyze the entire army's conduct through the rebuilding process and to evaluate its actions in the Atlanta Campaign, which followed. Since such a task is too massive for a single article, a simpler path, the monitoring of one unit, has been taken. This study, therefore, follows Brig. Gen. Arthur M. Manigault's brigade, explores all available sources regarding its soldiers' actions and opinions, and determines both how the brigade responded to the rebuilding process and how it performed in the field.

Manigault's command, a composite brigade, was typical of the Army of Tennessee. Its regiments—the Twenty-fourth, the Thirty-fourth, and Twenty-eighth Alabama and the Nineteenth and Tenth South Carolina—were recruited in 1861, brigaded at Corinth in 1862, and placed under the command of Colonel, later Brigadier General, Manigault in early 1863. A part of Thomas C. Hindman's division, this brigade was the best-drilled unit at Corinth, had fought well in the Perryville campaign and at Stone's River, and had drawn praise for its performance at Chickamauga. Yet these same troops were also implicated in the collapse of November 25. Soldiers from the Twenty-fourth Alabama had abandoned the brigade and their own position on the ridge after Deas's and Holtzclaw's Alabama brigades had broken before advancing blue columns. Consequently Alabama troops and anyone associated with them were now indiscriminately labeled as cowards and greeted derisively by hoots of "Yaller-hammer, Alabama! Flicker, flicker, yaller-hammer!" Seeking to blame others for his own negligence and grasping at straws, Bragg placed on Manigault's men part of the blame for the debacle.[5]

Contrary to Bragg's misinformation, the brigade, with the exception of members of the Twenty-fourth, had neither broken nor abandoned the field precipitously. To the contrary, it was Col. William F. Tucker's Mississippi brigade and Brig. Gen. Zachariah Deas's Alabama regiments to Manigault's immediate left and right that had first given way. In the break that resulted, Manigault's men fell back a quarter-mile only after Union soldiers turned Tucker's captured cannon on them. At this point the brigade reformed and remained in its position until dark, guarding one of the several avenues of escape. The survivors then forded Chickamauga Creek and joined the retreat. It was a sad occasion, for 634 members of the unit, many of them prisoners, remained behind.[6]

Because they were helping to cover the army's withdrawal, Manigault's regiments did not reach Rocky Face, forty miles distant, until the afternoon of November 27. The men, part of the army's nearly 29,000 who successfully reached their destination, were tired, dispirited, and often without clothing, shoes, blankets, food, or weapons. Due to the almost constant rain they had struggled over roads that were little more than muddy quagmires by day and sheets of ice by night. The soldiers were also compelled to cross swollen rivers and creeks that were beginning to ice.[7]

Dalton, a small town on the Western & Atlantic Railroad, did little to relieve the feeling of despondency. The town was only a defenseless railhead ninety-six miles from Atlanta, bereft of food, ammunition, or shelter for the incoming soldiers. The brigade troops, like the rest of Bragg's men, had to sleep in the icy woods without tents and covering for weeks as they constructed shelters. An officer of the Twenty-fourth Alabama was quick to note that he was not very happy when he had "to sit up all night at the root of a tree by a sorry fire and a freezing rain falling upon me all the while." Still, Manigault's soldiers were more fortunate than most. At least they had arrived to find hot food waiting because their brigade commissary had heard the reports of the rout and had hastened his wagons and cooks to Dalton to prepare and cook rations.[8]

Although Joseph E. Johnston later observed that Dalton had "little to recommend it," for it had neither "intrinsic strength nor strategic advantage," the town nevertheless became the winter headquarters of the army. Campgrounds for each division were carefully selected within a three- to five-mile radius of the settlement to provide quarters for men and animals together with exercise yards for regiments and larger units. "Very comfortable quarters," wrote Capt. John S. Palmer, were constructed three miles south of Dalton to compensate for "the deficiency of tents." But the size and type of hut differed. Most resembled "chicken coops" with simple four-post construction. Because many companies did not possess a single ax, they had to borrow such tools and work, often at night, while others were not using them. Each hut, however, possessed a good clay chimney and a large fireplace that made the "domicile as comfortable a place as one could desire."[9]

Bragg was relieved of his command in early December, and Gen. Joseph E. Johnston replaced him three weeks later. Johnston arrived to find his army much smaller than reported, poorly fed, and inadequately equipped. One veteran indicated that its primary fare, bacon and cornbread, was less nutritious than that normally given to slaves and would in time cause scurvy among the troops. The general was briefed on Bragg's failings, on the latter's attempts to discredit many of his officers, and on the discord among units. Like many others at Dalton and in Richmond, he was apprehensive about the "confidence level" (or morale) of the army and could agree with historian Irving A. Buck that "troops may be defeated without their morale being destroyed, so long as they have the consciousness that it was only the fortune of war and not for bad conduct on their part, or even that it was through mistakes by their leaders." Knowing that both of these things had transpired and that a "sullen, dangerous demoralization" could follow, Johnston moved as quickly as possible to restore the "elan and the self-respect" of the men. It was necessary, however, that he not be too openly critical of his predecessor because a number of his soldiers and officers still remained supporters of Bragg. Accordingly, when some brigades cheered the new commander, he acknowledged their accolade. But when the soldiers of Hindman's and Stevenson's divisions neglected to offer the same recognition, he feigned not to notice.[10]

Taken aback by the living conditions he saw, Johnston pushed for their improvement. He wired Richmond to expedite the shipment of additional food (rice, potatoes, and sugar) and clothing to Dalton. He sought the cannon, weapons, ammunition, and draft animals necessary to make the Army of Tennessee campaign-fit. In this fashion and by his frequent visits to the camps Johnston, or "Old Joe" as he came to be called, gradually won the respect and often the admiration of his men.[11]

Families from across the South were even quicker to respond than the government in Richmond. By the end of December boxes of clothing, carpet, woolen blankets, shoes, nuts, and tobacco were arriving and continued to come until the need was met. "Treats," like sausage, spare-ribs, fresh hams, potatoes, dried fruit, coffee, onions, butter, fruits, brandy peaches, and cakes were much in demand; strangely enough, "a little salt and soap" were more sought after because "the latter is hard to be got while the former is dealt out very sparingly to us."[12]

As soon as adequate food and shelter were available, the preparation of the army began. Drill, previously little stressed in the Army of Tennessee, now received daily attention. Companies, battalions, regiments, and brigades were drilled twice a day for a total of three hours and were all inspected on Sunday. Divisions and corps with their artillery, ambulances, and supply wagons were reviewed at least once a month. Hindman's division, for instance, was maneuvered on March 16. The entire corps under Lt. Gen. John Bell Hood (Hindman's, Stevenson's, and Stewart's divisions) went on display the day after. On April 9, Lt. Gen. William J. Hardee (an authority on drill) had his corps (Bate's, Cheatham's, Cleburne's, and Walker's divisions) perform a sham battle. "Solid lines of infantry would move up within a few paces of each other & fire whole volleys into each others face," wrote one observer from Manigault's Brigade. "It was very exciting & the soldiers enjoyed the sport very much."[13]

Even more impressive were the grand reviews. On February 4, Johnston exhibited his entire force for the first time. "It was the largest parade of troops ever had on one field in the Confederacy [to date]," wrote Col. Newton Davis. "It was truly a magnificent sight. The field was about two miles long & we had three lines across it." Still more majestic was the review of April 20, when Joe Johnston paraded "forty to fifty thousand" infantry. "It is the opinion of all who are capable of judging that the Confederacy never had any better & perhaps never so good & well disciplined an army as we have here at present," wrote Davis. "All are in good health & fine spirits, cheerful & sanguine of success when they are brought to meet the enemy again on the field."[14]

While both the construction and maintenance of fortifications and the repair of local roads and bridges were also required, there was ample time for leisure. Reading (including newspapers and novels), socializing, games (including bullpen, town ball, leap-frog, cat, wrestling, and baseball), and visits by family and friends were all encouraged. Because many of Manigault's officers were masons, the brigade constructed a lodge and met nightly. Singing was a frequent pastime, and it was not unusual for groups to go from cabin to cabin serenading the occupants. On the evening of February 4, for instance, officers of the Twenty-fourth Alabama and a "brass band from a Tennessee Brigade" (probably Brig. Gen. Alfred J. Vaughan's) provided Manigault with "some music."[15]

Snowball fights, including battles between regiments and even divisions, were another form of recreation. Among the most memorable of these was a mammoth struggle between Hindman's and Stevenson's divisions on March 23. According to Robert A. Jarman, the day began when Edward Walthall's Mississippi brigade "routed" Zachariah Deas's Alabama brigade with snowballs and took possession of their camp. After a brief truce, the two brigades formed "in line of battle with field officers mounted" and attacked, routed, and captured Manigault's brigade. The three units soon united and moved against "Stevenson's division with a regular line of battle, skirmishers thrown out and all. . . . Charge after charge was made with only snowballs, and you could have heard the yelling and hallowing for miles." Years later few would recollect that this was a winter of abnormally cold weather, with frequent snowstorms, freezing rain, impassable roads, and bone-chilling winds. Instead, most soldiers joined Johnston in remembering Dalton fondly for its "pleasant days." It was, without question, the best winter quarters the army ever had, and the drill, work, games, and other activities were important factors in the re-bonding of the army.[16]

Positive changes also enhanced confidence. Regiments that had lost heavily were reinforced, reorganized, and, if need be, consolidated. Brigades and divisions were restructured to reverse the damage done by Bragg's vendetta, and reinforcements allowed Johnston to create new commands. He upgraded the commissary, supply, medical, and transportation systems, reorganized the artillery, and improved unit marksmanship. In June 1864 Lt. Gen. Leonidas Polk, who had helped to create the Army of Tennessee, marveled that he had "never known the army to be so well clad and shod and fed . . . or so well organized or so easily handled." Lt. Col. Irvine Walker of the Tenth South Carolina observed that the "discipline and organization [were] . . . perfected during this season of rest."[17]

In addition to logistical and organizational changes, Johnston won praise for his generous policy regarding furloughs. The plan allowed every soldier at least one ten-day trip home, with as many as 5,000 men absent at a time. It also permitted Manigault, his regimental commanders, and his officers to take their first leaves of absence from the war. In the process, as Captain Palmer observed, the policy "brought in a good number of men" because it allowed an immediate furlough for anyone who could furnish a new recruit. Alongside these new men, the sick, the wounded, and even those who had "overstayed their leave" were welcomed back, and by late April 1864 these and many other small changes minimized dissension and divisiveness. Morale was dramatically improved, and even the staunchest pro-Bragg men, including major generals William H. T. Walker, Edward C. Walthall, and Joseph Wheeler, Brig. Gen. Manigault, and Col. Newton Davis, gave Johnston his due. "Our army here, I think, is in better spirits than I ever saw it," indicated Davis on March 11, "and all seem to have the utmost confidence in their commanding general." Johnston, who had worked tirelessly to restore the army, was beginning to be compared to the much-lauded Robert E. Lee and was now cheered by troops whenever he appeared among them. Only one thing seemed to bother the men: "Genl. Johnston keeps his own secrets & nobody here knows what he intends to do."[18]

Nevertheless, Johnston's policies had prepared the men. By May 6, 1864 (that is, at the beginning of the spring campaign), Johnston had roughly 45,000 infantrymen and artillerymen, 4,000 cavalry, and 111 cannon. His infantry was divided into seven divisions commanded by Stewart, Hindman, Stevenson, Bate, Cheatham, Cleburne, and Walker; each fielded 5,000 to 7,000 men. These divisions were combined into two corps, the first under Hood and the second under Hardee. A third corps under Polk, containing 20,000 men in three divisions (commanded by French, Loring, and Walthall), was expected from Mississippi within the month. All units were also approaching pre-1863 strength. Hindman's division, for instance, reduced to 4,945 effectives on December 3, 1863, was back to 6,760 soldiers by April 30, 1864. Of this number, 1,838 men belonged to Manigault's brigade. To add to this, bragged one observer, there was "very little sickness," and the men were "better satisfied, more cheerful and contented than I ever knew them to be."[19] Thus in three short months Johnston was well on the way to accomplishing his major goal of refitting, reorganizing, and rebuilding the army. It remained to be seen, though, how well it would perform on campaign.

Unfortunately for Johnston, his opponent, Maj. Gen. William T. Sherman, had a force of 110,000 men in three armies that was better prepared, supplied, and equipped. In artillery Sherman possessed a two-to-one advantage in cannon, and if rifling and caliber were counted, the advantage was closer to three to one. In cavalry his edge was more than two to one, and in infantry, his strongest branch, the Union general possessed more than twice Johnston's initial manpower, with one of his three armies larger than Johnston's total force. Likewise, the equipping of some Union troops with Spencer, Henry, and Smith and Wesson repeating rifles (with magazines that held seven to sixteen shots) increased Sherman's advantage and made it more difficult for Johnston to engage the enemy on an equal basis.[20]

The campaign that began at Dalton (May 7–12) failed to produce a major tactical victory for either Federal or Confederate forces. Heedless of his own strength in troops and materiel, Sherman refused to engage Johnston's army at Dalton because it was too strongly fortified. Instead Union soldiers flanked the position by moving west of Rocky Face and south through Snake Creek Gap. To protect his supply line Johnston withdrew his army to Resaca (May 13–15) and prepared fortifications that Sherman assaulted on May 14. Unable to capture these and stung by two counterattacks, one by Carter Stevenson and the other by Alexander Stewart, Sherman again resorted to a flanking movement, a maneuver that he subsequently utilized repeatedly during the campaign. This time he forced Johnston to retreat via Calhoun (May 17), Adairsville (May 18), and finally Cassville (May 19). When a battle failed to materialize at the latter town, the Army of Tennessee continued its retreat to Cartersville (May 20), Ackworth (May 23 to 24), and New Hope Church (May 25).

To redeem sullied reputations, Manigault's men, like the rest of the army, were anxious to engage their enemy, but they were remarkably patient. The men disliked "retrograde" movements, but they cast the blame on Sherman for trying "to avoid a general engagement" and for "making every exertion to get to our rear," instead of meeting them on an open field. Cassville, however, was a test of their revitalized will. Johnston announced on the 19th at Cassville that he was prepared to fight, but when Hood and Polk counseled retreat, he complied. Capt. John S. Palmer of the Tenth South Carolina was stunned and angry that Johnston would again direct the "ill-fated" army south, and it made Newton Davis's heart "bleed to see the destruction of property [by Sherman's army]." He momentarily questioned what he was sacrificing his effort for. "I am completely tired out, dirty, sleepy & in a bad condition generally. It has been sixteen days since I changed my under-clothing & I reckon I am the dirtiest man you ever saw." Both men could only think "that Bragg would either have fought the enemy or been in Atlanta and fortified it by this time," and that "Johnston has been outgeneraled [again]." But confidence was so high that the Army of Tennessee did little more than complain. The men had confidence in their commander, a fact that Maj. Thomas Taylor of the Forty-seventh Ohio corroborated. "His [Johnston's] army exhibits less demoralization than any army I ever saw that has retreated so far," wrote Taylor. "We find very few stragglers, take very few prisoners."[21]

In the two months that followed, Johnston showed himself to be a master of retreat and trench warfare. Constant entrenching in red clay, a month of rain, deadly sniper fire, and minimal rations strengthened rather than weakened the will of the brigade to fight on. "We have learned to sleep in rainy weather, in mud and water as sound and well as in dry and pleasant weather," wrote one participant. Another commented that Johnston was managing "admirably" despite his limited resources and manpower; it was "perfectly astonishing how well our men have stood this trying campaign." Still another expressed himself even more forthrightly: "For nearly three months we have been retreating, but the morale of the army was better than when the campaign opened. . . . We had seen the retreat conducted without the loss of even a broken wagon wheel, and we had unlimited faith in the generalship of 'old Joe.' . . . We were willing to fight at any time and place he said so, believing that he would not ask us to fight unless the advantages were clearly on our side."[22]

Among the most difficult to convince, however, was the brigade's commander. Manigault admired Braxton Bragg's general efficiency and reluctantly gave Johnston credit for reforms at Dalton. As late as Resaca the general indicated that even though his current commander fought well, Bragg "would have managed the retreat [much] better." Still, the fact that Johnston's "superior generalship . . . proved correct in every point" at last brought Manigault into line with his men, and he, too, accepted that their commander "had given the men a reliance in their own superiority and a certain belief that they would eventually beat the enemy, save Atlanta, and recover the country as far north as Chattanooga."[23]

Less patient than his adversary, Sherman launched exploratory assaults on Stewart's division at New Hope Church and on Cleburne's division at Picketts Mill on May 25 and 27. When these were repulsed, Johnston instructed William Bate to attack Dallas on May 28. The failure of this thrust, even though well executed, discouraged Johnston, and he resorted to additional defensive lines, the first at Lost Mountain (June 4–18), a second at Kennesaw Mountain (June 18–July 2), and the third along Nickajack Creek (July 5–9). Two further battles, at Kolb's Farm (June 22) and at Kennesaw Mountain (June 27), were costly but inconclusive. By mid-July, Johnston and his army were positioned just north of Atlanta.[24]

Johnston's plan "to keep up the spirit of his army" by a skillful defense had kept Sherman at bay but had failed to protect north Georgia or meet the offensive expectations of Jefferson Davis. Accordingly, on July 17 the commander was removed. It was a crushing blow to brigade and to army morale. "It seemed impossible," Capt. John Stoney Porcher penned, but "it was true." James T. Searcy could not understand the logic behind the action. "General Johnston knows best," he wrote. "As long as our armies are intact and effective we have a country. The territory is not the thing to judge by in regarding our strength." Yet while soldiers might protest, shun their new commander, and threaten not to serve, the deed was irrevocable. Richmond was not interested in the opinion of the army.[25]

It was even more of a "calamity," noted Manigault, that John Bell Hood replaced Johnston. Although brave, he was "totally unfit for command of a corps," much less an army, and to replace Johnston at a critical point in a major campaign was a "hasty and ill judged" move that "contributed materially to the downfall of the Confederacy." Others expressed almost identical doubts. "Gen. Hood . . . was rash to a criminal extent," concluded Sergeant Pitt Chambers, and "we judged him to be lacking in those higher qualities that fit one for handling an independent army." When Robert E. Lee, commander of the Army of Northern Virginia, was consulted on July 12 regarding the proposed change, he noted "Hood is a bold fighter," but "careless." Lee added, "I am doubtful as to the other qualities necessary [for command]."[26]

Regretfully for Hood, the window of opportunity—eight days—was brief, and in that time he failed to win the confidence of the men. His credentials from Virginia, high casualties, and recent failures—Resaca, Cassville, and Kolb's Farm—preceded him, and his first order that "we would henceforth fight no more from breastworks and rifle pits," a way of saying that the men would attack, failed to "reassure" Johnston's soldiers. Hard-fought battles against the Federals at Peachtree Creek on July 20, at Bald Hill on July 22, and at Ezra Church on July 28 left nearly 12,000 dead, wounded, and captured, more than his predecessor had lost in the previous three months. The brigade, demoralized and disheartened, now began to conclude that their commander's "headlong way . . . costs more than it comes to." According to Col. Irvine Walker of the Tenth South Carolina the "struggle . . . the lives lost, the suffering inflicted, had all been for nothing," and many men were coming to the conclusion that they had "done their best and lost." A fourth and final attack at Jonesboro on August 31 was little more than a sham. The men were used up, "wholly disorganized," and acted more like "a mob in an open field." According to Maj. Thomas Taylor of the Forty-seventh Ohio, the advance was "the least determined of any I ever saw them make." Manigault agreed, noting that the "men did not behave as well as on any previous occasion," and he continued, bluntly, "[the men] have long since lost confidence in their leaders."[27]

Although not destroyed, the Army of Tennessee was now all but finished as an effective military force. Reduced to less than 30,000 men, a force equal to that which had retreated to Dalton on November 27, 1863, it had lost over 30,000 men by death, capture, and desertion in less than two months, had been defeated in four open battles, and was again without equipment, food, and supplies. Even worse, it remained under the command of Hood, who would complete its ruin by December 1864 at the battles of Spring Hill, Franklin, and Nashville.[28]

A definitive history of the army or the entire Georgia campaign, for that matter, was not the purpose of this study. The real goal was to determine, in microcosm, how Bragg's shattered army was rebuilt and how effective it became. The evidence, as seen through the eyes of one brigade, suggests that the work at Dalton was well done, and that the Army of Tennessee improved as a fighting force while under Johnston's command. Although the testimony of those involved also suggested that Joseph E. Johnston was not able to develop the offensive potential of the army as well as he might have, most agreed that he had maintained his troops' morale and confidence in him, preserved the army, and kept casualties to a minimum.[29] Contemporary Union and Confederate opinion agreed that his generals—Bate, Brown, Cheatham, Clayton, Cleburne, French, Hardee, Stewart, Walker, and Walthall—had performed well offensively during the campaign. Some historians suggest that if Johnston had been better served by two of his corps commanders, Leonidas Polk and John Bell Hood, the Confederate offensive capability would have been enhanced.[30] By contrast, after Hood ultimately achieved complete command of the Army of Tennessee, he led it from one defeat to another and lost the confidence of the men. As Robert E. Lee had pointed out, Hood usually "tried to do too much with too little in too short a time," was "careless," and "lacked the high order of talent" to command an army. Those who remained with him did so for two reasons: "for the cause, not the general," and because Joe Johnston had, in retrospect, done his work well.[31]

NOTES

1. General Braxton Bragg (1817–1876). Newton N. Davis to Elizabeth Davis, December 2, 1861, Davis Family Papers, Alabama State Archives, Montgomery.

2. James L. McDonough, *Chattanooga: A Death Grip on the Confederacy* (Knoxville: University of Tennessee Press, 1984), 20–40, 61–67; Peter Cozzens, *The Shipwreck of Their Hopes* (Urbana: University of Illinois Press, 1994), 20–21; John Hoffman, *The Confederate Collapse at the Battle of Missionary Ridge* (Dayton, Ohio: Morningside Press, 1985), 25–26.

3. Shelby Foote, *The Civil War: Fredericksburg to Meridian,* vol. 2 of *The Civil War: A Narrative* (New York: Random House, 1963), 856. John S. Palmer to Harriet J. Palmer, October 17, 1863, Davis Family Papers, Alabama State Archives, Montgomery (cited hereafter as ASA); Newton Davis to Elizabeth Davis, November 14, 1863, Davis Family Papers, ASA. Hoffman, *The Confederate Collapse at Missionary Ridge*, 43–45, 70–73; Maj. Gen. Patrick R. Cleburne (1828–1865).

4. Jefferson Davis required Johnston to reoccupy "the country, upon the supplies of which the proper subsistence of our armies materially depends." He was further to avoid attacking fortified positions and to fight in the "open field." Joseph E. Johnston, *Narrative of Military Operations* (New York: Appleton, 1874), 267–91.

5. Arthur M. Manigault, *A Carolinian Goes to War: The Civil War Narrative of Arthur M. Manigault* (Columbia: University of South Carolina Press, 1983), 4–21; Foote, *The Civil War: Fredericksburg to Meridian,* 867. Brig. Gen. Arthur M. Manigault (1824–1886); Brig. Gen. Zachariah Deas (1819–1882); Brig. Gen. James Holtzclaw (1833–1893); Maj. Gen. Thomas C. Hindman (1828–1868).

6. In a letter published in the *Charleston Daily Courier* on December 16, 1863, Manigault clarified a report of the Battle of Missionary Ridge (published by the *Courier* on December 5, 1863) that "Manigault's Brigade on our right gave way on the lst charge of the enemy." He stated that it was "entirely incorrect" and that he would not comment further as he was unwilling to throw blame on others. *Charleston Daily Courier,* December 16, 1863; Newton Davis to Elizabeth Davis, November 29 and December 2, 1863, Davis Family Papers, ASA; Hoffman, *The Confederate Collapse,* 23–24.

7. Thomas L. Connelly, *Autumn of Glory* (Baton Rouge: Louisiana State University Press, 1971), 271–77.

8. Moultrie Ball, "Colonel Julius Theodore Porcher and Captain John Stoney Porcher of the 10th South Carolina Regiment, Confederate States Army," Charleston: unpublished, no date, 65; Newton Davis to Elizabeth Davis, November 29, 1863, Davis Family Papers, ASA.

9. Johnston, *Narrative of Military Operations,* 277; John S. Palmer to Harriet J. Palmer, December 22, 1863 Davis Family Papers, Alabama State Archives, Montgomery; Manigault, *A Carolinian Goes to War,* 140–44.

10. Johnston, *Narrative of Military Operations,* 261–302; Newton Davis to Elizabeth Davis, December 24, 1863 Davis Family Papers, ASA; James T. Searcy to Stella Searcy, December 1, 1863 Davis Family Papers, ASA; Irving A. Buck, *Cleburne and His Command* (Jackson, Tenn.: McCowat-Mercer, 1959), 172. General Joseph E. Johnston (1807–1891).

11. Foote, *The Civil War: Fredericksburg to Meridian,* 117–218; Craig Symonds, *Joseph E. Johnston* (New York: Norton, 1992), 249–56; Newton Davis to Elizabeth Davis, March 11, 1864 Davis Family Papers, ASA; Albert Castel, *Decision in the West* (Lawrence: University Press of Kansas, 1992), 364.

12. On December 3, 1863, Col. James H. Pressley, commander of the Tenth South

Carolina Regiment, thanked the women of Darlington District for forty pairs of socks, twenty pairs of drawers, eighteen shirts, and "a lot of meal, bacon, hams, rice, peas, soap, pepper, etc." *Charleston Daily Courier,* December 10, 1863. On December 12, Corporal J. W. Jackson brought "boxes of goods to the fourteen members of Co. K in camp." After distributing the clothing, each member "had several shirts and prs. of pants and drawers. . . . I have distributed the surplus blankets to Co. M. Have also loaned the surplus blankets to those who were entirely destitute." John S. Palmer to J. S. Palmer, December 14, 1863, Davis Family Papers, ASA. A week later the Tenth and Nineteenth South Carolina Regiments received "a bale of blankets, one hundred and sixty in number, one hundred prs. of shoes, a halfbox of tobacco, three barrels of ground nuts, two hundred prs. White flannel shirts" from the Central Association of South Carolina (a women's relief organization). John S. Palmer to Harriet J. Palmer, December 22, 1863, Davis Family Papers, ASA.

13. Newton Davis to Elizabeth Davis, February 4, 9, 14, and April 9, 1864, Davis Family Papers, ASA. Lt. Gen. John Bell Hood (1831–1879); Lt. Gen. William J. Hardee (1815–1873); Maj. Carter L. Stevenson (1817–1888); Lt. Gen. A. P. Stewart (1842–1908); Maj. Gen. William Bate (1826–1905); Maj. Gen. Benjamin Cheatham (1820–1886); Maj. Gen. W. H. Walker (1816–1864).

14. Newton Davis to Elizabeth Davis, February 4 and April 20, 1864, Davis Family Papers, ASA.

15. Manigault, *A Carolinian Goes to War,* 163; "History of the Twenty-Fourth Alabama Regiment," ASA, 34; "History of the Twenty-Eighth Alabama Regiment," ASA, 50; Saul Emmanuel, "An Historical Sketch of the Georgetown Rifle Guards and as Co. A. of the Tenth Regiment, South Carolina Volunteers" in "The Army of the Confederate States," Georgetown, S.C.: unpublished, 1909, 21; Newton Davis to Elizabeth Davis, February 4 and 20, 1864, Davis Family Papers, ASA.

16. Newton Davis to Elizabeth Davis, March 23, 1864, Davis Family Papers, ASA; Robert A Jarman, "The History of Co. K 27th Mississippi Infantry," Jarman Papers, Mississippi Archives, Jackson, 26–27. Newton Davis's description (March 23) is in some respects even more complete: "Snow falling commenced yesterday morning & has been kept up, justly generally ever since. It first commenced with two or three on a side & then increased to a company & from a company to a regiment from a regiment to a brigade & finally from a brigade to a division on a side. It was magnificent though to see two divisions arrayed against each other with banners flying & bugles sounding & the men all around with snow balls advancing to the charge. The fight between the divisions lasted two or three hours. It was the most exciting sport ever witnessed. First one line would be driven back & then the other. Charge after charge would be made by the opposing forces with a yell that could be heard for miles around. Just imagine to yourself six thousand men arrayed against each other in a line half a mile long with snow balls flying incessantly from one end to the other."

17. Lt. Gen. Leonidas Polk (1806–1864). Manigault, *A Carolinian Goes to War,* 163–68; Cornelius Irvine Walker, *Rolls and Historical Sketch of the Tenth Regiment, South Carolina Volunteer In the Army of the Confederate States* (Charleston: Walker, Evans & Cogswell, 1881), 107; Joseph H. Parks, *General Leonidas Polk, CSA: The Fighting Bishop* (Baton Rouge: Louisiana State University Press, 1962), 380.

18. John S. Palmer to Esther S. Palmer, January 1, 1864, Davis Family Papers, ASA; Parks, *General Leonidas Polk,* 380; James T. Searcy to George Searcy, November 29, 1863, Davis Family Papers, ASA; letter from Dalton, February 25, 1864, Davis Family Papers; *Charleston Daily Courier,* March 2, 1864; Newton Davis to Elizabeth Davis, February 4, March 11,

April 6, 1864, Davis Family Papers, ASA. General Robert E. Lee (1807–1870); Maj. Gen. Joseph Wheeler (1836–1906); Maj. Gen. Edward Walthall (1831–1898).

19. "History of the Twenty-Fourth Alabama," 36–37; Manigault, *A Carolinian Goes to War*, 178; Castel, *Decision in the West*, 104–12; Newton Davis to Elizabeth Davis, March 11, 1864, Davis Family Papers, ASA. Maj. Gen. Samuel G. French (1818–1910); Maj. Gen. William W. Loring (1818–1886).

20. Castel, *Decision in the West*, 112–16. General William T. Sherman (1820–1891).

21. Newton Davis to Elizabeth Davis, May 17 and 21, 1864, Davis Family Papers, ASA; John S. Palmer to J. S. Palmer, May 22, 1864, Davis Family Papers, ASA; Johnston, *Narrative of Military Operations*, 320–24; Albert Castel, *Thomas Taylor's Civil War* (Lawrence: University Press of Kansas, 2000), 119.

22. Newton Davis to Elizabeth Davis, June 19, 1864, Davis Family Papers, ASA; John S. Palmer to Esther S. Palmer, June 19, 1864, Davis Family Papers, ASA; William Pitt Chambers, *Blood and Sacrifice: The Civil War Journal of a Confederate Soldier* (Huntington, W.Va.: Blue Acorn Press, 1994), 156.

23. Manigault, *A Carolinian Goes to War*, 158, 183–84, 256.

24. Johnston's strategy from the beginning was "to stand on the defensive, to spare the blood of our soldiers by fighting under cover habitually, and to attack only when bad position or division of the enemy's forces might give us advantages counterbalancing that of superior numbers." Johnston, *Narrative of Military Operations*, 318. At Resaca on May 14, Carter Stevenson and Alexander Stewart, under Hood's direction, attempted to turn Sherman's left flank. The assault personified Johnston's view of the advantages to be gained from Sherman's "bad position." A second assault, also under Hood, by Stewart on May 15 was in pursuit of the same aim. Neither was well planned. Fourteen days later William Bate sought to exploit a weak section of the Federal line at Dallas but failed. Sherman's men, taken by surprise, referred to the probe as "a fearful assault" and reported that "Hardee's entire command, estimated by prisoners to be 29,000," was in front of them. Castel, *Thomas Taylor's Civil War*, 123.

25. John F. Marszalek, *Sherman: A Soldier's Passion for Order* (New York: Free Press, 1993), 269; Castel, *Decision in the West*, 352–62; Manigault, *A Carolinian Goes to War*, 192–206; James T. Searcy to Evelyn S. Searcy, undated, Davis Family Papers, ASA; Hugo Black, a member of Hardee's Corps, said that his men were "so opposed to the change" that "they will not fight under Hood." Hugo Black to Mary A. Black, July 20, 1864, MSS, 31f, Atlanta Historical Society, Atlanta; Ball, "Colonel Julius Theodore Porcher," 74.

26. Manigault, *A Carolinian Goes to War*, 200; Chambers, *Blood and Sacrifice*, 157; Castel, *Decision in the West*, 352–53.

27. Chambers, *Blood and Sacrifice*, 157; Walker, *Rolls and Historical Sketch of the Tenth Regiment*, 116; F. Jay Taylor, ed., *The Secret Diary of Robert Patrick, 1861–1865* (Baton Rouge: Louisiana State University Press, 1959), 199–200; Manigault, *A Carolinian Goes to War*, 246; Castel, *Thomas Taylor's Civil War*, 178.

28. Castel, *Decision in the West*, 542.

29. The purpose of this study is not to debate the merits or failings of Joseph E. Johnston; it is intended to reflect contemporary opinion. Suffice it to say, though, that the bulk of the officers and men in the Army of Tennessee endorsed Johnston and his strategy of retreat and army preservation, or had faith in their ultimate success in battle or in wearing Sherman down. Col. Newton Davis, on the other hand, initially welcomed Hood because he would fight. Yet Davis indicated ruefully on August 17, 1864, that "I had over three hundred men when we left Dalton and now I have but one hundred and twenty left,"

knowing full well that most were lost under Hood. Newton Davis to Elizabeth Davis, August 17, 1864, Davis Family Papers, Alabama State Archives, Montgomery. Most scholars (for example, Albert Castel, Bruce Catton, Thomas Connelly, Nathaniel C. Hughes, Lloyd Lewis, John Marszalek, William Scaife, and Wiley Sword) agree in general that Johnston's work at Dalton and his handling of the Army of Tennessee inspired confidence among the troops. Although some scholars (that is, Richard McMurry, Stephen Davis, and Steven Woodworth) point out Johnston's failings as commander, they are nevertheless unable to gainsay his effective control of his army.

30. Polk, Hardee, and Hood were personal friends of President Davis and assigned by him to the Army of Tennessee. Known as "Old Reliable," Hardee possessed ability and experience, while Hood, a proven and brave division commander, was unfamiliar with higher command responsibilities. On the other hand, Polk was an experienced soldier and beloved by his men, but he lacked drive. When Polk and Hood combined against Johnston and refused their full support to their commander, Hardee was effectively isolated. Lee and Stewart were able, active, and well-trained soldiers who executed their orders punctually. Had they served Johnston together with Hardee, the chances of the Army's success would have been improved. See Sam Davis, *Soldier of Tennessee* (Baton Rouge: Louisiana State University Press, 1999); Herman Hattaway, *Stephen D. Lee* (Jackson: University of Mississippi Press, 1976); Nathaniel C. Hughes, *Gen. William J. Hardee* (Baton Rouge: Louisiana State University Press, 1865); Symonds, *Joseph E. Johnston,* and Connelly, *Autumn of Glory,* regarding the Polk-Hood alliance and the abilities of Lee and Stewart.

31. Castel, *Decision in the West,* 352–53; Chambers, *Blood and Sacrifice,* 157.

ON THE HOME FRONT

THE SOUTH CAROLINA ORDNANCE BOARD, 1860–1861

(1945)

Frank E. Vandiver

November of 1860 found the people of South Carolina almost unanimously in favor of secession. The presidential election of that month had defeated what little hope there was for compromise. There was really little of the compromise spirit left in the people by this time. They had had enough of that in 1832 and again in 1850. Tired of shilly-shallying, they were for "separate State action" and nothing else. The feeling that Lincoln and Hamlin would defeat the southern presidential candidates, Breckenridge and Lane, caused Governor William H. Gist, of South Carolina, to hint at the possible necessity of legislative "action for the safety and protection of the State" as early as October of 1860.[1]

In the event of secession, and on all sides this was looked upon as a foregone conclusion, several important questions would present themselves. First was the problem of secession itself. South Carolinians felt that no problem was presented by seceding, except that of negotiating certain questions regarding public property with the federal government. Secession was nothing, more or less, than the inalienable right of those who had entered into a compact, to withdraw from it when that compact was perverted to use against them. In view of this idea, it was natural that there was a general feeling that no war would develop as a consequence of secession.[2] The opposite opinion was, however, held by a minority of well-informed men.[3] If this latter group was correct, and war did result, the defense of the state would be the primary concern of all. Events were to show that the minority were unfortunately correct. Before this was clear, however, the military protection of the state had already claimed the attention of many citizens. Arms were a necessity, and it is to the various efforts of South Carolina to provide them that this paper is devoted.

The South Carolina legislature, on the first day of the called session, November 5, 1860, took up the matter of protecting the state. Mr. John Cunningham, from the House Committee on the Military, offered resolutions allowing the governor to draw on a sum of $100,000, appropriated December 16, 1859, for military emergency.[4] On the eighth, the defense of the state had become so important that a resolution was introduced in the House to appropriate $1,000,000 for that purpose.[5]

"A Bill to Arm the State" was introduced on the same day. This bill did not pass but, nevertheless, caused wide interest. The Bank of Charleston offered to take $100,000 of the $400,000 bond issue called for in the bill. The Exchange Bank of Columbia showed itself to be no less a patriotic establishment by saying it would take its full quota of this sum.[6] In addition to these measures providing funds for military purposes, the governor was authorized to issue arms to new volunteer companies, which were properly organized, with their full quota of personnel.[7]

Wishing to establish a permanent state military organization, the legislature directed that a joint military committee meet during the coming recess of the assembly, and prepare a plan for arming the state and setting up a permanent military bureau. This joint committee was to report a bill on the first day of the reassembling of the legislature.[8]

While the General Assembly was concerning itself with matters of public defense, the public was active in its own behalf. Volunteer companies were formed throughout the state and tendered their services to the governor. Many members of the state militia formed volunteer units and reported themselves at the disposal of the chief magistrate. In most instances this presented a serious problem. As these organizations reported, they expected the state to arm and equip them.[9] There were, of course, some exceptions. The Waccamaw Light Artillery supplied one-third of their corps of ninety men with Maynard rifles, Colt pistols, swords, and horse equipment at their own expense, but requested the state to furnish sixty rifles and cap boxes, sixty swords, sixty pairs of pistols and holsters, and ammunition for a battery of 6-pounders as well as for the rifles.[10] Other companies were even more resourceful than the Waccamaw Artillery. The Charleston Zouave Cadets, in need of "knapsacks, blankets, and other accoutrements necessary for active duty in the field," appealed for public help. Through the columns of the *Charleston Daily Courier*, they asked the people to help raise $1,000 for their equipment.[11]

Some companies received aid from public-spirited associations, formed mainly as committees of safety. One such was the "Winyah Association of 1860." This was organized with an executive board "empowered to look to the safety and good order of the District; to aid the Officers of Companies in providing the necessary arms and munitions, until the State authorities can act. Also in directing and promoting all matters necessary to the public good, which are contemplated by the Resolutions forming the Association." The society was to cease to exist as soon as the government of the State was duly organized for defense.[12]

Agents for various firearms of more or less repute, as well as agents for the country's best weapons, recognized a potential gold mine in the troubled secession area. Merchants also saw the chance for rich profits and stocked all kinds of guns. Lucas and Strohecker, of Charleston, had on display specimens of Colt army and navy pistols.[13] H. F. Strohecker, of the same city, was prepared "to equip any citizens, volunteers or Minute Men, with all necessary apparatus."[14] He had Colt revolvers, carbines, and rifles; Maynard rifles and shot guns; Sharps rifles and carbines; Adam's pistols[15] and Smith and Wesson seven shooters.

Luckily for the state, the arms companies were primarily concerned with selling their products and not so much disturbed over who bought them. General A. J. Gonzales, agent for the Maynard Arms Company, Washington, D.C., offered the military model of the Maynard rifle at the same price paid by the United States. This was $33 per gun for orders of not less than thirty; otherwise the price would be the standard $40.[16] He was, of course, angling for orders from the many volunteer companies in the process of organizing.

While a general sentiment in favor of boycotting northern business was rife at this time,[17] South Carolinians did not carry this to the extent of refusing to buy munitions of war from their northern neighbors. South Carolina was one of the largest purchasers of arms from the New Haven Arms Company, Connecticut, and also purchased a great deal of arms from Cooper and Pond, of New York.[18] Notwithstanding the trade with northern arms factories, the problem of securing guns and ammunition became so acute that some of the officers of the state infantry service petitioned the legislature for aid to help establish an armory.[19] Governor Gist was of the opinion that it would be important for each individual state to set up an armory "or that two, three or four states should unite for that purpose. We should not be dependent on the North, or a foreign country, for our weapons of defense, lest in the hour of need the supply may be withheld from us."[20] While such an armory was not actually established, the idea behind the discussion concerning it will serve as an example of the efforts put forth to equip the state troops for field service.

All of these undirected and disorganized efforts to obtain weapons could have led to confusion. Some system was certainly needed to coordinate the state's exertions in this direction. In order to meet this necessity, the legislature, on the first day of its regular session, November 26, 1860, reported "A Bill to establish a Board of Ordnance and an Ordnance Bureau, and for other purposes." The bill, which was ratified December 17, 1860 (three days before the state seceded), provided that a Board of Ordnance be established whose members were to be the governor, the adjutant and inspector general of the state, an ordnance officer, and three other persons to be appointed by the governor. The chief executive of the state was to be president, *ex-officio,* of this group, any four of whom were to constitute a quorum. The board was to "engage a fit and competent Ordnance

Officer," also an *ex-officio* member. He was to hold the rank of colonel of artillery, being commissioned by the governor. His salary was to be $3,000 per annum.

The duties of the board included that of examining into "the condition of all ordnance, small arms, ordnance stores, ammunition, gun carriages, and other equipment, shot, shell, and so forth, belonging to the State." In order to carry out this assigned task, the board was granted authority to call on other state officers "who have such matters in charge," for reports on the condition and location of the above munitions. It was granted free access to the state arsenals, magazines, and depots when necessary. It was also responsible for the storage and safe keeping of state war material. Ten thousand dollars were to be added each year to the military contingent fund to defray the expense of a corps of guards the board was to employ to guard the magazines, arsenals, and armories.

The board was made the disbursing agent for certain funds appropriated for it by the legislature, for the purchase of improved ordnance material. Any arms so purchased were not, however, to be issued to the ordinary militia or state volunteers, except in cases where they were pressed into service or special duty. The ordnance officer was to inspect all arms and ordnance purchased by the board. He had the added duty of establishing an ordnance department and was to perform such other duties as the board might direct.[21]

For the position of ordnance officer, a man with a good understanding of mechanical problems would be needed. The choice fell upon Edward Manigault. He had been engineer and superintendent of the Charleston and Savannah Railroad;[22] hence he was a man amply qualified for the position.

Colonel Manigault's task was not one to be envied. Some 17,000 muskets had been shipped to the Charleston Arsenal by United States authorities between January 1, 1860, and January 1, 1861, but this number was comparatively small when needed to meet the impending storm. The legislature immediately recognized the vital nature of the task assigned to Manigault, and placed the sum of $400,000 at his disposal. Later, however, this was to be cut to $150,000.[23] Taking stock of the ordnance resources of the state, Manigault reported on January 9, 1861, that there were in store at the South Carolina Arsenal, 686 rifle muskets of the latest pattern; 5,928 percussion muskets, models of 1842 and 1852; 5,000 flint locks, altered to percussion, model of 1842; 600 flint locks; 267 calvalry pistols, percussion; 501 cavalry pistols, flint locks; 45 carbines; 1,630 cavalry sabers, and 101 artillery swords.

In the hands of the state troops[24] were 11,430 muskets, smooth bore, percussion, model 1842; 5,720 muskets, smooth bore, altered to percussion, model 1822; 2,800 rifles, percussion, without bayonets; 500 Hall's breech-loading rifles; 300 percussion pistols; and 805 flint lock pistols.

In the matter of heavy ordnance, Manigault reported that he had in store the following pieces, obtained in 1851–52: six 8-inch Columbiads; thirty-two

24-pounder siege guns; four 8-inch siege howitzers; five 10-inch Sea Coast mortars; and two 10-inch siege mortars. Also, he had the following pieces, acquired prior to 1851: twelve 18-pounder guns; five short 18-pounders; twenty-three long 12-pounders; seven short 12-pounders; three 10-inch mortars. This gave a total of ninety-nine pieces of ordnance, exclusive of the four complete batteries of field guns in Charleston, each composed of four 6-pounder guns, and two 12-pounder bronze howitzers, also excluding eighteen bronze 4-pounders and twenty iron 6-pounders.[25]

The cause of secession had supporters spread over the length and breadth of the country. When it became known that South Carolina had "resumed her independence," northerners as well as men from all parts of the South, deluged Governor Francis W. Pickens, who had succeeded Gist on December 10, 1860, with offers of their services. Many propositions came in the mails of ways to reduce Fort Sumter. The Board of Ordnance, as well as the governor, was inundated with letters offering newly invented arms for the consideration of the state. John B. Read, of Tuscaloosa, Alabama, brought to the attention of Governor Pickens his projectile for rifled guns. "By the explosion of the powder the wrought iron portion is forced into the grooves of the gun, and the rotation thus communicated to the projectile secured its striking upon its apex."[26] David Looney, of Louisville, Kentucky, offered to allow the state to test a unique weapon known as "Porter's Rifle." This gun could be fired nine times in four seconds and, when empty, could be reloaded by the substitution of a small cylinder for the empty one (an operation reputed to take only three seconds). It was claimed that 1,000 men armed with the Porter gun "can discharge nine thousand shots in four seconds, eighteen thousand in ten seconds, or twenty-seven thousand in fifteen seconds."[27] This gun interested Pickens, as did some of the other innovations suggested. On occasion the Ordnance Board would inquire about these inventions with a view to purchasing them.[28] The board and Colonel Manigault did inquire frequently about arms up for sale.[29] The purchase of arms was entered into by the board on a fairly large scale. They dickered with a Colonel S. Bobo of Spartanburg to get him to cast shot and shell for the state in the Spartanburg Iron Works.[30] An order was placed with the Hazard Powder Company of Enfield, Connecticut, for 50,000 pounds of cannon powder and 10,000 pounds of musket powder. Manigault said that all powder obtained from this firm in the past had given satisfaction.[31] The one rolling mill in the South capable of heavy work was put to use by the board. J. R. Anderson and Company of Richmond, Virginia, were given orders for mortar shells and shot for Dahlgren guns.[32]

Some of the ordnance supplies issued by the board brought invectives down on its head. Major A. M. Smith, commanding a battalion of the First Regiment of South Carolina Volunteers, on Sullivan's Island, wrote Manigault: "In yesterday's guard reports the officer of the Guard reports that in the discharge of pieces of the old guards eleven Muskets out of twenty four failed to fire. In an engagement with the enemy I had as soon have that much sand in my gun as the cartridges we now have."[33]

It is a wonder that the Ordnance Board did not receive more criticisms than it did. It was evidently considered as much a general military board as an ordnance board. The legislature at one time toyed with the idea of letting the board fix the scale of pay and rations of volunteers accepted for state service.[34] It was required to issue arms not only to the land forces of the state but to the Coastal Patrol as well.[35] It was concerned with the matter of sending arms to Florida. The board informed Governor Pickens that 4,000 United States muskets and bayonets could be sent to Florida without detriment to South Carolina.[36] Florida had seceded on January 11 and was in need of arms and ammunition. Pickens sent all he could to aid in Florida's efforts to prepare.[37]

The State Ordnance Department was bound to run into the same trouble that plagued Colonel Josiah Gorgas, chief of ordnance of the Confederacy, during the whole course of the Civil War; namely, lack of manufacturing facilities. While the state would encounter this on a much smaller scale, it was bound to have its own particular problem. The sources of both the Confederacy and the various states would be the same; conflicts would develop between state and Confederate ordnance officers. South Carolina in the antebellum period never showed much interest in manufacturing enterprises. Manufactures and manufacturing were just beginning to come into their own when the outbreak of the war cut them, along with everything else, short. South Carolina was another of the "Cotton States" which had no heavy industry with which to aid the sorely pressed Confederate States, or to supply its own needs.

On April 5, 1861, the state turned over to the Confederacy such arms, ordnance, and munitions of war as was thought proper by the state authorities. Though the board continued to function on matters relating to state troops, militia, and so forth, it was no longer a completely independent organization, since the Confederate Ordnance Department assumed charge of the ordnance for all Confederate commands.

NOTES

1. Proclamation, October 12, 1860, in *Journal of the House of Representatives of South Carolina, Called Session of November, 1860* (Columbia, 1860), 5.

2. See, for example, the *Charleston Daily Courier* (cited hereinafter as *Courier*), November 14, 17, and 24, 1860, quoting respectively, the *Augusta Democrat, Yorkville Enquirer,* and *Spartanburg Express.*

3. Jefferson Davis was one of this group. Jefferson Davis to Col. W. P. Johnston, Nov. 18, 1877, in *Journal of Southern History,* May 1944, 211; also "Santee" to the editors of the *Courier,* November 26, 1860.

4. *House Journal, Called Session, 1860*, 13–14. The Senate concurred in this on November 9. *Senate Journal*, 30.

5. It did not carry.

6. See the *Courier*, November 14 and 26, 1860. This is not to be confused with the $400,000 loan mentioned earlier.

7. *House Journal, Called Session*, 1860, 46. This resolution was introduced and passed on November 13.

8. *House Journal, Called Session*, 41, 44.

9. See, for example, petition of the Charleston Artillery, reported in the House, November 28, 1860, in the *Courier*, November 29 and petitions of the Palmetto Guard, December 20, 1860. The Rutledge Mounted Rifles, December 24, 1860, and January 1, 1861; the Calhoun Artillery, December 25, 1860; the Marion Rifles, January 26, 1861; and the Lexington Light Dragoons, February 11, 1861, in Miscellaneous Military Papers of the South Carolina Ordnance Board (cited hereinafter as S.C. Mil. Papers), manuscript in the Library of Congress. Microfilm copies of these papers are in the Ramsdell Microfilm Collection, University of Texas Archives.

10. Petition of the Waccamaw Artillery to [the Board of Ordnance?], January, 24[?], 1861, S.C. Mil. Papers. They received the rifles, sabers and ammunition.

11. Zouave Cadets to the Public, in the *Courier*, November. 14, 1860.

12. *Courier*, November. 15, 1860, quoting the *Pee Dee Times*, November 14, 1860. The idea of committees of safety was a carryover from the troubled times of 1849. In February and March of that year many district meetings were held throughout South Carolina. "Nearly every one of these meetings provided for the appointment of a committee of safety or vigilance for the district to call meetings when necessary, and to correspond with similar committees." C. S. Boucher, *Secession and Cooperation Movements in South Carolina, 1848–1852*, in *Washington University Studies* (Concord: N.H.), set. 4, vol. 5, no. 2 (1918): 78–79.

13. *Courier*, November 7, 1860.

14. Ibid., November 12, 1860.

15. Alabama already had 300 of these and had 200 more on order. *Courier*, October 29, 1860, quoting the *Montgomery Mail*. Many merchants were convinced of the salability of firearms and military equipment at this time. *Courier*, November 12, 13, 14, 15, 17, 24, and December 8, 1860.

16. *Courier*, November 17, 1860.

17. Ibid., November 21, December 1 and 6, 1860.

18. Ibid., November 26 and 28, 1860.

19. Ibid., December 1, 1860.

20. Governor's *Message No. I*, in *Courier*, November 27, 1860. The governor said that Major R. S. Ripley, a South Carolinian, had offered to establish an armory for the South, "in Georgia, Alabama or South Carolina, according as may be agreed on by those States. All he asks is, that each of the three States named should contract with him for fifty thousand dollars worth of arms annually, for five years, and extend their patronage for a short period thereafter; the arms furnished to be up to a standard model, to be determined upon and delivered at prices fixed by competent authority, and to be subject to the proper military inspection, in parts, by State officers, those of each State to inspect the arms for that State. This would be preferable to having an Armory, and would preclude the necessity of burdening each State with an extensive establishment, dependent upon it for management by salaried officers, and would require no expenditure by the State until its value would be received." The governor thought that this was the best plan for keeping up the state's supply

of arms and said that the governors of Georgia and Alabama approved it and intended to submit it to their respective legislatures. He recommended that South Carolina take a share in the proposition and bind herself to take $50,000 worth of arms per year, for the five-year period. He was in favor of opening negotiations between the three states for the armory site. It is apparent that this scheme did not materialize, for we find Ripley a brigadier general in Lee's army in 1862.

21. "An Act to establish a Board of Ordnance" in *Acts of the General Assembly of the State of South Carolina, Passed in November and December, 1860, and January*, 1861 (Columbia: 1861), 856–58. This act incorrectly bears date of passage as November 13, 1860. It was introduced November 26, and ratified December 17, 1860. See *House Journal, Regular Session, Commencing Monday, November 26*, [1860] (Columbia: 1860), 7, 226.

22. See advertisement of the Charleston and Savannah Railroad in the *Courier*, November 24, 1860. Mr. D. E. H. Manigault of Austin, Texas, a nephew of Edward Manigault, stated in a conversation with the writer, September 16, 1944, that his uncle was an engineer. The writer is indebted to Mr. D. E. H. Manigault for furnishing this information.

23. "An Act to authorize the issue of Certificates or Stock to provide for the Military Defense of the State," in *Acts of the General Assembly of South Carolina, 1860, 1861*, 951–52. This act was ratified December 22, 1860. "An Act to raise supplies for the year commencing in October one thousand eight hundred and sixty," in *Acts of the General Assembly of South Carolina, 1860, 1861*, 839, ratified January 28, 1861.

24. There is some doubt as to whether Manigault, in his report, meant that these arms were in the hands of the State troops, or in the Charleston Arsenal, as he headed this portion of his report *"Small Arms in late U. S. Arsenal (now in possession of State Troops)."* Since the first list of small arms was given as the arms in store, exclusive of those in the hands of the militia, the statement given in the text is probably correct.

25. List of ordnance compiled by Col. Edward Manigault, January 8, 1861, MS, Pickens and Bonham Papers, Library of Congress, microfilm copies in Ramsdell Microfilm Collection, University of Texas Archives. There is another list of ordnance on hand in South Carolina, December 1860, in *Journal of the Convention of the People of South Carolina*, 4th Sess., 1862, 606. This gives 103 pieces of heavy ordnance, 66 pieces of field artillery, 27,407 muskets and rifles, 2,271 pistols, 2,648 swords and sabers, and 20,400 pounds of powder.

26. John B. Read to Gov. F. W. Pickens, December 15, 1860, S.C. Mil. Papers.

27. Circular, David Looney to F. W. Pickens, January 21, 1861, S.C. Mil. Papers. In a personal letter to Pickens, January 16, 1861, Looney had given the rate of fire as 9,000 in 4 seconds, 18,000 in 12 seconds, or 27,000 in 25 seconds. S.C. Mil. Papers.

28. Looney to Pickens, January 16, 1861; W. Alston Hayne to the Board of Ordnance, February 8, 1861, S.C. Mil. Papers.

29. See Charles S. James to Edward Manigault, February 1, 1861; Gen. A. J. Gonzales to Pickens, December 20, 1860, S.C. Mil. Papers.

30. Col. S. Bobo to Dr. Cannon [?], January 21, 1861, and to [Manigault?], January 30, 1861, S.C. Mil. Papers.

31. Col. Edward Manigault to Col. Hazard, January 16, 1861, S.C. Mil. Papers. An endorsement on the back of this letter read: "Note. Col. Hazard had been up before *Grand Jury of United States Court* but fortunately before he had received my letter."

32. Telegrams: J. R. Anderson & Co. to Pickens, March 2, 1861, Pickens and Bonham Papers; J. R. Anderson & Co. to Manigault, March 12, 1861, S.C. Mil. Papers; Thos. H. Wynne to Pickens, March 1, 1861, Pickens and Bonham Papers.

33. Maj. A. M. Smith to Edward Manigault, March 2, 1861, S.C. Mil. Papers.

34. See Senate proceedings in the *Courier,* December 8, 1860.

35. Lt. Henry A. Mullins to the Board, January 21, 1861, S.C. Mil. Papers.

36. James Jones, Chairman of the Board of Ordnance, to Pickens, January 19, 1861, in Pickens and Bonham Papers; also *American Annual Cyclopedia and Register* of *Important Events* of *the Year* 1861 (New York: D. Appleton & Co., 1867), vol. 1: 646.

37. Governor M. S. Perry of Florida asked Pickens, on March 15, for 5,000 pounds of cannon powder. Telegram, Perry to Pickens, March 15, 1861, in Pickens and Bonham Papers.

THE WORK OF SOLDIERS' AID SOCIETIES IN SOUTH CAROLINA DURING THE CIVIL WAR

(1938)

James Welch Patton

The enthusiastic zeal with which the women of the Confederacy exerted themselves in support of the southern cause was one of the distinctive features that characterized the War for Southern Independence. Women aided in the creation of the Confederate armies by encouraging the willing and goading the reluctant among their relatives and acquaintances to enter the military service of the southern states, and they had scarcely completed the painful duty of bidding the newly recruited regiments farewell when they were called upon to assume the endless task of supplying these soldiers with many of the material comforts and necessities required by the participants in modern warfare.

From the very outset of the conflict, it was evident that, in the face of an imperfect system of transportation, a relative lack of manufacturing industries, and the blockade which the Federal government would likely impose, the resources of the Confederacy would be inadequate to compete with the almost unlimited resources of the North, unless some means of counteracting this disparity between the two sections could be devised. Beginning with the spring and summer of 1861, therefore, thousands of women throughout the South devoted themselves to the labor of supplementing the supply of clothing, foodstuffs, flags, tents, gun cases, cartridges, medicines, bandages, and numerous other articles which the Confederate government was unable to provide in sufficient quantities for the use of its armies.

The energetic manner in which the southern women undertook these difficult tasks is impressive. They labored over heavy tents, overcoats, jackets, and pants, knit socks and made shirts, provided food for passing soldiers, concocted medicines, scraped lint, and prepared bandages, often toiling into the late hours of the night and until their delicate fingers were stiff, swollen, and bleeding from overwork. With her own labor supplemented by that of her slaves, one South Carolina woman supplied an entire company of soldiers with all of its necessities,[1] and another woman in the same state was able, through her own efforts, to provide a company with clothing made from wool that was grown, carded, spun, and woven on her own plantation.[2] A North Carolina woman uniformed a whole company at her own expense and traveled about for the entire length of the war, attending to the wants of the sick and distressed and soliciting funds for relief work. Writing to Governor Vance in August 1864, she estimated that she had collected goods and supplies to the value of half a million dollars.[3]

But essential as were the exertions of such individuals, it soon became apparent that more effective work could be accomplished through cooperative endeavor. Since the usual problem was that of equipping companies rather than single soldiers, collective activity afforded an opportunity for the pooling of resources and a division of labor. The inadequate number of spinning wheels, looms, and sewing machines could be more readily utilized to the limits of their capacities; funds and raw materials could be more easily solicited and collected from the government and other sources; and a more efficient distribution of the supplies would be facilitated. Likewise, a less tangible but equally important accompaniment of group activity was the evolution of an *esprit de corps* to a degree hitherto unknown among the women of the South, a development which furnished an obvious relief from the trials and heartaches occasioned by the war. Individual efforts were therefore supplanted to a considerable extent, during the early months of the conflict, by cooperative agencies known as soldiers' aid societies.

Such societies were formed in every section of the South. Usually beginning as informal gatherings of women who had come together for the purpose of manufacturing soldiers' supplies, they met in private homes, town halls, courthouses, churches, school houses, or wherever else a convenient place of assembly could be secured. Each society had an appropriate name, a constitution,[4] formally elected officers, and written rules of procedure. Although clergymen and other male speakers were frequently invited to appear at the meetings, for such purposes as offering prayers, giving advice on matters that lay beyond the realm of feminine experience, or making patriotic addresses, the actual management and work of the associations were accomplished almost without exception through the efforts of the women themselves.

No accurate estimate of the number of these organizations formed in South Carolina has been made, but it is certain that their activities in this commonwealth were extensive. One hundred and twenty-four societies were listed in an account compiled by Mrs. Augustine T. Smythe, Miss Mary B. Poppenheim, and Mrs. Thomas Taylor,[5] and a more thorough investigation would doubtless reveal the existence of many others. They were to be found in every portion of the state, from Georgetown to Pendleton and from Beaufort to Chesterfield.

The names adopted by the South Carolina societies were both varied and descriptive. Some were commonplace and unimaginative; others were distinctive and, in a few instances, picturesque. A list of titles selected at random might include such designations as: the Soldiers' Relief Association of Aiken, the Soldiers' Aid Society of Cheraw, the Young Ladies' Hospital Association of Columbia, the Auxiliary Soldiers' Relief Association of Summerville, the Sabbath School Relief Society of Spartanburg, the Knitting Society of Abbeville, the Lower Bridge Sewing Society, the Mountain Creek Home Guard Society, the States' Rights Society and the Palmetto Girls' Society of Charleston, the Rehoboth Aid Society of Edgefield, the Hospital Club of Anderson, the Lamont Association of Grahams, the Parnassus Aid Society of Marlboro, and the Wild Cat Ladies' Benevolent Association of Lancaster.[6]

The aims of these societies were almost entirely of a practical nature. "The object of this association," reads an excerpt from the constitution of the Soldiers' Relief Association of Charleston, "is to provide garments for our soldiers in the field, and hospital stores and other comforts for the sick and wounded."[7] The Bethany Hospital and Soldiers' Aid Association of Edgefield County announced as its main purpose, "the immediate relief of the sick soldiers from our midst," and then the indiscriminate favoring "of all weary soldiers in our cause."[8] The Hospital Aid Society of Spartanburg asserted its objectives as being "to provide garments, hospital stores, and other comforts for our sick and wounded soldiers, and, secondly, to furnish underclothing, socks, and other articles needed for our soldiers in the field—these objects to be carried out by voluntary contributions of money, material, and labor."[9]

The various phases of the work accomplished by such organizations are most extensively illustrated in the achievements and experiences of the Greenville Ladies' Association in Aid of the Volunteers of the Confederate Army, the original minutes of which have been preserved and are now deposited in the library of Duke University.[10] This society held its first meeting on July 19, 1861, and continued its labors without interruption until May 1, 1865, when a detachment of Stoneman's raiders, passing through upper South Carolina in pursuit of Jefferson Davis, plundered the association storeroom, and, as vividly recorded in the last paragraph of the minutes, stripped the place "of every article it contained, leaving the Society without the means of carrying on any further operations."[11]

The objects of the Greenville association were stated as, "firstly, to relieve the sick and wounded among the soldiers, by forwarding to them linen, underclothing, cordials, bed ticks, socks, &c.; secondly, to make winter clothing for the Volunteers in the Confederate Army."[12] To this end, the members of the society cut out and made up uniforms and various other garments which, together with boxes of food and hospital stores, they dispatched to the front for the use of soldiers from the vicinity of Greenville. They contributed cloth, foodstuffs, medicines, and money from their own resources and solicited such supplies from others, sponsored lectures and other entertainments for the purpose of raising funds,[13] fed and otherwise attended to the needs of passing soldiers, sent nurses to the battlefields, and in a few instances aided in burying the dead.

An examination of the lists of articles that were sent to the front by the members of this society affords the most concrete evidence of the substantial character of its activity. Between July 21 and December 14, 1861, for example, the association dispatched twenty boxes and three bales of supplies to the hospitals in Virginia and those on the South Carolina coast. Included in these shipments were: 280 shirts, 180 pairs of drawers, 160 pairs of socks, 14 dressing gowns, 4 pairs of pants, 1 vest, 1 scarf, 120 pocket handkerchiefs, 190 sheets, 5 counterpanes, 70 comforts, 10 bed ticks, 14 blankets, 2 quilts, 50 pillows, 165 pillow cases, 2 curtains, 144 towels, 12 pounds of herbs, 15 pounds of tea, 21 pounds of spice, 80 pounds of sugar, 3 pounds of arrowroot, 8 pounds of hoarhound candy, 20 jars of jelly, 14 cans of fruit, 4 bottles of pickles, 16 bottles of tomatoes, 100 bottles of wine, cordial, and brandy, 25 pounds of soap, 24 tin spoons, 70 tin cups, 80 tin plates, 70 tin pans, 1 ½ bushels of apples, ½ bushel of sweet potatoes, 1 ham, 20 loaves of bread, 3 dozen eggs, 60 chickens, and a quantity of pins and needles, linen, Bibles, testaments, tracts, newspapers, magazines, and books.[14]

Equally substantial achievements resulted from the efforts of other South Carolina societies. "The patriotic ladies of York," announced a local newspaper in August 1861, "are up and doing their utmost in behalf of the sick and wounded soldiers. They have already forwarded a large and valuable box of hospital stores, and on Tuesday next they will have a *tableaux* in the Masonic Hall for the purpose of raising funds to procure necessary supplies of clothing; etc., for our soldiers during the coming winter."[15] On September 20, 1861, Coffin and Pringle of Charleston, forwarding agents for the South Carolina Hospital Aid Association,[16] acknowledged the receipt of: two boxes of supplies from the Ladies' Relief Association of Williston, eight boxes from the Soldiers' Relief Association of Providence Church, St: Matthews Parish, one box from the Ladies' Soldiers' Aid Society of Manning, one box from the Grahams Turn Out Association, two boxes from Abbeville, and one bale of blankets from the ladies of All Saints Parish; also $50.00 from the Ladies' Auxiliary Association of James Island, $20.00 from Upper St. James, Goose Creek, and $20.00 from St. Helena Church, Beaufort—the last named item being the proceeds derived from the sale of a bracelet contributed by a young woman.[17] During the same month the Soldiers' Relief Association of Aiken made three shipments, which included: 60 pairs of drawers, 60 pairs of socks, 60 flannel shirts, and 60 cotton shirts, together with books, papers, and sundries, to the Aiken Allen Guards at Camp Pillow, Tennessee; 43 pairs of drawers, 60 pairs of socks, 61 flannel shirts, 71 cotton shirts, 19 pairs of pants, and 19 jackets to the Richardson Guards; and

84 pairs of pants, 79 pairs of socks, 88 blankets, 5 comforts, and sundry other articles to General Bonham's Brigade at Flint Hill, Virginia.[18]

Typical illustrations of the work accomplished by the societies during the second and third years of the war are found in the experiences of the Charleston Soldiers' Relief Association, which received in donations between April 21 and July 21, 1862, 52 flannel shirts, 506 cotton shirts, 314 pairs of drawers, 384 pairs of socks, 33 handkerchiefs, 40 towels, 62 mattresses, 45 bed sacks, 8 pairs of pantaloons, 69 sheets, 71 pillows, 91 pillow cases, 38 fans, 5 dressing gowns, 91 mosquito nets, 10 pairs of slippers, 12 caps, 30 quilts, and 4 comforts, in addition to a large amount of wine, liquors, and hospital nourishment of all kinds;[19] and in the exertions of the Spartanburg Sabbath School Relief Association, which sent to the front for the use of soldiers in May 1863, 2 quilted comforts, 1 mattress, 16 shirts, 11 pairs of socks, 1 bushel of dried peaches, 1 ½ bushels of dried apples, 2 hams, 1 piece of dried beef, 2 bottles of blackberry wine, 2 bottles of catsup, 1 bottle of honey, 1 package of mint, and 24 dozen eggs, as well as a quantity of grits, meal, rye, barley, peas, bread, crackers, and rice.[20]

Nor were the boxes sent during the closing months of the war less substantial in content. Included in a Christmas box packed by the women of Chesterfield in December 1864 were hams, flour, fruit, butter, eggs, lard, preserves, cakes, biscuits, and meal.[21] A box provided by the Summerville Ladies' Relief Association in January 1865 contained 14 feather pillows, 9 pairs of socks, 1 gallon of whiskey, 1 gallon of vinegar, 1 peck of peas, 1 cake of suet, 2 fans, and a bundle of linen rags.[22] Articles supplied by the Soldiers' Relief Association of Charleston at about the same time included 286 cotton shirts, 233 flannel shirts, 267 pairs of drawers, 198 pairs of socks, 179 pairs of pants, 23 pairs of shoes and slippers, 19 comforts, 18 pairs of blankets, and 36 scarfs and handkerchiefs.[23]

The preparation of these supplies required an enormous amount of labor. "The days and weeks were spent in working and toiling for the soldiers," wrote a South Carolina woman many years later; "far into the night our women would ply their needles, getting ready to send out the monthly boxes. . . . How you would sew for them [the soldiers]! How you would knit for them, and how you, with your delicate white hands, would make the palmetto cockade for their caps, and how you would send them letters of love, sealed with your tears !"[24] In the minds of many women the emergency was so great as to be considered a justification for work on the Sabbath or during the suspense that obtained while great battles were in progress; and others were so intensely preoccupied with their duties that they were observed knitting while on visits and as they rode in carriages.

One of the greatest concerns of the women of South Carolina was to see that the hospitals, both large and small, had the necessities as well as the comforts which would aid in the alleviation of suffering. Under the more favorable circumstances this meant the supplementing of staples provided by the government with luxuries and delicacies from private kitchens; under unfavorable conditions, which frequently existed, it meant the supplying of staples as well as luxuries. In their efforts to achieve these objectives, women scoured the countryside for supplies; they deprived themselves of luxuries at their own tables; they established hospital kitchens; they solicited contributions of money and materials; and, in numerous other ways, ceaselessly strove to transform the resources at their disposal into objects of immediate use.[25]

As in other sections of the wartime South, bazaars and fairs were extensively utilized by the women of South Carolina for the purpose of raising funds with which to procure hospital supplies. Probably the most elaborate bazaar in the whole history of the Confederacy was held in the hall of representatives in the old State House at Columbia in January 1865. "To give a just description of this royal festival, with its delightful accessories," said the effusive account of a local newspaper, "would require a pen dipped in the hues of a thousand rainbows, or the power to catch the fantastic shapes that live in the changing pictures of a kaleidoscope."[26] For several weeks previous to the event, the women of the South Carolina capital, both residents and refugees, ransacked garrets and cellars, closets and trunks, in an effort to produce articles that might tempt the purses of the crowds which were anticipated. Contributions were levied on all sides; products of the needle and culinary arts were brought forth; and gold subscribed by Confederate sympathizers in England was converted into curiosities, ornaments, and other objects that could not be secured in the blockaded South. From domestic sources came blankets, yards of calico and flannel, shoes, home-knit socks and stockings, shawls, silverware, dolls, cakes, bread, and even a live calf; from abroad came penknives, pins, hairpins, Parisian bonnets, ostrich plumes, sugar plums, almonds, and various other rarities. In front of the speaker's desk was placed a huge booth garlanded with evergreens and Spanish moss, and surmounted by a banner emblazoned in letters of gold with "A Tribute to Our Sick and Wounded Soldiers." On either side of this structure were semicircles of other booths, each marked with the shield of one of the Confederate states and managed by representatives of these respective commonwealths. For days gay throngs crowded around the booths, nonchalantly paying fabulous prices for whatever articles that might strike their fancy, while both participants and visitors were astonished that so much finery and luxury could be gathered among a people whose resources were supposed to be so limited.[27]

In addition to furnishing supplies, the soldiers' aid societies often sent members of their organizations to work in the hospitals of South Carolina and those established for South Carolina troops in other states. An entry in the minutes of the Greenville Aid Association in September 1861, for example, makes mention of packing "two boxes for Mrs. Benson and Miss Ingram to take with them to

Brentsville, Virginia . . . where both were to act in the capacity of nurses."[28] Among the most outstanding services of this sort performed in South Carolina were those of Louisa Susanna McCord, a daughter of Langdon Cheves and the widow of David J. McCord, a distinguished lawyer of Columbia. After serving as president of the Columbia Soldiers' Relief Association and the Ladies' Clothing Association, she resigned these duties in 1862 in order to give her whole time to the military hospital established in the buildings of the South Carolina College. In the midst of this activity there came the news that her son had been killed at Second Manassas, but her work continued "patient and cheerful and tender in its ministrations in the hospital; it was also capably executive. She managed the scheduling of the assistant nurses, planned the provisioning of the larder, that was often meager and largely dependent upon gratuitous contributions. She regulated the convalescents, she wrote letters for them, talked with them, soothed the restless, gave Christian comfort to the dying."[29]

Although not actually connected with the soldiers' aid societies, the most skillful and devoted of all the South Carolina women who nursed disabled Confederates were doubtless the members of the various Roman Catholic sisterhoods. They constituted the only class of women in the state who were possessed of formal training in nursing and hospital management, and they worked among the sick and wounded in camp, in hospital, and on the battlefield with the calculated self-abnegation and efficiency that was traditional among such orders of holy women. Largely northern or else foreign in origin, wearing habits strange to Protestant soldiers, and observing no distinctions of race or section in their ministrations, they were naturally received with suspicion at first; but when they proved by silent deeds that their only aim was to relieve suffering humanity, they won the confidence and admiration of both the soldiers and the people of the state generally. With thirty years of experience in the care of the sick behind them, the Sisters of Our Lady of Mercy in Charleston performed signal service in the hospitals of that city, especially in Roper Hospital, where between thirty and thirty-five of them were on duty. In answer to a plea from the Bishop of Richmond in 1861, they also sent members of their order to serve as nurses at White Sulphur Springs, Virginia, where they worked and suffered until the end of the war.[30]

Another important feature of the work of the soldiers' aid societies was the organization and maintenance of wayside homes. These institutions were small hospitals or rest rooms which were established by women at various points in the Confederacy for the purpose of taking care of the numerous sick and wounded men who were dropped off or left stranded by the inefficient railway service. The first wayside home was established in Columbia in March 1862, when a clergyman of that city called the attention of the Young Ladies' Hospital Association to the fact that there were many ill and needy men stranded at the local railroad station. These young women immediately equipped a room at the station which they called "The Soldiers' Rest." When this room became inadequate to accommodate the large number of soldiers who desired to make use of its facilities, the women of Columbia secured larger quarters, capable of housing one hundred men and feeding three hundred. At the same time, the services of older women and men ward masters and nurses were called in to relieve the supposedly more sensitive young women of "the grim work to be done" and "the ghastly sights to be seen."[31] The extent of the activities of these women is illustrated by Mrs. Thomas Taylor's account of their work during an emergency created by the arrival of a large number of men from a recently fought battle. This writer recalled seeing "Mrs. Bryce with a huge coffeepot in her hand, standing in the Wayside Kitchen; Mrs. Fisher, with a large spoon, stirring something on the stove; and the invaluable Dinah Collins, making up something and turning a portly figure and kindly face to one and any who spoke to her, and at the same time giving directions which kettle to get warm water from."[32]

The wayside homes established at other places in the state had histories similar to the one in Columbia. At Anderson a committee of women met every afternoon train. "With pitchers of buttermilk, and a bottle of whiskey, we would go through the cars," wrote Mrs. Sylvester Bleckley, "and if any sick soldiers were on board we ministered to their wants."[33] The women of Chester were described in May 1863 as "having now in full operation a comfortable Wayside Hospital for sick and wounded soldiers," which "would offer to any such a quiet rest, and refreshments, when they may be either going to or coming from the wearisome toils of the battlefield."[34] At Abbeville two women met each train that came in, and if there were soldiers on board too sick to go on they were cared for at the wayside hospital established there. If they were able to go on, a hack was furnished, often to Washington and Elberton, Georgia, distances of thirty and forty miles.[35]

"Were it not for the exertions of the Southern women," wrote an observant English traveler in contemplating the work of the soldiers' relief societies, "the volunteers [of the Confederacy] would have been ill provided for."[36] Such a statement might also have been made of the soldiers' aid societies in South Carolina.

NOTES

1. Mrs. Thomas Taylor et al., eds., *South Carolina Women in the Confederacy* (Columbia: State Committee United Daughters of the Confederacy, 1903 and 1907), vol. 1: 196–97.

2. Ibid., 100.

3. Clyde Olin Fisher, "The Relief of Soldiers' Families in North Carolina During the Civil War," *South Atlantic Quarterly* 16 (January 1917): 71. See Francis B. Simkins and James W. Patton, *The Women of the Confederacy* (Richmond, Va.: Garrett and Massie, 1936), 19–21, for other examples of individual relief work.

4. For typical constitutions see those of the Ladies' Charleston Association, *Charleston Courier*, July 30, 1861, and the Bethany Hospital and Soldiers' Aid Association of Edgefield County. Taylor et al., *South Carolina Women in the Confederacy* 1: 67.

5. Ibid., vol. 1: 21–25; vol. 2: 91–92.

6. Ibid., vol. 1: 21–25; vol. 2: 91–92.

7. Ibid., vol. 1: 109.

8. Ibid., vol. 1: 67.

9. Ibid., vol. 2: 39.

10. These records, consisting of two bound volumes and several additional loose sheets, were preserved after the war by the vice-president of the association, Mrs. William Pinkney McBee. Upon her death in 1901, they passed into the possession of her daughter, Mrs. C. M. Landrum of Greenville, by whom they were presented to Duke University in 1936. At the request of Professor W. K. Boyd, the author of this article has recently undertaken and completed the task of preparing these minutes for publication in a forthcoming issue of the *Trinity College Historical Society Papers*.

11. Minutes of the Greenville Ladies' Association, May, 1, 1865.

12. Ibid., July 19, 1861.

13. For example, a lecture by Paul Hamilton Hayne on June 30, 1864, the proceeds of which amounted to $95.25, and a strawberry fete during the preceding month, at which $3,361.25 (old issue currency) was raised. "Minutes of the Greenville Ladies' Association," May 30, June 20, and July 4, 1864.

14. *Charleston Mercury*, January 10, 1862.

15. *Yorkville Enquirer*, quoted in *Charleston Courier*, August 20, 1861.

16. A semi-official organization formed in July 1861 for the purpose of establishing hospitals for sick and wounded South Carolina troops in Virginia. Under the direction of the Rev. Robert W. Barnwell, a professor in the South Carolina College who resigned his position to undertake this work, the association established eight hospitals in 1861 and 1862. These hospitals depended upon the soldiers' aid societies in South Carolina for a large portion of their supplies. See *Report of the South Carolina Hospital Aid Association in Virginia, 1861–1862* (Richmond, Va: Mac-Farlane and Fergusson, 1862), reprinted in Taylor, *South Carolina Women in the Confederacy* 2: 93–120.

17. *Charleston Courier*, September 20, 1861.

18. Ibid., October 12, July 30, August 1, August 10, August 19, August 23, and November 22, 1861, and March 6, 1862, for typical lists of contributions made by other South Carolina organizations during the first year of the war.

19. *Charleston Mercury*, July 21, 1862.

20. Ibid., May 21, 1863.

21. *Charleston Courier*, January 3, 1865.

22. *Charleston Mercury*, January 10, 1865.

23. *Charleston Courier*, February 20, 1865.

24. Mrs. Sylvester Bleckley, "The Women of the Piedmont," *The State* (Columbia), March 7, 1906.

25. The manufacture of substitutes for drugs and medicines was also an important phase of this activity. See Simkins and Patton, *The Women of the Confederacy*, 138–39.

26. *The South Carolinian* (Columbia), cited in *New York Herald*, January 29, 1865.

27. Taylor, *South Carolina Women in the Confederacy* 1: 217–18, 243–47.

28. Minutes of the Greenville Ladies' Association, Sept. 12, 1861.

29. Jessie Melville Fraser, "Louisa C. McCord," *Bulletin of the University of South Carolina* 91 (October 1920): 35–36.

30. Ellen Ryan Jolly, *Nuns of the Battlefield* (Providence, R.I.: Providence Visitor Press, 1927), 287, 293.

31. Mary Boykin Chesnut, *A Diary from Dixie* (New York: Peter Smith, 1929), 205–6; Francis W. Dawson, ed., *Our Women in the War: The Lives They Lived—The Deaths They Died* (Charleston: News and Courier Co., 1885), 2–4.

32. Taylor, *South Carolina Women in the Confederacy* 1: 94.

33. Ibid., 364–65.

34. *The South Carolinian,* May 17, 1863, quoted in Taylor, *South Carolina Women in the Confederacy* 2: 9.

35. Taylor, *South Carolina Women in the Confederacy* 1: 69.

36. Samuel P. Day, *Down South; or an Englishman's Experiences at the Seat of the American War* (London: Hurst and Blackett, 1862), vol. 1: 127.

DISSATISFACTION AND DESERTION IN GREENVILLE DISTRICT, SOUTH CAROLINA, 1860–1865

(2001)

Aaron W. Marrs

When a divided Democratic Party lost the 1860 presidential race to "Black Republican" Abraham Lincoln, calls for secession in South Carolina gained urgency and volume. Major secessionist figures visited the upcountry to urge residents there to support a separated South. Greenville District warranted special attention: for decades, the district had resisted the rhetoric of secessionists. Proslavery arguments did not instantly turn Greenville residents to the secession movement since many of them did not own slaves. In addition, Greenville was home to one of the state's most ardent unionists, Benjamin F. Perry. Yet in late 1860 the district delivered a disunionist mandate in line with the remainder of the state. Although Perry ran for a spot as a delegate to the secession convention, he suffered resounding defeat, and a slate of secessionists represented Greenville District. Had Greenville District cast its lot with the secessionists, or was this election an isolated incident? An examination of contemporary documents, both from Greenville residents and the military officers responsible for the area, shows that residents quickly began to tire of war. Bands of deserters became a serious problem for Confederate officials, and dissatisfaction and desertion continued until the end of the war. In short, the fatigue of war and a Confederate government that threatened liberty more than the feared Union Army led to early desertion and dissatisfaction with the war effort.[1]

The period leading up to the secession convention is worthy of brief analysis because it includes an outburst of disunionist fervor from a previously unionist district. Other historians have examined this time and the question of independent white farmer support for the Confederacy. In his *Origins of Southern Radicalism,* Lacy K. Ford Jr. argues that upcountry yeomen supported secession to preserve their independence from the encroaching influence of manufacturers and the government. Admittedly yeomen supported slavery because "slavery for blacks guaranteed the freedom of common whites." But the drive for secession came principally from a desire to preserve independence from rapacious capitalists and an intrusive government.[2]

In "Mobilization for Secession in Greenville District," James Gettys proposes that prolonged exposure to secessionist rhetoric in district newspapers persuaded the electorate to support disunion. For example, the conciliatory *Patriot and Mountaineer* became uncompromising after Lincoln's election, trimming its banner from "The Rights of the South and the Union of the States" to "The Rights of the South." Immediately after the election, the newspaper described a meeting at Greenville courthouse where people of every political stripe joined to denounce "Aggression."

The following January the newspaper demanded a "Confederacy of Slaveholding States." Greenville's other newspaper, the *Southern Enterprise*, was always more unyielding. It headlined a story about an abolitionist's death with "One Wiped Out," approvingly documented the departure of southern students from northern colleges, argued that southerners should write their own textbooks, and promoted support of southern manufactures. The newspaper urged a turnout of at least 2,000 voters at the election for the state secession convention. Gettys's conclusion is unsatisfying because he does not fully establish the link between the content of the newspapers and the actions of the electorate—after all, secessionist editors operated in Greenville prior to 1860 to little avail.[3]

There is some evidence that the newspapers did not always represent popular opinion. First, Perry did not suffer defeat until running for a seat in the secession convention, despite the rising voices of the newspaper editors. Second, although the election of 1860 was lopsided, voter turnout was low—only about half of Greenville's registered voters participated, less than the *Southern Enterprise*'s hopeful estimate of 2,000. Third, the strong statewide momentum for secession may have convinced upcountrymen in and out of Greenville that secession was a foregone conclusion. Perry was one of the few unionists in the entire state to run for a delegate's position. With no unionists to vote for, opponents of secession in the upcountry may have simply stayed home. Even if those who stayed home supported secession, they were obviously not motivated enough to demonstrate their support by voting.[4]

Thus the picture of rabid disunionism shown in the newspapers is tempered by the secession convention election. Although Greenville District supported the movement for secession and the war, any initial enthusiasm for secession turned into anger toward the Confederate government as the situation grew worse for residents. Sources of home-front dissatisfaction fell into four main categories: the shortages of goods and speculation, poor crops, impressment of goods by the Confederate army and the army's inability to pay debts, and constant demands for slave labor to build coastal defenses.

Since the majority of the Civil War was fought in the South, the region as a whole faced the problems of commodity shortage and speculation; Greenville District was no exception. The Confederate government refused to handle wartime relief, preferring to leave that problem to the individual states. As early as 1861 speculation (buying supplies and selling them at an exorbitant profit) was practiced in Greenville District. Shortages struck necessities like paper, and residents were forced to experiment with alternatives to commonplace items like coffee, which were now luxuries.[5]

Beginning in 1862 an influx of refugees from Charleston drove commodity prices even higher; one farmer lamented that "Our village is full of Charlestown People fled from The City Provision is higher than I Ever knew before." The depressed situation led him to wish that the war would end so he could once again "Sit Down by our own fireside and Enjoy ourselves as in Days that is gone by." Difficulty even struck the *Southern Enterprise,* which announced in 1863 that it could no longer extend credit to advertisers or subscribers. The newspaper had shrunk to a single sheet of paper. Shortage and speculation made mere survival difficult; in desperation, residents turned to their government for help.[6]

In 1863 the government finally began to address the problem. Governor Milledge Luke Bonham issued a proclamation making it illegal to ship certain foods out of the state. He asked the General Assembly to extend this prohibition further than his limited powers would allow. Although the General Assembly did not pursue this particular legislation, it did establish a series of relief boards composed of local residents. These boards had the authority to distribute aid, in cash or in kind, and drew funds from local taxation, making success difficult in depressed districts.[7]

Although the initial act mandated that the boards would last until four months after the conclusion of the war, patchwork legislation appeared each year to renew the purpose of the boards, occasionally change their composition, and expand their power. The first piece of renewal legislation, for example, appropriated $600,000 for needy families, demonstrating that the initial tax had been insufficient. By 1863 manufacturers were required to pay a tax in kind to the boards, and by 1864 sheriffs were given the power to seize goods if a manufacturer refused to turn them over. Farmers were required to supply both the Confederate Army and indigent families with their crops. In short, relief efforts experienced problems from the outset—neither the districts nor the state government could successfully shoulder the burden. The constant tinkering with renewal legislation shows that efforts were haphazard, and the high demands placed on farmers made their own survival more difficult.[8]

The problems of shortage and speculation were exacerbated by the second reason for growing dissatisfaction in the upcountry—poor crop yields. In 1862 farmer Alsey Albert Neves wrote to his sons in the Confederate Army that he had difficulty raising even a hundred pounds of corn that year: "so you will say sorry farming for 10 hands so say I but I no that I never tried harder to make a large crop than I did this year but faild but I dont mind that." The Confederate quartermaster stationed in Greenville, Alfred Ward Grayson Davis, called the 1862 wheat crop "almost a total failure." Unfortunately the new year did not bring improvement. A less optimistic Neves told his sons in 1863 that "upland is not good at al it has bin two wet for anything." In particular, "corn crops is very sorry worse than they was last year there will not be near as much corn maid this year as last." In 1864 corn shortages struck Davis's son and successor as Greenville post quartermaster, Charles Lewis Davis. In July of that year he complained to an army captain that "I have to send below to buy corn as there is not enough here to subsist the people." Farms also suffered from the calls for conscription—when the farmers were called to serve in the army, farmland was simply abandoned.[9]

Ostensibly trying to improve matters, the government imposed its authority on individual farmers, running against any desire for freedom from governmental control. In an effort to focus agricultural production on food, the General Assembly made it a high misdemeanor to distill cereal grains and fruits into "spirituous liquors." In addition several laws attempted to curtail the production of cotton, the cash crop that had brought such prosperity to the upcountry in the 1850s. The General Assembly demanded that farmers return to growing food and limited them to three acres of cotton per "hand," which it defined as a slave within a certain age group. This legislation was intensified over time—by 1864 the ratio was narrowed, the definition of "hand" was tightened, and the law was extended to the end of the war.[10]

The Confederate Army's struggle to secure adequate resources led it to a policy of impressment. Confederate officials set prices for goods and took what they needed, leaving a family only enough to survive. The intrusiveness of impressment and the inability of the Confederate government to pay its debts constituted the third main source of home-front dissatisfaction. The Davis family's increasingly agitated letters document the problems of securing supplies. The untrustworthiness of the currency may have led many farmers and manufacturers to withhold their goods from the quartermaster. When they did sell, manufacturers were not afraid to demand market prices for their goods. For example, one cotton factory refused to sell its shirtings at the price set by the quartermaster, demanding fifty cents per unit instead of thirty-two. Charles Davis complained that it was impossible to get the supplies that he required without a policy of impressment. To his credit, Davis tracked down at least some improper impressments and attempted to have the owners reimbursed.[11]

By 1864 Greenville District residents were increasingly dissatisfied with Davis and his government's financial woes. On July 10, 1864, Davis noted that "I have not had a dollar since the 25th March last and am very much inconvenienced for the want of it, as parties are very clamorous for there pay." In that letter he asked Hutson Lee, chief quartermaster for South Carolina, Georgia, and Florida, for $15,000; two weeks later he practically begged for nearly four times that amount. By October the local stage company declined to transport soldiers at a lower rate than civilians, and Davis estimated his indebtedness at $80,000. Davis's laments would continue until the end of the war. Greenville merchants simply refused to support their government by continuing to extend credit to its agents.[12]

The fourth condition that angered Greenville residents was the constant demand for slave labor to build defenses on the coast. Since the upcountry held fewer slaves than the low country, demands for slave labor were galling not only because laborers were needed at home but also because upcountry slave-owners were unwilling to fund the low-country defense. Owners were initially given the option to commute service by paying eleven dollars per month per slave. As the war continued, such options were removed; by September failure to send slaves was a misdemeanor and punishable by a two-hundred-dollar fine per slave. Some slaveholders preferred paying the fine to parting with their slaves. One proclamation pleaded in vain for slaves, commenting both on the depreciated Confederate currency and the need for workers: "Some of the Districts in this Division have paid fines heavily. The money has been useless. . . . If you would serve your country, send your negroes to do the labor."[13]

Eventually, 10 percent of all slaves became liable for coastal labor. Governor Bonham realized that the call for slaves "has created more dissatisfaction and discontent than any other duties the Citizens have had to perform" but also recognized the necessity of protecting Charleston. He continued to demand that the General Assembly call for additional laborers. By 1864 Greenville District had been drained of slave labor; an army officer noted that much of the district was depressed and could send no more slaves.[14]

Difficult conditions at home provided strong temptation for soldiers to return and care for their families. Poor conditions in the army and the lack of necessities also contributed to desertion. Sickness, for example, could deal a crushing blow to companies keeping close quarters, and soldiers faced economic problems as well—Charles Davis was no more successful in obtaining funds for soldiers' wages than he was in obtaining funds for his debts. With horrible conditions and death possible even off the battlefield, it is scarcely surprising that some men preferred not to serve. As deserters returned to the hilly regions of the Greenville District, the governments in Columbia and Richmond had to respond. Desertion was treated locally, through the payment of bounties for individual deserters, and also formally by the government through troop movements and legislation.[15]

Desertion was initially handled locally on an ad hoc basis. Alfred Davis appointed Captain Foster to report the names of deserters in Greenville District. In addition Davis stationed J. H. Gaillard at the railroad depot to examine soldiers' papers and to turn in deserters. Just two days later Gaillard detained two men within the conscript age who had not yet reported for service. Despite this early success, the Confederates were not ready for the problem—Davis complained about the lack of instruction on how to punish deserters.[16]

Local newspapers carried warnings and announced bounties for deserters. One issue of the *Southern Enterprise* devoted a full three and one-half columns to the names of men missing from General Braxton Bragg's army and said "we presume that many of those whose names are found in the list were captured recently by the enemy." The newspaper published notices declaring that men should report by a certain date or return to camp to have their furlough examined. In June 1863 the army offered thirty dollars each for twenty-three Greenville-area deserters. All but three, who showed no occupation, were listed as farmers. Such advertisements continued throughout the year. By November the rewards for some deserters had been raised to seventy-five dollars, clearly indicating the importance that the army placed on securing as many men as possible.[17]

Advertisements alone were not sufficient to return soldiers to their posts. The General Assembly finally addressed the issue in September 1863, fining sheriffs a thousand dollars if they refused to act on information regarding the location of a deserter. The penalty for advising someone to desert or hiding a deserter was five hundred dollars and a one-year jail sentence.[18] Finally the army sent troops to round up delinquents and deserters. J. A. Keller, patrolling the Greenville District in March 1865, wrote that "Stragling and Desertion is still very common. On the 14th instant we arrested 15 men, going as they reported to their homes, without papers of any kind. Yesterday the 15th we arrested 9 men, 7 without papers. The other two had papers, which they owned to be forged. From what I can learn, in the Districts of Union, Spartanburg and Greenville the citizens have been almost overrun by Deserters and absentees from the army."[19]

The deserter groups in the mountains continued to be a threat until the end of the war. Regular troops were involved in the effort to round up deserters. General Joseph Johnston sent troops from Mississippi to collect deserters from the Sixteenth South Carolina Infantry. Members of that regiment took the opportunity to return to Greenville when marching from Charleston to Jackson, Mississippi. Governor Bonham coordinated troop movements with North

Carolina Governor Zebulon Vance since the mountainous border was a popular spot for deserters.[20]

Finally for three months a Captain McGuire patrolled northern Greenville District. He had no qualms about shooting deserters, particularly those who fired on his own men.[21] McGuire needed a force of about fifty to complete his work, and found the approval of at least one Greenville resident: "I saw him yesterday and think him pretty smart he has taken some 8 or ten and killed one or shot him so that he is sertain to dye. . . . I think a few more to get the same fare will bring the Torys and Deserters to there sences if the last one of them was dead. . . . the country would be a heap better off than it is McGuire said that the man that hurts one of his boys shall have fifty balls through his hide."[22]

By October, McGuire was considered "a turer [terror] to torys and deserters." After collecting more men and killing several as well, McGuire finally retired from the area in November. Despite his work the army still needed to send troops to the area in 1864, and a letter writer in 1865 commented that "all the reserves" in nearby Union district had been sent to scour the mountains for deserters.[23]

The desertion rates for some companies in the Sixteenth Regiment, drawn largely from Greenville, ran as high as 30 percent. The problem of desertion in South Carolina eventually drew the attention of Confederate officials, illustrating both the gravity of the problem and their inability to perceive the issues underlying desertion. In a letter to Superintendent of the Bureau of Conscription John Preston, Major C. D. Melton blamed desertion on the fact that "the people . . . are poor, ill-informed, and but little identified with our struggle. They have therefore been easily seduced from their duty." While correct that Greenville residents had grown "little identified" with the Confederacy, Melton evidently believed that their reaction was the result of misinformation, not genuine dissatisfaction.[24]

Melton enclosed three letters he had received from John Ashmore with his letter to Preston. Ashmore described the high organizational level of the deserters with their small mobile bands and systems of signals and warnings. Deserters even fortified their positions—Ashmore requested a six-pound cannon to demolish a log barricade that had been erected near Gowensville, in Greenville District. In his most hysterical letter to Melton, Ashmore predicted that deserters could easily bring the enemy into the area, noted that conscripts were afraid to arrest deserters because they feared reprisals, reemphasized the organizational level of the deserters, and described the burning of homes and factories. Worst of all, deserters defended themselves with Confederate arms that they had taken with them. Evidently these yeomen now viewed the Confederate government as a greater threat to their liberty than Lincoln, the president who had troubled them just three years earlier.[25]

Preston passed the letters on to Secretary of War James Seddon, who forwarded them to General Robert E. Lee, calling for "decisive measures." Lee's measured response confirmed that troops had been sent to North Carolina and South Carolina to arrest deserters. He could recommend no further action. Almost simultaneously Assistant Secretary of War John A. Campbell passed a letter that he received to President Jefferson Davis, noting that "the condition of things in the mountain districts . . . menaces the existence of the Confederacy as fatally as either of the armies of the United States." Unfortunately, the Richmond government was unable to devise an appropriate response.[26]

As war continued, desertion made the already difficult process of securing troops even harder. In 1864 Preston announced that his bureau's mission would soon be moot because there were too few men to recruit. Troops continued to patrol the mountains, and their work was not entirely fruitless—from September 1862 to January 1865, over 2,500 South Carolinian deserters returned to service. Prosecution of deserters—demonstrated by petitions for writs of habeas corpus proving that the petitioners were not liable for service—continued in Greenville. But deserters were still problematic in the Greenville community. In 1864, 28 men presented a petition to Captain A. J. Boyles, the district enrolling officer, demanding that the Greenville jailer receive additional help because the jail was frequently filled with deserters. Charles Davis requested a guard to keep "incendiaries and rogues" away from his stables in January 1865.[27]

At war's end, Confederate leaders were still out of touch with general opinion. In March 1865 Secretary of War John Breckinridge could only lamely suggest to General Lee that he attempt to work with local authorities to "awaken a more wholesome state of public feeling. I know of nothing else that can be added to the means already employed to remedy this evil." Clearly Breckinridge was unable to address the problem adequately. A "wholesome state of feeling" could not be achieved through continued exhortation and hollow rhetoric; people had tired of war and wanted simply to be left alone. Yeomen farmers of the upcountry had now soured to the message that provoked a more eager response after Lincoln's election.[28]

Desertion in South Carolina should not be exaggerated. In terms of the absolute number of deserters, South Carolina ranked tenth in the Confederacy, far below states like North Carolina and Tennessee. Unionist sentiment was weaker in South Carolina than in states that came late to the Confederacy—like North Carolina and Virginia. But for the men who did desert or for their families who remained discontented at home, the list of complaints was long. The government had become intrusive and inadequately responsive to the needs of the people. White conscription and impressment of slaves drained needed labor from the farms. Demands for slave labor to defend the coast angered men who had fewer slaves than the plantation owners in the low country. Columbia issued edicts that limited the amount of cotton a farmer could grow. Poor weather decimated cash and subsistence crops alike. Cries from wives and children encouraged desertion, and conditions in the army were miserable enough to provide ample reason as well. Economic ruin prevented the Confederate Army from adequately arming, clothing, and feeding its troops. Manufacturers refused to extend credit to a Confederate Army hobbled by a rapidly depreciating currency.[29]

In short, the fatigue of war and the inability of the Confederate government to address pressing problems led to desertion and dissatisfaction in the Greenville District. After briefly rallying to the secessionist cause, residents of the district retreated to their desire to remain independent and asked only that the government leave them alone. Describing the fierce resistance that he faced from the deserters in the mountains, John Ashmore lamented that "they swear by all they hold sacred that they will die at home before they will ever be dragged forth again to do battle for such a cause." For these upcountrymen, the initial promise of the Confederate government had turned into a fight in which they wanted no part.[30]

NOTES

1. For a description of speeches delivered in Greenville before the secession convention, see Susan Louisa Burn to Charles Burn, December 6, 1860, Burn Family Papers, South Caroliniana Library, University of South Carolina, Columbia (hereafter SCL).

2. Lacy K. Ford Jr., *Origins of Southern Radicalism* (New York: Oxford University Press, 1988), 337, 351, 354.

3. James Gettys, "Mobilization for Secession in Greenville District," MA thesis, University of South Carolina, 1967, 91. *Patriot and Mountaineer* (Greenville), April 10 and November 22, 1860; January 3, 1861. *Southern Enterprise* (Greenville), December 22 and 29, 1859; January 12, April 26, and November 29, 1860.

4. Stephen Alan West, "From Yeoman to Redneck in Upstate South Carolina, 1850–1915" (PhD diss., Columbia University, 1998), 233–39. Perry lost the election, 1,342 to 225.

5. Mary Elizabeth Massey, "The Effect of Shortages on the Confederate Homefront," *Arkansas Historical Quarterly* 9 (1950): 176. West, "Yeoman to Redneck," 245. Frances Neves to William Neves and John Neves, December 11, 1861; Frances Neves to William Neves, December 24, 1861; Frances Neves to William Neves, John Neves, and George Neves, February 14, 1862, Neves Family Papers, SCL. The Neves family resided in Mush Creek, Greenville District.

6. James Farr to "Dear Son," May 19, 1862, Farr Family Papers, SCL; *Southern Enterprise* (Greenville), January 16, 1863.

7. Milledge Luke Bonham, "Proclamation," April 10, 1863, Governor Milledge Luke Bonham: Proclamations of Governor Bonham, South Carolina Department of Archives and History, Columbia (hereafter SCDAH); Milledge Luke Bonham, *Message No. I of His Excellency, M. L. Bonham, to the Legislature, at the Extra Session of April, 1863* (Columbia, S.C.: Charles P. Pelham, 1863), 4–5 (hereinafter Bonham, *Message No. I*); South Carolina General Assembly, *Acts of the General Assembly of the State of South Carolina, Passed in December, 1861* (Columbia, S.C.: Charles P. Pelham, 1862), 15–16.

8. South Carolina General Assembly, *Act of the General Assembly of the State of South Carolina, Passed in December, 1862, and February and April, 1863* (Columbia, S.C.: Charles P. Pelham, 1863), 137–39 (hereinafter General Assembly, *Passed* . . .); General Assembly, *Passed in September and December, 1863* (Columbia, S.C.: Charles P. Pelham, 1864), 191–94; General Assembly, *Passed at the Sessions of 1864–65* (Columbia, S.C.: Charles P. Pelham, 1866), 239–44; William Frank Zornow, "State Aid for Indigent Families of South Carolina Soldiers, 1861–1865," *South Carolina Historical Magazine* 57 (1956): 84–86.

9. Alsey Neves to William Neves, John Neves, and George Neves, September 26, 1862, Neves Family Papers, SCL. Alfred Davis to Colonel Abraham C. Myers, December 11, 1862, "Post Quartermaster, Greenville, SC, Letters Written, December 8, 1862–April 25, 1865," SCL. Alsey Neves to William Neves and John Neves, August 2, 1863; Alsey Neves to William Neves, John Neves, and George Neves, September 4, 1863, Neves Family Papers, SCL. Charles Davis to Captain M. S. Hanckel, June 7, 1864; Charles Davis to Captain C. H. Rhett, July 30, 1864; Charles Davis to Major G. W. Cunningham, July 24, 1864, "Post Quartermaster, Greenville, SC, Letters Written, December 8, 1862–April 25, 1865," SCL.

10. Ford, *Origins of Southern Radicalism*, 337, 247, 254; General Assembly, *Passed in December, 1862*, 111–12, 113–17; General Assembly, *Passed in September and December, 1863*, 200; General Assembly, *Passed at the Sessions of 1864–65*, 249.

11. Alva Dozier Gaskin, "Conscription and Impressment in South Carolina, 1860–1865" (MA thesis, University of South Carolina, 1926), 51. Alfred Davis to Captain G. J. Crafts, January 21, 1863; Charles Davis to Major Hutson Lee, October 4, 1863; Charles Davis to General Alexander R. Lawton, October 10, 1863; Charles Davis to Mr. J. T. Britt, March 27, 1864; Charles Davis to Mr. B. W. Williams, November 18, 1864, "Post Quartermaster, Greenville, SC, Letters Written, December 8, 1862–April 25, 1865," SCL. West, "Yeoman to Redneck," 246. Frank L. Owsley, "Defeatism in the Confederacy," *North Carolina Historical Review* 3 (1926): 450.

12. Charles Davis to Hutson Lee, July 27, 1864; Charles Davis to Hutson Lee, October 5, 1864 (two letters on that date); Charles Davis to Lawton, March 3, 1865; Charles Davis to Major Norman W. Smith, July 10, 1864, "Post Quartermaster, Greenville, SC, Letters Written, December 8, 1862–April 25, 1865," SCL.

13. John Hammond Moore, *Southern Homefront, 1861–1865* (Columbia, S.C.: Summerhouse Press, 1998), 130; *Southern Enterprise* (Greenville), September 10, 1863. The state was split into four divisions for supplying slaves for the coastal defense. Slaves constituted 32.2 percent of Greenville District's population, compared with low-country districts like Beaufort (81.2 percent) and Georgetown (85 percent). Percentages from "Historical United States Census Browser," fisher.virginia.lib.edu/census (accessed December 6, 2000).

14. Milledge Bonham to General G. T. Beauregard, January 15, 1863, Governor Milledge Luke Bonham: Letters and Telegrams Received and Sent, SCDAH; Bonham, *Message No. I*, 6; General Assembly, *Passed in December, 1862*, 105–8, 110–11; General Assembly, *Passed in September and December, 1863*, 175–76; General Assembly, *Passed at the Sessions of 1864–65*, 224–26. Initially slaves were selected from the portion of slaves liable for road duty. Colonel John Black to Captain H. W. Feilden, May 10, 1864, in U.S. War Department, *The War of the Rebellion: A Compilation of the Official Records of the Union and Confederate Armies* (Pasadena, Calif.: Broadfoot, 1985) (hereafter *Official Records*), serial 1, vol. 53: 332.

15. Owsley, "Defeatism in the Confederacy," 448; Ella Lonn, *Desertion during the Civil War* (1928; rpt., Lincoln: University of Nebraska Press, 1998), 7; James F. Sloan, diary, January 20, 1862–March 25, 1862, Sloan Papers, SCL; Charles Davis to Lawton, December 8, 1864, "Post Quartermaster, Greenville, SC, Letters Written, December 8, 1862–April 25, 1865," SCL.

16. Alfred Davis, advertisements, January 12, 1863; Alfred Davis to Colonel John S. Preston, January 14, 1863; Alfred Davis to Beauregard, January 17, 1863, "Post Quartermaster, Greenville, SC, Letters Written, December 8, 1862–April 25, 1865," SCL.

17. *Southern Enterprise* (Greenville), January 29, April 9, June 11, July 9, and October 8, 1863; the June 25, 1863, issue also includes a separate advertisement for three more deserters, also offering thirty dollars each; August 27, September 3, and October 8, 1863 (later issues include repeats of the earlier advertisement); November 10, 1863 (this particular advertisement was repeated on November 26 and December 3, 1863).

18. General Assembly, *Passed in September and December, 1863*, 177–78.

19. J. A. Keller to Colonel John M. Obey, March 16, 1865, SCL.

20. General Joseph Johnston, "Proclamation," June 18, 1863, Governor Milledge Luke Bonham: Proclamations of Governor Bonham, SCDAH; Major C. D. Melton to Preston, August 25, 1863, *Official Records,* serial 4, vol. 2: 769; Bonham to Zebulon Vance, August 22, 1863, *Official Records,* serial 4, vol. 2: 741; Vance to Bonham, August 26, 1863, *Official Records,* serial 4, vol. 2: 765.

21. Frances Neves to William Neves, Neves Family Papers, SCL, August 4, 1863.

22. Alsey Neves to William Neves, John Neves, and George Neves, Neves Family Papers, SCL, September 4, 1863.

23. Alsey Neves to William Neves, John Neves, and George Neves, October 11, 1863; Alsey Neves to William Neves, John Neves, and George Neves, October 18, 1863; Emma Neves to William Neves, November 25, 1863, Neves Family Papers, SCL. Feilden to Black, April 29, 1864, *Official Records,* serial 1, vol. 35, part 2: 455. "Mother" to "My dear Charlie," January 6, 1865, Sims Family Papers, SCL.

24. For desertion rates in the Sixteenth Regiment see *Compiled Service Records of Confederate Soldiers Who Served in Organizations from the State of South Carolina* (Washington, D.C.: National Archives and Records Service, 1958), rolls CW 0820–CW 0825, SCDAH. For Melton quote see Melton to Preston, August 25, 1863, *Official Records,* serial 4, vol. 2: 769–70.

25. John Ashmore to Melton, August 7, 1863, *Official Records,* serial 4, vol. 2: 772; Ashmore to Melton, August 16, 1863, *Official Records,* serial 4, vol. 2: 773; Ashmore to Melton, August 17, 1863, *Official Records,* serial 4, vol. 2: 774. The Bureau of Conscription was headquartered in Richmond. Melton was commandant of the camp for conscripts in Columbia. Ashmore was the chief enrollment officer for the districts of Anderson, Greenville, Pickens, Spartanburg, and Union, headquartered in Greenville.

26. Preston to James Seddon, further notations by Seddon and General Robert E. Lee, August 29–September 15, 1863, *Official Records,* serial 4, vol. 2: 768–69. Lee does not specify who has been sent to the mountains, but this letter may refer to McGuire. John A. Campbell, endorsement on a letter from Lieutenant-Colonel George Lay to Preston, September 7–8, 1863, *Official Records,* serial 4, vol. 2: 786.

27. Preston to Seddon, April 30, 1864, *Official Records,* serial 4, vol. 3: 354; General James Chesnut to Seddon, June 18, 1864, *Official Records,* serial 1, vol. 53: 342; Major-General George Stoneman to Major-General George H. Thomas, April 19, 1865, *Official Records,* serial 1, vol. 49, part 2: 407–8; Preston to John Breckinridge, February 1865, *Official Records,* serial 4, vol. 3: 1099–1110; Various vs. B. B. McCreery, February 4, 1864, Greenville Clerk of Court: Writs of habeas corpus relating to conscription law, SCDAH; Citizens of Greenville, South Carolina, petition to A. J. Boyles, August 27, 1864, Greenville Clerk of Court: Correspondence of the clerk concerning local conduct of the Civil War, SCDAH; Charles Davis to Colonel W. W. Perryman, January 9, 1865, "Post Quartermaster, Greenville, SC, Letters Written, December 8, 1862–April 25, 1865," SCL.

28. Breckinridge to Robert E. Lee, March 1, 1865, *Official Records,* serial 1, vol. 46, part 2: 1275.

29. Lonn, *Desertion during the Civil War,* 231; Daniel Crofts, *Reluctant Confederates: Upper South Unionists in the Secession Crisis* (Chapel Hill: University of North Carolina Press, 1989), xv, xxi.

30. Ashmore to Melton, August 7, 1863, *Official Records,* serial 4, vol. 2: 772.

THE PROBLEM OF RELIEF FOR THE FAMILIES OF CONFEDERATE SOLDIERS IN SOUTH CAROLINA

(1994)

Patricia Dora Bonnin

On May 1, 1861, a notice in the pages of the *Edgefield Advertiser* appealed to readers for help in aiding the families of soldiers: "Citizens will please come to anyone of our number without a more special call and contribute as they may think proper. No appeal is needed in a case like this, where all will esteem it a privilege to lend their aid."[1]

Even during these early days of the Civil War the citizens of Edgefield, South Carolina, realized that a commitment had to be made to ensure the survival of the mothers, wives, and children of Confederate soldiers. As the war continued, and hopes for a short war faded, the necessity of relief became more pressing for the local government and also for the government of South Carolina. However, efforts to help the families of soldiers were unsuccessful in dealing adequately with the suffering which plagued many women and children in South Carolina.

While many factors determined the effectiveness of relief, this paper concentrates primarily on the motivational elements behind the development of relief. Motivation might have affected the extent to which aid could solve the problems on the home front. The paper also examines the manner in which relief was administered in Edgefield, South Carolina; relief agencies had no guidelines in distributing aid, a lack which probably resulted in an unfair system.

Although local attempts were made in Edgefield to help the families of soldiers, these endeavors soon fell short of what was necessary, and the state government stepped in to provide aid. The Journals from the General Assembly of South Carolina indicate several measures taken to afford relief for the families of soldiers. Bills enacted during the first year of the war to help these families placed the responsibility of distributing money on local relief boards.

Families received varying amounts of money from the state depending on their local board and the wealth available in their own district. This system did not serve the needs of the most destitute families. Later, the legislature established a general state fund to alleviate the problems poor districts faced.

Edgefield relief records from October 1862 through January 1863 provide a great deal of information about the measures taken for the relief of soldiers' families in South Carolina. These records indicate the amount of money given to suffering families and who distributed the money; the funds distributed were intended to last for two months. These records also vividly demonstrate the problems which arose from the absence of guidelines: families were at the mercy of their relief board officers. These men could capriciously give more money to one family and less to another.

The relief accounts reveal a number of discrepancies in how much aid families received. Among families with four children all under the age of ten, some received considerably more money than others. The reports do not explain differences in amounts distributed. It might be that some families could not prove they needed more funds or maybe the person distributing money was more partial to families he knew and liked. Until more evidence is found, one can only conjecture.

One distributor, G. D. Huiet, appears to have been more uniform. For the wives and widows of soldiers, the amount was $2.50. For every child they had under ten years old, they received an additional $2.50. For children between the ages of ten and fourteen, the amount was $2.00. The records filed by Luke Culbreath show no patterns for the amount of money given, and the totals are higher than those filed by Huiet. One woman with two children under ten received $11.85, while another woman with two children under ten received $9.35. To one woman without children Culbreath gave $7.90. This is over five dollars more than Huiet gave to women without children.[2] The differences in amounts allocated by the relief boards in Edgefield indicate a problem with the state legislation. No regulations determined the distribution of funds, so each board member handed out money as he saw fit. This proved unfair to families in desperate need.

As expected, families belonging to the planter classes were not in need of relief in Edgefield. A comparison of names of families on relief in 1863 to the Census records of 1860 shows that heads of households on relief tended to be farmers, millers, or factory workers. The census also shows the economic status of families before the war, including the value of real and personal property. Most families on relief had no real estate before the war. However, it appears as though the relief board did not favor those families with less property. For example, the Howard family had more real estate than most families on relief, yet it received almost five dollars per person. On the other hand, the Jordan family had no real estate before the war and received only $2.50 per person. The census also provides information on widows who had older sons eligible for the army. For example, Ann Gray is reported as being widowed and receiving $10.88.[3] The reason for this large sum of money may lie in the fact that she had six sons in the army.

Relief records for Edgefield list 444 families in November and December of 1862. One year later, the board of relief from Edgefield counted 727 families on its rolls for relief with over $30,000 distributed.[4] This might reflect changing conscription laws as more and more men left for service. A list in the Edgefield newspaper named forty deserters for April in the final year of the war. The names of twenty out of forty deserters match the relief records of 1863.[5] One of the deserters, W. L. Coleman, was even a former member of the relief board.

In studying these records and the limitations of relief, we need to understand what might have motivated the government to develop a relief system. In a practical sense, the government could not place the needs of the home front before those of the army, but it also could not ignore the problems arising from suffering behind the lines. Through relief, the government might have hoped to forestall threats to the war effort, such as destruction of army property and public dissent. The government also appears to have acted in a somewhat fatherly manner in trying to shelter the women of the South while the men were away.

The practicality of relief must first be placed into context of what the government could realistically accomplish. Economic instability restricted South Carolina's capacity to respond to army needs, let alone the needs of families. The economic problems of the South have long been viewed as the strongest factors behind the Confederacy's failure to continue the war. Douglas Ball contends that the defeat of the South was attributable to the inadequate management of finances. The government, confident of a short war, failed to create practical fiscal policies. The South also lacked the leadership essential to developing effective economic strategy, including survival on the home front.[6]

Aside from the Confederate treasury's inadequacy and Congress's inability to handle fiscal administration, the Confederacy was also plagued by a dogmatic faith in "King Cotton." Southerners simply believed that foreign powers would assist them because of the importance of cotton.[7] This short-sighted faith, however, was not vindicated; other countries began to increase their production of cotton by almost 800,000 bales between 1862 and 1864. The dreams of an embargo were never fulfilled for the South.[8]

While the South could not use cotton to force other countries to intervene on its behalf, the cash crop could be used as a basis for security on bonds and loans. The Confederate Treasury Department issued cotton certificates which it hoped to sell in Europe. During the war the Treasury circulated $1,500,000 in cotton certificates, and in late October 1862 Confederate agents began negotiations for a loan with a French agency. After several modifications, the loan amounted to $15,000,000 using cotton as security. The South continued to depend heavily on the influence of "King Cotton" as the agents of the Produce Loan Office were forced to increase purchases and induce planters to satisfy the demands of the Confederacy created by the cotton certificates and the French loan.[9]

The reliance on cotton suggests its power to raise revenues, but this dependence kept the South at the mercy of cash crops. It prevented many planters from raising the food crops needed to keep the home front and the army strong enough to endure the war. The government of South Carolina realized the need to reduce the amount of cotton produced despite the pressure to supply crops to the Produce Loan Office. In the journals of the Executive Council this concern appears for the first time in March 1862: "Resolved: That an address be issued by the Governor and Council to the planters of the State, urging on them the necessity of planting large grain crops, and not more than one tenth of their usual crop of cotton for the present year."[10] On the motion of Colonel Hayne, the resolution was changed to state that not more than one-fifth of the usual cotton crop be permitted in order to facilitate a smaller crop for the year.[11]

In April 1862 the House was prepared to punish those who planted an amount of cotton which exceeded a certain quantity during the duration of the war. The House read the bill once and then ordered it to lie on the table. Attempts to limit the production of cotton continued to appear in the journals, and continually were ordered to lie on the table and did not surface for consideration again.[12]

These endeavors to control the production of cotton illustrate how the government tried dealing with imbalance of crop production. The journals of the General Assembly do not, however, indicate whether this legislation was effective in providing more food crops for the state. In addition, the government's insatiable demands for food and cloth, combined with the northern blockade, brought on drastic shortages and skyrocketing prices early in the war.[13]

The legislative records also illustrate how South Carolina tried dealing with the economic hardships which befell the South. The House of Representatives addressed the problem in December 1862: "Resolved: That it is the opinion of the Legislature of South Carolina that one of the chief causes of the present high prices of all the necessaries of life is the redundancy of the currency, there being in actual circulation two hundred fifty millions of dollars in treasury notes, when one hundred million would afford an ample supply for the business of the country."[14]

The House concluded by offering two remedies for the financial instability of the South. The first called for a tax of general application to produce a demand for the treasury notes in circulation. The second remedy entailed the investment of all surplus in the funded debt of the Confederate states by unanimous consent of the people. The House then resolved that the Confederate Congress should impose a heavy tax on the property and businesses of the country. The House also agreed that the duty of all southerners was to invest in the stocks and bonds of the Confederate States of America. The House believed that these resolutions would be the best means by which to bring about relief for both the government and the people.[15]

In an economy plagued by a depreciated currency, combined with the inability of the government to encourage the production of grains instead of cotton, the distribution of relief could not rely on monetary aid. As the Confederate dollar bought less and less, less was available to purchase. In response to shortages and escalating prices, the South Carolina legislature deliberated on the distribution of goods. In the House of Representatives journal of 1863 there is a resolution which placed the responsibility of supplying goods to families on the shoulders of the relief boards. The resolution calls for the distribution of provisions in lieu of money.[16]

Through offering provisional aid, the government hoped to avoid several undesirable situations as a result of suffering and want. The legislature realized the need to prevent dissent and dissatisfaction with the war. The bread riots which occurred in cities such as Richmond and Columbia were an indication that women would not passively allow their families to starve.

A letter received by the Executive Council in March 1862 indicates the necessity of providing goods to families. A Marion district resident informed the council that the salt warehouse had been looted by "certain citizens."[17] During the next several months the General Assembly took action to provide salt for the families of soldiers. To avoid the looting of private holdings and perhaps those belonging to the army, the government assigned the distribution of salt to the boards of relief. The bills which deal with the responsibility of salt dispensing do not indicate how much salt the boards possessed, nor do they inform the officers of how much salt to give to each family.

Aside from protecting private and perhaps military interests, the government might also have wanted to assume the distribution of goods to prevent public dissent. The bread riots threatened to destroy unity and exhibited images of discontent throughout the South. Newspaper editors chastised women for their unpatriotic and selfish behavior, but the suffering of women and children could not be ignored. The displays of violent behavior on the part of women also threatened existing beliefs that women were the exalted protectors of southern culture.

The implementation of relief might then be seen as a way to pacify the outcries of women and an attempt to preserve the traditional roles of women. The untraditional actions of women threatened to disrupt national unity which was crucial for the South's ability to carry on the war. Legislation devised to provide necessary goods and prohibit extortion can be seen as a method of placating angered women and restoring faith in the Confederacy. A governor's message from Edgefield's Milledge Bonham reflects the government's awareness that the lack of protection for the families of soldiers could result in destitution.[18] Although the government might be concerned with avoiding discontent among the soldiers, there must have been also an understanding that the home front must need to be dealt with in a manner which would not foster discontent.

While discontent threatened unity on the home front, desertion plagued the Confederacy's ability to meet Yankee forces. Men fled from the battlefield for various reasons, the most compelling of which was to return home to their starving families. South Carolina's legislative records indicate the growing worries over the high rates of desertion. Bonham's message to the General Assembly in 1863 hints at the reasons for the abandonment of army posts. He states that in most cases deserters probably did not leave the army with the intent to betray their country.[19] In response to Governor Bonham's message, the Senate not only introduced legislation to apprehend deserters more effectively, but also to cure part of the problem—the suffering faced by many soldiers' families.

Relief for families was perhaps not viewed as a direct method of trying to keep soldiers in the army, but government officials were probably anxious to take steps to protect war interests. In a message to the General Assembly, Governor Bonham explains that it is the state's duty to protect every soldier's family against want. He urged the men of the government to increase the aid distributed by the boards of relief and, if necessary, to raise taxes for that purpose.[20] Bonham's message does not refer to the need for aid as essential to the continuation of the war effort, but we can perhaps speculate that his suggestion was motivated by a pragmatic understanding of a relief system. By protecting the families of soldiers, the governor must have realized that he was also making an effort to prevent men from leaving the war front.

While the government appears to have used relief efforts in a practical manner, there is no evidence that these were conscious motives. The same can be said for paternalistic influences. In looking at the paternalistic motives behind the development of relief, we must keep in mind that this paternalism played a large role in the culture of the South before, during, and after the war. This discussion will not attempt to understand southern paternalism in its entirety. Instead, the idea of paternalism will be used to understand why the government of South Carolina would have felt compelled to develop a system of relief. We have already seen what the government might have hoped to accomplish through aid programs for the benefit of soldiers' families. This discussion will deal more closely with the abstract factors which can be seen at work in the legislation of South Carolina.

A discussion of paternalism in the South before the Civil War is beyond the scope of this paper, but it is important to have a general understanding of cultural influences on government officials before the war. In southern society, male dominance was not only a prevailing characterization, it was also strengthened by customs and laws.[21] White women were considered physically weak and dependent upon male protection, direction, and control.[22]

In the midst of war, women began clinging to familiar foundations of paternalism in the form of appeals to the government. After all, it was this newly established government which had called their fathers, husbands, and sons into service. The journals of the Executive Council contain a number of letters from women pleading for the exemption of their husbands or sons. The applications of women such as Elizabeth McRae and Harriet Beckwith requested the exemption of sons in the service. The application of Mrs. McRae was sent to a committee to be investigated, while Mrs. Beckwith's application was sent to the adjutant general for a decision.[23]

Although the journals only provide limited information concerning the letters for exemption, we can see by the number of letters that many women were turning to another tangible form of paternalism left in their lives—the government. Most of the letters received by the Executive Council appear only once and were referred to the adjutant general.[24] The response of the adjutant general is not provided in the pages of any legislative journals. According to George Rable, many letters to the government seeking exemptions, or aid, were filed without an answer.[25]

Military necessity prevented the government from responding favorably to the letters of struggling women, but these applications reveal the way in which many women viewed the duties of the government. What then was the government's attitude toward women? On February 6, 1863, a bill came before both the House of Representatives and the Senate which set forth the ideals expected of southern women:

> Whereas the Women of the South have contributed to the prosecution of our present struggle for independence all the aid and comfort their gentle but heroic hearts could devise, as well by the encouragement of their applause by the manifold products of their skill and industry; and whereas the soldiers of the South, ever brave and patriotic, have been doubly fired to the discharge of their duties by the lovely charities and devoted sympathies of these patriot sisters in a common cause; therefore, be it resolved unanimously that this General Assembly hereby testifies admiring appreciation of their services, and warmly accords to them the praise of having contributed largely to the rapid progress of

our country's deliverance from the threatened vengeance of a foe who seeks to desolate the homes of which they are the ornament and pride.[26]

This bill provides an unrealistic image of southern women during the war. The true struggles of women were ignored in this praise-filled resolution which made the women of the South seem saint-like. Rather than dwelling on the many sacrifices women endured in terms of emotional destruction and physical want, the government tried offering a patriotic piece of propaganda. Praise, however, did not fill empty stomachs.

Despite the eloquent praise of women found in bills such as this, nothing indicates that the government felt it owed women any aid. Instead, we find in his message of 1862 that Governor Pickens believed relief was an obligation to soldiers.[27] Any actions taken toward the development of relief must then be understood as the government's desire to carry on the tradition of paternalism. In the absence of soldiers, the government had to become the protector of women. The earlier discussion on extortion provides examples of how the government dealt with a woman's ability to protect herself and her family while the men were away. In his address, General Harlee only names the families of soldiers to be the group endangered by exorbitant prices. The bill dealing with extortioners stipulates that the fines go toward the benefit of relief boards. Both target families as the sole victims of extortion. It might suffice to say that the government tried to protect these women solely out of compassion for their struggles, but then women are referred to in the light in which the government sees them: the *families of* soldiers. Women were not referred to as individuals, but rather as belonging to the soldiers. The government's role was to take the place of absent fathers and husbands.

The role long held by husbands and fathers did not occur overnight; Rable explains that the government was slow to assume the responsibilities of general welfare. It was the men, not the government, who were supposed to provide for and protect women. These notions of masculine honor and individual responsibility could not easily be ignored.[28] The government's actions and rhetoric indicate the paternalistic influences at work. Whereas it might appear overly simplistic to claim that the government saw itself as the temporary provider for women and children, it must be remembered that those holding state offices spent their lives believing that white women needed to be sheltered.

Although paternalism and pragmatism may not have been conscious imperatives behind the development of relief, it appears that these were compelling factors behind the actions of officials. The Edgefield relief records supply details about the local relief efforts, but this is only part of the larger question of relief. In order to find out more about the disparities between the money given by one board member in comparison to another, other studies should analyze the relief records for the following years. The manuscript Census from 1870 also should be compared with the relief records to find out whether families on relief recovered after the war and if they still lived in Edgefield. A larger study on the topic might reveal the effectiveness of the relief system within the state of South Carolina and throughout the Confederacy.

NOTES

1. *Edgefield Advertiser,* May 1, 1861.
2. Record of the Soldiers' Board of Relief, Edgefield District, South Carolina, 1863, South Carolina Division of Archives and History (SCDAH).
3. Records of the Soldiers' Board of Relief, Edgefield District, South Carolina, 1863, SCDAH.
4. *Reports and Resolutions of the General Assembly, 1863*, South Carolina General Assembly, SCDAH, 325.
5. *Edgefield Advertiser,* April 12, 1861.
6. Douglas Ball, *Financial Failure and Confederate Defeat* (Urbana: University of Illinois Press, 1991), 1–8.
7. Ibid., 11.
8. Ibid., 65.
9. Richard Cecil Todd, *Confederate Finance* (Athens: University of Georgia Press, 1954), 44–50.
10. *Journals of the South Carolina Executive Councils of 1861 and 1862,* 112.
11. Ibid., 112.
12. *Journal of the House of Representatives of the State of South Carolina, 1862,* 389–410.
13. George Rable, *Civil Wars* (Urbana: University of Illinois Press, 1989), 92.
14. *Journal of the House of Representatives of the State of South Carolina, 1862,* 87.
15. Ibid.
16. Ibid., 156.
17. *Journals of the South Carolina Executive Councils of 1861 and 1862,* 186.
18. *South Carolina Senate Journal 1863* (Columbia: Pelham State Printers, 1863), 10.
19. Ibid.
20. *Journal of the House of Representatives of the State of South Carolina, 1863,* 74.
21. Orville Vernon Burton, *In My Father's House Are Many Mansions* (Chapel Hill: University of North Carolina Press, 1985), 99.
22. Anne Fior Scott, *The Southern Lady* (Chicago: University of Chicago Press. 1970), 4–6.
23. Ibid., 90.
24. *Journals of the South Carolina Executive Councils of 1861 and 1862,* 152, 182.
25. Rable, *Civil Wars,* 86.
26. *South Carolina Senate Journal 1863,* 259.
27. *Journal of the House of Representatives of the State of South Carolina, 1862,* 11.
28. Rable, *Civil Wars,* 104.

EMANCIPATION, RACE, AND SOCIETY

FATEFUL LEGACY

White Southerners and the Dilemma of Emancipation

(1977)

Dan T. Carter

When the Civil War ended in April of 1865, the victorious North was deeply divided over two crucial questions: what was to become of the white South, and what was to be done with the two and a half million freed slaves? White southerners had plunged a peaceful nation into a nightmare of bloodshed and destruction. In the minds of most northerners, secession appropriately symbolized the final act of southern estrangement. It was not simply that the region adhered to archaic political ideas and an immoral and outmoded system of human labor, the South was antagonistic in every respect to the spirit of modernism. It was agrarian in an age which increasingly emphasized industrialism, and it was generally conservative and antagonistic to new ideas in a young nation which encouraged liberal social and intellectual experimentation.

Were these wicked, sinful and backward people therefore to be welcomed back as erring brothers? Or were they to be held at arm's length until they exhibited a properly penitential spirit; until they were "Reconstructed" in a form more suitable for membership in the nation they had spurned in 1861? To put the matter bluntly: just how worthy of citizenship were these proud southerners?

The second question was inextricably interwoven with the first. The Emancipation Proclamation, and later the Thirteenth Amendment, outlawed slavery but did little to define the future status of the freedmen of the South. Were they to be given the full rights and privileges of citizenship? Or were they to be granted some status halfway between chattel slavery and complete political equality?

In the best of times, these would have been difficult problems, but these were not the best of times. A legacy of antebellum and wartime hatreds clouded the issues, and solutions were all too often shaped by grasping attempts to cultivate political and economic power, as Republicans sought to protect their narrow majority and Northern Democrats attempted to regain the political support of their Democratic brothers in the South. Above all else the nation faced this crisis without the healing leadership of Abraham Lincoln.

Under these circumstances, it is not surprising that the triumphant North was like a noisome Tower of Babel in the spring of 1865. In dealing with the white South, some conservatively counseled compassion and immediate political reconciliation. Others insisted that such talk was folly. The South had spurned the union; it should be readmitted only after it had proved its loyalty and reliability. In many respects, the new president Andrew Johnson seemed to mirror this schizophrenic attitude with his harsh promise that "traitors would be punished" and his remarkably lenient policy toward the defeated South.

As far as the freedmen were concerned the political landscape seemed only slightly less chaotic. Most northerners were willing, indeed insistent, upon granting civil rights to the freedmen of the South. Blacks should be allowed to hold property, to sue and be sued, to testify in court, to be secure in their persons and property: in short to be treated as equals before the law. But there was little substantial support for full political rights for southern blacks. In the past decade, more than a dozen American historians have analyzed and described northern racial attitudes in the years before and during the Civil War, and their conclusions are depressingly similar. The majority of northern whites feared and despised blacks as well as the institution of slavery, and their opposition to southern expansionism in the 1850s more often than not reflected white racism rather than a genuine concern for the plight of the antebellum slave.

Nevertheless, within less than three years after the war had ended, the Congress of the United States had adopted the most far-reaching civil rights legislation in our history. The Fourteenth and Fifteenth amendments had been launched on the road to ratification, and the era of "Radical" Reconstruction had begun.

In seeking to unravel this mystery of causation, historians have approached the question from a number of perspectives. In an earlier era, Reconstruction was attributed to an atmosphere of national hatred and revenge carefully choreographed by such Republican Radicals as Thaddeus Stephens, Charles Sumner, and "Beast" Ben Butler.

More recently there has been a tendency to deemphasize the role of the Radical Republicans. What seems clear from the evidence is the basic conservatism of most Republicans and their genuine reluctance to adopt coercive measures against the South. Eric McKitrick probably captured this new direction best in his 1960 biography of Andrew Johnson when he argued that it was the violent resistance of the white South to any change that led to the adoption of Radical Reconstruction. White southerners made a number of fatal blunders in the immediate postwar period, says McKitrick. They ignored Johnson's modest Reconstruction requirements and instead adopted black codes which severely restricted the civil and economic rights of the freedmen. They elected to local and state office the very secessionists who had precipitated the war and plunged the South into racial turmoil by using violence, murder, and even assassination to strike down any proponents of political rights for blacks. In short, the recalcitrance of the white South in 1865, coupled with Johnson's personal inflexibility and political ineptitude, forced a reluctant Republican congress to adopt the very Reconstruction measures white southerners had feared and opposed.[1]

But why did southerners make such a horrendous miscalculation for the second time in five years? What drove them toward their own political self-destruction? These are questions which have been answered less satisfactorily.

The problem is more perplexing to me, because of the intellectual changes in southern society in the immediate postwar period. The peculiar defensiveness of the region before 1860 had always exaggerated the appearance of unity within the region. As W. T. Couch observed in 1933, the life of the South had always been characterized by class divisions and "wide differences in political, economic, racial, educational and religious faiths." Defeat shattered the facade of unanimity among white southerners which had triumphed in the antebellum period. For one brief almost euphoric period, white southerners seemed to speak their minds bluntly and without the restraints which had characterized southern debate since the days of Jefferson and Madison. In a July 4, 1865, speech, Georgia's provincial governor declared of the old South, "We abused mankind when they differed with us." Southerners had carried their opposition to men's thinking "to such an extreme, that men among us who dared to differ . . . were arraigned, not by law or before a legal tribunal, but before vigilantee [sic] societies and personally abused." Civilization was driven from the land, charged the provincial governor of Georgia, and "law and order was suppressed by lawless men." Under the title "Things Passing Away," the Raleigh, North Carolina, *Standard* compiled a staggering indictment against the "bigotry, terrorism and repression" of the prewar South and urged southerners to turn these practices forever aside. And the *Standard* called for complete, free, and open debate on all issues. The time for a "false unity" had passed.[2]

With the political and intellectual unity of the antebellum period fractured, southerners were often free to voice their self-doubts and questions concerning southern society. For those who had secretly favored change in southern society, but who had muted their calls for reform because of the necessity of unity and cohesion, the shambles of the old society seemed to suggest that a new day was dawning; the defeat of 1865 would be a beginning rather than an end. "I am very frank to say that I do zealously favor reconstruction," wrote the president of North Carolina's Trinity College in July of 1865. And his cheerful acceptance of change echoed across the South. "We should forget the past," an enthusiastic Mississippi lawyer wrote his wife six months after the war was over. "We must create language, literature and art; we must develop science." The South's antebellum life of ease and prosperity built upon slavery had been a curse which had dulled the sensibilities of the region. The abridgement of this false prosperity "will be the dawn of a New Era."[3]

Such summonses to a New South were not always couched in such vague generalities. In particular, one is struck by manifestations of what Paul Gaston would later call the "New South Creed." In every town, every hamlet of the South, southerners of various political persuasions strained to understand the implications of the war. And the most compelling lesson that seemed to emerge was the failure of antebellum institutions and ideas.

All during the 1840s and 1850s, J. D. B. DeBow's *Review* had been the forum for those southerners who supported manufacturing interests. William Gregg, James Taylor, Joseph Henry Lumpkin, Richard F. Reynolds, A. H. Brisbane, Daniel Pratt: such men had zealously supported economic diversification and industrialization as essential for the future of the South. As the war approached, however, their arguments had been increasingly muted by southerners' suspicion that industrialism was incompatible with the South's institutions—particularly slavery. Now that slavery was gone and the vaunted King Cotton strategy had been exposed as a hollow mockery, the proponents of industrialization stood vindicated.

Such ideas were not completely new, but there were some striking differences between the antebellum and postwar advocates of modernization. Postwar reformers not only supported industrialization, they were much more likely to bluntly attack the plantation system. The radical reformation in the labor system wrought by the abolition of slavery challenged the keystone of southern society, plantation agriculture. Some reformers welcomed this change; others accepted it reluctantly, but beginning with this common ground they proposed more substantial alterations in southern agriculture, alterations which would result in the breakup of landholding patterns, the abandonment of staple crop production, and the creation of a white yeoman farming class.

"Now that slavery no longer exists, it has become a social necessity to break up and abandon the plantation system," argued the Augusta *Chronicle and Sentinel* in June of 1865, and such heresy soon echoed through every major rural magazine published in the postwar period. *The Field and Fireside,* a North Carolina magazine devoted to the elevation of agriculture and the promotion of "Pure and Dignified Literature," called upon southern landowners to "divide and sub-divide" their immense plantations.[4]

Writers, particularly in the Southeast, seem to have accepted the notion that staple crop production was strictly a thing of the past. "The knell of African slavery in the South, in our judgment doomed cotton as king," declared the Raleigh *Sentinel.* And, while the plant would continue to be produced throughout the South, cotton—as well as rice, sugar and tobacco—would inevitably go into a decline in the South. As a committee of the South Carolina legislature concluded, the prevailing argument that the staple crop product of "plantation system is best adapted to the South" was a casualty of the war. There was still a place in the southern scheme of things, "but there is now an even greater place for the small farm."[5]

In the wake of defeat, therefore, Jefferson's vision of a region of small yeoman farms was reborn, not simply as a complement to the great landed estates, but a replacement. To southerners who were well aware of the differences between the shabby, run-down, and dilapidated nature of most southern agriculture and the well-kept fields of northern farms, it was a beguiling prospect. Within ten years, said one North Carolina newspaper, plantations with their centralized labor system would be replaced by "small, neat flourishings and improved farms."[6]

In some respects, of course, this tale of self-reconstruction was little more than an updating of the old antebellum Whig program: internal improvements, the development of complementary manufacturing interests, the diversification and modernization of American agriculture. For some southerners, however, reconstruction was more than this. In practical terms they were much more likely to welcome industrialization per se as an end within itself; they were much more likely to express open criticism of the plantation system and the large landholding system per se. But the essential difference was of a cast of mind, an outlook which was subtly different. What was needed, declared Thomas Settle of North Carolina, was not simply "railroads, canals, steamboats, factories, workshops, cities, towns, beautiful villages and neat farm houses"; what was needed was to "bury a thousand fathoms deep" the ideas and feelings of the past and to recast the spirit of the South in a mode of "universal progress."[7]

Georgia Judge O. A. Lochrane argued in the summer of 1865 that the great war was a chasm which separated the old South from the new. It was difficult for men to "shake down their convictions like apples from a tree," he admitted. "But the lessons of the past years are unmistakable." Unless an "improved and enlightened civilization" emerged from the ashes of the South, unless the backward customs and attitudes of the region could be swept away, the South would blindly relive the mistakes of the past. "We must be men, not monuments. . . . Let not pride, prejudice, and folly blind us and lead us stumbling backward over a wilderness of graves." The South, he concluded, had to be "reconstructed" in a mold more in keeping with the "enlightened spirit of the age."[8]

Given this remarkable burst of political candor and openness, given this near surrender to the very social and economic forces that had stood against the South, it is obvious that the essential problem was the future of the emancipated slave. What was to become of the freedmen? This was not a question of the racist South versus the idealistic North. Racism permeated the North as well as the

South. But there were unmistakable differences between the two regions. Northerners watched the results of Emancipation with mild concern, and a kind of quizzical curiosity as an experiment to be followed with interest and even some limited commitment. To white southerners, however, it was the crucial question of their generation, and they watched this massive experiment in freedom not with idle curiosity, but with passionate, involved commitment. On the outcome of this "experiment" rested the future of the South.

Thus no question so preoccupied southerners after the war as that of the future of the freedman and his role in southern society. The "negro question" was on everyone's lips in the weeks after the end of the war, reported a Mississippi parson in the spring of 1865.[9] Six months later, northern travelers to the South still found it the main topic of conversation with the southerners they met. "Everybody talks about the negro, at all hours of the day, and under all circumstances," reported the Boston journalist Sidney Andrews in his postwar travels. "Let conversation begin where it will, it ends with Sambo."[10] While concerns covered every phase of the future of black-white relations, the central preoccupation (at least initially) was over the degree to which the freedmen would continue to furnish the labor supply of the region.

The public pronouncements of white southerners were usually sober calls for a measured attempt to work with free labor, coupled with warnings that the future of such experiments was entirely dependent upon the leeway given to the South in working through this difficult period of readjustment. Privately, the observations of most southerners were a mélange of fear, uncertainty, and deep pessimism, leavened only occasionally by a grudging and guarded optimism. Their misgivings stemmed from their own proslavery pronouncements, the historical experiences of emancipation in other societies, and the wartime experiments of a few ex–slave owners with free black labor.

It was an article of faith, so commonly held it was seldom necessary to explicitly state it, that the freedman was inherently indolent and opposed to physical exertion. It was the carefully controlled use of force by the slave owner which (for his own good) kept the slave at work, maintained the economic viability of southern agriculture, and incidentally, returned a profit as well. Nor were such misgivings based upon idle speculation. Free black labor had been tried on a massive scale in the islands of the Caribbean, first in French Haiti and later in the British possessions. In his antebellum paean to the slave society, William Grayson summed up white southerners' perceptions of the results of this bleak experiment in freedom:

> The Bright Antilles, with each closing year,
> See harvests fail, and fortunes disappear;
> The cane no more its golden treasure yields;

> Unsightly weeds deform the fertile fields;
> The negro freeman, thrifty while a slave,
> Loosed from restraint, becomes a drone or knave;
> Each effort to improve his nature foils,
> Begs, steals, or sleeps and starves, but never toils;
> For savage sloth mistakes the freedom won,
> And ends the mere barbarian he begun.[11]

Such descriptions of the lapse into indolence and the resulting decline in the economies of the Caribbean islands were standard fare in the antebellum period, and they struck home with particular force as southerners faced a similar situation. In the first issue published after Emancipation, the Georgia magazine *Southern Cultivator* morosely described the depressing statistics of economic disintegration in the wake of the emancipation of Caribbean blacks, while the economic "expert" of the South, J. D. B. DeBow, recited equally gloomy statistics. Under slavery, the islands of the Caribbean had been a "fairy land of perpetual beauty," "astonishing fertility" and "enormous riches." Since the slaves were freed, however, land values had declined 80 percent, the currency had become worthless, plantations were abandoned and, in Jamaica alone, exports had declined 300 percent from 1809 to 1854.[12]

Such a litany of foreboding recurred again and again in the postwar press of the South. Blacks, freed from the imperatives of work, "gradually retired from labor"; content to work just enough to get by, went the refrain, they thus became marginal subsistence farmers at best and destroyed the agricultural productivity of the region. It was scarcely necessary to reiterate the facts of such depressing events, noted South Carolina's W. W. Boyce. "The Black race is proverbially indolent and improvident, and we cannot shut our eyes to the facts of history. All readers are familiar with the experiment of emancipation in Jamaica."[13]

Even more conclusive was the experience of white southerners during the war in their attempts to work with free labor. As soon as the Union soldiers had entered southern soil, the institution of slavery began to crumble. Experiments with free labor were made in a number of locations—notably the famous Port Royal District of coastal Carolina. But there were also a good number of plantations worked by free labor in the Delta region after Federal troops moved south from Vicksburg. In some instances, plantations were leased to northern investors, while the Federal government occasionally assumed direct responsibility. In others, "loyal" southerners were allowed to retain their plantation, and it was these latter experiments that were most discouraging.[14]

From Terrebone Parish in Louisiana a sugar plantation owner recounted in June of 1865 the effects of "free labor" upon agricultural production in that area. In 1861 he had produced 600 hogsheads of sugar on his plantation. In

1863, the first year of his experiment with free labor, production declined to 260 hogsheads. When he tried to reassert "discipline," the freedmen rebelled and he produced less than 90 hogsheads in 1864.[15] It was hardly a description to arouse hope and enthusiasm among southern planters. Such discouraging accounts of the effects of Emancipation were reprinted in southern newspapers and common knowledge by the spring of 1865.

In part, the bleak assessment was colored by the bitterness which southerners expressed when they discovered that their faithful slaves were neither slaves nor faithful once they had the opportunity. Dr. Elias Henry Deas, a rice planter on the Cooper River near Charleston and a prominent South Carolina physician, had confidently predicted during the war that—regardless of the outcome—his faithful slaves would remain by his side. Instead, as soon as the Federals arrived, they scattered in every direction. Hurt and bewildered initially, his surprise turned to rage as he bitterly told his daughter of their perfidy. The younger ones he could accept, he said, "but the old ones in a great many instances are no better than the young." All his life, said Augustin Taveau of Charleston, he had unquestionably believed that the South's slaves were "content, happy and attached to their masters." The events of the spring of 1865 shattered this comforting illusion. "Good master and bad master, all alike shared the same fate." The freedmen reacted with duplicity and treachery. "We have all been labouring under a delusion."[16]

The misgivings over the suitability of freedmen as laborers seemed amply borne out by events during the late spring and summer of 1865. At times, the private correspondence and personal diaries of southern landowners seemed little more than a litany of complaints over the disastrous qualities of the freedman as laborer. "The negroes you hire work about one half their time and are idle the balance," recorded David Schenck in his diary in June of 1865. As a class they were "idle, improvident and roguish." "Our negroes" did as they pleased, complained Samuel Agnew of Tipton County, Mississippi, going off in the wagon daily "and not giving their master's concerns any attention." Complaints of indolence and laziness had been standard fare throughout the antebellum period, and rare indeed was the slave owner who boasted of the work habits of his property. Deprived of ultimate authority, however, and facing economic deprivation and bankruptcy in many instances, the white southerner's concern over the alleged shiftlessness of his charges became a raging anger.[17]

Complaints of thievery by the freedmen vied with those of laziness in the months after the end of the war. "You can not yet fully conceive the annoyance we have from the miserable conduct of the negroes," complained a Sidney, Alabama, planter. "They steal everything that they can secret." Whenever an implement, tool, or livestock vanished, said Josi Borden, he was quick to question his hands, but he raged "nobody ever knows anything about it." "There is so much stealing going on down here you never saw the equal to it," a South Carolina girl wrote her cousin. "You cannot have a hog or cow unless you keep it in your yard." To leave an article of clothing outside to dry was to make a certain involuntary donation to charity. In contrast, Mrs. Anna R. Salley, the wife of an Orangeburg, South Carolina, farmer, denied to an aunt that the freedmen were responsible for all the theft that existed in the months after the war. "The whites are as much to be dreaded now as the blacks." But it was far too easy to simply blame the freedmen for any unexplained disappearance of property.[18]

Equally disconcerting to southerners was the movement of blacks away from the labor-starved plantations to the villages, towns, and cities of the South. In the contemporary literature, in the writings of later historians, and even in the works of novelists, the theme of the exodus became a powerful element of the drama of Emancipation. The city of Richmond was a sea of "negro and Yankee, Yankee and negro, ad nauseum," wrote Lucy Walton in her diary. "I am frequently stopped by piles of negro goods and chatter issuing from the gates of their old homes . . . as they start off to some fancied Elysian fields of Freedom. . . . The streets are thronged with Negroes of all shades." In Charleston, an elderly planter described with shocked amazement the "swarms of negroes" as they wandered up and down the streets, engaging in raucous behavior, petty thievery, and nightly fighting. In the year after Emancipation, a Charleston grand jury complained that mobs of blacks roamed the cities "attacking innocent citizens at will" and jeopardizing the persons and property of law-abiding citizens.[19]

What seems apparent is that the myth of the urban exodus serves to illustrate the renewed visibility of blacks rather than their actual massive influx into towns and cities. Before 1865, freedmen had been in a relatively small minority; slaves had gone into town only on errands and specific assignments. As a result, blacks were—if not a rare sight—at least a small minority. After Emancipation, however, the trip to town became one of the most visible symbols of freedom. The freedom to move about freely was a cherished one, particularly on the weekends. On the other hand, it was such a striking departure that whites were likely to view it as revolutionary and to resist such a change at every point. As a result, the question of "trips to town" became a prime source of conflict, particularly at contract time when whites tried to write into their contract arrangements provisions against leaving the plantation without permission. The laborer "must be confined to the plantation for a series of years," concluded a Louisiana sugar planter. If blacks were allowed to move at will from plantation to plantation and to vanish into nearby towns and villages whenever the whim attracted them, "it would be far better" and "cheaper to abandon these lands, however productive in former times." The freedmen, on the other hand, steadfastly resisted such prohibitions against their freedom of movement.[20]

Nor was it simply a matter of reasserting labor stability. The prospect of "barbarism" and "savagery" was suggested again and again by southerners gloomily viewing the postwar era. As the Atlanta *Daily Intelligencer* observed in the first weeks after Appomattox, the "Cyclopedia of Commerce" confirmed what was common knowledge; in every society where black slaves had been emancipated, the result was that the freedmen receded quickly into a "savage state." This, said the *Daily Intelligencer,* was an "indication of what we are to expect from a similar policy. Already there were signs of the "shockingly degraded condition of the Negro."[21]

The sharp dichotomy between northern and southern whites' conceptions of the nature of society (and the character of the Negro) can nowhere be seen better than in the insurrection hysteria which swept through the South in the summer and fall of 1865, culminating in the widespread belief that the freedmen would "rise" on Christmas Day of their first year of freedom and plunge the South into a bloody holocaust. There is not the time here to review the full circumstances of this bizarre episode in southern history, but the events are plain enough. Between August and December of 1865, huge sections of the Southeast and Southwest—primarily in the black belt region—became convinced that blacks were going to rise, slaughter the whites, and seize the land for themselves. The Insurrection Panic of 1865 was extraordinary proof of the way in which white southerners had become prisoners of their own fears and illusions. There is not one iota of evidence to support this panic: and yet thousands of white southerners were convinced they were on the verge of a racial Armageddon.[22]

The fear of a black uprising was only one facet of the gloomy outlook of white southerners. Even if the region should be spared a war of the races, its economy ultimately would be crippled by the gradual extinction of the region's black workforce. "The negro race will now run out," a former governor of South Carolina glumly predicted in 1865. With the "strong arm of the white man" withdrawn, they will pass from the North American continent in three generations.

A Georgia bishop sadly agreed. He insisted that he had the "highest interests" of the former slaves at heart, but no amount of instructing or teaching could forestall the inevitable. "Avarice and cupidity and ignorance will do for their extinction what they have always done for any unprotected inferior race. Poverty, disease, intemperance will follow in their train and do the rest." There was a sonorous ring of certainty to all these easy and glib predictions. Ethnography, history, and plain common sense were all summoned to document the obvious. The "mulattoes" as an inferior "hybrid" race would be the first to go, observed the New York *World.*[23] Very shortly, however, the blacks would sink into their natural state of barbarism and savagery.

A considerable number of white southerners saw evidence of their pessimism confirmed in the conditions of blacks during the postwar period. A committee of Calhoun County, South Carolina, citizens insisted that already the blacks were "diminishing at a fearful rate. The common estimate of their loss since 1860 is 1,000,000 of lives, or one quarter of their whole number."[24] Other observers recounted tales of huddled blacks pulled together in overcrowded, unsanitary conditions, "dying of disease and want." Such a process was accelerated by the refusal of the blacks to attend to each other. "They will often see a fellow-laborer, and even a near relative, die for want of a cup of gruel, or of water, rather than lose a few hours' sleep in watching," declared a Mobile doctor. While a correspondent of the Georgia *Enquirer* concluded his observation of the condition of blacks' health with the sarcastic observation that the "day will come when a Yankee will exhibit among the 'Cowikees' a bush negro as a curiosity, charging 25 cents admission fee."[25]

Such pronouncements occasionally sprang from something approaching an exercise in wish fulfillment. Nevertheless, this belief in black extinction was more than a prefabrication. And this may be seen in one of the most bizarre adventures of the postwar South: the immigration craze of 1865. The grandiose schemes to bring European whites into the South were compounded of fantasy, fear, hope, and ignorance, and they illustrated the complex emotional and intellectual currents of the postwar South.

With the days of the freedmen numbered, "population like capital will seek its equilibrium," said the *Southern Cultivator*. "The vast wave of [European] immigration . . . [to the North] will not now stop there." Attracted by the South's mild climate, rich farmland, and mineral wealth it would "flow over and fertilize the whole South with the moveable wealth this population will bring."[26] Joseph Cannon and William Holden of the North Carolina *Daily Standard* also suggested the inevitability of European immigration now that the most productive lands of the region were available at such low prices and the Negro was no longer a competing factor.[27]

For the proponents of southern modernization, such a development was long overdue. It meshed perfectly with their dream of reshaping southern society. The European immigrant would become the sturdy yeoman of the Jeffersonian dream. If all the large southern plantations and farms were divided into smaller family-size farms to be cultivated by "responsible" European immigrants and northern white labor, "instead of the large worn-out, unproductive fields so much the rule in former days, they would soon be substituted by small, neat, flourishing and improved farms." The postwar editor of the Augusta *Chronicle and Sentinel* poured scathing ridicule on the "obsession" of the antebellum southerners to own land—regardless of its productivity. The results of such a policy had been disastrous, he told his readers in the summer of 1865. White southerners had become enmeshed in the single-crop cycle, and the plantation system had left the region progressively poorer except in a few extremely rich areas of the delta. But slavery at least had been a compelling factor in this system. With the institution gone, the time was ripe to strike for an independent white yeomanry composed of northern and European immigrants.[28]

The quest of southerners for European and northern immigrants was a fool's errand, as many perceptive southerners soon came to realize. As *The Farmer* concluded glumly in 1867, the emigration from Europe would "never flow into the South as it does to the North West. We have not the inducements that are held out by the new states." Few emigrants were willing to work for wages on the washed-out lands of the Southeast or the malarial swamps of the delta when they could homestead great sections of fertile land in the West.[29] The direction of postwar immigration confirmed such pessimism. During the first year after the war, 250,000 immigrants came to the United States. About 100,000 settled in New York. Illinois received 22,000 immigrants, Wisconsin 9,000, Pennsylvania 25,000, and Ohio 13,000. In contrast, the entire South received less than 3,000 immigrants with the great majority settling in Virginia and Tennessee. It was hardly the stuff of which giant movements were made.[30]

Even when southerners succeeded in bringing groups of immigrants to settle in the South, their experiments were almost uniformly disastrous. J. Floyd King, the son of a wealthy Georgia planter (Thomas Butler King) came out of the war with little more than his good name and a record of service in the Confederacy. He had gone north in the summer of 1865 with grandiose plans to start a saw mill on his old family plantation, but he found few backers. Instead, he soon became an enthusiastic agent of the American Emigrant Company. With his background in planting and his distinguished southern connections, the AEC selected him for a major experiment in emigrant labor. In the fall of 1865 he sailed from New York with a cargo of 213 Dutch, Danish, and German immigrants and a commitment to lease a 22,000-acre Louisiana Delta plantation.[31]

While King started with high hopes he quickly inherited a nightmare. Shortly after he landed in New Orleans, he almost lost his entire contingent when a local planter offered them jobs at more than the AEC had promised. With a little help from local parish officials he managed to get them up river to the plantation near Natchez, Mississippi, where they had been promised there was comfortable housing and ample food. When they saw the dilapidated slave shacks and tasted their first meal of moldy fatback and stale cornbread they sat down and refused to work. Even when King frantically began repairing the cabins and promised fresh beef and bacon each day, he had little success. By the end of January he had lost half his labor force, and each roll call revealed a diminished number of laborers. The "experiment," he frankly conceded, was a failure. "So far in this experiment I am satisfied that where the negro will work, he is the most profitable laborer, so much thro his education in cotton culture as anything else; the Emigrant is much the more expensive to feed and keep, and at present he is ignorant of the manner in which the plant is made to grow and to produce to the best advantage."[32]

That was the crucial phrase: "*where the negro will work.*" Historians have understandably focused upon the actions of southern whites which seemed to have had the greatest effect on national policy: the adoption of the black codes and the election of antebellum secessionists for example. It is equally important, however, to examine the state of mind of white southerners as they approached the postwar era. As a group, they were convinced that economic recovery was tied to a restoration of dependable black labor. They were equally convinced that blacks would not work without legal and physical coercion. Above all, they were fearful that the freedmen and women were teetering on the verge of "barbarism" and mass violence.

Under these circumstances, it is no justification for the violent abuses of postwar white southerners to say that they were swept along by fears and illusions which severely constrained their intellectual freedom of action. Some would make a modest break with the past. For most the emotional habits were too deeply embedded. Even when the worst apprehensions had been dispelled, the deep scars of slavery would remain. In the tortured mental and emotional landscape of the postwar South, reality had blended with illusion; in a world turned upside down white southerners had lost their bearings. In that respect, the events of the postwar period in southern society became something like a Greek tragedy. The flaw was a racial perspective tragically distorted by two hundred years of slavery. Both slave and master had become victims of the peculiar institution.

Given the bleak range of alternatives for the postwar period, it is no wonder that younger—and sometimes more radical—historians have longed for an "iron fist" which would have forced the white South to yield to change regardless of these racial blinders. Given the nature of northern racism and the general national reluctance to expand the power of the federal government, I find this a rather dubious form of historical Monday-morning quarterbacking. As Judge Lochrane so accurately put it, it was indeed difficult for men to shake down their convictions like apples from a tree.

NOTES

1. McKitrick's general conclusion has been sustained by a number of later studies, notably Michael Les Benedict's *A Compromise of Principle: Congressional Republicans and Reconstruction, 1863–1869* (New York: W. W. Norton and Co., 1974).

2. W. T. Couch, *Culture in the South* (Chapel Hill: University of North Carolina Press, 1934), vii–viii; Macon *Daily Telegraph*, July 5, 1865; Raleigh *Daily Standard*, August 8, 1865.

3. Braxton Craven to Bishop Edward Ames, July 24, 1865, Braxton Craven Papers, Duke University Library, Durham, N.C.; Charles Wallace to Wife, October 1, 1865, John Clopton

Collection, David Rubenstein Rare Book and Manuscript Library, Duke University.

4. Augusta *Chronicle and Sentinel,* June 28, 1865; *Field and Fireside,* quoted in *The Farmer* 1 (August 1866): 322–23.

5. Raleigh *Sentinel,* January 24, 1866; *Report of the Special Committee of the General Assembly of South Carolina on the Subject of Encouraging European Immigration and to Correspond with Governments, Societies and Persons* (Charleston: Joseph Walker, 1866), 14.

6. Raleigh *Sentinel,* October 27, 1866.

7. Notes of Thomas Settle speech, March 1867, in Settle Papers, Southern Historical Collection, Wilson Library, University of North Carolina, Chapel Hill.

8. Macon *Daily Telegraph,* August 3, 1865.

9. Samuel Agnew Diary, May 29, 1865, Southern Historical Collection, Wilson Library, University of North Carolina, Chapel Hill.

10. Sidney Andrews, *The South Since the War* (Boston: Ticknor and Fields, 1866), 22.

11. William J. Grayson, *The Hireling and the Slave, Chicora and Other Poems* (Charleston: McCord & Co., 1856), 34.

12. J. D. B. DeBow, "The State of the Country," *DeBow's Review* 1 (February 1866): 141.

13. W. W. Boyce, "President Johnson's Plan of Reconstruction," *DeBow's Review* 1 (January 1866): 74.

14. For a brief description of these wartime experiments with free labor, see Bell I. Wiley, *Southern Negroes, 1861–1865* (New Haven, Conn.: Yale University Press, 1938), 230–59.

15. See letter to the editor in the *New Orleans Times,* reprinted in Houston *Tri-Weekly Telegraph,* June 7, 1865.

16. Elias Horry Deas to Daughter, May 5, July 15, August 15, 1865, Deas Papers, South Caroliniana Library, University of South Carolina, Columbia; Augustin L. Taveau to William Aiken, April 24, 1865, Taveau Papers, David M. Rubenstein Rare Book and Manuscript Library, Duke University, Durham, N.C.

17. David Schenck Diary, June 14. 1865, Southern Historical Collection, Wilson Library, University of North Carolina, Chapel Hill; Samuel Agnew Diary, July 24, 1865, Southern Historical Collection. Complaints of idleness among the freedmen were so common it would be impossible to list the citations from postwar planters' manuscript collections.

18. Josi Borden to Doctor (Illegible), October 2, 1865, "In Reconstruction Miscellany," Folder 46, Manuscript, Archives and Rare Books Library, Emory University, Atlanta; D. to Cousin, September 10, 1865, Hemphill Papers, David M. Rubenstein Rare Books Library, Duke University; Anna Salley to Aunt, November 13, 1865, Bruce, Jones, Murchison Family Papers, South Caroliniana Library, University of South Carolina, Columbia.

19. Lucy Walton Diary, April 25, 1865, David M. Rubenstein Rare Book and Manuscript Library, Duke University; Ellas H. Deas to Daughter, May 5, 1865, South Caroliniana Library, University of South Carolina, Columbia; Report of Charleston Coroner's Jury, July 5, 1866, in James L. Orr Papers, South Carolina Department of Archives and History, Columbia.

20. Letter in Houston *Tri-Weekly Telegraph,* June 7, 1865.

21. Atlanta *Daily Intelligencer,* June 16, 1865.

22. Dan T. Carter, "The Anatomy of Fear: The Christmas Day Insurrection Scare of 1865," *Journal of Southern History* 42 (August 1976): 345–64.

23. *DeBow's Review* 2 (July 1866): 313; New York *World,* quoted in the Atlanta *Daily Intelligencer,* July 15, 1865.

24. Committee of Calhoun Citizens, "The Future of South Carolina," *DeBow's Review* 2 (July 1866): 441.

25. Josiah Nott, "The Problem of the Black Races," *DeBow's Review* 1 (March 1866): 269, 281; Columbus *Georgia Enquirer*, September 29, 1865.

26. *Southern Cultivator* 23 (August 1865): 118.

27. Raleigh *Daily Standard*, August 2, 1865.

28. Raleigh *Sentinel*, October 27, 1865; Augusta *Chronicle and Sentinel*, June 28, 1865.

29. *The Farmer* 2 (February 1867): 35–36.

30. "Emigration at New York and the Emigration Board," *Merchant's Magazine* 57 (September 1867): 191.

31. J. Floyd King to Anne Lin, December 24, 29, 1865, King Family Papers, Southern Historical Collection, Wilson Library, University of North Carolina, Chapel Hill.

32. J. Floyd King to John Mallery, January 18, 1866, King Family Papers, Southern Historical Collection, Wilson Library, University of North Carolina, Chapel Hill.

THE FREEDMEN'S BUREAU AND ITS CAROLINA CRITICS
(1962)

Martin Abbott

Unlike their posterity, South Carolinians in 1865 experienced little sense of romance in viewing the Lost Cause of the Confederacy; instead they felt only the anguish of failure and the agony of defeat. They were thus in no mood to welcome what they regarded as the effort of their conquerors to redefine the fundamentals of their life. They chafed under the military occupation of Union troops, and they looked with scorn upon the missionary endeavors of northern teachers and reformers who followed in the wake of Federal armies. And they expressed a particular resentment over the presence of the Freedmen's Bureau, whose operations involved the most explosive of all questions in the South, that of trying to define the new relationship between the freed slaves and their former masters. The creation of Congress in the closing months of the war, the bureau had been charged with a broad responsibility for the general welfare of southern Negroes as they moved along the path from slavery to freedom. It was expected to assist as many of the former slaves as possible in becoming landowners; to play a major role in defining the new status of the Negro as a free worker in a slaveless economy; to relieve destitution among the blacks by providing food, clothing, and medical care; and to supervise a program of Negro education.

From the beginning white Carolinians evinced a hostile suspicion of the bureau, fearing that its enthusiasm for helping the former slave would lead it to disturb, and even disrupt, the traditional relationship between Negro and white. No matter how circumspect it might be, the bureau was bound to incur the sullen displeasure, if not indeed the angry opposition, of the white population. The agency, therefore, faced a formidable task, one that would require a large measure of tact and discretion. Unhappily, Rufus Saxton, who served as head of the bureau in the state during 1865, possessed neither of these qualities. He suffered from the delusion that earnest intentions and honest emotions were enough to provide a solution for the serious problems before him; and whether wittingly or not, he managed by his initial words and actions to convey an impression that he regarded the well-being of the freedmen as somehow apart from that of the rest of society. Consequently, his administration succeeded in antagonizing a sizeable part of the white population.[1]

Opposition to the bureau first crystallized during the summer of 1865 as its officials undertook to resettle hundreds of freedmen on lands that had formerly belonged to the whites. Its control over such lands had grown out of wartime legislation by Congress, which had authorized federal agents to seize certain kinds of property within the reconquered areas of the Confederacy and then had directed that all such property be turned over to the bureau upon its creation. The bureau was expected to distribute the land among the freedmen by selling or leasing it to them in small plots and on convenient terms. Thereby a dual purpose might be served. Many of the former slaves would be encouraged to establish an economic independence with which to bolster their political freedom; and, secondly, the bureau could use the income from such sales and rentals for the support of its work—a vital consideration, since Congress had not appropriated any money for its initial operations.

In South Carolina the total of such property at the disposal of the bureau amounted to more than 300,000 acres of land. Under Saxton's direction agents and officers proceeded immediately to locate dozens of Negro families on 40-acre plots, either as tenants or as purchasers. The dispossessed white owners and their spokesmen promptly raised a sharp outcry against such proceedings. Typical was the comment of the Charleston *Courier,* which termed the presence of the bureau "anomalous and unnecessary" and then declared: "Those are the real enemies of the Freedmen who seek to instill into them, that they can either be prosperous or progressive except by . . . frugality, sobriety, and honest, consistent toil."[2] Another paper echoed this view: "We do not say that all Northern men who come South are of the class alluded to, but we do say that all who prowl through the country, teaching the Negroes . . . that the lands are to be given to the colored people . . . are the vilest and meanest sect that ever disgraced the annals of civilization."[3]

In time the original owners were able to reclaim most of their property as a result of President Johnson's reconstruction policy, since the presidential program provided for a restoration of all rights, including those of property, to all who secured pardon. Thus, South Carolina and the rest of the South were relieved of the threat of wholesale confiscation; but among the whites of the state resentment toward the bureau for its role in the affair lingered on.

During the same time white hostility toward the bureau was further inflamed as a result of its work in defining and regulating the new conditions of labor between the emancipated slaves and their former masters. Actually, of course, the heart of the matter lay in the hard necessity of both races having to unlearn more than two hundred years of habit, custom, and attitude fashioned by slavery. In light of what slavery had come to represent in the life of the South during the antebellum years, its disestablishment raised questions which time and experience alone could answer. Many of the freedmen in 1865 appear to have believed that Emancipation was going to usher in some sort of millennium, while many of the whites seem to have felt that the new code of race relations could be easily established within the traditional framework. As for the bureau, a large number of its agents labored under utopian delusions about the nature of postwar southern society. Each of the three groups thus viewed the matter in a different light; each approached it in a different spirit and from a different direction. In such a setting misunderstanding and ill-will among the groups were inevitable.

No one was quite sure of how to proceed in trying to impose some degree of order upon the chaos that prevailed in the state's agriculture. Many of the planters and farmers, faced with the devastation of war and a critical shortage of capital, sought to improvise arrangements with the freed Negro workers. Large numbers of Negroes, bewildered and excited by their changed status, wandered away from the farmsteads to test out the strange new freedom. The bureau, hampered by inexperience and limited funds, labored to devise a system of contract labor that would advance the Negro's economic welfare. It established rules governing wages and other conditions of employment and then endeavored to see that written contracts between the freedmen and their employers were drawn up to conform to such provisions.[4] White employers soon began to protest against the bureau's rules and regulations, as well as against its methods of enforcing the contracts. They were angered, for example, by the instances in which a few overzealous agents, at the close of the growing season, nullified those labor agreements which they defined as unjust to the Negro workers, even though the terms had been approved at the beginning of the season by some other bureau official. Governor James L. Orr and other spokesmen complained vigorously about the practice.[5]

Still another action that antagonized the whites was the practice of some bureau agents in collecting from the employer a fee of up to fifty cents for each laborer hired under an approved contract. An official in the district of Greenwood was reliably reported to have earned about two thousand dollars in such fees during one year. No doubt, the decision by the bureau's leaders to prohibit the practice at the beginning of 1866 was prompted in large part by the nature and number of white complaints about it.[6] Yet not even this prohibition could erase the feeling of farmers and planters that they had been dealt with unfairly.

The entire program of the bureau in the area of labor relationships encountered growing criticism from the whites. Some expressed a fear that the agency was opening up an "irreconcilable antagonism between the former owner and the freed slave" by encouraging the Negro to believe that every labor concession by an employer was "only so much wrung from the white man by compulsion." Others were persuaded that the bureau's policy would force planters to turn entirely to white labor for their needs; still others were convinced that the mere presence of the agency encouraged "the ignorant and the indolent" to abandon their jobs in order to flock around bureau headquarters to get free rations or to make trivial complaints. Many complained that bureau officials allowed Negro workers to violate their contracts with impunity while sternly forcing white employers to abide by their terms.[7] Indeed, a common feeling was that the greater the distance to the nearest bureau office, the greater the prospects for agricultural stability and prosperity. Typical of a widespread view was one newspaper's description of the bureau as composed of "negrophilists, professed humanitarians and sharp speculating characters" whose garments always gave off "the stench of the grave yard."[8]

One finds the same theme stressed over and over by white critics: agricultural affairs in the state could never be stabilized until white Carolinians, who best understood the Negro, had the unfettered right to control and regulate his employment. One of the state's leading judges summarized the feelings of a great many when he declared that the people of South Carolina were "greatly embarrassed by the presence and interference of the Freedmen's Bureau" by which the Negroes were "taught to be suspicious of their old masters . . . and encouraged to distrust their counsel." The bureau, concluded the judge, "is a great, useless, expensive, and mischievous machinery, which seems to be kept up simply to grind taxes out of the people for the support of cunning politicians, excited lunatics, and political preachers."[9]

The bureau also stirred up criticism among the whites of the state by its endeavors in the realm of education for the freedmen. Seemingly, the objections were prompted less by opposition to education itself than by a fear that political indoctrination was being practiced under the guise of schooling. Planters, for example, did not hesitate to establish schools for the children of Negro workers on their plantations; nor was it uncommon to find native whites engaged as teachers in such schools. One planter probably spoke for many in urging that "if we educate the black man, allow him to read, speak, hear speeches, vote and exercise the privileges of a FREE MAN, it derogates nothing from our own character . . . but raises him *towards a level,* at least, with us."[10] Whites then do not appear generally to have opposed schooling for the Negro, but rather the bureau's variety of it. A leading newspaper in the state asserted its belief that "the Northern people, under the auspices of the Government, and the immediate direction of that incubus, the Freedmen's Bureau," had established institutions under teachers who "maligned and traduced the Southern people" and who often taught "insolence and hatred more than anything else."[11] Holding such a view, many white spokesmen urged young Carolinians to take up the challenge of teaching the freedmen. One editor declared: "We want teachers . . . *of us* . . . who will leave politics outside of the schoolroom doors."[12] A planter made a typical plea in calling for native whites to take "the mental and moral development" of the freedmen into their own hands, so as "to leave no room for the ingress of these Northern moths into the social hive."[13] But there is little evidence that young men or women responded in any great number to such calls, leaving the bureau to educate the freedmen, and white spokesmen to criticize and condemn its efforts.

Perhaps more important than any of the foregoing in creating hostility toward the agency was the turn of political events during 1867 when Congress extended the franchise to adult males among the former slaves. White spokesmen were soon declaring that the bureau's main activity had come to be that of indoctrinating the Negroes with the political principles of the Republican Party. One newspaper expressed a common view in asserting that the agency had become transformed into nothing more than "a gigantic, radical party machine" under the central direction of General O. O. Howard, who was "a natural fanatic—one of the psalm-singing sort from New England."[14] Even William H. Trescot, a prominent leader of unusual moderation, could write that in South Carolina the Negroes who were generally inclined to trust the judgment of whites in most matters turned to bureau officials and other northerners for advice on political questions.[15]

Actually there is no solid evidence that the bureau in South Carolina ever used its position to any great extent for the purpose of politics. During the whole period of the agency's operation about two hundred different individuals were employed by it; yet of this number, not more than twenty-five or thirty can be identified as having engaged in politics, even in a minor sense, during their tenure of office or after leaving their bureau position.[16] Therefore, charges by white leaders that the institution's main concern was to serve the Republican Party simply do not appear to be borne out by the facts.

Yet a few agents and officers did concern themselves with the Negro's political fortunes, thereby lending credibility to the charges of Carolina critics. Rufus Saxton, for example, shortly after becoming head of the bureau in the state, publicly urged a large gathering of freedmen to draft a petition to the president demanding that the franchise be given them; Robert K. Scott, Saxton's successor, undoubtedly used the prestige and influence of his office during the closing months of his tenure to secure the governorship of the state for himself in 1868; and still a handful of other officials used their bureau positions for advancing their own political ambitions or the general cause of Republicanism among the former slaves.[17] Their number was small and their influence limited, yet their activity was enough to help fashion a stereotyped image in the minds of most whites in the state.

In addition to charging the bureau with political behavior, white spokesmen made other accusations. One editor, in commenting upon the order issued from Washington which forbade agents to engage in planting operations, expressed the hope that a similar prohibition might be imposed upon those "running saw mills, and otherwise speculating in and profiting by the 'sweat of the freedman's face.'"[18] Another journalist complained in 1868 that the bureau had cost the taxpayer fifteen or twenty million dollars, most of which had been pocketed by agents rather than used for the benefit of the Negro. "It is a very easy thing for a Radical to appear as the friend of the colored people, when he is getting a good salary for it," the writer concluded.[19] A planter described the agency "as a kind of sinecure for abolition pets to creep into . . . draw pay, and do little or nothing beneficial to the darkies."[20]

The whites, in sum, leveled a constant barrage of varied criticism against the bureau. They charged it with subversion of social relationships between Negro and white; with serving political ends; with encouraging idleness among the freedmen; with fostering misunderstanding between the two races; and with condoning incompetence, dishonesty, and fraud among its personnel. On occasion white feeling toward the agency threatened to erupt into physical violence against some of its officials. At Kingstree, for example, feeling became so strong against the local representative of the bureau that a detachment of troops had to be sent for his protection. In the district of Darlington, according to another officer, the people demonstrated a deep contempt for the bureau as well as for everything and everyone from the North. Most of the citizens, he wrote, were "miniature Hamilcars, bringing up their Hannibals."[21]

Yet despite such episodes and despite the general disposition of the whites to denounce the agency, one finds a curious paradox involved in their attitude. They often enough expressed scorn for the institution in general; yet, in their dealings with the individual representative, they frequently found him a responsible, well-meaning individual. John W. De Forest, a highly urbane and literate agent who was stationed in Greenville, wrote that although he was sometimes the victim of coarse insults from some of the townspeople, on the whole he found an air of hospitality that would have permitted him to be accepted into the society if he had wished. And even as it was, he found himself invited by the whites to numerous breakfasts, dinners, teas, and picnics.[22] At Abbeville a group of eminent citizens upon learning that the local agent was to be transferred elsewhere, requested his retention there in a petition which observed: "In our judgment his course has been approved by all fair minded men, both white and black; and we take pleasure in saying that . . . Capt. Perry has labored earnestly to discharge faithfully and impartially the very delicate duties of his office."[23] A group of whites in Orangeburg sent a similar petition relative to the agent there.[24]

On numerous occasions military officers, many of whom were also serving as bureau officials, were highly praised for their conduct. One was reported by a local paper to have served "with such discretion and impartiality . . . as to have commanded the esteem and respect of all classes of our people"; another was described as having performed his duties in a way that had "elicited the praises of all"; still a third was characterized as a man of "unwearied patience" whose "evident desire to administer Justice" was so highly regarded that members of the local bar were preparing a written testimonial to his "official worth and merit." In the city of Anderson the retiring commander took the unusual step of having a card published expressing his appreciation for the conduct of the townspeople during his tenure. "I have found them a friendly and quiet people who are well disposed and accept the situation in good faith," he declared.[25]

Most surprising of all, perhaps, were the endorsements given by the whites to Robert K. Scott's administration of bureau affairs from early 1866 until mid-1868. The Charleston *Daily News,* for example, while rejecting the assertion of northerners that the planters of the state would like to see the bureau continued, went on to declare: "The writer, and others not a few, whose opinions he knows, freely admits the integrity of purpose and propriety of deportment of General Scott." Under him the entire institution, which had been so "utterly odious" under his predecessor, had become at least tolerable and "by contrast, most agreeable."[26] Another leading paper, while disclaiming any particular friendship for the bureau, voiced its belief that Scott had conducted the affairs of the agency with "judgment and sound discretion" and had endeavored to control it "for the benefit of those for whom it was designed."[27] Another evidence of the general regard for Scott can be found in the petitions sent by leading citizens of the state to President Johnson, one saying that his "general administration has been beneficial" and another declaring: "Genl. Scott is well and favourably known to both Freedmen and Planters, both of whom have full confidence in his ability and integrity of purpose."[28]

A description of this contradiction in white attitudes is easier to give than to analyze. On the one hand leaders of white public opinion were relentless in their attacks upon the bureau as an institution; they questioned its need, doubted its work, and challenged its purpose; they professed to view it as an intruder, a usurper, an added distraction in an already distracted society. On the other hand, they were quite willing in the majority of instances to recognize, and even to pay tribute to, the worth of the individual bureau agent. And it has been the former attitude rather than the latter reality which has impressed itself upon the written record of the state's history. In 1879, for example, one Carolina author who had witnessed Reconstruction drew up a harsh indictment of the bureau, characterizing it as an agency that had spread "its filthy meshes all over the State. These were, at first, mere swindling machines in the hands of sharpers. Afterwards party contrivances were superadded for the political bondage of the black man, far more galling than those world-abused 'chains of slavery.' These man-traps furnished appropriate schooling for that rapacious crew who afterwards revelled in the treasury of the State."[29] Writing thirty years later a biographer of Wade Hampton offered an evaluation which, though more restrained, was hardly less negative. "The Freedmen's Bureau," he commented, "though in its origin beneficent in intention, did much more harm than good to the negroes themselves. By free rations they were encouraged to be idlers and vagrants, and by constant interference between them and the whites . . . the mutual kindly regard for each other originally entertained was weakened, or changed altogether."[30]

One is entitled to ask the question of why, in the annals of the state, the unfavorable picture of the bureau should be unrelieved by any reference to the many instances in which contemporary Carolinians, though opposing the bureau in general, displayed acceptance and even endorsement of its individual representatives; or why it should have continued to be charged with wrongs it never committed. And one is further entitled to venture an answer that the main reason can be found in the post-Reconstruction attitude of white Carolinians about the whole of their Reconstruction history. Having known and survived the vindictive wrath of the Radicals as well as the grim excesses of the carpetbag government in the state, whites after 1876 were unable to see anything but evil in the entire experience. Thus, they could not or would not admit that the bureau had been, or could be, viewed in any light other than as a manifestation of the spirit of the times. In this sense, the institution has received less than its just verdict at the hands of history.

NOTES

1. For this estimate of Saxton, see Martin Abbott, "The Freedmen's Bureau in South Carolina, 1865–1872," PhD diss., Emory University, 1958.

2. Charleston *Courier,* December 27, 1865.

3. Columbia *Daily Phoenix,* June 4, 1867.

4. Martin Abbott, "Free Land, Free Labor, and the Freedmen's Bureau," *Agricultural History* 30 (1956): 150–56.

5. J. L. Orr to R. K. Scott, December 6, 1866; R. K. Scott to O. O. Howard, November 1, 1866, records of the Bureau of Refugees, Freedmen, and Abandoned Lands, National Archives, Washington (hereafter BRFAL).

6. J. L. Orr to R. K. Scott, May 12, 1866, BRFAL.

7. Yorkville *Inquirer,* January 25, 1866; Sumter *Watchman,* May 30, 1866; Columbia *Daily Phoenix,* May 30, 1866; Charleston *Daily News,* August 13, 1866; Fairfield *Herald,* January 30, 1867.

8. An article from the *National Record* reprinted in Sumter *Watchman,* December 20, 1865.

9. Fairfield *Herald,* October 10, 1866.

10. Keowee *Courier,* April 27, 1867. Regarding white teachers in Negro schools, see the Sumter *Watchman,* June 5, 1867, and the Columbia *Daily Phoenix,* July 2 and September 3, 1867.

11. Columbia *Daily Phoenix,* September 21, 1866.

12. Ibid., April 3, 1867.

13. Keowee *Courier,* June 9, 1866.

14. Newberry *Herald,* August 28, 1867.

15. William H. Trescot to Andrew Johnson, September 8, 1867, W. H. Trescot Collection, Library of Congress.

16. See chapter 2 of Abbott, "The Freedmen's Bureau in South Carolina."

17. Ibid. Also see Charleston *Courier,* May 13, 15, 1865.

18. Columbia *Daily Phoenix,* May 23, 1866.

19. Abbeville *Banner,* September 30, 1868.

20. Yorkville *Inquirer,* September 13, 1866.

21. R. K. Scott to J. L. Orr, December 17, 1866, Freedmen's File, South Carolina Department of Archives and History, Columbia. George Pingree to R. K. Scott, September 24, 1867, BRFAL.

22. J. W. De Forest, *A Union Officer in the Reconstruction* (New Haven, Conn.: Yale University Press, 1948), 46.

23. Citizens to R. K. Scott, no date, BRFAL.

24. Citizens to R. K. Scott, July 27, 1868, Freedmen's File, South Carolina Department of Archives and History.

25. Orangeburg *News,* June 20, 1868; Camden *Journal,* May 16, 1867; Sumter *Watchman,* November 15, 1865; Charleston *Courier,* September 14, 1865; Newberry *Herald,* June 27, 1866; Columbia *Daily Phoenix,* May 10, 1866.

26. As reprinted in the Columbia *Daily Phoenix,* June 5, 1866.

27. Columbia *Daily Phoenix,* December 25, 1867.

28. Citizens to President Andrew Johnson, August 24, December 4, 1867, BRFAL.

29. John A. Leland, *A Voice from South Carolina* (Charleston: Walker, Evans and Cogswell, 1879), 34.

30. Edward L. Wells, *Hampton and Reconstruction* (Columbia: State Co., 1907), 75.

EDGEFIELD RECONSTRUCTION
Political Black Leaders
(1988)

Orville Vernon Burton

Historical literature has only recently begun to deal adequately with the question of where black leadership came from and how that leadership functioned on the local level. The political power that blacks acquired during Reconstruction gave the black community prestige and status, increased their wealth, and opened up to them nonagricultural occupations and roles. Primarily because of the political revolution, blacks began moving from traditional occupations into all areas of Edgefield society. Because the elected black political leaders were spokesmen for the community and yet are still so unknown, this paper explores individual biographies of these men and their relationships to Edgefield society and the Republican Party during Reconstruction.

Renewed interest in Afro-American history has produced long-needed studies of black leaders. The Reconstruction period and South Carolina's black leaders have received their share of attention, and several biographies have emerged as has the pathbreaking prosopographical study by Thomas Holt, *Black Over White*.[1] Yet, biographies have usually been of the most prominent South Carolina black leaders from Charleston or other cities; they have not as a rule dealt with how black leadership functioned at the rural local level or how and why black leaders got support. The question still remains: whence cometh local black rural leadership?

In 1865 most blacks in the upcountry of South Carolina were still slaves. By 1868, blacks had organized politically and were beginning to govern the state where they had once toiled as the property of other men. The study of a community is ideal for getting a sense of the local black leadership, and the study of a community like Edgefield is ideal for getting a sense of rural black leadership. The Edgefield *Advertiser* commented in 1867 that "There is one blessing at least in our having no railroad; and this is that the Wilsons [Senator Henry], Kelleys

[William D. 'Pig Iron'] and other dirty Radical emissaries who are traveling through the South, cannot conveniently come among us."[2] The achievements of Edgefield's black leaders were theirs alone.

Historians have noted that enterprising blacks from the coastal communities moved to the upcountry and established themselves in leadership positions.[3] This assertion was first made in the 1868 Constitutional Convention by a white Republican from Edgefield's next-door neighbor, Barnwell County, to Robert Brown Elliott, Edgefield's representative. He charged that Elliott and other blacks had used Barnwell and Edgefield to get themselves elected to the convention because the Charleston delegation had been filled.[4] There is some truth to this accusation. Edgefield black people certainly benefited from contact with Afro-Americans from outside the area, but most of the Afro-American political leadership came from Edgefieldians.

Robert Brown Elliott was one of the newcomers. A black carpetbagger, he went into the interior to organize voters and began his political career by winning election to the convention from Edgefield District. According to some accounts, his wife was a former Edgefield slave, and although he never actually lived in Edgefield he traveled through the county during Reconstruction to address mass audiences.[5] He was such an accomplished speaker that even the conservative spokesman for the Democratic white elite, the Edgefield *Advertiser,* commented on his elocution and his effectiveness. Although the *Advertiser* believed Elliott was too smart and educated for his devoted Edgefield supporters, the paper reported that Edgefield blacks were devoted to Elliott; "they worship him, and receive him with profound adulation."[6] Elliott was always controversial, and the whites both respected and feared his daring. When he was in charge of the 1870 Census for South Carolina, he told all census enumerators in Edgefield County to encourage black men to join the state militia.[7] The bourbon historian John Reynolds found Elliott particularly dangerous since as a black leader he had "sought actually to dominate and humiliate the white race."[8]

Another newcomer to Edgefield was John Bonum, the former slave of a hatter. He had operated a small store in Charleston before he left the coastal region to organize black voters for the constitutional convention. He was successful and was himself elected as a delegate from Edgefield.[9]

Another delegate was Prince R. Rivers, a former coachman from Beaufort, who had also moved to Edgefield District in 1865. A recognized leader among Beaufort slaves, he had been among the black delegation from Port Royal to the Republican National Convention in 1864.[10] He had also been one of the first Afro-Americans from South Carolina to join the First South Carolina, the black regiment in the Union Army. Rivers was an extremely disciplined soldier whose organizational skills were soon put to good use as a noncommissioned officer of black troops in the First South Carolina, whose commissioned officers were all white. General David M. Hunter took Rivers north in 1862 as an example of what a black soldier could be. While in New York, Rivers was attacked by a white mob infuriated by the chevrons on his uniform, and he successfully held his assailants at bay until the police arrived. He was devoted to the Union and bitter in his denunciation of the white southern secessionists.[11] When asked whether blacks would rebel against their white masters if they had military equipment and knowledge to give such an attack a chance, he replied "Yes, sah . . . only let 'em know for sure—for sure, mind you—dat de white people means right; let 'em know for sure dat dey's fightin' for themselves, and I know dey will fight."

Rivers was described by Col. Thomas Wentworth Higginson, the Union white commander of the First South Carolina, as "an imposing figure being six feet high, perfectly proportioned and of apparently inexhaustible strength and activity." He commented on Rivers's dark color and his aura of command: "if there should ever be a black monarchy in South Carolina, he [Rivers] will be King."[12] Even the white conservative historian of Edgefield who remembered the handsome Rivers admitted that the "Black Prince . . . was not by any means a bad specimen of humanity."[13]

Rivers had been an officer in Newberry County with the black troops who had tried and executed a Confederate soldier for stabbing one of their comrades. Soon afterwards he became an active Republican organizer in Edgefield and commanded Afro-American troops throughout the Edgefield area in 1865 and 1866.[14] Rivers inspired former slaves and struck fear in the hearts of whites. In 1870 an alarmed white Edgefieldian wrote that Prince Rivers was marching "through Edgefield County, at the head of armed companies, with fixed bayonets, making political and incendiary speeches, telling the freedmen to apply the torch and burn up the white people."[15]

The only other non-Edgefieldian Afro-American Reconstruction political leader was Samuel J. Lee, and he had lived so close to Edgefield while a slave that he was almost a native. Lee had been a slave on Samuel McGowan's plantation just over the Edgefield line in neighboring Abbeville District when the war ended. He worked for the federal government briefly in Alabama, and was twenty-two years old when he settled near Hamburg. Although in 1868 he described himself as a farmer, he was already known for his facile mind in debate, his ability as a public speaker, and his courage in standing up to whites.[16] Both Lee and Rivers became leaders of political groups and had considerable influence in the South Carolina House of Representatives. Lee became the Speaker of the House. Both he and Rivers continued to exercise influence in Edgefield County even after the areas in which they lived became part of Aiken County in 1871.

After Lee and Rivers left Edgefield County, other black leaders from Edgefield were natives of that county. Afro-American leaders emerged from within the Edgefield community as organizers and presidents of local Union Clubs. Ned Tenant, Spencer Dearing, John Mobley, David Harris, and Henry Barnes were all Union Club presidents.[17] John Mobley and David Harris were among those who, with Elliott, Bonum, and Rivers, attended the 1868 Constitutional Convention.[18] Local black leaders after 1870 also received initial training as officers in the militia. The officers of the first two companies formed were all ex-slaves from Edgefield, and all became political leaders: "Co. A. Carey Harris, Captain; John Carroll, 1st Lt.; Augustus Simkins, 2d Lt.; Co. B. George Morgan, Cpt.; Archie Weldon, 1st Lt.; Jesse Jones, 2d Lt."[19]

The first black Republicans elected to the state legislature were elected on a ticket with whites. In 1868 David Harris, Lawrence Cain, Prince Rivers, Samuel J. Lee, and John Gardener shared state political office with local whites Truman Root and John Wooley as state legislators.[20] Truman Root received numerous threats on his life, his home and store were attacked, and he was ostracized by old friends and even by his own daughter. This successful antebellum merchant, Episcopal church leader, and respected community member left Edgefield for Atlanta before his legislative term expired.[21] Another white elected state senator was Frank Arnim, a carpetbagger who settled in Hamburg after serving in the Union Army.[22]

In the first years of Reconstruction, white Republicans held local and county positions and dominated the local levels of authority. This is probably why they were the targets of the Democratic elite's ire rather than black politicos, who, in the first years of Reconstruction, were considered to be simply misguided.[23] The white Republican was seen as a traitor to his race by the Edgefield Democratic elite. The Edgefield *Advertiser* in 1867 announced that they preferred a black over a scalawag or white carpetbagger: "we can trust a Southern black man when we cannot trust a white traitor or a Yankee speculator in negro votes. . . . Give us the Southern negro, every time, before either a domestic or an imported Radical."[24] In 1868 the newspaper vehemently commented that "nary a nigger" had an office of importance in either the state or local spheres and queried "Why do they so tamely suffer this great wrong at the tender hands of their Radical friends?"[25]

As Reconstruction progressed, more and more blacks were elected to local office, so that by 1876, the impression of Black Reconstruction had been formed. Even those who had lived through the era seemed to have forgotten the large role whites had played in implementing the Republican reforms. A native Edgefield historian wrote that in Edgefield "from 1868 . . . nearly all representatives and county officers were negroes."[26] In reality, most local black leaders were still officers of their Union Clubs when the 1870 Census was enumerated and had not yet assumed roles of authority as local civil servants. By the summer of 1870, however, the newspaper reported that blacks were getting more of the political offices and remarked: "It is well. It pleases us. By all means let us have decent negroes instead of dirty white men."[27]

However, this attitude changed as elected black officials fought for the aspirations of the freedmen. At first, when the light-skinned mulatto Lawrence Cain, former slave of an Edgefield druggist, took an active lead in the political organization of black people, the Edgefield *Advertiser,* vocal organ of the local Democratic elite, had only the highest praise for Cain. In 1866, Cain invited the white community to observe the progress of the young black scholars he had taught in the local school he established after Emancipation, and the newspaper remembered Cain as a leading white citizen's favored "pet" when a slave and complimented his "genteel manner" and his "good sense and good feeling." After Cain began to organize the blacks politically, however, and ran successfully in several elections, the editors could not find words adequate to defame this same man.[28] A contemporary chronicler of South Carolina Reconstruction demonstrated this changed attitude: the "genteel" Cain now appeared "offensive to the white people" of the Edgefield area because of his "swagger and bad character."[29]

Lawrence Cain and David Harris, another Edgefield ex-slave, were among the first group to serve in the state legislature. Cain emerged as the rival of scalawag Philip A. Eichelberger, a former Confederate officer. Cain and Harris both lived in Edgefield Village, were landowners, and declared personal estate in the 1870 Census enumeration and local tax records. Samuel J. Lee, Prince Rivers, and John Gardener were elected to the legislature in 1868 from the Hamburg area. Lee and Rivers became substantial landowners during Reconstruction. In 1870, Lee, whose occupation was "commissioner of court," had real estate valued at $550 and personal estate at $400. Eventually he had a lot in town and a farm of over 100 acres three miles outside of town. Rivers, in 1870 a "trial justice," owned $250 worth of land, $500 personal estate, and eventually built up his landholdings to 226 acres. Gardener, like Cain, was a schoolteacher. He owned personal estate valued at $500 and property valued at $1,000.[30]

All among the first group of legislators were literate, and all except the Methodist preacher Harris served in the Union Army during the war or immediately afterwards. Military pay probably enabled these black men to purchase land. Cain, Lee, and Rivers all continued their association with the military and were commanders in the state militia during Reconstruction.[31] Rivers was forty-three years old in 1868, and Harris was fifty-two. Lee was twenty-three; Cain, twenty-four; and Gardener, twenty-five. This first group of black representatives from Edgefield were all self-assured, proud men who stood up to whites. Young former Union soldier John Gardener, whose school was two miles from Hamburg, would not tolerate abuse from whites and nearly lost his life because he refused to cower before a white Edgefield landowner. James Shinall was returning from Augusta and passed Gardener's schoolhouse at recess when some students frightened his team of horses. Shinall angrily rebuked the black children, and Gardener emerged to defend them. The local white newspaper reported: "Word engendered between the white and black adult, until the former felt it obligatory to punish the latter with a hammering." Shinall severed the unarmed Gardener's jugular.[32] Gardener survived the knifing, but he was the only Afro-American representative elected in 1868 who did not return to state office in 1870. Gardener, who had amassed a personal fortune by then of $1,500, remained active in local politics and became Intendant of Hamburg.[33]

Blacks in any positions of authority upset white notions of social order, but black law-enforcement officers were particularly threatening. But even worse, as far as whites were concerned, was the tendency of Afro-Americans to elect assertive, self-confident men to these positions. Augustus Harris was such a man. In 1864 Harris left the plantation where he had been a slave all his life, moved to Edgefield Village, and set up a shop. In 1868, a white man entered Harris's store, having mistaken Harris's presence at Democratic rallies as his support of that party. He informed Harris that Democratic victory in Edgefield was assured that year since "there was a party of one hundred men headed by a Captain, and the party known as the Ku Klux Klan, and that party was intending . . . to put a Radical to sleep, and then take the tickets from him, in order to defeat the election." Harris, a "Union Republican Club Member," who had gone to the Democratic meetings only to find out what they were planning, drove the white out of his shop. In 1870, Harris was chosen one of the two Edgefield constables. Addison Forrest, another Afro-American, was the other constable. Carey Harris, another former slave from Edgefield District, became the town marshal. The county jailer, Pickens Stewart, who was an ex-slave from Edgefield District, had twice as many white prisoners in his jail as black prisoners.[34]

The 1870 Census listed fourteen state militia men in one census grouping headed by Mack Brooks. All except Barentine Wilson, son of an antebellum free black farmer and landowner, had been slaves, and all appear to have been from the Edgefield area. Mack Brooks had been "born in the State, and raised in the town of Edgefield," and in 1868 he had testified that his occupation was hostler.[35] David Harris Jr., like Barentine Wilson, was from one of the prominent black families. He was the only state guard not listed in the militia census grouping headed by Mack Brooks. Instead he was listed with the rest of the members of his family in the household of his father, the preacher-politician and legislator David Harris Sr. Membership in the state militia was a prestigious occupation within the black community and acceptable for the sons of the community leaders.

These militiamen had a great deal of courage, since many Edgefield white men carried weapons and were quite willing to challenge the rights which the federal and state governments had granted the freedmen. Indeed, by 1872, in two separate incidents, both Augustus Harris and Addison Forrest, Edgefield

Reconstruction political black leaders, had been shot while serving warrants on Edgefield white men.[36]

While these black law officials represented hope to blacks, they represented anarchy to whites. A carpetbagger Republican described the reaction of white South Carolinians to black militiamen as "mob panics."[37] The Edgefield *Advertiser* saw the influence of black troops as "intense demoralization. . . . Wherever they are that place is deeply and damnably accursed. The contagion of their influence extends not only to persons of their own color, but also to many white people who are white only as regards their skin."[38] The Edgefield *Advertiser* in 1870 complained of the black militia "who guard the jail in our public square" that they are "darting out in full force upon white men, pell mell and with guns, raging, fierce profane, blaspheming, insulting, bloodthirsty."[39] The black militia, and especially the jail guard "composed of twenty odd negroes . . . are a fruitful and never ending cause of trouble, dissension, violence, and expense."[40] A conservative white historian who remembered the black militiamen in Edgefield wrote that they represented "the great disintegration of the old order of things that was taking place all around. . . . [Black militia were used to] humiliate and mortify the old masters and rulers."[41]

The year 1872 was a presidential election year. Blacks were encouraged by the Democratic landowners to support the old abolitionist Horace Greely who headed the Liberal Republican ticket instead of voting to reelect President Grant. At the Edgefield municipal elections, in fact, some Democrats were elected along with white and black Republicans on a fusion platform called "The People's Ticket."[42] Since 1870, Edgefield Afro-Americans had been demanding more black leaders. Lawrence Cain and David Harris had written to the new governor as early as 1868 encouraging the appointment of black magistrates.[43] White Republicans were concerned that blacks might try to have them removed from office.[44] Hamburg blacks insisted that a black trial justice should be appointed,[45] and Black Republicans from Edgefield demanded the dismissal of a white trial justice who they thought discriminated.[46] Similar petitions and letters demanding more jobs for Edgefield blacks were sent to governors Moses and Chamberlain.[47] This idea was echoed by black leaders in the state government. Robert C. Delarge claimed "we want more black men in office."[48] Afro-American leader Major Martin R. Delaney pursued the same theme when he told Edgefield blacks: "I take the ground that no people have become a great people who have not their own leaders . . . and black men must have black leaders. We must be the directors of our own people and let it be known that . . . no one else can lead black men."[49] For the election in 1872, Edgefield Afro-Americans continued to agitate for more blacks in offices on all levels. John Wooley, a native white Republican, announced: "The question of color having been raised by the leading colored men of Edgefield County, I respectfully withdraw from the canvass, as a candidate for the State Senate. I wish to let it be known that I endorse Grant and Wilson and the Republican Party of South Carolina."[50] Native Edgefieldian Dr. John A. Barker was the only white Republican from Edgefield to be elected a state representative after 1872, and he was reelected each term from 1872 to 1876.[51]

In 1872, Lawrence Cain was elected state senator and served there until Redemption. Preacher David Harris, nearing sixty years of age, decided not to run for state office again. He did, however, remain active within the party councils. Rivers and Lee were elected to the legislature from the new county of Aiken, and a new slate of black state representatives was elected from Edgefield.[52] Augustus Simkins, who had lived all his life as a slave in Edgefield County and was a harness maker, was elected to the legislature in 1872. At the time of his election, he owned a considerable personal estate and operated a shop in the town where he hired other artisans and day laborers.[53] Paris Simkins, son of Col. Arthur Simkins and a slave woman, Charlotte, was also elected a state representative. He was only twenty-three years old in 1872 but was a barber who owned his own shop.[54] Limus Simmons, who had been a slave on one of Governor Francis Pickens's large plantations and who continued working as a tenant after Emancipation, renting a piece of land from Pickens, also became state representative. In 1872 he was thirty-five years old. He owned his own thirty-three-acre farm valued at $150 and claimed personal estate worth $225. Dark-skinned David Graham had been a slave on a large plantation who had worked as a farm laborer and later became a tenant, and finally a landowner, was active as an officer in the militia, a major church leader, and was elected state representative.[55] At the same election in 1872 another ex-slave and militia leader, John Carrol, was elected the first black coroner of his native Edgefield.[56]

In 1874, Archie Weldon replaced Simmons in the state legislature. Weldon had also been a farm laborer in 1870, and one of the few blacks renting farms as tenants in the 1870 Census. In 1874 blacks captured even more powerful political offices on the local level. Jesse Jones, militia officer and a former Edgefield slave, was elected clerk of the county court.[57] Edgefield "born and bred" Ned Tennant, who had mustered black troops against white forces commanded by Matthew Culbraith Butler and by other whites, was elected county commissioner.[58] John Carrol, the coroner, became the first black sheriff of Edgefield, and young mulatto Harrison N. Bouey, a schoolteacher, was elected probate judge.[59] George Morgan, militia captain and the former slave driver who became foreman for Francis Pickens and Pickens's widow, Lucy, was reelected school commissioner and served with other black members of the county school board.[60] Andrew Simkins, the half-brother of state representative Paris Simkins, was elected superintendent of education. Blacks were wardens, intendants, solicitors; they held positions at every level of county and town government by 1874.[61]

Edgefield's black political development may have been aided by emissaries, but unquestionably the post-slavery black leadership was homegrown. All native Edgefield blacks elected to public offices were literate. As shown by their military participation and by personal encounters, they were also proud men who stood up to whites. As Reconstruction progressed, opportunities for political office became open to more and more people. Blacks demanded more and more powerful political positions and got them. Although those such as Rivers or Cain who had served in the Union Army retained their importance, other less-well-established blacks also began to play major roles in Edgefield politics. Even though Afro-American political leaders of Edgefield were drawn mainly from the soil and economic elite of the community, by the end of Reconstruction the political structure had opened to include even prosperous farm laborers, and the occupational structure was opening so that talented Afro-Americans could move up the social mobility ladder.

In conclusion, Afro-American leaders readily assumed the political responsibilities of the post–Civil War era. Common problems, relative homogeneity, strong kinship ties, and developing economic and occupational possibilities promoted political solidarity of the black community in Edgefield. The Afro-American church also was a source of strength for black leaders in their political commitment. The church's emphasis on traditional kinship structures and community service inspired black males to apply the ethics learned in their churches to the political problems of the postwar period. The churches helped black leaders to see that their authority was not dependent upon whites, but derived directly from the black religious community and the autonomy of their own families. Thus, with church and family as sources of and spurs to black freedom and dignity, black leadership blossomed in Reconstruction Edgefield.

NOTES

1. For example, Okon Edet Uya, *From Slavery to Public Service: Robert Smalls, 1839–1915* (New York: Oxford University Press 1971); Peggy Lamson, *The Glorious Failure: Black Congressman Robert Brown Elliott and the Reconstruction in South Carolina* (New York: Norton, 1973); Victor Ullman, *Martin R. Delaney: The Beginnings of Black Nationalism* (Boston: Beacon Press, 1971); Thomas Holt, *Black Over White* (Urbana: University of Illinois Press, 1977); Howard N. Rabinowitz, *Southern Black Leaders of the Reconstruction Era* (Urbana: University of Illinois Press, 1982).

2. Edgefield *Advertiser*, May 22, 1867.

3. Joel Williamson, *After Slavery: The Negro in South Carolina During Reconstruction* (Chapel Hill: University of North Carolina Press, 1965), 369–71.

4. *Proceedings of the Constitutional Convention of South Carolina, Held at Charleston, S.C., Beginning January 14th and ending March 17th, 1868. Including the Debates and Proceedings* (rpt., New York: Arno Press, 1968), 391; also cited in Lamson, *Glorious Failure*, 54.

5. Lamson, *Glorious Failure*, passim. There is no agreement about Elliott's wife. Julian Mims, "Radical Reconstruction in Edgefield County, 1868–1877," MA thesis, University of South Carolina, 1969, 26, asserts that he married an Edgefield native; Williamson, *After Slavery*, 176–77, says he married one of the Rollin sisters of Columbia; Lamson, *The Glorious Failure*, 31–33, does not choose either of these alternatives but concludes that there is "total confusion on the subject."

6. *Edgefield Advertiser*, August 18, 1872.

7. Ibid., Sept. 18, 1870; August 22, 1872. Elliott to P. J. Eichelberger, June 2, 1869, Letter Book of the Adjutant and Inspector General, 1869–70, South Carolina Department of Archives and History, Columbia; also cited in Lamson, *Glorious Failure*, 87–88.

8. John Schreiner Reynolds, *Reconstruction in South Carolina, 1865–1877* (Columbia: State Printing, 1905), 367.

9. John A. Chapman, *A History of Edgefield from the Earliest Settlements to 1897* (Newberry, S.C.: Filbert H. Aull, 1897), 257.

10. Willie Lee Rose, *Rehearsal for Reconstruction: The Port Royal Experiment* (Indianapolis: Bobbs-Merrill, 1964), 316.

11. Ibid., 192, 273; Williamson, *After Slavery*, 16, 27; Mims, "Radical Reconstruction," 27–29.

12. Thomas W. Higginson, *Army Life in a Black Regiment* (Boston: Lee and Shepard, 1890), 56–57; James M. McKim, *The Freed Men of South Carolina* (Philadelphia: Willis P. Hazard, 1862), 19.

13. Chapman, *History of Edgefield*, 259.

14. Ibid., 251, 253; Reynolds, *Reconstruction*, 6.

15. *Edgefield Advertiser*, September 15, 1870.

16. George Brown Tindall, *South Carolina Negroes, 1877–1900* (Columbia: University of South Carolina Press, 1952), 146, 286.

17. *Report of the Joint Investigating Committee on Public Frauds and Election of Hon. J. J. Patterson to the United States Senate made to the General Assembly of S.C. at the Regular Session, 1877–78* (Columbia: Calvo & Patton, State Printers, 1878), 709, 695, 702, 708, 698. *Edgefield Advertiser*, July 31 and August 8, 1867; August 4, 1870.

18. *Edgefield Advertiser*, February 12, 1868; Chapman, *History of Edgefield*, 257; Reynolds, *Reconstruction*, 77.

19. *Edgefield Advertiser*, June 2, May 5, September 15, 1870.

20. Ibid., June 17, 1868; Chapman, *History of Edgefield*, 259; Reynolds, *Reconstruction*, 107.

21. John P. Campbell, *The Southern Business Directory and General Commercial Advertiser* (Charleston: Press of Walker and James, 1854), vol. 1: 311; *Edgefield Advertiser*, May 8, 1867; *Report of the Joint Investigating Committee on Public Frauds and Election of Hon. J. J. Patterson*, 703, 678, 683–88.

22. *Edgefield Advertiser*, June 17, 1868; Chapman, *Reconstruction*, 257; *Report of the Joint Investigating Committee on Public Frauds and Election of Hon. J. J. Patterson*, 705–6; Reynolds, *Reconstruction*, 106; Mims, "Radical Reconstruction," 20–21.

23. *Edgefield Advertiser*, July 24, 1867.

24. Ibid., August 7, 1867.

25. Ibid., March 11, 1868.

26. Chapman, *Reconstruction*, 91.

27. *Edgefield Advertiser*, August 4, 1870.

28. Ibid., July 11, 1866; December 15, 1870; January 12, 19, 1871; January 25, February 29, and March 21, 1872; January 16, February 3, 1873.

29. Reynolds, *Reconstruction*, 365.
30. Edgefield County Deed Book, SSS, 344–45; TTT, 447–48 and OOO, 624–25. Also noted in Mims, "Radical Reconstruction," 33.
31. Tindall, *South Carolina Negroes*, 286; Williamson, *After Slavery*, 385; Joan Reynolds Faunt and Emily B. Reynolds, *Biographical Directory of the Senate of the State of South Carolina* (Columbia: South Carolina Archives Department, 1964), 191; Mims, "Radical Reconstruction," 25, 29.
32. *Edgefield Advertiser*, April 21, 1870.
33. Ibid., Oct. 6, 1870; Chapman, *History of Edgefield*, 259; Reynolds, *Reconstruction*, 150–54.
34. *Report of the Joint Investigating Committee on Public Frauds and Election of Hon. J. J. Patterson*, 690–91; *Edgefield Advertiser*, March 17, 1870.
35. *Report of the Joint Investigating Committee on Public Frauds and Election of Hon. J. J. Patterson*, 685.
36. *Edgefield Advertiser*, September 29 and October 13, 1870; November 12, 1871.
37. Louis F. Post, "A 'Carpetbagger' in South Carolina," *Journal of Negro History* 10 (January 1925): 49.
38. *Edgefield Advertiser*, January 3, 1866.
39. Ibid., August 18, 1870.
40. Ibid., December 8, 1870.
41. Chapman, *History of Edgefield*, 258.
42. *Edgefield Advertiser*, March 28 and April 4, 1872.
43. Lawrence Cain et al. to R. K. Scott, November 2, 1868, in the Papers of Robert K. Scott, South Carolina Department of Archives and History, Columbia, hereinafter cited as the Scott Papers; also see Ned Simkins et al. to R. K. Scott, March 13, 1869, Scott Papers; Mims, "Radical Reconstruction," 36.
44. Phillip A. Eichelberger to R. K. Scott, December 9, 1870, Scott Papers.
45. "Hamburg citizens" to R. K. Scott, September 18, 1871, Scott Papers.
46. Joseph E. Coleman et al. to R. K. Scott, July 6, 1872, Scott Papers.
47. H. N. Bouey to D. H. Chamberlain, July 17, 1876; Paris Simkins to Chamberlain, July 18, 1876 in the Papers of Daniel H. Chamberlain, South Carolina Department of Archives and History, Columbia, hereinafter cited as the Chamberlain Papers. Lawrence Cain and John McDevitt to F. D. Moses, October 1874, in the Papers of Franklin D. Moses Jr., South Carolina Department of Archives and History, Columbia, hereinafter cited as the Moses Papers.
48. *Edgefield Advertiser*, June 30, 1870.
49. Ibid.
50. Ibid., September 5, 1872.
51. Mims, "Radical Reconstruction," 85.
52. Ibid. *Edgefield Advertiser*, August 22, October 24, and November 28, 1872.
53. *Report of the Joint Investigating Committee on Public Frauds and Election of Hon. J. J. Patterson*, 696–97; *Edgefield Advertiser*, June 9, 1870.
54. *Edgefield Advertiser*, June 27, November 28, 1872; Lawrence C. Bryant, ed., *Negro Lawmakers in the South Carolina Legislature, 1868–1902* (Orangeburg: School of Graduate Studies, South Carolina State College, 1968), 22; Mims, "Radical Reconstruction," 26; Chapman, *History of Edgefield*, 190.
55. *Edgefield Advertiser*, June 6, July 7, and August 22, October 10, 1872; *Report of the Joint Investigating Committee on Public Frauds and Election of Hon. J. J. Patterson*, 704;

Chapman, *History of Edgefield,* 91; Francis W. Pickens to J. L. Orr, February 16, 1866, in the Papers of James L. Orr, South Carolina Department of Archives and History, Columbia, hereinafter cited as the Orr Papers.

56. Chapman, *History of Edgefield,* 417.

57. Ibid.

58. *Report of the Joint Investigating Committee on Public Frauds and Election of Hon. J. J. Patterson,* 708–9; Chapman, *History of Edgefield,* 260, 417.

59. Chapman, *History of Edgefield,* 417; Harrison N. Bouey to William Coppinger, May 23, 1877, in the American Colonization Society papers, Letters Received, vol. 227 (on microfilm reel 16a, 141), Library of Congress, Washington D.C.; W. D. Ramey to D. H. Chamberlain, July 5, 1875, Chamberlain Papers.

60. *Edgefield Advertiser,* June 24, 1868; October 24, 1872.

61. Ibid., October 10, 1872. Chapman, *History of Edgefield,* 417. Letters and Petition to the Governors of S.C., 1868–1876, Scott, Moses, Chamberlain Papers.

THE NEW REGIME

Race, Politics, and Police in
Reconstruction Charleston, 1865–1875

(1994)

Laylon Wayne Jordan

The torchlight procession, some three hundred black people "yelling and hooting" and stepping to a band, began peacefully. But on King Street someone in the procession fired off a revolver. The culprit was immediately handed over to the police by some of the others. But men and boys in another part of the procession, thinking that a shot had been fired at them from within a shop on Smith's Lane, began raining "brickbats" on the building "to the ruin of the window glass and crockery, and the great danger of the [white] occupants." A larger crowd gathered. The appearance of an impending row was so great that a harried policeman dispatched a young boy to the Citadel to fetch a detachment of soldiers, but the disturbance was over when they arrived. And thus the great parade, "keeping up an unearthly noise," completed its circuit of the city.[1]

Twenty-one months passed. It was May 1869, a scene of jubilation. Despite the early hour, a throng of blacks assembled around City Hall, awaiting the great event, the inauguration of Mr. Pillsbury. Faces that had been frowning since November last because it had appeared that their champion might be denied his electoral triumph were wreathed with smiles, and the topic of animated conversation was "the new regime." "Loud talk there was of a clean sweep of the city officials to make room for the loyal, and it was agreed by . . . the masses, that all the top rails would have to be removed to make room for the bottom."[2]

In 1869, a mid-point in the era of Reconstruction, great issues the nation has wrestled with ever since were being contested, nowhere more passionately than in Charleston, the first city of the Old South. The prewar regime had been swept away with slavery; the unheard of—racial democracy—was bidding to become normal. After four years of federal military interventions, changes in federal, state, and local constitutions and laws, pivotal civil lawsuits, and sometimes riotous demonstrations, black Charlestonians were realizing an extraordinary, if incomplete, expansion of their new freedom. Many black people remained poor, condemned by lack of property or skills or prejudice to do menial work. Residing in eastside neighborhoods like low-lying and unhealthy "Rottenborough," they died at a rate twice that of whites. But they were working for themselves, and they sat on juries and open streetcars and voted and shared political power.[3]

Appointments to bureaus like police had become commonplace. Just a decade earlier, the Charleston Police Department, following the example of cities like London and New York, had assumed the modern urban pattern of organization, function, routine, and dress. It was paramilitary, composed of officers and men appointed by the mayor, officers for the mayor's term and sergeants, "roundsmen," and privates during "good behavior." It was a full-time, day-and-night police, of a size varying between one hundred and two hundred men, depending upon the city's ability or willingness to fund it, and at all times the most expensive item in the city budget. It had plainclothes detectives and a few horsemen—when federal authorities took over the police power at the end of the Civil War in 1865 they confiscated fifty-six police horses—but its primary reliance was on uniformed patrolmen on walking "beats." Officers, especially captains or chiefs, were typically men of some substance, property, education, and military experience. The lower ranks were filled by unskilled wageworkers and featured a large number of Irish, the lowliest ethnic group.[4]

Subjected to the ravages of accident and a cruel civil conflict, gutted by fire, strangled by a naval blockade, and pounded by cannon, Charleston lay in ruins in February 1865, when the Union Army, including several black units, completed its conquest and began the task of cleaning and repairing the smoke-blackened remnant and reorganizing essential services, including law enforcement. For some months army officers governed and troopers with red-flannel badges patrolled the streets. But within the context of military occupation a provisional civilian administration and police bureau were permitted to form, both initially elected or appointed under antebellum laws and customs and both leaving blacks out. Meanwhile, although decent housing was difficult to find and business of all kinds was prostrated, Charleston swelled with "a pitiable herd" of homeless freedmen from the country. The air crackled with tension and sporadic violence born of the fevers of war, race, and novel circumstances.[5]

Union Army commanders knew they sat on a powder keg. While white folk wished, if they did not expect, a substantial restoration of the old regime, Radicals in Congress worked out a plan which amounted to revolution from above, and politicized blacks, frustrated by economic hardship and the limitations of their new freedom, threatened a revolution from below. General Daniel Sickles, local army commander between 1865 and 1867, was a Radical whose sympathies lay with real change. By the time the federal Congress under Radical influence enacted into law its political and moral judgment that southern government and "colored loyalists" should not be left under "restored rebels" but reorganized under Army supervision and new leadership with effective guarantees of full black citizenship, Sickles was already embarked on that course.[6] An enlightened despot, he shaped elections and manipulated freedom of speech and assembly by curbing public meetings "tending to revive . . . hatred and resentment against the government of the United States," but approving—and attending—rallies mounted by friends of the Union—an interracial Republican Party coalition of blacks, native whites willing to accept a new order ("scalawags"), and black and white newcomers from the North ("carpetbaggers"). He insisted on legal equality— "all laws . . . applicable to all inhabitants"—and imposed biracialism in civil courts. Sickles's command tried and sentenced black men for "resisting and attacking" policemen and conductors during an 1867 protest against racially segregated streetcars. But orders from his office subsequently integrated public transportation in Charleston, and blacks came to rely on his aid. However, it was his successor, General R. H. Canby, on most issues less venturesome, who integrated the police in 1868. Altogether, the changes amounted to a veritable reconstruction of public life.[7]

One of the more important manifestations of change was a new politics which confronted the Charleston mode of former times, a politics of "betters" based on inside maneuvering by men of wealth, virtue, and capacity within a single party, the Democracy, which could assume the common white man's support. The tactics by which the new Republican Party rose to power under the protecting arm of federal authority emerged logically from the necessity of mobilizing the freedmen, a majority—or near majority—among city voters when enfranchised in 1868. The political style owed something to Jacksonian Democracy, a prewar phenomenon which had minor impact in Charleston. It was direct and participatory, "democracy with wings," featuring ringing appeals and torchlight rallies of the faithful that were almost religious rites complete with a messiah whose name was Lincoln.[8]

In the fall of 1868, the first city elections in which blacks participated gave the mayoralty to Gilbert Pillsbury, an educator and old abolitionist whom idealism and careerism had borne southward with the Freedmen's Bureau, and Republicans swept the first post-military city council. But the near-absolute racial cleavage was not carried even to the next election. Although electoral irregularities and Democratic legal appeals long-delayed the inauguration of the Pillsbury regime, Democrats heard a clear political message: they must at least appear to accept black aspirations for full citizenship and include black men on their tickets or forever fail. As they moved to do the politically necessary thing, the political scene abruptly shifted. Two years later, a black minority, following the lead of "blacks of the better sort,"[9] antebellum "free people of color," who were alienated by Republican excesses of egalitarianism, taxes, and corrupt and unwise spending (especially in state government) or won over by expressions of Democrat good will, voted for Democrats. Stripped of exclusive racial coloration, Democrats and Republicans now took turns putting together intricate combinations of ethnic (German and Irish), white, and black voters in elections which brought out large numbers of voters. It was difficult to get a fair canvass. Republicans "imported" voters from the countryside; both sides used intimidation and repetitive voting. Campaign rhetoric was hot and election days tense and occasionally marred by violence. But after Pillsbury's term, the Democrats elected German-born General John Wagener and ran the city from 1871 to 1873, and the Republicans resumed their regnum with George Cunningham, a Tennessee native, in 1873. When Cunningham succeeded himself in 1875 at the head of a "reform" ticket of middle-of-the-road politicians, "both white and colored men," Republicans and Democrats, selected by leaders of both parties to reflect "respectability, property qualifications, intelligence and honesty,"[10] the revolution had been domesticated, "the mad religious energy of the crisis period . . . [having] burned itself out."[11]

Table 1. Mayoral Elections—City of Charleston 1865–1879[12]

Year	Winning Candidate Vote	Losing Candidate	Vote Total
1865	Gaillard (D)		
1868/9	Pillsbury (R) 5,065	Lesesne (D) 5,043	10,128
1871 (1)	Wagener (D) 5,586	Pillsbury (R) 4,809	10,395
1873	Cunningham (R) 6,706	Wagener (D) 5,491	12,197
1875	Cunningham (R) (2) 6,219	Wagener (D) 4,017	10,236
1877 (3)	Sale (D) 5,288	Flemming (D) (4) 1,924	7,212
1879	Courtenay (D) 4,463	Gayer (D) 2,191	8,314
		Sale (D) 1,660	

Notes
1. Five thousand blacks were properly registered to vote in Charleston in 1871.
2. Independent Republican—or Reform Republican.
3. All registered voters in 1877 totaled 9,586.
4. Independent Democrat.

Black officials never controlled the city administration. A black never headed either party's ticket, and although black men held one-half of city council seats between 1867 and 1877—the first freedman, Frank Brown, was elected as a Democrat along with John Wagener in 1871—and such appointments as clerk of council, clerk of the city, and coroner, they seem to have been content to follow white leadership.

As William Hine suggests, they were no Radicals but most concerned with employment and careers within the system.[13] The same thing must be said of the black men who served as policemen. At a time when several hundred able-bodied black residents of Charleston were underemployed in the private sector and when ordinary labor brought $1.25 to $1.50 for a ten-to-twelve-hour workday (about $30 a month) a job with a base salary of $50 a month for an eight-hour day had great appeal, even if subject to the vagaries of politics. From the first appointment by military-appointee George W. Clark in 1868 came a rush of black men, like the Irish before them, into blue and gold uniforms. After 1869 they comprised one-half of the force during Republican administrations and a somewhat smaller part when Democrats controlled city hall. Despite a rapid turnover, there was never a shortage of applicants.[14]

Table 2. Summary of Police Data[15]

Year/Party Men/Officers*	Number of Men	Number of Blacks	Holdovers from Year Men/Officers	Budget ($1000s)
1857/D	188/9	0/0		100
1867/D	88/5	0/0		
1869/R	126/5	40/0		90+
1872/D	91/5	21/0	11/0 (67)	68
1876/R	101/5	54/2		
1882/D	113/5	9/1	20/1 (77)	80
1885/D	71/5	1/1		

*Officers = captain, first and second lieutenants.
Men = sergeants, roundsmen, privates.

The spectacle of former slaves in blue uniforms representing the majesty and authority of the law epitomized the political revolution. Actually black policemen ranged from freedmen, probably the majority although the backgrounds of most are shrouded in obscurity, to at least one case of prewar freedom and wealth. To opponents of the experiment it was another role for which blacks were socially unprepared and even racially unfit. According to one view, given voice by William Gilmore Simms, blacks were more fit for a life of brigandage and crime, and he could point to what he considered conclusive evidence: in August 1869, early in Pillsbury's administration, the *Charleston Courier* announced that of 817 persons committed to the city jail in the previous twelve months, three-quarters were "colored."[16] But other voices replied that the explanation was social and economic, not personal or racial, that it was the brutalization of slavery, want, and ignorance, and that the cure must also be economic and social. In this spirit, Pillsbury once said that "for the security of life and property, for the promotion of peace and good order in the community, to say nothing of moral well-being, I would rather have in each ward school accommodations for all of suitable age, with power to enforce attendance, than cordons of police, or even garrisons of armed soldiers."[17]

Unfortunately, successive city administrations felt compelled by old indebtedness and diminished public revenues to slash the budget of both schools and police.[18] From 1866 into the 1870s the numbers of policemen and arrests showed a downward trend without corresponding evidence of declining lawlessness. The private watchman made a comeback: in 1872, a year in which Charleston County suffered through one murder a month, watchmen for hire were more numerous than policemen.[19] Meanwhile, the staged issuance of pistols and rifles in 1869 and 1870, emblematic of an official conclusion that demands of law enforcement had outrun the traditional armament of nightsticks and whistles, did not eliminate an old nemesis of lawmen, abuse at the hands of the public. Three assaults on policemen were reported in a single day in 1870, one with racial overtones. There was at least one case each week during December 1872.[20]

No black ever won appointment as captain or chief. The most imposing policeman of the era was a white man, Henry W. Hendricks, who was lieutenant of detectives at the end of the Civil War and chief during two Republican administrations, 1869–71 and 1873–75, and the fusion term of Mayor Cunningham which followed. A by-the-book advocate of law and order, he was not popular with any party or faction. Early on, he earned the animosity of Democrats for dumping white officers for black. But the most general complaint focused on his excess of zeal and heavy-handed methods, whether dealing with criminals, stray dogs, or unruly crowds. Ultimately he was respected as an earnest if hard bureaucrat. Even after escalating political violence in 1876 laid bare a deep racial schism within his department, one Democrat remembered that he "acted well and promptly" to limit the damage. The most notable black policeman was George Shrewsbury. The son of a "free person of color" who was also a businessman-butcher and a slaveholder before the war and member of city council in the Cunningham administration after, he rose rapidly in the early 1870s to the rank of lieutenant and chief of detectives—not entirely because of good connections—served well, and died violently in late 1876 in a dispute with a white man over a "colored woman."[21]

The department was heir to the characteristic ill of political spoilsmanship: the best qualified applicant was often not chosen, and rapid turnover hindered development of the one who was. Pillsbury once mocked his own creation: "Our Detectives.—The right arm of the police force; efficient and effective . . . [in] catching hogs, reporting obstructions, and arresting window shutters. . . . May they soon take to catching burglars." The unguarded sentiment was part of a general apprehension at certain times—for example in 1869, when Pillsbury offered his assessment—that the city faced unprecedented danger. At other times, for example when during Cunningham's second administration a relatively veteran force had been assembled, public confidence in the reliability and discipline of the police experienced a tremendous inflation.[22]

A garrison of federal soldiers, about eight hundred men, was still maintained in and around the city, at the Citadel and elsewhere, into the middle 1870s, and in truth their presence, and the federal power they represented, was a most important reason the races and parties strove to get along.[23] Still, with the decline of the Radical Republicans at Washington, the withdrawal of black units, and the coming of new commanders, the stance of the army changed. Held in barracks except on election days when they were deployed at the polls, the soldiers still tried to balance a political and racial see-saw, only now, mirroring emerging sentiments back home, they tended to sympathize with and tilt toward the traditional leadership and "home rule." And, naturally, relations between the army and black and white communities evolved. In a defining moment toward the end of 1875, officers of the First and Fifth United States Artillery regiments, the one rotating out and the other rotating in for garrison duty, were "handsomely entertained" at the Charleston Hotel by the cream of old Charleston society, including leading men of the Washington Light Infantry, German Fusiliers, and Palmetto Guards.[24]

A few days earlier, after a "fair and free election," perhaps the first of the era in the city, Charleston for the first time since the Civil War showed its approval of an incumbent administration by voting its continuance. Mayor Cunningham, elected as a Republican in 1873, would preside over a coalition council and hand the spoils of office to Democrats about as readily as Republican, to white as black men. The new government was forward-looking and upbeat, despite dark economic clouds, and committed (or reconciled) to the "new regime," the racial status quo. By its sensibility and moderation it won the support of the city's most powerful Democratic voice, the *News and Courier,* and the "entire confidence of the public," according to its editor.[25] As 1876, the United States' centennial year, loomed benignly ahead, city council, white and black, Democrat and Republican, native and "carpetbagger," issued under Cunningham's signature a mellow proclamation of goodwill to all and gratitude to "a smiling Providence . . . for His many mercies to us as a community."[26]

Thus on the eve of Redemption, the "Red Shirt" Revolution of 1876, Charleston made progress on the difficult road to racial justice, political equilibrium, and peace. The balance was precarious. The interest and influence of the federal government was receding: this had been dramatically underscored during 1875 by the Supreme Court's Cruikshank decision and President U. S. Grant's decision not to send soldiers into racially torn Mississippi. Rural areas of South Carolina had not established viable race relations and simmered on the edge of civil and race war. Everywhere, even Charleston, white reactionaries ached for the full restoration of the old regime. State government was in gridlock. Republican extremists, disturbed by the merging curses of racial and party moderates, exerted themselves to secure a baseline beyond which compromise was not acceptable. The legislature's nomination of William J. Whipper, a Radical and corrupt black legislator, to the judicial bench of the Charleston circuit just before Christmas 1875, was fashioned to provide a test of Republican loyalty, rebuke the increasingly moderate and reformist Republican governor, Daniel Chamberlain, and outrage the many Charlestonians who were not Whipper partisans. "Black Tuesday," as the day of the nomination was styled in the city by the sea, foreshadowed the coming storm.[27] In the new year Charleston would go through an ordeal of racial incidents (while the state and nation went through memorable elections) and emerge with black and white communities polarized, fusion-politics and the racially mixed police department discredited, the new order on the way to extinction, the federal presence liquidated, and the old largely restored, including a virtually all-white corps of police.[28]

NOTES

1. Charleston *Courier* (sometimes designated as *Daily Courier*), August 16, 1867.
2. "Inauguration of the New Mayor and Aldermen," *Courier*, May 4, 1869.
3. Thomas D. Morris, "Equality, 'Extraordinary Law,' and Criminal Justice: The South Carolina Experience, 1865–1866," *South Carolina Historical Magazine* 83 (January 1982): 15–33; George Tindall, *The Negro in South Carolina, 1877–1900* (Columbia: University of South Carolina Press, 1952), 190–200; William C. Hine, "Black Labor in Reconstruction Charleston," *Labor History* 25 (Fall 1984): 506; "Bill of Mortality," *Courier,* January 8, 1873; "Important Improvement," *Courier,* February 3, 1873.
4. Laylon Wayne Jordan, "Police Power and Public Safety in Antebellum Charleston: Emergence of a New Police, 1800–1860," *South Atlantic Urban Studies* (Columbia: University of South Carolina Press, 1979), vol. 3: 122–40.
5. See remarks of Alderman Ravenel, *Courier,* July 7, 1866. For the fall of Charleston see *Courier,* February 20, 1865; Martin Abbott, *The Freedmen's Bureau in South Carolina* (Chapel Hill: University of North Carolina Press, 1967), 37–38; *Courier,* October 19, 1865.

6. The premise is expressed in "The Question of Reconstruction: Letters from Chief Justice Chase to President Lincoln," April 11 and 12, 1865, *Courier*, July 7, 1865. A good, brief treatment of Sickles in Charleston is in Walter Fraser Jr., *Charleston! Charleston!* (Columbia: University of South Carolina Press, 1989), 275–85.

7. Arrival of Maj. Gen. Sickles, *Courier*, November 25, 1865; "Military vs. Civilian Law," *The Mercury* (Charleston), August 8, 1867. William B. Gatewood Jr., "'The Remarkable Misses Rollin': Black Women in Reconstruction South Carolina," *South Carolina Historical Magazine* 92 (July 1991): 177. The Special Orders, Headquarters of the Second Military District, Charleston, are housed in the South Carolina Department of Archives and History, Columbia. The quoted passage is from the preamble of an order issued over Sickles's signature on January 1, 1866.

8. Fraser, *Charleston! Charleston!* 285; *Daily Republican* (Charleston), July 6, 1867 (Sickles address to rally); "Negro Torchlight Meeting," *Charleston Mercury*, August 16, 1867; "The Republican Meeting," *Courier*, June 2, 1869.

9. D. E. Huger Smith, *A Charlestonian's Recollections, 1846–1913* (Charleston: Carolina Art Association, 1950), 140.

10. *New York Tribune*, quoted in "The Charleston Election," *News and Courier*, October 11, 1875.

11. Crane Brinton's words, on the phenomenon of "thermidor," the "last phase" of revolutions, in *The Anatomy of Revolution* (New York: Vintage Books. 1965), 208. For a treatment which emphasizes the "reactionary" and ephemeral qualities of the 1875 election, see E. Culpepper Clark, *Francis Warrington Dawson and the Politics of Restoration, 1874–1889* (University: University of Alabama Press, 1980), chapter 3. There is a good summary in Fraser, *Charleston! Charleston!* 288–99. See table 1.

12. Schirmer Diary, October 1, 1873; Charleston newspapers in respective years: *Courier News, News and Courier, Mercury, Daily Republican*; Fraser, *Charleston! Charleston!* 276, 288, 292, 301, 303.

13. William Hine, "Frustration, Factionalism, and Defeat: Black Political Leadership and the Republican Party in Reconstruction Charleston, 1865–1877," PhD diss., Kent State University, 1979, 246, 367–88, 457, 469.

14. Before Pillsbury's election, Republican Robert DeLarge declared that be knew 400–500 men who were eager for police badges if Pillsbury won. Hine, "Frustration, Factionalism, and Defeat," 133, 180, 331. See table 2.

15. Charleston Police Department Records, City Archives: Charleston City Directory and Yearbooks of the City of Charleston. 1857–85; "Proceedings of Council," *Charleston Daily Courier*, August 30, 1869; *New York Herald*, November 13, 1876; Fraser, *Charleston! Charleston!* 296; Melinda M. Hennessey, "Racial Violence during Reconstruction: The 1876 Riots in Charleston and Cainhoy," *South Carolina Historical Magazine* 86 (April 1985): 105.

16. Simms to John E. Cooke, May 9, 1868, in Mary C. Oliphant, ed., *Letters of William Gilmore Simms* (Columbia: University of South Carolina Press, 1956), vol. 5: 131; "City Affairs," *Courier*, September 1, 1869; "Crime and Pauperism," *Courier*, December 12, 1872.

17. "Pillsbury Inaugural," *Courier*, May 4, 1669; *Daily Republican*, February 18, 1871 (editorial).

18. *Daily Republican*, January 7, 12, 1870; *News and Courier*, November 4, 1872. It is not certain how many policemen are enough. With 125 officers in 1869, Charleston had 2.5 officers per 1,000 population, with 90 officers in 1872, 1.8. By comparison, Boston, Massachusetts, in recent years had 4 officers per 1,000 population, but San Diego, California, only 1.2. See Ramsey Clark, *Crime in America* (New York: Pocket Books, 1971), 119.

19. "City Affairs," *Courier,* August 13, 1869; for occupations see *City Directory Charleston, 1872–1873* (Charleston: Walker, 1873); Police Reports, *Courier,* July 19, 1866 (for June arrests); *Courier,* October 26, 1869 (for July-August-September); *News and Courier,* October 25, 1876 (for September); the numbers of arrests were, respectively, 348, 298 (avg.), and 269. Brian W. Dippie, "The Winning of the West Reconsidered," *Wilson Quarterly,* Summer 1990, 76, reports that Dodge City, Kansas, a contemporary cattle town with a reputation for mayhem, had five homicides in its worst year, 1878.

20. "City Affairs," *Courier,* August 13, 1869; Tindall, *Negro in South Carolina,* 159–62; *Daily Republican,* January 1, 1870; *Courier,* December 6, 16, 20, 27, 1872.

21. "A New Detective Police Force," *Courier,* July 20, 1866; "Our Detective Police," *Mercury,* August 26, 1867; "The Canine War" and "The War on the Bicycles," *Courier,* June 5, 1869; "Quick Work," *Courier,* July 22, 1869; "A New Appointment," *Courier,* October 20, 1869; "The Riot of the Eighth," *News and Courier,* November 23, 1876; Alfred B. Williams, *Hampton and His Red Shirt* (Charleston: Walter, Evans, and Cogswell, 1935), 121; Toomer Porter, *Led On! . . . An Autobiography* (New York: Arno Press, 1967), 196–98; "All About a Woman," *News and Courier,* November 24, 1876; "The Shrewsbury Inquest," *News and Courier,* November 25, 1876.

22. "A Sentiment," *Courier,* September 3, 1869; "Policeman on a Bender," *Courier,* August 16, 1869; "Beware of Burglars," *Courier,* September 3, 1869; "Incendiarism," *Courier,* September 11, 1869; Smith, *Charlestonian's Recollections,* 138–59; *News and Courier,* August 28, 1875.

23. Historian Edward Ayers laid down the general rule: areas in the Reconstruction South where blacks were in the majority and federal troops were present suffered less racial violence than areas where whites were in the majority and the army was far away. See his *Vengeance and Justice* (New York: Oxford University Press, 1984), 159.

24. Smith, *Charlestonian's Recollections,* 141–42; *News and Courier,* December 7, 1875. Just four years earlier, the Washington Light Infantry had organized a Rifle Club to defend "Southern Ways" against Yankee and blacks alike. Receipt Book of Rifle Club, 1871, Washington Light Infantry Papers, Special Collections, Marlene and Nathan Addlestone Library, College of Charleston.

25. "A Striking Contrast," *News and Courier,* December 7, 1875.

26. "The New City Council," *News and Courier,* November 30, 1875; *News and Courier* editorial, December 2, 1875. Symptomatic of the prevailing centrism was the mortality of newspapers of the political margins. In the fall of 1871 a Democrat, Jacob Schirmer, celebrated in his diary the death of the *Daily Republican,* which was shut down "for want of nourishment"—subscribers and advertisers—after several stormy years. He did not note that that paper had survived the *Mercury,* the journal of ultra-conservatism which had fought a bitter rearguard action against "the Negro policy" during the period of military rule, by a few months, or that the field was left to the moderate *News and Courier,* merged under the ownership and direction of English-born Francis Warrington Dawson. See Schirmer Diary, September 9, 1871, South Carolina Historical Society, Charleston; "The Great Issue," *Mercury,* August 20, 1867; and Clark, *Francis Warrington Dawson,* chapter 2.

27. Eric Foner, *Reconstruction: America's Unfinished Revolution, 1863–1877* (New York: Harper and Row, 1988), 564–74; Clark, *Francis Warrington Dawson,* chapters 2, 3. A particularly well documented example of a white Charlestonian who never saw anything in the "new regime" but "rascality and robbery" is Jacob Schirmer, a retired merchant; see Schirmer Diary, November 30, 1876.

28. Fraser, *Charleston! Charleston!,* 298–303; "The Summerville Election," *News and Courier,* June 15, 1876; "A Queer Day in Court," *News and Courier,* June 15, 1876; Schirmer Diary, May 15, October 25, 1876; Walter Allen, *Governor Chamberlain's Administration in South Carolina* (New York: G. P. Putnam's Sons, 1888), 153–208, 421–23; Melinda S. Hennessey, "Racial Violence during Reconstruction: The 1876 Riots in Charleston and Cainhoy," *South Carolina Historical Magazine* 86 (April 1985): 101–12; *New York Times,* November 9, 1876; "The Walter Inquest," *News and Courier,* November 22, 1876; "Council and the Police," *News and Courier,* November 22, 1876; Foner, *Reconstruction,* chapter 12; Tindall, *Negro in South Carolina,* 299–300; Charles A. Lofgren, *The Plessy Case* (New York: Oxford University Press, 1987), chapter 1.

A RECONSIDERATION
The University of South Carolina during Reconstruction
(1974)

John Herbert Roper

All state universities are garments which must be altered from time to time to fit the people of the state. The University of South Carolina in particular has felt the growth spurts of Carolinians; often a seam has been rent or a button lost before the tailors in the General Assembly and elsewhere could modify the clothing. When examining such an old suit of clothes one must not judge the "fit" by too modern standards. The baggy pants and narrow ties, the suspenders and celluloid collars, the cravat and the afghan all served a purpose for the wearer in his own day and age.

In the same vein the historian must approach an institution of an older day by the light of the purpose demanded of it in its own time. Thus, the antebellum South Carolina College emphasized classical Latin and Greek studies to the exclusion of modern foreign language, oratory over modern sciences, and a certain leadership style over contemporary studies. The college, in short, trained the leaders of the state: from its halls came Governor George McDuffie, Senator James H. Hammond, and political statesman Robert W. Barnwell. The school's historians, Maximillian LaBorde in 1859, and, more recently, Professor Daniel Walker Hollis, have both recognized this role.[1]

However, no one has yet acknowledged that the Reconstruction University of South Carolina, from 1873 to 1877, performed an analogous duty. Then the cloth of the university was cut around a pattern for a black student body, a student body which would figure just as prominently in leading its race as the college alumni had in leading whites. Beginning with 1932 and the publication of Francis Butler Simkins's and Robert Hilliard Woody's study, *South Carolina During Reconstruction*, those troubled years of Yankee rule have been reinterpreted by several scholars. Acknowledging the nationwide corruption and the economic depression which stymied reform in the administration of

President Ulysses S. Grant, these revisionists have insisted that substantive good emerged from the Reconstruction era. Perhaps now is the time to reconsider one of the grander and bolder experiments: the effort to integrate racially a southern state university.

The model for behavior in the South Carolina College had been the southern Christian gentleman, a well-mannered, cultured individual who understood the complexities of life from the *code duello* to the *code noir*. Those leaders went down to unhappy defeat before the triumphant Union hordes. Their replacements at leadership posts were not all despicable despots "on the make." Many were also fine Christian gentlemen who happened to be trained in the less grandiose society of Puritan New England.

As the black historian W. E. B. DuBois observed, the massive educational project for the uncounted Negro illiterates of the South was directed in this New England fashion.[2] From the dirt floors of one-room schools to the sedate setting of the famed University of South Carolina, the freedmen learned solid American values: honesty, morality, responsibility, industry, thrift, ingenuity, and, of course, religiosity. Through the new fabric of education were spun the threads of the Puritan work ethic and of patriotism.[3]

For the new sable clientele, many of whom had slaved in the fields only a few years before, classical training could not have been more extraneous. As a matter of fact, as Dr. Hollis demonstrated, the white university between 1865 and 1873 also had moved in the direction of pragmatic education, adding courses in medicine, law, engineering, and modern foreign languages. But with a practically all-black university after 1873, the board of trustees structured a curriculum to guide a semiliterate student into college-level instruction.[4]

To ease this steep incline, the university built a Preparatory Department, a maximum of four years of fundamental grammar, mathematics, and reading for those most scarred by slavery's enforced ignorance. Between the Preparatory Department and the freshman class, the trustees also placed a sub-freshman class, to further prepare the preparatory student for the university. Thus, while the new curriculum did not meet the high college standard, an AB degree from the Radical university was no meaningless honor: only sixteen men, all of whom accomplished much in later life, received AB degrees during the four school terms.[5]

Another knotty problem with both the postwar white university and the Radical university concerned money. A severe economic depression in 1873 dictated that a strong young man should stay on the farm and help the family; in those years, the sacrifice of a healthy teenager from the household was too dear an expense for even the noblest educational mission. Thus began the scholarship program, whereby one student per county could earn twenty dollars a month for living expenses. Conservative opponents scoffed at this measure; even the

Republican state superintendent of education, Justus K. Jillson, protested that unworthy politicians collected the money fraudulently.[6] On the other hand, Owen L. W. Smith, a veteran of both slavery and the Union Army, sent his money home to a starving, ill-clad family in South Georgia.[7] Like much Reconstruction legislation, the scholarships helped a few worthies, were exploited by a few greedy, and served as a progressive precedent despite abuses.

To direct this new curriculum, the trustees selected a faculty which was a curious blend of professional and propagandistic ability. The Reconstruction faculty divided into two camps, one of which educated and one of which publicized. Although the publicists took their scholarship seriously, and although the scholars campaigned politically, there remained a qualitative difference between the two camps. Benjamin B. Babbitt, Anson W. Cummings, T. N. Roberts, and Henry J. Fox lived in the fishbowl of political activism, public relations work, and the gospel of social reform. Richard T. Greener, William Main, and Fisk P. Brewer spoke on the hustings as well, but their passion was for the quieter, more solid side of education. It took both to keep the university going, for the state money, the black patronage, and the northern praise came because of the publicists; but the new students stayed because of the quiet scholars.[8]

Decades after 1877, the Radical alumni mirrored what they were taught as teenagers by northern Methodist tutors. Of these tutors, Anson W. Cummings and Benjamin B. Babbitt probably exerted the most direct influence on student behavior. These two, alternating as chairman of the faculty and as guest chaplain in the State Senate, lived in the public eye. From obscure backgrounds, each had burst onto the southern scene, infuriating the native whites while ingratiating themselves with Radical reformers. Neither boasted real academic prowess, but each man left his indelible label on the graduates of the school. Babbitt and Cummings also kept in touch with the General Assembly, sending forth invitations to chapel services, convocations, exhibitions, and commencements.[9]

Much like Cummings and Babbitt in sentiment, but less successful in student relations were Henry J. Fox and T. N. Roberts. Unlike the former two, Fox and Roberts had trouble grappling with the discipline problems posed by the young blacks they praised. Finally, the black scholar Richard T. Greener used his influence with the student body to smooth discipline in the classes of Fox and Roberts.[10]

Fox carried the word to the northern reading public, writing in the *Methodist Quarterly Review*. In those pages, the minister combated the full range of Negrophobic stereotypes, including shiftlessness, dishonesty, slovenliness, slowness, and childishness. There Fox laid out the story of reform at the University of South Carolina; he told of strict discipline, gentlemanly demeanor, and orderly habits instilled in his student body. Again, Fox emphasized the central nature of religious instruction to the curriculum.[11]

None of these figures—Fox, Babbitt, Roberts, or Cummings—could have taught at the old college. Not only were they heretical, but they had not attained the academic standards of the college professors. But on their black students these men placed a mark which stayed. Decades later, in far-off Liberia, former pupils T. McCants Stewart, William H. Heard, and Owen L. W. Smith preached on manners and discipline, on cleanliness and godliness, on truth and industry.[12] As late as the 1920s, William Sinclair in language straight from the old Radical faculty refuted the whole range of Negrophobic stereotypes.[13]

If the four publicists instilled certain models for behavior, three genuine scholars gave the talented black students the weapon of knowledge for the upcoming racial turmoil after 1877. These three were Fisk P. Brewer, Richard Greener, and William Main. Although Brewer and Greener occasionally entered the political lists to break a lance or two for the mission, their primary interest was academic. Main seemed to adhere strictly to the business of classroom education at which he excelled.

Fisk Parsons Brewer came to Columbia with the greatest reputation of the new faculty. Part of an old antislavery family, Brewer joined the abolitionist American Missionary Association on his graduation from Yale. The Congregationalist minister also taught ancient languages at Yale and served in the Greek consulship. At USC, Brewer instructed in Latin and Greek, while trying to place some of his better pupils in responsible teaching positions with the AMA schools. He published several scholarly articles on coin collecting between 1873 and 1877; and he left a scrapbook of the Radical university, which may be seen today in the South Caroliniana Library on the USC campus.[14]

William Main was younger than any professor except Richard Greener, but his was the best example of disinterested professionalism. When hired in 1873, Main was slightly over thirty and a decade before had received a master's degree in engineering from the University of Pennsylvania. His specialized training did not stop there, for he also garnered an advanced degree in mining engineering from the Polytechnic College of Pennsylvania. A well-traveled, multitalented young man, Main traversed the continent, holding jobs from Colorado to Lake Superior and from Lake Superior to Philadelphia. On the shores of the Great Lakes and on the slopes of the Rocky Mountains, the scientist labored in chemical and metallurgical laboratories. Returning to the Quaker City, Main worked as an analytical chemist before coming to Columbia. Generally, Main avoided politics.[15] The scholastic background and personal dedication of this academic carpetbagger gave the lie to one cynic's appraisal of the faculty as "unknown or known only to be despised."[16]

Like Main and Brewer, Richard T. Greener hailed from an Ivy League school and earned plaudits as an academician rather than as a publicist. But Greener by his presence was a special entity: he was black, the first such black graduate from Harvard, and living proof of the Negro's capacities.[17] His unique position as a black teaching blacks at the University of South Carolina made Greener a key liaison between the sable student body and the professors. Thus he could smooth feathers ruffled by the sub-freshman misbehavior which so rankled his cohorts, Fox and Roberts.

Besides teaching philosophy, he lectured the sub-freshmen and preparatory students in Latin. In the library, Greener made a contribution to the school itself, a contribution appreciated by white students long after Reconstruction. He repaired the damage done to the library—apparently by vandals—and wrought order out of the chaos by cataloguing the collection of over thirty thousand volumes. His report on this project, submitted to Congress, earned him membership in the American Philological Association of Newport, Rhode Island.[18] William J. Rivers, a respected professor from the antebellum college, visited Columbia and praised the black man's management of the library.[19] Despite all his many works, Greener's major impact on his students was as a symbol of black aspirations.

Unfortunately, the Modern Foreign Language and the Medical schools were conspicuous failures. Constant change in teacher personnel plagued the former, sheer student apathy the latter. Dr. John Lynch, a native Carolinian, taught only one medical student, who received no degree. In the Foreign Language Department, three German immigrants who spoke little English struggled to make the freedmen understand thick Prussian accents. None of these German teachers taught for as long as two years at USC.[20]

If the Medical College and the Foreign Language School on balance slowed the advancing mission, the Law School raced ahead in the first wave of the Radical offensive. The most distinguished university pupils, Richard Greener and state treasurer Francis L. Cardozo, took LLB degrees. More importantly, law professors Cyrus D. Melton and Franklin J. Moses Sr. reached across the chasm between Conservative and Radical. Each jurist grew up in the state; Melton held a South Carolina College degree; both served the Confederate cause. During Reconstruction, Melton and Moses climbed high in the legal structure of the state by virtue of Radical friends, but both remained friends with many of the Conservative opposition.[21]

This Radical faculty, threatened on so many sides by hostility and misunderstanding, lost their jobs when the Red Shirt hero officially became governor in the winter of 1877. Ironically, Wade Hampton, a southerner of sterling ancestry and sparkling war service, was led into doing what even William Tecumseh Sherman could not do: he closed the University of South Carolina. The faculty thus thrown out on its ears soon fell victim to unwarranted opprobrium in the histories written by men ideologically outraged by radicalism. In a calmer day, the records of personal ability and achievement left by this faculty have been examined and found worthy. Those records have been preserved largely in the South Caroliniana Library. But the faculty's greatest personal achievement, as for all teachers, was testified to by almost two hundred black students who lived and worked after Redemption.

As in antebellum days, graduates distinguished themselves as political and social leaders at the far corners of the world, the nation, and the state; they served at foreign embassies, at the nation's capital, and in the state legislature. For example, William H. Heard, Owen L. W. Smith, and Richard T. Greener gained posts in the Diplomatic and Consular Service; George W. Murray and Thomas E. Miller went to Congress to represent South Carolina; and Heard, Miller, and Joseph D. Boston sat in the state assembly.[22]

Also, as in the antebellum college days, former students went back to the rural communities and shaped lives from the more mundane settings of the church, the insurance company, the small business, and the one-room school building. Thus, Cornelius C. Scott, George W. Clinton, and Ambassador Heard tended the flocks of church congregations; Robert L. Smith in Texas and Isaac L. Purcell in Florida built small feudatories; and William M. Dart and Alonzo G. Townsend labored in the common school classroom.[23]

Times were hard both economically and socially around Columbia between 1873 and 1877. Some of the townspeople launched a clandestine guerilla activity against the black campus, annoying faculty and students without disturbing the federal troops encamped nearby. One night, a gang of local vandals swept into the university, breaking windows and firing pistols into the air. Later, Professor Henry J. Fox's favorite horse was injured by pranksters. The anonymous school official who warned of danger lurking in "Columbia's dark, tree-lined streets" did not exaggerate.[24] Ku Klux Klan actions just north of Columbia were especially vicious, and three prominent black assemblymen had been slain by political assassins.[25]

Undaunted by such pressure, the young men busied themselves with extracurricular affairs. Some scholars were grown men, elected officials grimly struggling with the ignorance imposed by slavery. Others, younger boys, appeared on the floor of the General Assembly in auxiliary roles as secretaries and assistants. Also, during the summer recess many men carried the torch of knowledge to the desperate illiterates down home. On the campus, the blacks maintained two debating clubs, the "Clariosophic" and the "Ciceronian." The advanced students performed at chapel and at exhibitions, which were all open to the public.[26] This kaleidoscope of activity which angered local Conservatives quickened the heartbeat of reformers across the country who believed in the Radical mission of racial uplift.

The best and most active students attended the law lectures of Melton and Moses. Francis L. Cardozo, mulatto secretary of state, obtained the highest law grade recorded.[27] Cardozo had been a key figure in the campaign to clean up the fraud-ridden state land commission, allotting at least some good land to deserving families.[28] Close behind Cardozo in the law school were Professor Richard Greener and Walter Raleigh Jones, the personal secretary to reform-minded Governor Daniel H. Chamberlain.[29]

Cardozo brought five young Howard University students down to USC: C. C. Scott, T. McCants Stewart, William M. Dart, John M. Morris, and Paul J. Mishaw. Each of these Charlestonians wrote a conspicuous record on the academic ledger of the university while dominating much of the other activity. Stewart, Dart, Scott, and Morris also joined fifty-nine other students in teaching common school children during the summer recess.[30]

There were other students who kept somewhat lower profiles on the Reconstruction horizon. Classical graduates Alonzo G. Townsend, Thaddeus Saltus, and John J. Durham conducted prayer meetings on Wednesdays, while John M. Morris assisted in the Preparatory Department.[31] There were also students too young to distinguish themselves in the short life span of the radical university. These latter unknowns, together with their more famous colleagues, used the values and training from the University of South Carolina in the turbulent racial squalls after 1877.

Victory for the Red Shirt Redeemers in the winter of 1876–77 closed down most of the Radical projects, including the university experiment. The next decades found the "old S.C.U. boys" as busy as before, but now most were far removed from white vision. Fifty graduates and alumni have been located. These men fell into specific groupings of professions or vocations, although several men acted in more than one field during a long and active life. Not surprisingly, the men who could be found lived among the "talented tenth" of the businessmen and professionals. Dominant careers were civil service (fourteen), political office (fourteen), the ministry (twelve), law (eleven), and college teaching or administration (ten). Seven men worked as journalists or writers; seven in business; five as physicians; four in the foreign service; three as land-owning farmers; and two, apparently, as menial laborers.[32] Civil service jobs, political appointments, foreign service, and even college positions all represented political plums of various sizes and tastes. The nature of these plums indicated political activism, an activism practiced at the university and continued by ties of loyalty knotted in the dormitory.

One of these Radical products, Richard Greener, left USC for a full life as educator—at Howard University Law School—as diplomat—ambassador to Russia—and as a political figure—a "regular" Republican called on often to speak in the Middle West where he eventually made his home. Greener earned biographical sketches in *Appletons' Cyclopedia of American Biography* and the *Dictionary of American Biography*.

Another part of the university mission reached the shores of Africa, carried there by graduates William Heard, Owen Smith, and McCants Stewart. The first two preached a messianic Puritan work ethic to the native Liberians from their official pulpits as ambassador to Liberia; Stewart served as professor in the Liberian national college at Monrovia.[33]

Politicians who kept working in South Carolina were Tom Miller and George Murray, two men who became bitter rivals. The former, a light-skinned "canary-bird," operated the State College for Negroes at Orangeburg. Miller also served in the state General Assembly from 1876 to 1888, and in the United States Congress from 1888 to 1892. His old classmate Murray, in fitting contrast, was an ebony Negro who replaced Miller in the House in 1892 and was elected again in 1896.[34]

Of the educators who sprang from USC, William A. Sinclair gained the greatest notoriety. A passionate exponent of the old Radical mission of equality, Sinclair served at Howard University as financial secretary. He spoke out often on black capability, helping in 1905 to found the National Association for the Advancement of Colored People, for which he officiated in Philadelphia and St. Louis.[35]

Strangely, none of these distinguished alumni swung the political and economic clout of Whitefield McKinlay, a man few whites knew. We may learn of him today through the Carter Godwin Woodson Papers in the Library of Congress. Shortly after Redemption in 1877, McKinlay quietly moved to Washington, part of the general exodus of black intelligentsia to the capital after 1877. There he set up a real estate business and a law practice, quickly gaining the patronage of veteran black politicians like P. B. S. Pinchback of Louisiana and Robert Smalls, Thomas Miller, and George Murray of South Carolina.

Gradually, McKinlay reached further into local politics, lending money to and advising AME church leaders, Howard trustees, and a host of once-famous blacks out of work such as Robert Smalls and Pinchback. Sometime after William McKinley became president, the realtor came into contact with Booker T. Washington and began a long friendship. The Tuskegee lion liked Whitefield McKinlay, introducing him to the presidential secretary, William Loeb. Washington employed Whitefield McKinlay as an ombudsman for black grievances, someone who quietly got the Tuskegee messages to the White House. Through clandestine meetings and many cryptic telegrams, President McKinley devised his policy on black patronage: no Negro would be removed from office unless replaced by another Negro who met Booker T. Washington's approval.[36]

Along with Washington, Whitefield McKinlay fought for black rights—even for civil equality—but always behind the scenes. With William McKinley's successor, Theodore Roosevelt, Whitefield McKinlay and Washington held less influence. On the whole, however, Whitefield McKinlay appreciated Roosevelt's courage in the famed dinner invitation to Washington, TR's public affirmation of friendship with the black race.[37]

In 1908, William H. Taft became president, an event which signaled a further decline in Whitefield McKinley's national influence. And in 1912, the southern-born Woodrow Wilson and his southern cabinet ended Whitefield McKinley's power outside the limits of the District of Columbia. On the other hand, the realtor continued to dominate much local black financing. An amazing number of people relied on him for small and large favors, from the destitute orphans at Washington's Frederick Douglass Home to Bishop George Clinton; others, like Richard Greener and P. B. S. Pinchback, relied on his friendship to steer themselves for the gloomy days after 1900. One surprising aspect of McKinlay's correspondence was the accumulation of mail from USC friends. Some, like Florida lawyer Isaac L. Purcell, wrote to inquire about alumni; others, like John A. Simkins of Edgefield, wrote to lament the disappearance for blacks of the educational brass ring from life's merry-go-round.[38]

Whitefield McKinlay, C. C. Scott, and Thomas Miller retained a set of values from their university training; so did William Sinclair, George Clinton, T. McCants Stewart, and Richard Greener. These different men strung their thoughts out along a spectrum of political ideology. Their Radical professors had emphasized social equality as a goal; to reach the goal they offered the tools of black capability: old American ideals of thrift, industry, honesty, responsibility, Christianity, and hard-nosed business "gumption." Some former students dropped the goal of equality—at least for their generation—but McKinlay, Scott, and Miller used the tools of American ethics in their "separate but equal" existence. Other students loudly and boldly kept proclaiming the message of equality: Sinclair, Clinton, Greener, and Stewart diluted very little of the "fountains of knowledge" from which they had drunk at USC.

The Radical university certainly failed to train and to keep training a black leadership; only sixteen boys emerged with AB degrees over three and one-half years. Instead, the Radical university was a pregnant failure, full of suggestions for the future. In its classrooms and dormitories grew up a coterie of black pragmatists, some dedicated to sterling ideals, but nonetheless pragmatists who understood the ways to success in the United States. The racial war through which they struggled after 1877 would have been more difficult without the bonds of brotherhood formed and the tactical measures first practiced at the University of South Carolina.

NOTES

1. Daniel Walker Hollis, *College to University: The History of the University of South Carolina* (Columbia: University of South Carolina Press, 1956), vol. 1: 1–78; Maximillian

LaBorde, *History of South Carolina College* (Charleston: Walker, Evans, and Cogswell, 1859).

2. William Edward Burghardt DuBois, *The Souls of Black Folk* (Chicago: A. C. McClurg and Co., 1903).

3. See "Lectures," undated clipping in Fisk Parsons Brewer Scrapbook, Fisk Parsons Brewer Papers, South Caroliniana Library, University of South Carolina; and University of South Carolina Records (USC Records), University Archives, South Caroliniana Library.

4. "Report of the Chairman of the Faculty," 1873, USC Records, South Caroliniana Library.

5. "Report" and "Catalogues of the University of South Carolina," in *South Carolina General Assembly Reports and Resolutions of S.C. to the General Assembly* (Columbia: n.p., 1873–77).

6. "Resolutions," Justus K. Jillson to the Faculty, April 12, 1875, USC Records.

7. "Biographical Sketch of the Rev. Owen Lun West Smith, D.O., United States Minister to Liberia" (n.p., 1900[?]), 1–24.

8. See postcards addressed to the faculty, USC Records, 1873–77.

9. *South Carolina General Assembly Reports and Resolutions*; Brewer Scrapbook.

10. Cornelius C. Scott, "When Negroes Attended the State University," *The State* (Columbia), May 8, 1911.

11. Henry J. Fox, "Our Work at the South," *Methodist Quarterly Review* 4 (January 1874): 29–45; Fox, "The Negro," *Methodist Quarterly Review* 5 (January 1875): 79–97.

12. William Henry Heard, *The Bright Side of African Life* (Philadelphia: African Methodist Episcopal Publishing House, 1898).

13. Charles Flint Kellogg, *NAACP: A History of the National Association for the Advancement of Colored People, 1909–1920* (Baltimore: Johns Hopkins Press, 1967).

14. W. F. Brewer, "Sketch of Fisk Parsons Brewer," typed manuscript [1940] in North Carolina Collection, Wilson Library, University of North Carolina, Chapel Hill.

15. Cornelius C. Scott, "William Main," manuscript in Carter Godwin Woodson Collection, Manuscript Division, Library of Congress.

16. James Lawrence Reynolds, *History of South Carolina College* (rev. ed., Charleston: Walker, Evans, and Cogswell, 1873), vii.

17. *Appleton's Cyclopedia of American Biography* (New York: D. Appleton and Co., 1888); and Dumas Malone and Allen Johnson, eds., *Dictionary of American Biography* (New York: C. Scribner's Sons, 1918).

18. *Appleton's Cyclopedia*, 1888; Malone and Johnson, eds., *Dictionary of American Biography*, 1918.

19. Edwin Luther Green, *A History of the University of South Carolina* (Columbia: The State Co., 1916), 415–16.

20. Scott, "When Negroes Attended."

21. Clippings in Brewer Scrapbook.

22. Scott, "When Negroes Attended."

23. See entries under folders for Cornelius C. Scott, George W. Clinton, William Henry Heard, and Isaac L. Purcell in Whitefield McKinlay Papers, Carter Godwin Woodson Collection.

24. "Annoyance of 1875," undated clipping, USC Records; "Malicious Mischief," undated clipping in Brewer Scrapbook.

25. Allen W. Trelease, *White Terror: The Ku Klux Klan and Southern Reconstruction* (New York: Harper and Row, 1971), 349–80.

26. USC Records, 1873–77.

27. "Report to the Chairman of the Faculty," 1877, USC Records.

28. Carol Bleser, *The Promised Land: The History of the South Carolina Land Commission* (Columbia: University of South Carolina Press, 1965), 77.

29. "Report to the Chairman of the Faculty," 1871, USC Records.

30. *Catalogue of the University of South Carolina* (Columbia: University of South Carolina, 1876).

31. Scott, "When Negroes Attended."

32. Ibid.

33. Walter L. Williams, "Black American Attitudes Toward Emigration to Africa, 1877–1900," MA thesis, University of North Carolina, Chapel Hill, 1972, 88–123, 219–25.

34. George Brown Tindall, *South Carolina Negroes, 1877–1900* (Columbia: University of South Carolina Press, 1952).

35. Kellogg, *NAACP.*

36. Booker Taliafero Washington Folders, 1904–8, Whitefield McKinlay Papers, Carter Godwin Woodson Collection.

37. Ibid.

38. Whitefield McKinlay Papers, 1900–1918, Carter Godwin Woodson Collection.

THE POLITICS OF RECONSTRUCTION

WADE HAMPTON AND THE RISE OF ONE-PARTY RACIAL ORTHODOXY IN SOUTH CAROLINA

(1977)

Richard Mark Gergel

The Redemption Era in South Carolina politics, extending from the end of Reconstruction in 1876 to the rise of Tillmanism in 1890, has been remembered as a period of stability under the moderate patrician leadership of Wade Hampton. While occasional historians have asserted a reservation or two about the quality of Hampton's leadership, a general consensus has been achieved to the effect that white South Carolinians were able to restore their political supremacy while providing opportunities for black participation and involvement in the exercise of power. This traditional view, however, falls impressively short of a reasonable characterization of race relations in South Carolina. Indeed, it would be more precise to say that white Democratic control of the government was attained through a violent overthrow of the Republican Party. Moreover, once the Hampton-led Democrats gained power, they immediately initiated efforts to make their ascendancy permanent. In the process, they amended the election laws so as to eliminate reasonable supervision of the polls by impartial or Republican observers, decreased dramatically the number of polling places in majority black districts, employed persistent policies to siphon off much of the local Republican leadership, and developed a unique "tissue paper" mode of ballot box stuffing to neutralize the state's black majority of voters. These methods were systematic, purposeful, and conclusively effective. Wade Hampton's role was central.[1]

The mystique of patrician moderation, long a cornerstone of southern historiography, today constitutes a secure part of a received cultural tradition. The emphasis on the racially moderate or "tolerant" approach of the southern upper class has been contrasted in this tradition with the racism of the "redneck." A close examination reveals that such distinctions are not particularly helpful in understanding the biracial politics of South Carolina of the late 1870s. There exists a need to focus less upon the nuances in the political rhetoric and manners of white politicians and more on the effects of their acts on southern blacks. But before this matter may be pursued, the towering political presence of Hampton, the very symbol of southern racial civility, needs to be carefully reviewed.

Wade Hampton III, a scion of one of nineteenth-century America's great family fortunes, spent the first half of his life managing his vast holdings of prime cotton land and slaves. As secessionist passions grew throughout the South in late 1859, Hampton took his first step into the limelight by publicly attacking a proposal to reopen the African slave trade, then before the South Carolina General Assembly. Hampton realized that the drift toward secession and eventual war with the Union could in the long run only damage the interests of his class, and his speech was designed to cool secessionist tensions in the South while placating abolitionist feelings in the North. Though his ideas were warmly received in the North, Hampton was bitterly denounced throughout the South. Once the war began, however, Hampton immediately established and financed his own military unit, and eventually rose to the rank of lieutenant general in the Confederate Army.[2]

Rising from the war a local hero, Hampton quickly plunged into the uncertain politics of postwar South Carolina. At the time, some Radical congressmen were seriously discussing universal male suffrage as a method of insuring the continued viability of the Republican Party once the nation was reunited. Hampton realized that a moderate policy of suffrage, with an educational qualification, would weaken the Radical plan while not significantly affecting the traditional balance of power in South Carolina. He believed that the former slaves would follow the dictates of their previous masters, and thereby reinforce the political base of the aristocracy. Instead of following Hampton, however, the South Carolina General Assembly passed one of the South's most punitive Black Codes, which pushed the U.S. Congress toward universal suffrage. As the Radical-sponsored Reconstruction Acts neared approval in the national Congress, Hampton vigorously opposed them, both as chairman of the State Democratic Executive Committee and as a private citizen.[3]

Once the Reconstruction methods became law, however, Hampton encouraged his fellow South Carolinians to accept them, and began making efforts to "direct the negro vote." Hampton believed it was absolutely necessary to control the black vote because "now we are fighting for bread and life, and a desperate battle we are waging. . . . The revolution is not ended."[4]

Events moved too quickly for Hampton and his followers. The Republican Party was able to consolidate the state's black majority into the most potent political force in South Carolina. The Republican-controlled State Constitutional Convention drew up a new constitution in 1868 that provided for universal male suffrage, guaranteed civil rights for all, and created a public educational system. As State Democratic Executive Committee chairman, Hampton and several others sent a bitter note to Congress denouncing the new constitution. They claimed the result of the new document would be that "Intelligence, virtue, and patriotism are to give place, in all elections, to ignorance, stupidity, and vice. The superior race is to be made subservient to the inferior." Hampton and the others concluded that they would continue to fight for the white people of the state "until we have regained the heritage of political control handed down to us by our honored ancestry."[5]

As the Republicans firmly settled into control of the South Carolina government, Hampton, now virtually impoverished, was forced to remove himself from active participation in public affairs and to dedicate his energies to bankruptcy proceedings instituted against him in three states. Meanwhile, a small significant core of whites—led by generals Martin Whitherspoon Gary and M. C. Butler and participating in such organizations as the Democratic Party and the Taxpayer's League—never gave up hope of returning to power, even in the heyday of Radical rule. Their moment came in 1876, and was signaled by the tumultuous overthrow of the Republican Party by whites in Mississippi the previous year. Gary, Butler, and their associates decided that the Mississippi model proved the utility of a judicious use of fraud, violence, and intimidation. Like a military tactician, Gary began planning the campaign of '76.

Gary's proposal, which eventually came to be known variously as the "Mississippi Plan" and "Edgefield Plan," sought to unite the state's white minority and destroy the political organization of the black community. The plan called for the creation of Democratic Military Clubs "armed with rifles and pistols and such other arms as they may command." It required that each Democrat control the vote of one black "by intimidation, purchase, [or] keeping him away . . ."; recommended that Democrats disrupt all Republican meetings and demand "division of time"; and outlined a strategy for ballot-box stuffing in case the need arose. Gary invited political allies to his Edgefield County home and shared with them his proposal.[6]

The Gary system was not easily implemented, for black political rights were guaranteed in law and subject to specific protection through federal intervention. As a result, South Carolina Redeemers faced the tactical need to run a campaign of terror and fraud while at the same time publicly appearing to be participating in a legitimate political process. The Democrats associated with the "Edgefield Plan" were alert to the danger of the reinstitution of federal military rule should a violent uprising by whites appear to be taking place. It was in meeting this latter hazard that Wade Hampton was to prove himself most useful to the cause of Redemption.

In June of 1876, Hampton visited the state from his home in Mississippi. Appreciating the personal dimension that he could add to the campaign, Gary explained his plan to Hampton and asked him if he would accept the Democratic nomination for governor. Hampton readily accepted the offer.

The canvass was designed on two levels—one orchestrated by Hampton and the other by Gary—to deal with the dual problems of the campaign's image in the North and the permanent threat to Democratic control posed by the state's overwhelming black majority. Visible on one level was the pageantry of Hampton's tour across the state, described by one supporter as a campaign to "arouse the white population to secession or nullification madness." A corollary purpose, made necessary by the sheer numerical realities of race, centered on bringing as many black voters as possible into the Democracy. Moderate statements on the race issue by Hampton constituted the cornerstone of this latter approach. Meanwhile, Gary and Butler implemented a campaign of terror and intimidation designed either to push black voters into the Democratic column or to keep them home on election day. The Democratic canvass closely followed Gary's original plan. The most prominent ingredient consisted of 290 rifle clubs with 18,000 members. This force succeeded in massively disrupting the Republican campaign effort. Violence, intimidation, and even random murders were commonplace in the final weeks of the campaign.[7]

Election day was characterized by Democratic intimidation, repeat voting, and ballot-box stuffing. On the face of the returns Hampton defeated incumbent Republican Governor Chamberlain 92,261 to 91,127. Two formerly Republican counties, Laurens and Edgefield (Gary's home), gave Hampton heavy majorities, but only by voting 5,000 more men than lived in the two counties. Both parties contested various county results, and each claimed victory. A monumental struggle promptly ensued, and eventually dual governments were proclaimed, complete with two governors and two legislatures. The five-month battle for legitimacy was finally won in April 1877 by Hampton and the Democrats as part of the Compromise of 1877.[8]

Terror had brought white rule, but scarcely white hegemony—as convincingly demonstrated by the close balance of Democratic and Republican Party strength implicit in the returns of 1876. Thus a crucial task remained unaddressed: if white redemption was to be permanently inculcated into the political culture of South Carolina, this relative balance of party strength had to be fundamentally altered.

The struggle for power by the Democrats therefore moved from the terrain of electoral politics to the more complex level of negotiation and internal infighting. Gary's control of the situation, so visibly evident during the canvass itself, dwindled as Hampton asserted his leadership over the movement. Gary was on the outside as Hampton consolidated his hold on the state political apparatus, while at the same time negotiating secretly with Rutherford B. Hayes. Only one of many actors in the electoral campaign, Hampton moved his government into the State House in April of 1877 with full control over the Redemption movement.

Once in office, the Hamptonians moved quickly to consolidate their executive and legislative power. First, Hampton demanded the resignation of all legally elected Republican state officials and fortified the edict by ordering that their offices be padlocked. The governor contended that the Republicans had won their elections by fraud. All factions understood that the pro-Democratic Supreme Court would uphold the governor's order, and the resignations were soon forthcoming.[9]

Simultaneously, the Hamptonians moved to alter the balance of power in the House. Originally, sixty Republicans had won election to the House in 1876, compared to sixty-four Democrats. The Democratically controlled House agreed to accept the election of only thirty-seven of the Republican representatives, unseating twenty-three others. The greatest source of the purging was the seventeen-member Republican delegation from Charleston, whose seats "were arbitrarily declared vacant."[10]

To further weaken Republican influence, Hampton carefully used his patronage power to bring various opposition leaders into the Democratic fold. Working in close conjunction with local legislative delegations, Hampton co-opted many Republican officials, black and white, by appointing and reappointing them to various patronage positions. Given the acute agricultural depression in the South in 1877, the power of local patronage can scarcely be underestimated.

The Hampton patronage policy was aimed primarily at counties with black majorities and strong Republican organizations. For instance, Georgetown County, which was 85 percent black, had ten blacks selected out of thirty-seven appointments during Hampton's gubernatorial term. On the other hand, Greenville, with a black population of 33 percent, had just one black selected out of fifty-one county appointees. In some counties there appeared to be a conscious effort to reappoint the sitting Republican officials, as a method of co-opting the local leadership. Further, a substantial portion of the appointments were timed to coincide with either the five-month period in which the Hampton and Chamberlain governments were struggling for power or during the final months before Hampton's 1878 reelection bid. It is important to note that after 1878 when the Republican Party was no longer a political force in the state the Democrats were far less generous with their patronage positions.[11]

Another technique used by the Hamptonians to undercut local Republican strength was the nomination of black Democrats for offices in overwhelmingly majority black counties. This policy was pushed strongly by Hampton, particularly in the nomination of three black Democrats in a special election in Charleston in 1877. Between 1876 and 1890 at least one, and as many as six, black Democrats sat in the South Carolina House, all representing counties with black votes exceeding 65 percent.[12]

Though the purging of Republican executive and legislative officeholders and the shrewd utilization of patronage assured the Democrats of firm control over state government for the moment, a truly permanent hegemony required fundamental manipulation of the electoral process to neutralize the voting power of the state's substantial black majority. The centerpiece of the Democrats' strategy was a bill introduced by Senator Gary that decreased the number of voting precincts in low-country counties—with heavy black majorities—and separated the legal status of federal and state election procedures. In the process the "low road" and "high road" approaches of Gary and Hampton in 1876 were combined in a single concrete and decisive effort at suffrage restriction in 1878.

The decrease in the number of polling places in areas of concentrated Republican strength was intended to force voters to walk ten to twenty-five miles to cast their ballots. No precincts were left in thickly populated black townships, and in some counties polling places were so dramatically decreased that it was impossible for all the blacks to vote within the time allotted on election day. The second section of the Gary bill, calling for separate places for federal and state boxes, was designed to prevent federal supervisors from observing balloting procedures for state offices. Thus, the supervisors would be able to report on fraud only in regard to federal elections. The Gary bill sailed through the House and Senate in votes that went almost entirely along party lines. On March 22, 1878, Governor Hampton signed the act into law.[13]

To culminate the Redeemer's electoral "reconstruction," Hampton moved forcefully to prevent any Republican supervision of balloting procedures. First, in contravention of state law, Hampton refused to appoint, with a few exceptions, Republicans to county boards of canvassers. In their stead, the governor appointed pliant black Democrats. The boards were responsible for both supervision of the election returns and selection of poll managers. To be assured that the Redeemers' strategy of an unsupervised ballot was extended all the way down to the precinct level, State Democratic Party Chairman John Kennedy instructed his county chairmen, by secret memorandum, to inform their boards of canvassers to "appoint *proper* managers—all *Democrats*" (emphasis in the original).[14]

As the election of 1878 neared, Hampton reached the zenith of his power. Fully in control both of his party and of the state's electoral machinery, Hampton was prepared to begin his final campaign to destroy the Republican Party as a significant political force. Since his dubious victory of 1876, the governor had been able to siphon off a significant portion of the Republican leadership, while neutralizing much of the remaining threat through suffrage law alterations. At the Democrats' state convention in July 1878, Hampton was renominated and the moderate platform of 1876 was reconfirmed. Hampton and other party leaders were emphatic on their point of calling both races to the Democratic fold.

But beyond the public fanfare of good faith and fair play, the Democrats renewed their low-road efforts once again. In late August, State Democratic Party Chairman Kennedy sent a secret memorandum to his local chairmen outlining the campaign of 1878. He urged each chairman to run an "aggressive, but not violent" campaign that included "divisions of time" at all Republican meetings. Kennedy told the chairmen to have "a great show of men on horseback" and other such actions "as will impress the minds of our opponents with our settled and unwavering determination to carry the election." As in Gary's 1876 plan, each white Democrat was instructed to control the vote of one black, and in counties where it was "judicious" chairmen were urged to enroll Negroes as members. In regard to ballot-box stuffing, Kennedy instructed the local chairmen to do anything "that will swell our vote," but urged them to "try to stop all boasting of counting in. Let our motto be 'Still waters run deep.'" As mentioned earlier, Kennedy instructed all chairmen to make sure only Democrats were appointed as polling officials. Finally, Kennedy ordered the chairmen to destroy his letter, and to "leave nothing undone to carry your county."[15]

Meanwhile, the Republican Party, torn by dissension, weakened by Hampton's patronage policies, fearful of Democratic violence, and powerless to avert the frauds of the Party of Redemption, began its organizing effort for the campaign by deciding not to nominate a statewide ticket. The party, which had polled over ninety thousand votes just two years earlier, was in August 1878 a weakened structure ready to crumble. The Republican platform, the convention's only channel for its anger and frustration after two years of Hampton rule, constituted a scathing attack upon the Redemption government. It castigated the Democrats for the violence and frauds of the 1876 campaign and the ensuing special elections; attacked the Redeemers for their policy of "division of time," which disrupted the Republican canvass because of the fear of violence; accused the Democrats of unseating rightfully elected Republicans to swell the ranks of the dominant party; and criticized the Hamptonian legislature for passing the electoral law changes which decreased the number of precincts in predominantly Republican areas. Instead of pursuing state offices, the Republican Party of South Carolina—in a desperate effort to avoid complete destruction—decided to concentrate only on its local races.[16]

Hampton's campaign of 1878 was, therefore, no mere electoral canvass—it was an effort to end for all time the meaningful participation of the Republican Party in the democratic process of South Carolina government. Hampton's 1876 tone, full of moderation and conciliation, shifted in 1878. First, he declared that because of the continued presence of the Republican Party, South Carolinians were "not yet free." Drawing the parameters of the political terrain very narrowly, Hampton argued that there was no place in the Palmetto State's politics for any white man except in the Democratic Party. With ominous clarity, Hampton informed blacks that any race which "placed itself in opposition [to the white race] . . . must give way before the advancing tide and die out as the Indians have done. . . . It is the law of God." In another speech, Hampton firmly warned blacks that if they continued, what he called, "drawing the color line," then "they would be drawing it for their own destruction." The governor offered blacks an end to the violence and intimidation if they would join the Democratic Party. As the Hampton organ, the *Charleston News and Courier,* put the options: "if the negro does not vote with the Democratic Party, he must not vote at all."[17]

In conjunction with the strict "Democratic only" campaign of Hampton, a systematic strategy of violence and intimidation was initiated, at least in part, by State Adjutant General Moise. Instead of organizing into semisecret rifle clubs, the Democratic military clubs were made part of the state militia. Indeed, the local militias were ordered to meet to organize at the same times and places as the Democratic county ratification conventions. A school teacher in Beaufort County described the canvass: "political times are simply frightful. Men are shot at, hounded down, trapped, and held to [*sic*] certain meetings are over, and intimidated in every way possible." A Democratic newspaper in the same county stated: "In order to prevent our county falling into such hands [the Republican Party], any measures that will accomplish the end will be justifiable, *however wicked* they might be in other communities" (emphasis in the original).[18]

With virtually no supervision at the polls, election day provided the Democrats with the opportunity to demonstrate the utility of the new legal sanctions for ballot-box stuffing. A state law provided that when the total ballots cast at any box exceeded the number of electors recorded as voting, then the excess ballots would be removed. The law stated that poll managers—now almost all Democrats—would reach into the ballot box, and blindfolded, remove excess votes. The Democrats printed up prior to the election tissue-thin ballots, which were far smaller and of a different texture than the standard paper ballots. Democrats, in preparing to vote, would, as one eyewitness described: "fold as many (tissue ballots) as they saw fit in a regular ballot, and passing the latter into the narrow aperture of the padlocked tinbox, a quick tap, as it rested in the slit, drove it and dislodged the little ballots, which then had the appearance of having been legally cast."[19]

Once the polls were closed and the votes were counted, the managers would place the ballots back into the boxes and withdraw the excess. In "correcting" this excess vote, the blindfolded judges, guided by the tissue ballots, demonstrated a remarkable ability to remove only Republican ballots. The widespread use of this technique would, according to the *New York Times,* "stagger belief."

In the Second Congressional District, where no Republican served as an election official, nine out of every ten boxes had an "overflow." One precinct had an excess vote of over 2,500.[20]

The result was a decisive victory for the Democrats. The balance of power, originally very close in 1876—78 Republicans in the General Assembly compared to 79 Democrats—shifted to 150 Democrats and only 8 Republicans in 1878. At the local level, where the nearly 60 percent black majority apparently stayed loyal to the Republican Party, the Democrats managed to win 19,000 more votes than the Republicans.[21]

Hampton readily conceded the existence of terror and fraud in his 1878 election, blaming the violence on "the terrible moral obliquity visited on our people by Radical rule." On the floor of the United States Senate he again acknowledged the illegal activities, but defended the actions of his campaign by contending that "it was a case where the very civilization, the property, the life of the State itself, were involved."[22]

The 1878 election resulted in the utter destruction of the Republican Party in South Carolina. The violence, the ballot-box stuffing, the manipulation of election laws, and the abandonment of the state organization by the national party all contributed to its demise. The Republican Party continued to meet, biennially limping along as a patronage clique, but never ran another major race in South Carolina as a party that carried the hopes of the freedmen.[23]

The canvass of 1878 indicated that a thoroughly united white community, left to its own devices and undisturbed by the possibility of federal intervention, could subvert the voting power of the state's black majority with considerable effectiveness. The chapter of black aspiration was seemingly closed—certainly as long as whites were content to vote en masse under patrician leadership. But the sheer poverty of the state insured that the great mass of the white electorate would someday strive to express its own aspirations. Such a schism within Democratic ranks would inevitably push the white dissenters into a coalition with their impoverished black neighbors. When this time came—with the Greenbacker movement in 1882 and the agrarian insurgency of the early 1890s—the Democrats moved step-by-step toward permanent legal disenfranchisement.

Thus, Hamptonian politics provided the most significant contribution to the political culture of South Carolina between the Civil War and the civil rights movement. By defining the ends and offering the means to achieve them, Wade Hampton gave to South Carolina the one-party racial orthodoxy that shaped the politics of the state for the next nine decades.[24]

NOTES

1. The near-Olympian moral position achieved by southern conservatives as a result of historical literature growing out of the mature Dunning tradition of Reconstruction came under telling assault in a pioneering essay by C. Vann Woodward, "Bourbonism in Georgia," *North Carolina Historical Review* 16 (January 1939): 23–35, written in 1938. Woodward's theme has been subsequently pursued by Joel Williamson, *After Slavery: The Negro in South Carolina During Reconstruction, 1861–1877* (Chapel Hill: University of North Carolina Press, 1965); Joel Williamson, *Origins of Segregation* (Lexington, Mass.: D. C. Heath, 1968); and to a lesser extent, by Francis Simpkins in his studies of Pitchfork Ben Tillman. The reputation of Wade Hampton—one of the primary bases of the historical assumption about "patrician moderation"—has survived these revisionist studies. Modern scholarship necessarily builds upon the pioneering work of these men.

2. G. G. Vest, "A Senator of Two Republics," *Saturday Evening Post*, February 20, 1904, 8; David Duncan Wallace, *The History of South Carolina* (New York: American Historical Association, 1934), vol. 3: 158; Alexander K. McClune, *Recollections of Half a Century* (Salem, Mass.: Salem Press Co., 1902), 407; William Arthur Sheppard, *Red Shirts Remembered* (Atlanta: Ruralist Press, Inc., 1940), 85–88.

3. W. E. B. DuBois, *Black Reconstruction* (New York: Harcourt, Brace and Co., 1935), 412; Wallace, *History of South Carolina* 3: 237, 254–55; Alfred M. Waddell, "An Address Delivered to the Colored People By Their Request at the Wilmington Theatre, July 26, 1865" (Wilmington: Daily Wilmington Herald Office, 1865), 3–11. Hampton sent a letter to Waddell in 1865 informing him that the Wilmington speech was an exact statement of his feelings. Letter in Alfred M. Waddell Papers, Southern Historical Collection, Wilson Library, University of North Carolina at Chapel Hill.

4. Letter from Wade Hampton, March 31, 1867. Wade Hampton Papers, South Caroliniana Library, University of South Carolina.

5. Wade Hampton and Others, *The Respectful Remonstrance on Behalf of the White People of South Carolina, Against the Constitution of the Late Convention of the State, Now Submitted to Congress for Ratification* (Columbia: Phoenix Book and Job Power Press, 1868), 6, 12. For a background on Republican rule in South Carolina during Reconstruction, see Joel Williamson, *After Slavery: The Negro in South Carolina During Reconstruction, 1861–1877* (Chapel Hill: University of North Carolina Press, 1965); Peggy Lamson, *The Glorious Failure: Black Congressman Robert Elliott and Reconstruction in South Carolina* (New York: W. W. Norton Co., 1963); Henry Allen Bullock, *A History of Negro Education in the South* (Cambridge, Mass.: Harvard University Press, 1967), 56.

6. Election Plan, 1876, Martin W. Gary Papers, South Caroliniana Library, University of South Carolina. "Division of Time," was a Democratic campaign technique in which armed men on horseback would attend Republican rallies and demand an equal portion of the speaking time, in an effort to intimidate the attendants.

7. Paul Leland Haworth, *The Hayes-Tilden Disputed Presidential Election of 1876* (Cleveland: Burrows Brothers Co., 1906), 136; Hampton Jarrell, *Wade Hampton and the Negro: The Road Not Taken* (Columbia: University of South Carolina Press, 1949), 59–60; Francis B. Simkins and Robert Hilliard Woody, *South Carolina During Reconstruction* (Chapel Hill: University of North Carolina Press, 1932), 335; "The Political Condition of South Carolina" *Atlantic Monthly* 39 (February 1877): 177–94, reprinted in John H. Moore, ed., *When South Carolina Was an Armed Camp: The Reconstruction Essays of Belton O'Neall Townsend*

(Charleston: Home House Press, 2013), 49–73; Lamson, *Glorious Failure,* 245; Edward Maxwell, "Hampton's Campaign in South Carolina," *South Atlantic,* 1878, 422; *Appletons Annual Cyclopedia* (New York: D. Appleton and Co., 1886), vol. 16: 720; "South Carolina in 1876: Testimony as to the Denial of the Elective Franchise in South Carolina at the of South Carolina," *Atlantic Monthly,* 1877, 177–94; Lamson, *Glorious Failure,* 245; Edward Maxwell, "Hampton's Campaign in South Carolina," *South Atlantic,* 1878, 422; *Appletons Annual Cyclopedia* (New York: D. Appleton and Co., 1886), vol. 16: 720; *South Carolina in 1876: Testimony as to the Denial of the Elective Franchise in South Carolina at the Elections of 1875 and 1876 Taken under the Resolution of the Senate of December 5, 1876* (Washington: Government Printing Office, 1877), 233; and Francis B. Simkins, "The Election of 1876 in South Carolina," *South Atlantic Quarterly* 21 (1922): 336.

8. Haworth, *Hayes-Tilden Disputed Presidential Election,* 145; *South Carolina in 1876,* 578; Lamson, *Glorious Failure,* 265; and C. Vann Woodward, *Reunion and Reaction* (Boston: Little Brown and Co., 1951), 19, 32, 147, 219–20.

9. *New York Times,* April 15, 1877. "A South Carolinian," "The Result in South Carolina," *Atlantic Monthly,* January 1878, 3. George Brown Tindall, *South Carolina Negroes, 1877–1900* (Columbia: University of South Carolina Press, 1952), 17. Included among the Republican resignations were those of Lt. Governor R. H. Gleaver, Attorney General Robert Brown Elliott, and Secretary of State Henry E. Hayne.

10. Tindall, *South Carolina Negroes,* 16–17; *New York Times,* June 4, 1877; *Charleston News and Courier,* May 31, June 1, 1877. As a result of the refusal to seat the Charleston delegation, a special election was held and through massive ballot-box stuffing and terror, the Democrats overcame a previous Republican majority of 6,000 votes. Hampton later admitted that the Democrats stuffed as many as 5,000 ballots in that special election. *Congressional Record,* 46th Cong., 2nd Session, 3755.

11. Hampton Appointment Book and Subject File, South Carolina Department of Archives and History, Columbia; William J. Cooper, *The Conservative Regime* (Baltimore: Johns Hopkins Press, 1968), 34, 88. Hampton appointed 117 blacks to positions out of a total of 1,400 selections.

12. Tindall, *South Carolina Negroes,* 23; Hampton Subject File, South Carolina Department of Archives and History, Columbia.

13. *Journal of the Senate of the General Assembly of the State of South Carolina, 1877–78,* 20; *New York Times,* October 26, 1878; Wallace, *South Carolina History* 3: 325; Tindall, *South Carolina Negroes,* 68; Cooper, *Conservative Regime,* 94; Alruthens Ambush Taylor, *The Negro in South Carolina During Reconstruction* (Washington: Association for the Study of Negro Life and History, 1924), 290–91; J. Morgan Kousser, *The Shaping of Southern Politics* (New Haven, Conn.: Yale University Press, 1974), 50; and James Welch Patton, "The Republican Party in South Carolina, 1876–1895," *Essays in Southern History,* ed. Melvin Fletcher Green (Chapel Hill: University of North Carolina Press, 1949), 103. The significant role of election laws is not to be underestimated. J. Morgan Krousser, says: "Election laws and procedures did, in themselves, have very substantial impacts on both the scope of political participation and the mode of political activity in the South," 5.

14. *New York Times,* October 26, November 16, 1878; Patton, "Republican Party in South Carolina," 103; Robert Smalls, "Election Methods in the South," *North American Review* 151, no. 408 (November 1890): 594; letter from John D. Kennedy to McCall, Marlboro County Democratic Chairman, August 23, 1878, McCall Papers, South Caroliniana Library, University of South Carolina. As an example of Hampton's policy of circumventing the requirement that he appoint Republicans to boards of canvassers, the governor

appointed a black in Horry County as the minority representative, even though he was running as a Democrat for office in that very election.

15. *News and Courier,* July 29, 1878; *New York Times,* October 18, 1878; Tindall, *South Carolina Negroes,* 29; and letter from Kennedy to McCall, McCall Papers, South Caroliniana Library, University of South Carolina.

16. *News and Courier,* August 6, 9, 1878; Tindall, *South Carolina Negroes,* 31–32.

17. *New York Times,* April 8, August 24, September 27 (quoting the *News and Courier*), October 31, 1878; *News and Courier,* October 3, 1878; Cooper, *Conservative Regime,* 96.

18. *New York Times,* October 27, 1878; Rupert S. Holland, ed., *Letter and Diary of Laura M. Towne* (Cambridge, Mass.: Riverside Press, 1912), 288–89.

19. Edward Hogan, "South Carolina Today," *International Review,* February 1880, 114; Patton, *Republican Party in South Carolina,* 108–9.

20. *New York Times,* November 8, 11, 29, 1878; Cooper, *Conservative Regime,* 94–95. The heavy reliance on the *New York Times* is due to the absence of any local opposition press. The *New York Times* had a correspondent in South Carolina during the election.

21. *New York Times,* November 15, 30, 1878; Tindall, *South Carolina Negroes,* 41. The results from South Carolina and several other southern states were so obviously fraudulent that they forced President Hayes to admit that his "reconciliation policy" was "a failure." Stanley Hirshon, *Farewell to the Bloody Shirt* (Bloomington: University of Indiana Press, 1967), 49–50.

22. *Yorkville Enquirer,* January 23, 1879; *Congressional Record,* 47th Congress, Special Session, 373.

23. Patton, *Republican Party in South Carolina,* 95–111; Tindall, *South Carolina Negroes,* 43–44.

24. Tindall, *South Carolina Negroes,* 50–51; Taylor, *The Negro in South Carolina,* 292; Patton, *Republican Party In South Carolina,* 104–6; Kousser, *Shaping of Southern Politics,* 17–18, 27, 49, 92; *New York Times,* January 2, 1882; Harold Stine, "The Agrarian Revolt in South Carolina: Ben Tillman and the Farmer's Alliance," senior honors thesis, Duke University, 1974. See also Lawrence Goodwyn's definitive work, *Democratic Promise: The Populist Moment in America* (New York: Oxford University Press, 1976).

THE SOUTH CAROLINA CONSTITUTION OF 1865 AS A DEMOCRATIC DOCUMENT

(1942)

John Harold Wolfe

A recent and rather commendable development in the historiography of Reconstruction is the belated consideration of the positive contributions of the so-called Radical regimes in the various southern states. However, in revealing much that hitherto has been overlooked, many of the present-day historians retain the great weakness which marred the work of their predecessors—they do not give a complete or entirely accurate picture. To present such a picture is indeed very difficult when one is dealing with only a short period. Nevertheless, even an approach to a scientific interpretation cannot be reached unless the writer carefully weighs the positive contributions of both provisional and Radical Reconstruction. In this brief study an attempt is made to fill out the picture in regard to a particular phase of provisional Reconstruction in one of the states. In spite of the fruitful research of scores of capable students, many similar studies remain to be done before the complete story can be told.

That one of the purposes of the South Carolina Constitutional Convention of 1868 was to democratize the government of the state is well known, but that the convention of 1865 had gone far toward achieving that result generally has been overlooked. The democratization which was accomplished in 1865 resulted partly from the demands of South Carolinians and partly from the insistence of the president of the United States that a "republican form of government" be established.

Even though white manhood suffrage had existed since 1810, such practices as property qualifications for holding office, the control of the senate by the lower part of the state through the parish system, and the election of the governor, the presidential electors, and most of the other officials by the legislature made South Carolina virtually a political oligarchy. In fact, the statement of a northern newspaper reporter who attended the convention of 1865 that "the longings of South Carolina are essentially monarchical" and that even many of the common people "would readily accept the creation of orders of nobility," while obviously exaggerated, may have seemed true to an outsider.[1]

Aware of these undemocratic features, Andrew Johnson suggested that certain changes be made before South Carolina ask for the restoration of local civil authority.[2] With the support of the president, the provisional governor, and some of the delegates from the lower part of the state, the people of the upcountry hoped that at last they would obtain the constitutional modifications for which they had been striving so long. Earlier changes had been prevented largely by the refusal of the low country–controlled senate to permit the calling of the convention which probably would make the more populous upcountry dominant in both houses of the legislature and provide more directly democratic methods of choosing other state officials. That such a convention must have met eventually is undoubtedly true, but that it assembled in 1865 is to be accounted for mainly by the demand of the president of the United States rather than by the final acquiescence of the low country. However, before the delegates reached Columbia it was generally agreed that the long delayed reorganization now would take place and that there would be as much interest in solving local problems as in meeting federal demands.[3]

In a transitional period, either the evolutionary or the revolutionary process may be followed. The preference of both President Johnson and most South Carolinians in 1865 was the former. But would the state be permitted to adjust herself gradually and of her own accord to the new conditions? Because of the part she had played in the secession movement, there was more outside interest in her conduct than in that of any other southern state. It was soon evident that the Radicals desired punishment and a period of probation. Obviously the *New York Tribune* did not trust South Carolina.

> This state, having been the first and most rampant in rebellion, will probably be the last to receive the benefits of reconstruction. All other Southern States will in a short time be under civil rule again, while South Carolina will be suffered to undergo privation a year or two before she can be relieved of military domination. That is the proper government for her at the present time; for it is a question whether a sufficient number of loyal and trustworthy white natives can be found in that State to fill the civil offices. Therefore the Palmetto State will probably have to be content for the present with military rule.[4]

In the meantime, however, the people of South Carolina were accepting the results of the war quietly. A traveler passing through the state in July wrote that

"Not one among the marvellous events of the war seems to me more marvellous than the almost perfect tranquility into which South Carolina has returned."[5] Some of those most interested in the future of the state feared that the situation might best be described as discouragement or even apathy instead of mere quietness.[6] In spite of all his searching, Sidney Andrews could find no evidence that anyone desired to continue the war.[7] But the attitude of repentance demanded by the Radicals seemed entirely lacking. When Perry, shortly before his appointment as provisional governor, expressed regret over secession and the war his tone was severely criticized by the northern press. Having opened his remarks with the statement that "This meeting of the citizens of Greenville is one of deep humiliation and sorrow," he later attributed the existing deplorable conditions in the southern states to the folly of secession. "Mr. Chairman, I will here frankly say, as I have often said during the past four years, that there was not a man in the United States who more deeply regretted the secession of the Southern States than I did at the beginning of the revolution. There is not now in the Southern States anyone who feels more bitterly the humiliation and degradation of going back into the Union than I do. Still, I know that I shall be more prosperous and happy in the Union than out of it."

These words and the comparison of Lincoln and Johnson to the decided advantage of the latter were more than the Radicals could stand.[8] Perry's opposition to nullification in 1832 and to secession in 1860, his refusal to leave the Democratic Convention in the latter year, and his undisguised love for the Union were all ignored. The *New York Tribune* declared that "If there be in South Carolina no better timber than this wherefrom to fashion a provisional governor, we think the manufacture might have been wisely postponed. . . . From the beginning to the end of this harangue there is no recognition of that large body of the people of South Carolina who are not humiliated."[9]

Other northern periodicals used a similar tone, and even the *New York Times* had an editorial on the danger of too much talking.[10] When he was in Washington a little later, Perry explained to the president and several members of his cabinet the circumstances under which he had made the speech. Johnson and Seward readily understood, but at the request of the former he gave an explanatory statement to the newspapers.[11] However, the *New York Tribune* then retorted that if it was necessary to speak in that manner, South Carolina was not ready for civil rule.[12]

The campaign for seats in the convention was free from spectacular events. The provisional governor and other leaders were very desirous that nothing happen which might interfere with early restoration. At least one prominent candidate who was known to oppose the abolition of slavery and would so vote if elected was persuaded to withdraw from the race.[13] The election passed off quietly, and in many places the number voting was smaller than normal.[14] One reason given for the small vote cast was the revocation by military order of the right of magistrates to give the oath of amnesty. The right was restored by the president, but too late for the people generally, in some districts, to avail themselves of the information.[15] Governor Perry, seconded by the press of the state, declared that the convention was composed of the "ablest, wisest and most distinguished men in South Carolina . . . that no political assemblage in South Carolina had ever surpassed it in virtue, intelligence and patriotism."[16] Twelve had sat in the secession convention, and most of them had taken part in the war on the side of the Confederacy.[17] There were, of course, the mediocre along with the able. The average age of the delegates seems to have been between forty-five and fifty, with perhaps a dozen young and about the same number of old men.[18]

A few of the individual members deserve mention. James L. Orr had been Speaker of the national House of Representatives, a leader in the secession convention in spite of his Unionist inclinations, and later a member of the Confederate Senate. Francis W. Pickens, a former congressman, had been governor when Fort Sumter had been taken. Alfred Huger had been postmaster of Charleston for many years. Samuel McGowan had been a major-general in the Confederate Army. John Farrow had been a member of the congress at Richmond. The provisional governor's son and secretary was a delegate from Greenville. John A. Inglis, also a leader in the secession convention, was a chancery judge. Franklin J. Moses, of Hebrew descent, formerly an ardent secessionist whose activities had not been limited to South Carolina, had been a member of the State Senate for many years. James P. Boyce was president of the Baptist Theological Seminary in Greenville.

From the beginning of the convention every effort was made, especially by the leaders, to prevent action or word which might embarrass the president in his restoration or reconstruction policy. The delegates chose as permanent president Judge D. L. Wardlaw, a man with a long record of public service from the northwestern part of the state. When one member suggested that the rules of order used in the convention of 1860 might be adopted, James L. Orr quickly remarked that he thought that as little reference as possible to that convention would be desirable. This advice was followed, and a different set of rules was used.[19]

In his message Governor Perry urged the delegates to look to the future instead of "dwelling on the past, and grieving over its errors and misfortunes." Slavery was dead and must be so declared in a new or amended constitution. He recommended that the basis of representation in the senate be changed so that the small, thinly populated low country parishes would no longer be given a voice in the state government unwarranted by their population and property. The extension of manhood suffrage to all freedmen was opposed on the ground that they were not ready for it and that such a step would give to the large landowners "a most undue influence in all elections." Perry called to the attention of the delegates the provisions of the constitutions of several of the northern states requiring the ownership of property for all voters. "If the New York qualification of a freehold for a person of color were adopted in South Carolina very few of the freedmen in this state would ever be able to exercise the right of suffrage. In North Carolina, Tennessee, and perhaps other slaveholding States, free negroes formerly were entitled to vote, but it is understood that they seldom saw fit to exercise the franchise."[20]

The Radicals, who wanted no color distinction, Perry said, forgot "that this is a whiteman's government, and intended for white men only; and that the Supreme Court of the United States has decided that the negro is not an American citizen under the Federal Constitution." He recommended that the governor be elected by popular vote, that he be given more power and an adequate salary, and that the legislature no longer be an "Electoral College for the State."

Perry felt that the great cause of disunion had been removed and that "In less than ten years we shall realize in the loss of slavery a blessing in disguise, to ourselves and our children." South Carolina should set "a bright example of loyalty to the other Southern States" in "cheerfully performing all the obligations to the Federal Government." He was gratified that those most active in the late war were cheerfully accepting its results, and he condemned the less active ones who were "less inclined to acquiesce in the inevitable results of the war."

In general the governor's message was favorably received by the press of the state, but many northern periodicals severely criticized his remark that the Radicals forget "that this is a white man's government." The *New York Tribune* asserted that they might be excused for forgetting what they had never known and warned that "South Carolina must present herself at the door of the House next December with quite other words and more repentant lips if she looks to see those doors fly open to her delegation."[21]

The important problems which finally came before the convention were those connected with the ordinance of secession, slavery, and the reorganization of the state government. On the second day the ordinance of secession was repealed with only three dissenting votes.[22] Again the *New York Tribune* and *Harper's Weekly* registered their disapproval, declaring that annulment and not repeal was demanded.[23] But the *New York Times* had stated on the day the convention met that repeal would satisfy the federal government,[24] and even the Radical correspondent of the *Boston Advertiser* and the *Chicago Tribune*, although he thought that the ordinance should have been annulled, considered the matter of little consequence, since "the whole Confederacy, late and so called, could not coerce her into again taking up arms against the general government."[25]

Because of the part slavery had played in bringing on the war, the question of its abolition was one of the most important problems to be considered. It was generally admitted that the institution was dead, but there was considerable discussion as to whether the convention or the legislature should be the one to declare it so, and how the declaration should be phrased. Evidence shows that many of the delegates expected the slave owners to be compensated.[26] At least eight different emancipation propositions were introduced. Of these, two made no mention of how slavery was being abolished; four stated that it had been done by the federal government in one way or another; and one seemed to imply that the convention was performing the act.[27] The tenor of the speeches and the voting showed that a small majority wished to record the "historical fact" that the federal government had been the emancipating agency, this no doubt being considered a point in favor of compensation.[28] Having decided upon the wording of the provision, the delegates then wrote it into the constitution, with only eight dissenting votes.[29] "So the fact was accomplished beyond all cavil, and South Carolina stepped into the ranks alongside Massachusetts,—joining hands with her to bear aloft the banner of freedom,—bowing to the logic of events rather than that of free speech,—convinced by cannon-balls rather than by arguments, yet, under the circumstances, turning from the things of slavery to things of liberty with commendable grace."[30] The convention seemed agreed that Negroes should be permitted to testify in all cases involving themselves or their property, but it was decided that the matter should be submitted to a special committee to be appointed by the governor, which would report to the legislature.[31]

Negro suffrage as such was not debated.[32] Andrews found that perhaps a score of the delegates had expressed themselves as being opposed to Negro suffrage in any form. He could find only six who definitely showed a more tolerant attitude, but the statement of one of the latter group is particularly interesting: "the idea that South Carolina might, within five years, admit negro suffrage, was not more startling than the idea would have been in 1860, that she would within five years declare slavery abolished."[33]

The basis of representation in the legislature had long been a major point of contention between the upper and lower sections of the state. Under the constitution of 1790 it was possible for the three low country judicial districts of Beaufort, Charleston, and Georgetown, with only one-fifth of the white population, to control the state government. After the amendments were passed in 1808, allowing each district to elect one representative for every sixty-second part of the white population of the state it contained and one for every sixty-second part of the taxes it paid, the upcountry gained control of the House of Representatives. However, the practice of combining districts in choosing senators was discontinued, thereby giving each district one senator and the city of Charleston two. This enabled the low country to retain control of the senate. The upper part of the state had made a substantial gain, but as its population grew it became more dissatisfied with a basis of representation which allowed a "rotten borough" to elect a senator and placed so much emphasis on wealth.[34]

The two sectional groups soon found themselves arrayed against one another in the convention of 1865. Andrews thought that there was as much difference in feeling as would have been the case if one group had come from "this State and the other from Indiana."[35] According to the same writer, George D. Tillman of Edgefield, the most influential upcountry leader, was "a genuine Red Republican in his disregard of what he called 'ancient rights and privileges'" and characterized the parish system as the "Chinese conservatism of Charleston."[36] The only hope of the low country lay in the limitation of the convention to the consideration of only those matters which must be dealt with in order to restore the state to participation in the federal government, but all such attempts failed.[37] Thus the parish system was abolished, and one of the most undemocratic provisions in the constitution of South Carolina was removed.[38]

Having decided to leave the number of members of the house of representatives at 124, the delegates engaged in a lengthy debate as to whether the Negroes—now that they were free—should be counted for representation purposes. This brought up the color issue with all its connections. Seeing a chance to regain control of the lower house of the legislature, the delegates from the low country, where most of the freedmen lived, made a stubborn fight to have the representatives apportioned according to property and the total population, instead of property and the white inhabitants. Andrews thought that the proposed change gained ground with debate, but it finally lost by the narrow vote of 51 to 59. Then the compromise of counting three-fifths of the Negroes was debated until the statement of several leaders that all or none should be represented caused it to be withdrawn. The next step was the reconsideration of the first proposal. In answer to the argument that Negro representation was a step toward Negro voting, Judge Edward Frost asserted that the Negro was a free man, but not ready for the suffrage. He did not think that the freedmen were asking for the voting privilege except when influenced by designing white men. "We must concede that the negro is a free man, having civil rights, having property rights, having the right to be represented in the body politic, and unquestionably destined at no very distant day to have political rights." For a time it seemed that at least the three-fifths compromise would be adopted, but finally some of the leaders who had been supporting the proposal to count all the Negroes stated that reflection had convinced them that the time had not come when they should be admitted into the body politic in any manner. It was then decided that the basis of representation should remain property and white population.[39]

Most of the controversial questions had now been disposed of, but the convention took several other important actions. The property qualification for holding office was abolished, and the practice of keeping similar state offices in

Columbia and Charleston was discontinued.[40] For a long time the more democratic upcountry had insisted that the presidential electors should be chosen by popular vote. Since the federal constitution assigns to the legislature the power to specify the method of choice, the convention could not fix the process of election; but it passed a resolution stating "That the election of electors of President and Vice-President of the United States should be made by the people of the State entitled to exercise the right of suffrage, and that the Provisional Governor be respectfully requested to communicate this resolution to the next Legislature."[41] Another step toward the democratization of the state government was the adoption of the provision that thereafter the governor should be elected by popular vote. He was to serve four years and might not hold office for two consecutive terms. His power was enlarged to the extent that he was given a partial veto which could be overruled by the majority vote of the whole representation in both houses of the legislature.[42] The lieutenant-governor, whose part in the government had been slight indeed, heretofore, was made president of the senate and given a vote in case of even division.[43] In all elections by the legislature the members must vote *viva voce* and their votes were to be recorded in the journals.[44]

White manhood suffrage was retained with the liberalization that emigrants from Europe who met residence requirements and had declared their intentions of becoming citizens were given the franchise. This was expected to encourage immigration.[45] An attempt was made to fix a uniform basis of tax assessment.[46] No provision was made for a referendum on the constitution or any action of the convention.[47]

The democratizing features of the new constitution and the other work of the convention were well summed up by Governor Perry in his final message:

> You have repealed the Ordinance of Secession, abolished slavery, equalized the representation in the Senate, given the election of the governor to the people, expressed your judgment in regard to the election of Presidential Electors by the people, established equal taxation throughout the State, and declared the responsibility of the representative to his constituency by viva voce voting in the Legislature. You have endorsed the administration of President Johnson, and pledged yourselves to cooperate with him in the wise measure he has inaugurated for securing peace and prosperity to the whole Union. And you have referred to a Commission the protection of the "Freedmen" and colored population of the State, whose business it will be to regulate the relative duties of employee and employer.[48]

The South Carolina Constitution of 1865

The Charleston *Courier* thought the constitution "Truly Republican in character, and can scarcely fail to meet with general commendation." As to the vital question of whether the convention had satisfied the federal government and the rest of the country, it was felt that it had "placed itself on an impregnable foundation, and may appropriately claim the support of the good and the wise in every section."[49] But there were those who viewed the matter from a different angle. Completely ignoring the democratic changes in the constitution, *Harper's Weekly* said:

> Either South Carolina as a State of the Union has the right to refuse to make any change whatever in her Constitution, and to claim the recognition of her Senators and Representatives in Congress exactly as those of New York are recognized, or the United States have the right to insist upon such conditions of her return as good sense and experience suggest. South Carolina, by the assembling and action of her Convention under the authority of the United States, has already yielded her claim. She acknowledges the authority of the United States to dictate the terms of her return. Let the United States not mistake weakness for generosity, nor expect a harvest of palms if they allow dragon's teeth to be sown.[50]

Although he approved the democratic features of the constitution so far as they went, Andrews thought that the failure to take the Negro into the body politic and the general attitude of the people that the state was more important than the federal Union were sufficient to warrant a delay in the restoration of South Carolina to her former relations with other states and with the federal government.[51]

The events succeeding the convention are in general well known. The elections were held and the legislature met. The president allowed the governor-elect to take office. Congress did not admit the senators and representatives chosen in the southern states. The investigating committee submitted its report, and with the Congressional Acts of 1867 the process of restoring the late Confederate states began anew.

Thus evolutionary process was supplanted by the revolutionary. The constitution of 1865 was followed by the constitution of 1868. The former document has been given scant attention by either the Conservatives or the Radicals. Both have taken it for granted or ignored it. To one group it had to be good; to the other it had to be bad. Neither recognized it for what it was, or at least might have been—a transitional document which represented a distinct stage in the democratization of the political structure of South Carolina. When compared to the constitution of 1868, it may seem conservative, particularly in regard to the color question. But if it is considered in the light of the document preceding it, the positive democratic features are easily seen. An indication that we are approaching the day when a broader perspective will enable us to study the South Carolina constitution of 1865 on its merits is the statement of the most recent and the ablest of the defenders of "Black Reconstruction" that the convention "took some advance steps" and that at least one action of that body "was a step toward democracy so far as the whites were concerned."[52]

NOTES

1. Sidney Andrews, *The South Since the War* (Boston: Ticknor and Fields, 1866), 386.
2. Benjamin Franklin Perry, *Reminiscences of Public Men With Speeches and Addresses, Second Series* (Greenville: Shannon & Co., 1889), 246–47.
3. A typical statement of the problems that would come before the convention may be found in the Columbia *Phoenix*, September 4, 1865.
4. *New York Tribune*, June 23, 1865, reprinted in the *Phoenix*, July 4, 1865.
5. *Nation* (New York), vol. 1 (July 27, 1865).
6. *Phoenix*, August 25, 1865; Charleston *Courier*, Sept. 4, 1865.
7. Andrews, *The South Since the War*, 95.
8. The complete speech was printed in the *Phoenix*, July 22, 1865; *New York Times*, July 20, 1865; and in several other papers in the state and in the North.
9. *New York Times*, July 20, 1865, quoted by John Porter Hollis, "Early Period of Reconstruction in South Carolina," *Johns Hopkins University Studies in Historical and Political Science* (Baltimore: Johns Hopkins University Press, 1905), vol. 23: 32.
10. *New York Times*, July 20, 1865.
11. *Phoenix*, August 15, 1865; Perry, *Reminiscences of Public Men*, 246–49.
12. *New York Tribune*, July 22, 1865, reprinted in *Phoenix*, July 31, 1865.
13. Perry, *Reminiscences of Public Men*, 277.
14. Charleston *Courier*, September 7, and Winnsboro *Tri-Weekly News*, September 5, 7, 1865.
15. *Phoenix*, September 12, 1865.
16. Perry, *Reminiscences of Public Men*, 274; Charleston *Courier*, September 14, 1865; *Phoenix*, September 9, 1865; and Sumter *Watchman*, September 27, 1865.
17. *Journal of the Convention of the People of South Carolina Held in 1860, 1861 and 1862, together with Ordinances, Reports, and Resolutions, etc.* (Columbia: R. W. Gibbes, 1862), 46; *Phoenix*, September 7, 1865.
18. Andrews, *The South Since the War*, 39.
19. Ibid., 45; *Journal of the Convention of the People of South Carolina Held in Columbia, S.C. September, 1865* (Columbia: J. A. Selby, 1865), 185–88.
20. *Journal of the Convention of the People 1865*, 11–19.
21. *New York Tribune*, September 20, 1865, quoted by Hollis, "Early Period of Reconstruction," 37. See also *Harper's Weekly* (New York), vol. 9 (October 7, 1865), and *Nation*, vol. 1 (September 28, 1865).
22. *Journal of the Convention of the People 1865*, 29; Andrews, *The South Since the War*, 52–53.
23. *New York Tribune*, October 17, 1865, and *Harper's Weekly*, October 14, 1865, respectively.
24. *New York Times*, September 13, 1865.
25. Andrews, *The South Since the War*, 85–86.

26. *Phoenix,* September 4, 7, 12, 13, 1865. James L. Orr, in a convention debate, expressed confidence that the slave owners would be compensated; *Charleston Courier,* September 22, 1865.

27. *Journal of the Convention of the People 1865,* 7, 19, 20, 22, 27, 30, 31, and 46.

28. Andrews, *The South Since the War,* 67.

29. *Journal of the Convention of the People 1865,* 64–65.

30. Andrews, *The South Since the War,* 67.

31. *Charleston Courier,* Sept. 29, 1865; *Journal of the Convention of the People 1865,* 41, 103, 121–123.

32. It is very interesting to note that Governor Perry, in an article published in 1873, stated, "I thought as a matter of policy and justice, that the intelligent property holders amongst the freedmen should be allowed to vote, and so stated in the original draft of my first message to the convention. But my friends advised me to leave out this recommendation, as it would only produce a division in the convention, and there was no probability of its being adopted. I did so, and have ever since regretted it, for if a qualified suffrage had been extended to the colored people, we might have avoided the second reconstruction and the Constitutional Amendment imposed by Congress." Perry, *Reminiscences of Public Men,* 275.

33. Andrews, *The South Since the War,* 89–90.

34. An interesting historical sketch of this problem is given in David Duncan Wallace, "The South Carolina Constitution of 1895," *University of South Carolina Bulletin* (Columbia: University of South Carolina, 1927), no. 197: 14–15.

35. Andrews, *The South Since the War,* 47.

36. Ibid., 80.

37. *Journal of the Convention of the People 1865,* 6, 22, 33–34; *Phoenix,* September 21, 1865; *Charleston Courier,* September 25, 1865; Andrews, *The South Since the War,* 80.

38. *Journal of the Convention of the People 1865,* 69–71. The new provision stated that "Each Judicial District in the State shall constitute one Election District except Charleston District, which shall be divided into three Election Districts."

39. *Journal of the Convention of the People 1865,* 79–82, 86–87; *Charleston Courier,* September 25, 1865; Andrews, *The South Since the War,* 69–75, 82.

40. Constitution of 1865, Article 1, Sections 13 and 14; Article 2, Section 3; and Article 11.

41. *Journal of the Convention of the People 1865,* 68; *Constitution of the State of South Carolina and the Ordinances, Reports and Resolutions Adopted by the Convention of the People Held in Columbia, S.C., September, 1865* (Columbia: J. A. Selby, 1866), 11.

42. Constitution of 1865, Article 2, Sections 2 and 21; *Journal of the Convention of the People 1865,* 112–13, 117; *Charleston Courier,* September 20, 28, 1865.

43. Constitution of 1865, Article 2, Sections 5 and 6.

44. Ibid., Article 1, Section 25.

45. Ibid., Article 4; *Charleston Courier,* September 28, 1865.

46. Constitution of 1865, Article 1, Section 8; *Charleston Courier,* September 19, 1865.

47. The South Carolina Constitution of 1868 is the only one that has ever been submitted to the people. Previous ones had been "put into force by the body that framed them on the old theory of the sovereignty of the people being possessed by the convention"; Wallace, "South Carolina Constitution of 1895," 22.

48. *Journal of the Convention of the People 1865,* 130. Not considering such an action a *sine qua non* for the restoration, the convention did not repudiate the Confederate debts. When Secretary Seward informed Perry that the president did expect repudiation, the convention had adjourned. Seward then expressed a desire for an official statement on the subject by

the legislature; *Senate Executive Documents, Treaty Documents and Reports,* 39th Congress, 1st Sess., No. 21, 200–201.

49. September 29, 30, 1865. A similar opinion was expressed in Sumter *Watchman,* October 4, 1865.

50. *Harper's Weekly,* October 14, 1865.

51. Andrews, *The South Since the War,* 391. He tried hard to be unbiased, but he never succeeded in understanding why South Carolinians did not repent of their "political sins" immediately. Although he was more sympathetic than many others of his group, he thought with them that the admission of the southern senators and representatives should be delayed.

52. W. E. Burghart Du Bois, *Black Reconstruction: An Essay toward a History of the Part which Black Folk Played in the Attempt to Reconstruct Democracy in America, 1860–1880* (New York: Harcourt, Brace & Co., 1935), 385.

ANDREW JOHNSON
The Second Swing 'Round the Circle
(1966)

Robert J. Moore

In the congressional election of 1866 Andrew Johnson made a famous and controversial "swing 'round the circle," a tour of several northern states, on behalf of candidates favorable to his views. His second "swing 'round the circle," the topic of this inquiry, is the revolution in historians' opinions of his personality and presidency. These opinions have come full circle since the first genuine historical accounts of Reconstruction and of the hapless successor to Lincoln.

The image of an obstinate, egotistical, crude, demagogic Johnson, unfit for the presidency, was firmly established early in this century by the first scholars to exploit the Reconstruction theme. His hardheadedness and his lack of dignity caused the defeat of his Reconstruction program and rendered him a leader without a party. These early historians did not question Johnson's honesty, but they heavily condemned other facets of his character. Lack of flexibility, dignity, and of tact were the keys to his lack of success, according to the gentlemanly, upper-middle-class historians whose interpretation was dominant for the first two decades of the twentieth century.

James Ford Rhodes, probably the most important writer in establishing this interpretation, was a well-to-do gentleman historian who moved in the best circles of Boston and Cambridge society. Socially, his delight was in congenial dining companions and good after-dinner conversation. Politically, his delight was in stateliness and moderation. William A. Dunning, a historian and political scientist whose seminars at Columbia University are still without parallel in their influence on Reconstruction historiography, was of a similar conservative bent. To gentlemen who adhered to the golden mean and who expected no less of their public servants, Andrew Johnson's blustery, "Give 'em hell, Harry," style of spontaneous stump speaking (to borrow a fitting modern analogy) was highly distasteful. To men who admired moderation and compromise, Johnson's refusal to make small concessions in order to win larger victories for his policies seemed inexcusable stubbornness.

Johnson's character defects were all the more grievous to Rhodes and Dunning because these defects doomed the presidential Reconstruction policy. A more capable and dignified chief executive might have salvaged much of Lincoln's plan of Reconstruction from the attacks of the Radicals and thus prevented what Rhodes and Dunning considered one of the most tragic eras in American history.

The prevailing attitude of Reconstruction historians toward the seventeenth president was epitomized by Rhodes: "Johnson, by habits, manners, mind, and character, was unfit for the presidential office, and whatever may have been the merit of his policy, a policy devised by angels could never have been carried on by such an advocate. The American people love order and decency; they have a high regard for the presidential office, and they desire to see its occupant conduct himself with dignity. . . . Johnson degraded the office, and he is the only one of our presidents of whom this can be said."[1] This view of Johnson was dominant for about the first two decades of this century. But challengers arose who were to exonerate the president from the charges of Rhodes and Dunning and to exalt his reputation to an unprecedented peak by 1930.

A major impetus to this dramatic change in historians' opinions was the availability of two sources of new evidence. The Andrew Johnson papers were acquired by the Library of Congress and made accessible to historians in 1905. These were of some importance in the change in attitude, but Dunning used them and saw no reason to revise his view. Of more importance for the reputation of Johnson was the publication of the *Diary of Gideon Wells* in 1910–11. This voluminous journal by Johnson's secretary of the navy showed Johnson in a favorable light and made a good brief on his behalf.

James Schouler was the first historian to make full use of these newly available materials for the defense of Johnson. In fact, he added a seventh volume to his history of the United States explicitly to vindicate a president who had been mistreated by historians. Schouler's Johnson was a courageous, strong, self-poised administrator. "He was stubborn in political opinions where he thought himself right, defiant, ready to fight for them; yet those opinions were just, enlightened, and such as only a sound and independent statesman could have formed."[2]

Andrew Johnson's reputation was carried to its summit of glory by five publications which appeared in the half-dozen years following 1924. Like all sympathetic portrayals of Johnson, these five adopted the central theme of the president as a courageous defender of the Constitution during its period of greatest trial.

The earliest of these exaltations of Johnson was a biography by Robert Watson Winston, a North Carolina politician and judge who retired at the age of sixty to return to college to prepare himself "to interpret the New South to the Nation and the Nation to the New South."[3] Winston was the most modest of the five authors in his claims for Johnson, but he left little doubt that he intended to rectify earlier misconceptions. He portrayed Johnson as the soul of virtue, wholesomeness, and simplicity, a man who stubbornly placed country above self. The Reconstruction president's vetoes of civil rights measures did not indicate that he was a bigot, but rather demonstrated his respect for the Constitution. As a defender of the Constitution Johnson belonged in the ranks of national heroes as "a plain, rugged, two–fisted American President, striving to do the right thing as best he could."[4]

Despite the works of Schouler and Winston, Lloyd Paul Stryker felt that Andrew Johnson had not received his due vindication at the judgment bar of history. This New York lawyer's biography of Johnson was designed to redress the balance and once and for all do justice to this man who was crucified in Abraham Lincoln's place. Stryker's biography was an elaborate advocate's defense of Johnson which upheld and justified the subject at all points in the most lavish terms, while it viciously attacked and vilified the enemies of Johnson. Stryker defended Johnson as being a temperate man, an honest man, and the great defender of the Constitution. He pointed out that at the time of impeachment Johnson had received numerous offers from former soldiers to defend him in the crisis. Therefore, Stryker contended that Johnson, had he chosen, could have started another civil war in which the forces of honor and respect for the Constitution would have been on his side, and the forces of dishonor and hypocrisy would have been on the Radicals' side. "No one can read Johnson's story without the temptation to regret that he did not put that bugle to his lips, and fight that war upon hypocrisy with bayonets. Stevens and Sumner had reveled long enough in their sadistic persecution orgies!" But Johnson chose the road of higher courage—the hemlock, if necessary.[5] Thus, in highly colored, spectacular style did Stryker marshal the case for the defense of both Johnson and the South.

If it can be said that each volume of Bancroft's *History at the United States* was a vote for Andrew Jackson, it can be asserted with equal validity that each page of Claude G. Bower's *The Tragic Era* was a vote for the Democratic Party of the 1920s. Bowers was a journalist whose party activism gained for him a career in the diplomatic service. He was the keynote speaker at the Democratic National Convention in 1928, the year before the publication of *The Tragic Era*.

Bowers was an admirer of Johnson who even defended the president's ill-fated "swing 'round the circle" in 1866. "Never in history had a president gone forth on a greater mission—to appeal for constitutional government and the restoration of union through conciliation and common sense; and never had one been so scurvily treated."[6] Bowers described Johnson as a man of complex nature—honest, inflexible, tender, able, forceful, and tactless. But it was fortunate for the United States that he had two passions—the Constitution and the Union. Bowers proclaimed Johnson one of the nation's greatest servants.

The book was the story of the Reconstruction period told in an exciting, dramatic, and colorful fashion. The popular, readable style made it probably the most widely perused volume on Reconstruction;[7] therefore, Bowers has been a powerful influence on the public's attitude toward Reconstruction and toward Andrew Johnson. Bowers indicated in his autobiography that the main contribution of *The Tragic Era* was to gain a more favorable interpretation of Johnson.[8] However, Bowers's influence on scholars has probably not been as great as on the general public since the reviews in scholarly journals were highly critical of the book. From the point of view of scholarly appreciation for *The Tragic Era,* Bowers had the misfortune of dramatizing and exaggerating the traditional interpretation just at the precise moment that that interpretation was beginning to come under attack.

As thorough as Winston's and more readable; as interesting as Bowers's or Stryker's and better researched—this is the manner in which a reviewer described George Fort Milton's *The Age of Hate: Andrew Johnson and the Radicals.* And the reviewer was correct. Milton, a journalist and active Democrat, unfolds a story which never loses interest and occasionally flashes with brilliance of style. The book is an exhaustive defense of Johnson and his policy which a few words or a couple of quotations will hardly exemplify. Milton believed history would ultimately rescue this man of firm character and honorable purpose from the slander against him. And Milton showed a new concern—to defend Johnson against the charge of being hostile to Negroes. "The truth was that the President was deeply interested in the negro's welfare, and warmly seconded southern efforts to that end."[9]

The final volume in that brace of five which brought Andrew Johnson's reputation to its peak by 1930 was *The Critical Year: A Study of Andrew Johnson and Reconstruction* by Howard K. Beale. This work is something of a watershed both in the interpretation of Reconstruction and in the assessment of Andrew Johnson. It is the first major analysis of Reconstruction that develops the economic interpretation suggested just three years earlier in Charles and Mary Beard's *Rise of American Civilization.* Beale's study of the election of 1866 convinces him that the major issues were economic and that the Radicals were basically motivated by economic considerations. The Radicals hammered on the emotional theme of Reconstruction in order to camouflage their real intentions—to maintain government in the hands of big-business, high-tariff, and sound-money interests. Reconstruction represented the method by which the new industrial class consolidated its control over the federal government.

To Beale, Andrew Johnson stood as the determined, though unsuccessful, bulwark against control by profiteers who plundered the public wealth. The president represented the agrarian, anti-plutocratic, common-man point of view and stood out as "one of the first great conservators of our national resources."[10] He was a courageous and sober man, a fairly able president whose policies were thwarted by the unfair tactics of the Radicals.

Though Beale lauds and defends Johnson, his inferred criticisms of Johnson's political judgment laid the groundwork for a whole new barrage of derogations which have undermined the high position of esteem to which Johnson's memory had been elevated by 1930. Beale especially emphasizes Johnson's failure to recognize the economic issues as the true issues of the campaign. Had he based the congressional election campaign of 1866 on the real economic issues rather than on the less important issue of reconstructing the South, Johnson could have bound the westerners and southerners to him in a great anti-monopoly party that would have been triumphant over the divided Radicals. Thus, he could have inaugurated a liberal economic policy as well as carried out his moderate Reconstruction policy. Now, one would assume that an able politician would discern the basic issues and select the ones on which he could ride to victory; therefore, Beale, in his effort to vindicate Johnson, seems simultaneously (and unintentionally) to relegate the Reconstruction president to a rather low order of political genius.

Since Beale's transitional work, the reputation of Andrew Johnson has been on the decline. This is in spite of some efforts to maintain his defense against an increasing avalanche of criticism. Those writers who have continued to praise the president's abilities, wisdom, and courage in recent decades are those who are attached to his policy of Reconstruction and are trying to defend that policy against the attacks of revisionists who look with more favor upon the Radical congressional plan of Reconstruction.

Two of the recent defenders of Johnson's reputation deserve no real notice. Their attempts are unworthy of their subject, even if their subject had been the worst president the United States ever had. One of them, George L. Tappan, wrote in 1954 a frothy little book which has no bibliography, no footnotes, and no index. His material is taken almost entirely from Lloyd Paul Stryker, whom he quotes abundantly. The other unworthy defender is Margaret Shaw Royall. Her bibliography contains sixteen titles, of which three are incorrect and a fourth attributed to the wrong author! Also, it is quite probable that the holder of Stryker's copyright could sue her for plagiarism. Neither Andrew Johnson nor historical writing is served by such as these.

A more reasonable, though not highly effective defense of Johnson, was published in 1960 by Milton Lomask. In a popularly written account of Johnson's presidency, Lomask portrays him as the defender of the Constitution against the attacks of the Radicals, who wanted to destroy the federal system and establish a sort of parliamentary government similar to England's. While writing in approving tones of the president's inflexible stand on constitutionalism and his paternal attitude toward Negroes, Lomask does see grounds for criticism. Johnson was tactless and did not compromise sometimes when he could have. He did not meet the Conservative Republicans halfway, and he failed to see the sincerity of their desire to extend civil rights to the Negro. Lomask's estimate of Johnson is favorable but reveals a glaring flaw: "a man of admirable character, incorruptible and patriotic, Andrew Johnson was one of the best political philosophers and one of the poorest politicians ever to sit in the White House."[11] While defenders of Andrew Johnson have been in evidence in the last few decades, they have been unequal to the task of maintaining his reputation against the gathering crescendo of criticism by recent historians of Reconstruction.

The most extensive and damaging critique is Eric McKitrick's *Andrew Johnson and Reconstruction,* published in 1960. McKitrick's chief theme is to demonstrate how Johnson "threw away his own power both as President and as party leader, how he assisted materially, in spite of himself, in blocking the reconciliation of North and South, and what his behavior did toward disrupting the political life of an entire nation."[12] Shortly after the war Johnson's position was very strong. Almost all the Republican newspapers supported him, and the Radicals were not yet a solid phalanx against him. He should have considered himself an agent of the victorious element in dealing with the defeated, but he refused to impose terms. And when the Congress reconvened he constantly tried to thwart its attempts to establish reasonable terms of peaceful settlement. Gradually, the whole Republican Party did begin to move toward the more extreme aims of Negro suffrage, exclusion of southern states, and anti-Johnson sentiment. But the men called Radicals did not cause this movement, in McKitrick's judgment. "If there were to be a real prime mover, a causal agent: such a role would have to be played by the one man—Andrew Johnson—whose behavior was critical in anything and everything the party did."[13] By his vetoes and his attacks, Johnson alienated more and more of his former supporters and forced the Congress toward a more radical position.

But thus far McKitrick has only damned Johnson for some of the weaknesses that even his best friends recognized. His criticism goes deeper; it penetrates to that central virtue upon which his defenders based his case—his constitutional position. McKitrick rejects the idea that Johnson's position on the Constitution was the only valid, sound, and honest stand while others' positions were dishonest and irrelevant covers for base motives. "Andrew Johnson was by no means the only man who cared immensely about the Constitution."[14] Of course, political arrangements underwent a change in such a tumultuous time as the emergence from Civil War, but the Constitution was still a real check on men's minds. So the granite figure of Johnson heroically maintaining the Constitution while all others would trample upon it begins to crumble.

David Donald, too, chips away at this constitutionalist image. He denies that Johnson's Reconstruction policies can be explained in terms of uncompromising attachment to the letter of the Constitution. No doubt the president, like most Americans, believed in the Constitution, but he was not an inflexible constitutionalist. For example, as military governor of Tennessee he imposed an oath which disqualified political enemies from voting, and as president he appointed provisional governors for southern states and gave instructions for the creation of new governments, all without constitutional authority. Donald explains Johnson's behavior on the basis of political considerations. And in his latest book, *The Politics of Reconstruction,* he gives Johnson credit for proving himself "a virtuoso of politics."[15] This shows an interesting change in Donald's assessment of the Reconstruction president; in 1956 Donald scored him for his "political ineptitude."[16]

Another blow to the view of Johnson as the pure constitutionalist fighting for principle is dealt by John and LaWanda Cox in *Politics, Principle, and Prejudice, 1865–1866* (1963). It has been customary to accuse the Radicals of acting for partisan political reasons while assuming that Johnson stood on sound, selfless, constitutional grounds. The Coxes document the partisan political ambitions and maneuvers of the Radicals' opponents. They deny that Johnson was primarily motivated by an inflexible adherence to the Constitution and to principle. He was influenced at least as much by political ambition and racial prejudice. He sought to develop a third party which would perpetuate his own power. He largely caused the impasse between himself and Congress by refusing to guarantee basic rights of citizenship to the Negro.

Here we encounter what appears to be the basic factor in the decline of Andrew Johnson's reputation among recent historians—his position concerning rights for Negroes. Reconstruction historiography has been dominated for the last two decades by historians who favor a position of equality for the Negro in American society. They have taken a new look at the relative values of the policies of Johnson and the Radicals. They have found that the Radical policies were designed to do for the Negro then what American society is trying to do for him now, and have decided that those policies could not have been all wrong. They have found that Johnson's program tended to inhibit the advance of the Negro and consequently have decided that that program could not have been all right.

As early as 1935 the Negro historian and civil rights activist W. E. B. DuBois was saying that the key to Johnson's career was his inability to overcome his prejudices and include Negroes in his concept of democracy.[17] Most of the biographers of Thaddeus Stevens have tended to portray Stevens as the sincere champion of the Negro while Andrew Johnson was an unfortunate or evil obstacle.[18] In a recent appreciative study of the role of abolitionists during the Civil War and Reconstruction period, James M. McPherson portrays Johnson as a racist who brought disaster upon himself by driving moderates into alliance with the Radicals.[19] W. R. Brock, a Cambridge University historian, generally concurs in this evaluation in his fresh analysis of the political and constitutional problems of the immediate postwar period.[20]

Perhaps the nearest approximation to a summary of the interpretation of Andrew Johnson now prevalent is found in Kenneth M. Stampp's new synthesis: *The Era of Reconstruction, 1865–1877* (1965). Stampp sees Johnson as the last of the Jacksonians, living in a static world, practicing the politics of nostalgia. At the end of the war Johnson set out to create agrarian democracies in the southern states, but the planter politicians defeated his purpose, maintained their dominance, and won his acceptance of their reorganized state governments. Johnson's violent, uncompromising behavior played a large role in forcing the moderate Republicans to join with the Radicals and assume control of the Reconstruction process. Furthermore, Johnson was unwilling to include the Negro in his democratic creed. It has been argued that race relations would have been better in subsequent years had it not been for the Radicals' program; however, Stampp says: "The truth is that, before the radical program began, the Johnson governments themselves had introduced the whole pattern of disenfranchisement, discrimination, and segregation into the postwar South. And there, quite possibly, matters might still stand, had Andrew Johnson had his way."[21]

This view of Johnson is fully as unfavorable to him as the Rhodes-Dunning interpretation. So, the reputation of Andrew Johnson has now made the full swing 'round the circle and returned to its early twentieth-century nadir. Such is the fate of presidents; such are the ways of historians.

NOTES

1. James Ford Rhodes, *Historical Essays* (New York: Macmillan Co., 1909), 217.
2. James Schouler, *History of the Reconstruction Period, 1865–1877*; this is volume 7 in a series entitled, *History of the United States of America Under the Constitution* (New York: Dodd, Mead and Co., 1913), 142.
3. *Who Was Who in America: A Companion Volume to Who's Who in America* (Chicago, A. N. Marquis Co., 1942–50), vol. 2: 587.
4. Robert W. Winston, *Andrew Johnson: Plebian and Patriot* (New York: H. Holt & Co., 1928), 512.
5. Lloyd Paul Stryker, *Andrew Johnson: A Study in Courage* (New York: Macmillan Co., 1929), 585–86.
6. Claude G. Bowers, *The Tragic Era: The Revolution After Lincoln* (Boston: Houghton Mifflin Co., 1929), 138.

7. Letter from Houghton, Mifflin & Co. to author, April 22, 1960. Its sales approximated 140,000 by 1960. As well as I have been able to determine, this is by far the largest sale figure for any book on Reconstruction (as of 1966).

8. Claude G. Bowers, *My Life: The Memoirs of Claude Bowers* (New York: Simon and Schuster, 1962), 208–10.

9. George Fort Milton, *The Age of Hate: Andrew Johnson and the Radicals* (New York: Coward-McCann, Inc., 1930), 286.

10. Howard K. Beale, *The Critical Year: A Study of Andrew Johnson and Reconstruction* (New York: F. Ugar Co., 1958), 217.

11. Milton Lomask, *Andrew Johnson: President on Trial* (New York: Farrar, Straus, 1960), 345.

12. Eric L. McKitrick, *Andrew Johnson and Reconstruction* (Chicago: University of Chicago Press, 1960), 14.

13. Ibid., 66.

14. Ibid., 95.

15. David H. Donald, *The Politics of Reconstruction, 1863–1867* (Baton Rouge: Louisiana State University Press, 1965), 23.

16. David H. Donald, "Why They Impeached Andrew Johnson," *American Heritage* 8 (December 1956): 103.

17. W. E. Burghardt DuBois, *Black Reconstruction: An Essay toward a History of the Part Which Black Folk Played in the Attempt to Reconstruct Democracy in America, 1860–1880* (New York: Harcourt, Brace & Co., 1935), 241–42, 332.

18. Fawn M. Bodie, *Thaddeus Stevens: Scourge of the South* (New York: Norton, 1959); Ralph Korngold, *Thaddeus Stevens: A Being Darkly Wise and Rudely Great* (New York: Harcourt, Brace & Co., 1955); Alphonse B. Miller, *Thaddeus Stevens* (New York: Harper, 1939); Thomas Frederick Woodley, *Great Leveler: The Life of Thaddeus Stevens (*New York: Stackpole Sons, 1937).

19. James M. McPherson, *The Struggle for Equality: Abolitionists and the Negro in the Civil War and Reconstruction* (Princeton, N.J.: Princeton University Press, 1964).

20. W. R. Brock, *An American Crisis: Congress and Reconstruction, 1865–1867* (London: Macmillan & Co., 1963).

21. Kenneth M. Stampp, *The Era of Reconstruction, 1865–1877* (New York: Knopf, 1965), 82.

RIGHTEOUS LIVES
A Comparative Study of the South Carolina Scalawag Leadership during Reconstruction
(2003)

Lewie Reece

Reconstruction was a profound revolutionary event in the political history of South Carolina. Where once government had been controlled by a small elite, under Reconstruction, the state came to experience a vibrant democracy. At the heart of that democracy was the leadership of the Republican Party, which dominated South Carolina politics from 1867 to 1877. Largely composed of African Americans, the Reconstruction Republican Party included only a small minority of white voters. While some of these white Republicans were carpetbaggers, many were native whites who, for a variety of reasons, associated with the Republican Party. Mocked as scalawags by their peers, they often played an important role in the workings of the party and played a key role in shaping its public policy, ideology, and electoral strategy.

This paper attempts to address the role of scalawag Republicans by examining four prominent scalawags who held positions of leadership: Simeon Corley, Edmund Mackey, Samuel Melton, and Alexander Wallace. All four of these men showed a willingness to extend to African Americans an opportunity to be treated as equals. Each developed close relationships with the African American community and was at least committed to political equality for African Americans. As a local party activist Corley encouraged African Americans to register to vote. Wallace aided African Americans in their struggles with racial violence in the upcountry. Melton and Mackey both served in the U.S. Attorney's Office where they prosecuted white Democrats who denied the civil rights of African Americans. Their participation in the events of Reconstruction hardly ended their influence in South Carolina politics. All four remained involved in Republican politics and attempted to protect suffrage for African Americans and white Republicans. These scalawags in South Carolina were not simply political opportunists but rather sought the creation of a new, different kind of politics in the state.

Alexander Wallace's early political career suggests the normal antebellum success story. Despite a limited education, he eventually became a successful planter and went on to serve several terms in the state legislature. When the war came Wallace evidently disapproved of secession enough to withdraw from public life and made no effort to serve in the Confederate Army. When the war was over he returned to active participation in politics, being reelected to the South Carolina legislature in 1865. Prior to the passage of the Reconstruction Act of 1867, which gave the vote to African Americans, Wallace's political career was little different from other South Carolina moderates. It is difficult to say precisely why he joined the Republican Party; possibly he saw it as an organization that best reflected the concerns of southern unionists. Yet once Wallace became a Republican he fully supported African American political participation. Wallace went on to serve four terms in Congress though as a congressman he kept a fairly low profile.[1]

Yet from the very beginning Wallace was vigilant in addressing acts of violence against African American and white Republicans in the upcountry. Wallace fully supported the intervention of the federal government and worked with a congressional investigating committee that examined activities of the Ku Klux Klan in his congressional district. The massive federal intervention in York County seemed to unite white and African American Republicans. Democrats complained that in the 1872 congressional election some African Americans prevented others from voting against Wallace.[2]

In the aftermath of the federal intervention against the Klan, Wallace was a consistent advocate of a federal presence to enforce voting rights. In 1874 when Attorney General George Williams adopted a policy of reconciliation toward Klan violence, Wallace complained that in a period of ten months, "only *three* men have been arrested in York County charged with KK offenses." Moreover, noting the upsurge of white paramilitary groups, Wallace demanded intervention from the Justice Department. In 1876 he struggled against tremendous odds to be reelected to Congress; Red Shirt paramilitary groups often directly attacked meetings that Wallace sought to lead. Wallace noted that these groups would "surround the meetings on horseback" and often had no purpose other than to break up gatherings of Republican voters. At one meeting they shouted down Wallace while physically threatening him.

In spite of Wallace's best efforts to be reelected, he was overwhelmed by the Democratic tide and was defeated. While Wallace's defeat marked the end of his official public involvement in Republican politics, he remained sufficiently interested in voting rights to commend Attorney General Charles Devens for his prosecutions of Democrats in South Carolina. Wallace also cared enough about the proposed repeal of the Enforcement Acts, which protected the voting rights of southern Republicans, to urge Republican Congressman James Garfield to get Republicans to resist Democratic efforts at repeal. Tell the president to "stand firm" in the crisis, wrote Wallace to Garfield in 1879, for South Carolina Republicans approved of the hard line national Republicans were taking on the issue. Thus Wallace's support for voting rights was a consistent policy from which he never wavered.[3]

If Alexander Wallace's political career demonstrates an enduring commitment to voting rights, the political activism of Edmund Mackey suggests the close connection between white and African American Republicans in the low country. Edmund Mackey was the son of Albert Mackey, one of the more prominent southern unionists who resisted secession. In a long political career Mackey served as the sheriff of Charleston County, an alderman for the city of Charleston, a state legislator, an assistant U.S. attorney, and a congressman. At the heart of Mackey's political career was a close intimacy between himself and African American politicians and voters. Such closeness was perhaps best demonstrated during an election riot in Charleston in 1876 in which African Americans rushed to Mackey's assistance to repel assaults by white Democrats. Yet for all Mackey's radicalism there were clear limits, for he broke temporarily with the Republican organization to run for Congress as an independent Republican in 1874. Mackey also strongly supported Governor Chamberlain in his efforts to reform and perhaps even deny some political appointments to African Americans. Yet when Republicans struggled for political survival in the election of 1876, Mackey strived to maintain the Republican organization and to prevent the Democratic takeover. As leader of Republicans in the State House, Mackey met the crisis of the competing houses with equanimity. It was hardly Mackey's fault that in the end forces outside his control prevailed. Yet 1877 marked not the end of Mackey's political career but rather a new phase of political activity.[4]

When President Hayes recognized Wade Hampton as his official choice for governor, he also sought to appoint Republicans who would be acceptable to the new regime. The position of U.S. attorney was extended to Lucius Northrop, a Conservative Republican, whom Edmund Mackey's uncle, the mercurial Thomas Jefferson Mackey, once described as a "republican by profession." Northrop, in putting forward his name for the office, sought to make it clear that he distinctly disapproved of the "constant use of the bayonet." As a result Mackey's selection as an assistant U.S. attorney was no doubt seen by Hayes as something of a sop to party regulars in South Carolina. As an assistant U.S. attorney Mackey proved to be a vigorous advocate of using the law as a means to achieve justice for African American and white Republicans. Such advocacy soon provoked the ire of the Charleston *News and Courier*. Mackey took great pains to point out to Attorney General Charles Devens that the complaints of the publisher, Democratic politician Francis W. Dawson, were the concerns of the guilty, who had directly participated in fraudulent ballot-box stuffing.

Further, along with U.S. Marshal R. M. Wallace, Mackey took an interest in protecting the life of African American Republican Edmund Deas. Deas, a prominent Darlington County legislator, was arrested as part of a campaign of intimidation and coercion launched by Democrats in the aftermath of the brutal 1878 elections. While Northrop did nothing to prevent Deas from being arrested and detained for several months, Mackey and Wallace made consistent efforts to secure his release. As Deas ruefully noted, "*Mackey* and *Wallace* & others had been advising him to take steps in my interest but he would not do it." A consistent willingness to help Deas suggests Mackey's personal connections with African American Republican politicians in general. It was this kind of relationship that could have induced Robert Smalls to endorse Edmund Mackey as a compromise candidate for a congressional Republican nomination in a district designed to elect an African American. That Mackey could be so readily accepted by African American delegates in the 1880 election also suggests that his political and personal conduct built a reputation of trust. Years after Mackey died—all too young—his old friend and African American Republican Congressman Thomas E. Miller complained that since the "death of Mackey" not enough was done to keep Republican voters listed on the registration rolls. That Mackey's death could be used to mark the end of an era says a great deal about the impact he made on low country Republican politics.[5]

Like his fellow scalawags, Simeon Corley too served in Congress, but he maintained more of a local orientation to Lexington County throughout his political career. Unlike the other three Republicans described in this paper, Corley was not someone who was born into a prominent family nor did he have an antebellum political career. Corley's early training was that of a tailor. In his autobiography Corley makes it clear that he took an interest in the issues of secession and Union in the prewar years. An advocate of temperance, abolition, and preserving the Union at all costs, Corley faced constant challenges. When secession did finally become a reality, Corley accepted it begrudgingly and evidently resented being "compelled to enter the Confederate army." At the end of the war, when Corley returned to South Carolina, his uncompromising unionism made him "a *lover* of the Union," and it was with real enthusiasm that he took the oath of allegiance to the United States."[6]

Corley's voice was not one that was heeded in South Carolina in 1865. Corley described his being defeated as a delegate to the constitutional convention that year as being primarily due to his "demanding more for colored men." After the passage of the Reconstruction Act, Corley became involved in the organization of the Republican Party, especially in Lexington County. Early party building took place fairly quickly in established urban centers such as Columbia and

Charleston, but outside those areas it required a more persistent effort. Aiding the party's efforts was the fact that many white conservatives refused to participate in the new registration of voters—as the Reconstruction Act required—and boycotted the elections held in 1868. Yet a sufficient number of white Union voters did participate in Lexington County, and Corley claimed a "majority of white voters" cast ballots for the Republican ticket. Corley clearly saw political affairs in South Carolina as an opportunity to arrive at a new start for both whites and African Americans in the state. "The wants of the white and colored race are precisely alike—their interests are identical." In Corley's view then, Republican policies were designed to aid the poor of both races. To deny rights to African Americans would only result in raising up those who would injure the rights not only of blacks but of whites as well. Thus, as a delegate to the Constitutional Convention of 1868, Corley advocated African American property ownership. While a member of Congress, he spoke in favor of the ratification of the Fifteenth Amendment to guarantee African American voting rights. He called for new approaches to public policy questions.[7]

The demise of Reconstruction did not mark the end of Corley's participation in politics. The election of 1880 proved to be critical at both the state and local levels, especially in Lexington County. Corley attempted to inform national political figures of the difficulties of South Carolina Republicans and also fought with both white and African American Republicans against the entrenched power structure of the Democratic Party. In the summer of 1880 Corley made a concerted effort to suggest the need of the national Republican Party's direct intervention. Corley believed that after Hayes betrayed South Carolina Republicans by handing over the state to Hampton, the result had been four years of despotism, which made Republicans eager to "throw off the shackles by which they are illegally bound." Corley also felt that if Republicans failed in this campaign it would mean "our last hope for good government is gone." He therefore suggested to presidential nominee James Garfield the importance of sending two or three good speakers who could campaign in each county and encourage Republicans to surge to the polls. Corley's suggestions evidently attracted considerable discussion at the headquarters of the national party, for William Chandler, who served as the *de facto* campaign manager for Garfield, suggested that Corley's ideas had merit. Yet Chandler concluded that there was an insufficient amount of time to "arouse the whole state" and, as a result, Corley and South Carolina Republicans were effectively on their own. Republicans did make a massive effort to carry the state for Garfield but were stymied everywhere by multiple acts of fraud by Democratic election officials. Yet in the aftermath of the election, Corley remained hopeful and sought to convince president-elect Garfield of the necessity of using federal power to ensure "*honest* and *fair elections*." Corley remained committed then to the issues of civil rights, which he believed would help to create a new kind of politics in South Carolina.[8]

Such activity carried the price of being an object of both physical and legal persecution by the Democrats. Democrats in the county suggested to Corley that he ought to go by the jail and pick out his cell. Turning to the one lawyer who, he believed, could influence a jury in Lexington County, one who would be able to stand up to the "bulldozing influences which will be brought to bear upon it by the political lawyers of the bar," Corley wrote to beg the influence of Samuel Melton. Few political alliances could seem more odd than that between Corley, the impassioned tribune of the poor, and Melton, the suave, sophisticated attorney with ties to the South Carolina aristocracy. What united these men was their politics, for in his own quiet way Melton was just as committed to civil rights as was Corley. Melton was a graduate of South Carolina College; he had developed a reputation as a gifted attorney in the prewar years, was a state legislator, and thus was connected to the political establishment in the state. When the secession crisis came, Melton, like many moderates, accepted its reality. In fact, unlike Corley, Melton eagerly embraced the Confederate cause and served as a colonel in the Confederate Army. Melton evidently was a true believer, for as late as March 1865 he was writing his wife that the suffering and pain of the South was a good thing in that it would make people "patriotic & true." Yet Melton accepted the demise of the Confederacy with good grace and, after passage of the Reconstruction Act, entered the Republican Party. In all likelihood he did so not out of a commitment to equality but more as an act of pragmatism.[9]

Through most of the Reconstruction period Melton preferred to remain in the background. Melton was clearly a moderate Republican but still a party regular. Melton was willing to publicly laud African American Congressman Robert Elliott for a speech in support of the radical Civil Rights Act of 1875. Yet Melton came to public recognition more for his close friendship with Daniel Chamberlain, who was elected governor in 1874. Melton and Chamberlain were involved in the ownership of the *Daily Union Herald,* a leading Republican newspaper, and formed a political partnership that sought to reform the Republican Party. On such a platform Melton was elected attorney general of South Carolina in 1874 and remained a close ally of Chamberlain for the next year. It was when Melton became convinced that Chamberlain was more interested in appeasing Democrats than reforming the party that he ended his alliance with Chamberlain and eventually resigned as attorney general.[10]

Like the other Republicans discussed in this paper, Melton's political career did not dead end with the Democratic seizure of power in 1877; rather it took a new form. In the immediate aftermath of Redemption, Democrats began a concerted program of persecution against the state Republican Party. They conducted countless investigations and filed frivolous charges of bribery, misconduct, and fraud against Republicans, hoping that the sheer volume of such suits could induce the federal government to stop prosecuting Democrats who participated in election riots. As one of the few Republicans Democrats would heed, Melton had to negotiate with Democrats in an effort to stop their campaign of persecution. In fact, Melton became a mediator between Governor Wade Hampton and President Rutherford B. Hayes. It was a task that Melton found useful in that eventually he was able to move Hampton to a compromise solution. Yet Melton evidently found absurd Hampton's contention that former Treasurer Francis Cardozo and Congressman Robert Smalls, both African American politicians, were guilty of massive fraud. The prosecution of Cardozo, Melton told Hayes, was "monstrous," and he served as Cardozo's attorney at trial. Yet the eventual compromise, which involved an end to both state and federal prosecutions and the pardoning of Republicans convicted before Hampton's kangaroo courts, brought the issue to an end. Melton accepted the compromise partly because he believed Hampton would allow fair elections in South Carolina and might even serve Republican interests. Hampton, Melton told President Hayes, was "desirous of having a strong and intelligent representation of our party in the Legislature," and having conceded an "honest ballot and a fair count" it might once more be possible to count "South Carolina for the Republic." Melton's estimate of Hampton was overly optimistic, but in all likelihood Melton did much to end the campaign of persecution.[11]

Melton remained an important figure in South Carolina politics throughout the next decade. Serving as U.S. attorney in the Garfield and Arthur administrations Melton made real efforts to end violations of voting rights. Despite being well aware of the difficulties of prosecuting election cases before juries of white Democrats, he remained vigorous in his attempts to do so during his tenure as U.S. attorney. Almost alone in a fight with the whole apparatus of the Democratic Party of the state, Melton concluded, "*this effort must be made.*" He was aware that as an "unflinching Republican" his views were all but discounted before a jury. Yet the larger interest of trying to secure the voting rights of African Americans and whites made that effort worthwhile. The results were in many ways predictable; juries refused to convict, but Melton's determination reflected a willingness to try to secure the full meaning of national citizenship for all people in South Carolina.[12]

An examination of the political careers of these four Republicans demonstrates a clear pattern. All four remained consistent advocates of civil rights, especially of voting rights, and while one can see necessity motivating some of their actions, certainly the intensity of their actions suggests that they came to their positions freely. Moreover, their advocacy of civil rights carried with it close association with African Americans. This is not to suggest that these Republicans overcame all racial prejudice, but their party activity made them willing to extend full political rights to African Americans. In their approach to political issues then, these scalawags fully accepted the idea of civic equality and remained committed to full public participation. Opportunism simply cannot explain the depth of their political careers nor the degree to which they remained involved in the issues of Reconstruction. Simeon Corley put it best when articulating this new politics in 1868: "Old South Carolina, politically as it was, is dead and buried with the past. New South Carolina, as it is, lives, and will continue to live on the bright pages of history in the future, as a free, progressive State of this great sisterhood, to the end of time."[13]

NOTES

1. The basic source on Wallace's early career would be the *Biographical Directory of the American Congress, 1774–1996* (Alexandria, Va.: CQ Staff Directories, Inc., 1997), 2004. Also useful for the contours of the antebellum period are Lacy K Ford Jr., *Origins of Southern Radicalism: The South Carolina Upcountry, 1800–1860* (New York: Oxford University Press, 1988), and Stephen W. Channing, *Crisis of Fear: Secession in South Carolina* (New York: Norton, 1970). Useful for background on southern politics during presidential Reconstruction are Michael Perman, *Reunion Without Compromise: The South and Reconstruction, 1865–1868* (New York: Cambridge University Press, 1973), and Dan T. Carter, *When the War Was Over: The Failure of Self-Reconstruction in the South, 1865–1867* (Baton Rouge: Louisiana State University Press, 1985). For describing the context of southern Republicans in Congress, see Terry Seip, *The South Returns to Congress: Men, Economic Measures, and Intersectional Relationships, 1868–1879* (Baton Rouge: Louisiana State University Press, 1983).

2. A. S. Wallace to My Dear Sir, December 4, 1872, Alexander S. Wallace Papers, South Caroliniana Library, University of South Carolina; Allen W. Trelease, *White Terror: The Ku Klux Klan Conspiracy and Southern Reconstruction* (1971; rpt. Baton Rouge: Louisiana State University Press, 1995), 362–80, 393, 395; Donald G. Nieman, *Promises to Keep: African Americans and the Constitutional Order, 1776 to the Present* (New York: Oxford University Press, 1991), 83–85; Richard Zuczek, *State of Rebellion: Reconstruction in South Carolina* (Columbia: University of South Carolina Press, 1996), 58, 82, 88–108. For an extensive discussion of Klan violence and the federal response, see Lou F. Williams, *The Great South Carolina Ku Klux Klan Trials, 1871–1872* (Athens: University of Georgia Press, 1996), and Eric Foner, *Reconstruction: America's Unfinished Revolution, 1863–1877* (New York: Harper and Row, 1988), 284, 430, 433.

3. D. T. Corbin to George H. Williams, March 28, 1874; A. S. Wallace to Williams, September 18, 1874; Wallace to Alphonso Taft, August 25, 1876; Wallace to Taft, September 8, 1876; Wallace to Charles Devens, October 18, 1878, Letters Received by the Department of Justice from South Carolina, Record Group 60, National Archives (hereinafter cited as LRDJSC); A. S. Wallace to James A. Garfield, May 5, 1879, James A. Garfield Papers, Library of Congress (hereinafter cited as Garfield Papers). For a good discussion of the retrenchment in federal policy see Nieman, *Promises*, 89–90. For the 1876 campaign of violence see Richard N. Current, *Those Terrible Carpetbaggers: A Reinterpretation* (New York: Oxford University Press, 1988), 350–57; Joel Williamson, *After Slavery: The Negro in*

South Carolina During Reconstruction, 1861–1877 (Chapel Hill: University of North Carolina Press, 1965), 408–12; and Peggy Lamson, *The Glorious Failure: Black Congressman Robert Brown Elliott and the Reconstruction in South Carolina* (New York: Norton, 1972), 239–49. Also useful for the context of violence and the 1876 campaign is Zuczek, *State of Rebellion*, 188–201.

4. For the basic facts of Mackey's life see *Biographical Directory*, 1429. Information on the Charleston riot of 1876 can be found in Wilbert L. Jenkins, *Seizing the New Day: African Americans in Post–Civil War Charleston* (Bloomington: Indiana University Press, 1998), 151–55, and Melinda M. Hennessey, "Racial Violence During Reconstruction: The 1876 Riots in Charleston and Cainhoy," *South Carolina Historical Magazine* 86 (1985): 100–112. For the context of Charleston politics in the period see William C. Hine, "Black Politicians in Reconstruction Charleston, South Carolina: A Collective Study," *Journal of Southern History* 49 (1983): 555–84. For the difficulties between reform and regular Republicans during Chamberlain's governorship see Williamson, *After Slavery*, 399–405; Current, *Those Terrible Carpetbaggers*, 133–48; and Lamson, *Glorious Failure*, 213–33. For Mackey's conduct during the contested election see Lamson, *Glorious Failure*, 255–57; and Williamson, *After Slavery*, 412–13.

5. T. J. Mackey to Robert K Scott, August 6, 1870, Robert K. Scott Papers, Ohio Historical Society, Columbus. L. C. Northrop to D. K. Carter, May 1, 1877, Rutherford B. Hayes Papers, Rutherford B. Hayes Presidential Center, Fremont, Ohio (hereinafter cited as Hayes Papers). E. W. M. Mackey to Charles Levens, November 20, 1878; Edmund H. Deas to Charles Devens, August 16, 1879, LRDJSC. Thomas E. Miller to E. A. Webster, April 15, 1890, Benjamin Harrison Papers, Library of Congress. William J. Cooper Jr., *The Conservative Regime, 1877–1890* (Baltimore: Johns Hopkins University Press, 1968), 105–7. For a discussion of the role played by the Justice Department in the aftermath of the 1878 elections in South Carolina and the South see Xi Wang, *The Trial of Democracy: Black Suffrage and Northern Republicans, 1860–1910* (Athens: University of Georgia Press. 1997), 159–62; Robert M. Goldman, *A Free Ballot and a Fair Count: The Department of Justice and the Enforcement of Voting Rights in the South, 1877–1893* (New York: Fordham University Press,, 2001); and Nieman, *Promises*, 100–101. For a discussion of South Carolina politics and the U.S. attorneys in the immediate aftermath of Redemption see Lou F. Williams, "Federal Enforcement of Black Rights in the Post-Redemption South: The Ellenton Riot Case," in *Local Matters: Race, Crime, and Justice in the Nineteenth-Century South*, ed. Donald G. Nieman and Christopher Waldrep (Athens: University of Georgia Press, 2001), 172–200.

6. For information about Corley's prewar views see Simeon Corley to Charles Lanman, July 28, 1868, Short Sketch of the Life of Simeon Corley, 1869, Simeon Corley Papers, South Caroliniana Library, University of South Carolina (hereinafter cited as Corley Papers); and Foner, *Reconstruction*, 299.

7. Robert B. Elliott to Charles Sumner, May 22, 1867; Simeon Corley to Sumner, December 10, 1867; B. F. Randolph to Sumner, November 23, 1867; Christopher C. Bowen to Sumner, May 22, 1867; Simeon Corley to Sumner, November 25, 1867; Corley to Sumner, July 5, 1867, Charles Sumner Papers, Houghton Library, Harvard University, Cambridge, Mass. Simeon Corley, "To the Voters of the Third Congressional District of South Carolina," April 4, 1868, Corley Papers. Simeon Corley, *Right of Suffrage: Speech of the Hon. Simon Corley of S.C. in the House of Representatives, January 28, 1869* (Washington, D.C.: Congressional Globe Office, 1869). For the lack of participation by many white Democrats in politics in the period see Perman, *Reunion*, 269–336; Williamson, *After Slavery*, 351–53;

and Julie Saville, *The Work of Reconstruction: From Slave to Wage Laborer in South Carolina, 1860–1870* (New York: Cambridge University Press, 1994), 151–95.

8. For the basics on Corley's political career see *Biographical Directory,* 864. Simeon Corley to James A. Garfield, August 30, 1880; W. E. Chandler to Garfield, October 15, 1880; Corley to Garfield, January 27, 1881, Garfield Papers. Union Republican Party of South Carolina, *Address of the State Executive Committee of the Union Republican Party of South Carolina* (Charleston: J. W. Hammond, 1880). For William E. Chandler's political career see Leon B. Richardson, *William E. Chandler, Republican* (New York: Dodd-Mead, 1940).

9. Simeon Corley to Samuel W. Melton, May 25, 1881, LRDJSC. Samuel W. Melton to Mrs. Melton, December 20, 1860; Melton to Mrs. Melton, April 25, 1861; Melton to Mrs. Melton, March 18, 1865, Samuel W. Melton Papers, South Caroliniana Library, University of South Carolina. Williamson, *After Slavery,* 374.

10. Lamson, *Glorious Failure,* 185, 202; Current, *Those Terrible Carpetbaggers,* 332–36, 344; Williamson, *After Slavery,* 399, 404.

11. F. L. Cardozo to R. B. Hayes, May 7, 1878; Samuel W. Melton to Hayes, May 22, 1878; Wade Hampton to Hayes, March 25, 1878; Melton to Hayes, April 8, 1878; William E. Earle to D. T. Corbin, March 9, 1878, Hayes Papers. Williamson, *After Slavery,* 414–16. Cooper, *Conservative Regime,* 29–32.

12. Samuel W. Melton to Benjamin Harris Brewster, March 1882; Melton to Brewster, January 30, 1882; Melton to Wayne MacVeigh, July 4, 1881, LRDJSC. Cooper, *Conservative Regime,* 105–6. Wang, *Trial of Democracy,* 199–200. See as well Goldman, *A Free Ballot and a Fair Count.*

13. Simeon Corley, "To the Voters of the Third Congressional District of South Carolina," April 4, 1868, Corley Papers.

WADE HAMPTON
Conflicted Leader of the Conservative Democracy?
(2007)

Fritz Hamer

In April 1877 Wade Hampton III, Confederate military hero, and now political "savior," declared to a Columbia crowd on his return from Washington that they should "forget we are Democrats or Republicans, white or colored, and remember only that we are South Carolinians."[1] Although Hampton may have used some political hyperbole to soothe a fractious electorate, as the now undisputed governor of the Palmetto State he seemingly wanted to convince white Democrats that blacks, most of them former slaves, should be allowed to participate in the political process. Of course the litmus test for this to happen had to be that African Americans repudiate the Republican Party. That party, which in the minds of many South Carolina whites had corrupted and nearly ruined the state since 1866, had championed the rights of the former slaves. While white Democrats appeared united in their hatred of the Radical Republican regimes of Reconstruction, the latter's rule in South Carolina had ended in 1877. Hampton now offered an olive branch, of sorts, to those black Republicans whom he had reviled for over a decade. And most of Hampton's Democratic allies supported the former general's overtures, for they expected that African Americans would have few alternatives.

But some of Hampton's allies in the 1876 election disagreed. Several former Confederate officers, among them Matthew C. Butler and Martin Gary, had no patience for reconciliation with blacks. In their minds, the battle for the state government, for the very integrity of a white-dominated South Carolina, was to eliminate all political opponents, white or black. In other words, neither the reviled Republicans of both races, nor, for that matter, any other African Americans, should be allowed to participate henceforth in the political process. Did Hampton believe that his prestige and personal qualities were strong enough to overcome such powerful hatreds, or was his Columbia rhetoric just that, something to offer the opposition until he and his lieutenants could eliminate them completely from the political arena? This paper will review his motives and relations with people up to the election of 1876, and will argue that both tendencies were at play. In the final analysis, however, Hampton represented white Democratic resurgence and retrenchment, and while he may have believed that former slaves could be a part of the political process, it would only be on his and his white lieutenants' terms. In their minds only whites had the ability, indeed the very right, to govern the state. But to find out what led Hampton to his "redeemer" leadership role in the crucial election of 1876, one must first review his background.

Until South Carolina's secession in 1860, Hampton's life had little to suggest that he would be embroiled in contentious politics. Although his grandfather had held prestigious military posts, first in the Revolution and later in the War of 1812, and his father also had attained distinction in the latter war, the family focus was to attain land, slaves, and wealth. When the third Wade was born in 1818, he became part of one of the most privileged families in the American South. The Hampton family already controlled vast acreage in the South Carolina Midlands, owned hundreds of slaves, and made millions of dollars from growing cotton. They had few social or economic peers. Wade Hampton III was not just a wealthy scion of a prominent family, but was also well educated and traveled, having attained a degree from South Carolina College and having toured extensively in Europe and the Northeast during his young adult life. Nonetheless, his most important purpose in life was to become a successful plantation manager who would direct vast estates of cotton lands from which the family would continue to derive great wealth. In 1843 he began to manage the family plantation in Mississippi, which included twelve thousand acres and nearly one thousand slaves. Hampton traveled regularly between these holdings and those in the Midlands of South Carolina in order to manage both. His favorite activities, hunting and fishing, could also be assuaged in such endeavors. Like his father and grandfather, Wade viewed politics as a secondary role in society that he reluctantly assumed. In 1852 Richland District constituents elected him for the first time to the South Carolina House of Representatives, and six years later the same voters elevated him to the State Senate. Although he served on legislative committees regarding federal relations, agriculture, and redistricting, he rarely spoke publicly and did not initially distinguish himself in either chamber. And not until his last years in the antebellum legislature did he even speak out on major issues before the legislature. In short, it seems that he served in the State House because his social position required it.[2]

Such modest political ambitions began to change as the rift between North and South grew more intense at the end of the 1850s. In fall 1859 Hampton spoke out against John Brown's raid on Harpers Ferry and warned that if the

North did not condemn this radical abolitionist, the Union could not survive. Although he did not lead the charge when Lincoln became the standard bearer as the Republican presidential nominee, the South Carolina planter supported plans for a secession convention if the Illinois lawyer were elected. Hampton not only voiced his support for the Minutemen, those groups of men in many communities around the state that prior to the national election supported secession, but he formally joined them. Throughout the fall 1860 electoral campaign season, groups of Minutemen held public demonstrations in their own regalia and published a manifesto supporting secession. In the wake of Lincoln's election victory, Hampton continued to support the calling of a secession convention, although he was not subsequently elected to that body. But when South Carolina seceded, Hampton immediately offered his services to defend the newly independent "nation." In the midst of the crisis, however, as South Carolina faced off against the Federal government over the status of Fort Sumter at the mouth of Charleston harbor, Hampton saw fit to leave the state in March 1861 to check his holdings in Mississippi. It was only after his return to the Palmetto State two weeks after Sumter surrendered that Hampton began to organize his now famous legion. The planter-turned-soldier became not only the legion's founder, but also its financier, using his vast wealth to pay for its soldiers' uniforms, equipment, and firearms. By late spring the Confederate high command ordered Hampton's Legion north to defend the newly anointed capitol in Richmond, Virginia.[3]

Hampton's many exploits as a military leader, first of his legendary Hampton Legion and then as cavalry commander of the Army of Northern Virginia, are well known. After the Confederate armies reorganized in spring 1862, the legion was split up, and its commander became a subordinate under the renowned cavalry general, Jeb Stuart. Upon this legendary figure's death in May 1864, Hampton's distinguished service and abilities led to his promotion as Stuart's successor in command of all Confederate cavalry in the Army of Northern Virginia. From Manassas to Gettysburg to Petersburg, the South Carolinian received many wounds in daring attacks against Federal cavalry and infantry. In the last months of the war Hampton went home in a doomed attempt to stop William T. Sherman's march through the Carolinas. Loyal and determined to war's end, Hampton's resilience seemed more tragic because of his own personal losses. First, his brother Frank fell mortally wounded at Brandy Station in June 1863. More than a year later, one of his sons, Preston, was killed in an engagement near Petersburg. To compound these tragic deaths, at the war's end Hampton's family home at Millwood, just outside Columbia, was burned to the ground by Sherman's troops. His holdings in Mississippi, including three steam cotton gins and 4,700 bales of cotton, were likewise lost. Perhaps Hampton's greatest capital loss, however, was the liberation of more than one thousand slaves. In spite of all his dedication to the southern cause, the state's most distinguished surviving Confederate military commander found himself virtually destitute financially and emotionally.[4] Despite his best efforts, Hampton could only recover a small portion of his holdings following his declared bankruptcy in 1868.

In the midst of such personal and capital losses Hampton was slow to accept the new social and political order dawning on postwar South Carolina. Although he rejected emigration to South America or Europe, a course that some of his former Confederate comrades had taken, he was slow to reconcile himself to the Confederacy's demise. In summer 1866 he wrote to his former commander-in-chief, Robert Lee, that "I am not reconstructed yet." Furthermore, he told Lee that "time will prove that you have not fought in vain." It is clear that Hampton would not easily concede that four years of bloodshed and personal loss had been a national and personal waste.[5]

As the defeated Confederate tried to cope with his own personal loss, the political and economic changes occurring within his state became more alarming. For a brief period it had appeared that former Confederates would be able to resume the reins of power with the blessings of President Andrew Johnson. But the Republican-controlled Congress soon refused to accept Johnson's lenient terms for the former Confederacy and reversed the president's Reconstruction policy with a series of laws in 1866 that imposed severe restrictions on most of the old leadership and required the southern states for the first time to accept former slaves as political and social equals. This was an affront, if not worse, to most whites such as Hampton. And they soon showed their opposition.

Hampton expressed this bitterness in greater detail in an 1866 letter to President Andrew Johnson. He denounced what he perceived as a vindictive Congress that was led by Radical Republicans who had usurped their authority and ignored the Constitution by forcing the southern states to adopt the Thirteenth and Fourteenth amendments without due deliberation by their respected white leaders. In short, to Hampton the amendments were forced upon the South illegally. He could also not accept that Congress had responded in such a manner in order to thwart the South Carolina legislature, which in December 1865 had passed a series of "Black Codes" that severely restricted the movement of freedmen and, essentially, returned them almost to the life of servitude that they had recently left. Nor could Hampton see the purpose of what he called the "corrupt" Freedmen's Bureau and "a horde of barbarians—your brutal negro troops" that imposed law and order in the South. Such organizations, he maintained, were an effrontery to whites, but especially to former slaveholders who had had virtual life-and-death mastery over blacks barely a year before. Such a response was natural for men like Hampton who had grown up and been taught that only they had the ability and right to govern the affairs of their state. Now that former slaves were free men to whom Congress had given political rights, Hampton could not fathom such a monolithic shift in social position, even if his beloved South had been defeated militarily.[6]

His bitterness slowly waned in the following months, but Hampton remained true to his upbringing as a planter and former slaveholder. Even though he advocated limited political rights for freedmen, he advised his white friends that they could still control the state legislature by controlling the black vote. Like planters of the antebellum era, Hampton and most of his class could not conceive that former slaves actually had the ability to behave rationally in the political arena. Many former slaveholders believed that freedmen were still inherently imbued with the secondary status they had possessed in slavery. African Americans needed people like Hampton to instruct them and "prevent" them from harming themselves. Such a conclusion came from the paternalist racist assumption that blacks were unable to think for themselves or realize their own best interests. In 1868 he told James Connor, a fellow Confederate veteran from South Carolina, that it was the duty of "every Southern man" to secure the "good will and confidence of the negro." It was even acceptable to send blacks to Congress, since Hampton considered that they could be trusted more than "renegade [whites] or Yankees." In conclusion he advised Connor that "respectable negroes" should be recruited. Presumably Hampton meant freedmen whom whites knew could be relied upon, whether by bribery or intimidation, to accept and serve southern whites in a loyal, that is, subordinate manner.[7]

The assumptions of Hampton and his associates were sorely tested during the following decade as the battle against Republican Party rule in the state ebbed and flowed. At first, most white voters tried to forestall the election of delegates to a new state constitutional convention mandated by Congress. Since the latter had required that a majority of the state's registered electorate ratify the convocation of such a convention, a large number of registered white voters never cast their ballots on election day in November 1867. Despite this unity, the vast majority of registered black voters (85 percent) who voted for such a body was sufficient to validate the elections for the constitutional convention that met two months later. Not surprisingly, the convention's majority of black delegates drafted a new constitution that ushered in tax and land reform, and the establishment of the first formal public education system in the state. Nonetheless, the former cavalry leader continued to believe that whites could influence enough freedmen so that Democratic conservatives could control the legislature when the next round of elections occurred in fall 1868. But Hampton's assumptions, as we will see, proved false.

The Radical Republicans' bold program threatened white Conservatives, who feared losing control of black labor and of political affairs to a Republican Party with majority black support. It was the intention of most white Democratic leaders to prevent this and take back the reins of power in order to forestall what they imagined would be political and social chaos. Although some whites, even Hampton for a time, advocated some peaceful accommodation with Republicans, many believed that only intimidation and violence against their opponents could resurrect white control. Former Confederates such as Martin Gary and Matthew C. Butler decried this perilous new order as an attempt to place the "negro over the white man" whereby Republicans were "at war with the noblest instincts of our [white] race." To those whites who tried to reach an accommodation by political means with former slaves, intransigent conservatives like Butler believed they were badly misled, if not traitors to their race. Butler and his supporters, known as "straight outs," began a campaign of intimidation and violence to attain future electoral victory for conservative Democrats. Such violence ranged from beatings to murder, one of the more extreme cases being the assassination of a black leader, Benjamin Randolph, in October 1868 while the latter was campaigning in Abbeville for a seat in the legislature. Several shots rang out at the local train station and killed him instantly. Yet even in this violent atmosphere blacks and their white Republican allies went to the polls in November and won a significant majority.[8] The Radical Republicans now began to implement their reform agenda—they raised taxes, implemented land redistribution, and installed a locally administered public education system.

Hampton could not legally run for political office because Congress had barred high-ranking Confederate officers from public service, yet his work behind the scenes was not impeded by the Republican victory of November 1868. Since his prediction that whites could control the black vote had proved illusory, he seemed to discard his hopes in that direction. Hampton now tacitly supported the Klan violence that accelerated in the wake of the 1868 elections. Active primarily in the upstate, bands of vigilantes, often clad in frightening regalia, intimidated and attacked white and black Republican supporters with impunity. Unable to end the violence, the Republican governor, Robert K. Scott, appealed to President Grant and Congress for federal troops to help stem the carnage. In April 1871, after the president invoked the Third Enforcement Act (commonly known as the Ku Klux Klan Act), federal troops soon arrested several hundred suspected Klansmen. Even though Hampton publicly spoke out against the violence, he nonetheless led a subscription effort on behalf of the accused for their legal defense. Although one historian has called the act timid and has suggested that it should have been imposed earlier and more forcefully, this action by the national government ended most of the violence. Hundreds were incarcerated, and trials were held. Unfortunately for the authorities, so many suspects turned themselves in that the courts and jails could not process the huge backlog that these arrests and surrenders had created in the justice system. This circumstance, coupled with the expert trial representation that the accused received through the moral support and the financial backing of people such as Hampton and Butler, assured that only a token number of accused Klansmen were convicted, and they generally received light prison sentences. Even though the violence came to an end, the pause proved only temporary. As the campaigning for the fall 1876 elections began in earnest, white conservative elements reignited their campaign of intimidation and violence. And this time Hampton led the effort by running for governor.[9]

Although former Confederates at all levels had eventually been given political amnesty by Congress in 1872, Hampton had remained too preoccupied with personal family issues and his poor finances to take a leadership role in the fight against the Radical Republicans at that time. His efforts to improve his finances collapsed when the insurance company he joined went into bankruptcy less than a year after his appointment to its board. Nevertheless, he still had a keen interest in the political future of his home state. Thus when old Confederate leaders approached him in June 1876 to be the Democratic Party's nomination for governor, he readily accepted.[10]

Hampton's social position and heroic role as a Confederate leader during the war made him the ideal standard bearer for the conservative Democrats. Unanimously nominated in the August party convention, the soldier-turned-politician started a campaign across the state from the upcountry to the low country, defending the virtues of his party and castigating the allegedly corrupt and spendthrift ways of the Radical Republicans. But Hampton's speeches and his obvious public appeal as a hero of the defeated Confederacy became more effective largely because of the private militia—the mounted Red Shirts—that bolstered his appeal and protected him in every community where he took his campaign. On the fall campaign swing through Anderson, Sumter, Winnsboro, and Yorkville, Hampton was met by an impressive entourage of local dignitaries, admiring young women, and scores, sometimes hundreds, of mounted Red Shirts. For one campaign rally in Winnsboro on October 16, 1876, an elaborate itinerary was created and fliers were posted throughout the community.[11] The arrangements outlined where the local Democratic dignitaries were to stand, the location of "colored clubs," and how the "mounted men" were to position themselves so that "colored people of both parties" could be admitted in front of them. In Yorkville a grand parade met Hampton at the train station and turned out for the Democratic nominee's stump speech where he appealed not only to whites, but also to blacks. As usual, he castigated the corrupt Republicans in Columbia and their governor, Daniel Chamberlain; then Hampton appealed for black support. Ironically, he told blacks that they had become "slaves to your political masters" and that to be "freemen they must leave the Loyal League" and join with him to bring "free speech, free ballot, a free press."[12] And yet just a decade before most of the blacks in the audience had been slaves for life to Hampton and to others of his class, chattels devoid of any rights whatsoever. Now fear prevented many black voters at these meetings from disagreeing openly while the Red Shirts stood ready to pounce on any dissenters in the crowd. Except in the low country where blacks outnumbered whites, few of these grand political rallies allowed the opposition to refute Hampton's claims.

In spite of Hampton's appeals on the stump and his professed opposition to campaign violence, his Red Shirt supporters ruthlessly used intimidation and violence throughout the upcountry to suppress Republican opposition. One Laurens County Republican group appealed to Governor Chamberlain for protection because no one "dares to speak nor act with respect of his franchise privileges without being in extreme danger."[13] Individual acts of violence sometimes expanded into major battles that led to injury and death on a large scale. Just as the campaign began in earnest, the Ellenton riots of September 1876 saw black militia carry on a running battle with Red Shirt companies for almost two days before federal troops intervened to end the carnage. At least fifty blacks and one white Red Shirt lay dead at its conclusion. At Cainhoy in the low country blacks and whites faced off again in similar fashion. Here the black militia got the better of the action, but still white Democrats inflicted nearly as many casualties on the Republicans before they fled. Despite such brutal violence occurring all around him, Hampton seemed to remain above the fray, outlining before black audiences why they should support his election. Through an alliance with the whites, he argued, "who owned the land . . . [and] pay the taxes," blacks could redeem the state "together." But, he warned, if they continued with their "carpet-bag friends [the Republicans]," they would lose any aid or support, presumably from whites, when needed.[14]

As Edmund Drago shows in his recent study, some former slaves seemed to take Hampton's words to heart, for the white Red Shirt clubs did possess black allies. There were at least eighteen black Democratic Clubs organized during the 1876 political campaign. It is difficult to determine how many of these clubs actually were formed by political coercion from whites or from genuine disillusionment by blacks with the Republican leadership. Evidence gathered by Drago suggests that these black organizations had members that joined for a variety of reasons, some from conviction, others out of necessity. Some African Americans felt that even if the Democrats were not their best political allies, they did not think that the Republican Party could protect them. In order to continue living and working in their communities, some former slaves consequently believed that they needed to gain favors from white Democrats who would protect and sustain them during and after the elections.[15]

Even though black allies for the Red Shirts did exist, it is clear that most African Americans remained loyal to the Republican Party despite the growing divisions within its ranks during the election campaign. And most of those black voters who switched their allegiance faced severe rebuke from fellow blacks, including their wives. Within most black communities such betrayal often led to expulsion from the household, and sometimes even physical assaults. But white intimidation by the Red Shirts and their allies was far greater. Even so, the results at the polls were very close when the November ballots were tallied. Although the conservative Democrats had a lead of just over one thousand votes across the state, this was initially nullified by the vote count in Laurens and Edgefield counties. County commissioners in these two districts reported voter fraud where Democrats received more votes than actual registered voters. This began the long stalemate over who had won the election. For the next several months both Republicans and Democrats claimed victory.[16]

In spite of this uncertainty Hampton declared himself the winner. He demanded that his Republican opponent step down. Backed by federal troops, Chamberlain refused. A potentially bloody riot almost ensued during the last days of November 1876 as both Republican and Democratic legislators claimed victory for themselves and proceeded to occupy the same chamber in the still-unfinished South Carolina State House, each group led by rival would-be speakers, E. W. M. Mackey for the Republicans and William H. Wallace for the Democrats. The tense situation continued for four days with both sides refusing to leave the chamber. Surrounded by federal troops, on the morning of the fourth day the Democrats reluctantly voted to leave voluntarily when the soldiers outside seemed poised to remove them by force. Meanwhile, disgruntled whites had begun to arrive in Columbia from many areas of the state to gather around the State House, seemingly bent on throwing out the Republican members regardless of the federal troops. Before violence could break out, Hampton displayed commanding leadership when he went before the mob and requested that it disperse. As it did so, his authority was manifest, while the legitimacy of the Republican governor and his party was irrevocably weakened.[17]

While Chamberlain tried to hang on with the aid of federal troops and congressional backing, Hampton had enough public support to have himself inaugurated governor in December 1876 even though he lacked legal authority. He declared in his acceptance speech that he owed much of his success to black voters who "rose above prejudice of race and honest enough to throw off the shackles of party." Yet even though Hampton publicly claimed this black support, others in his own party realized that the Red Shirt bands with their intimidation tactics and recourse to violence had really "won" the election for him, not any putative black crossover voters. A case in point: on election day in one Lexington precinct a Democratic observer admitted that only ten blacks voted the Democratic ticket. While it is difficult to assess how many blacks actually voted Democratic across the entire state, one historian estimates that probably no more than a hundred blacks in each county voted for Hampton and his party.[18]

Nonetheless, even without substantial black support Hampton would eventually force his Republican rival to resign his office. As he and Chamberlain disputed each other's legitimacy into the spring of 1877, Republicans' hopes that somehow their ticket could still win grew ever dimmer. Hampton and his Red Shirts advised their supporters to pay taxes to the Democracy—that is, his own Democratic Party's regime—not to Columbia, so that the Republican regime increasingly could not operate the daily duties of government. In fact the power of the conservative Democrats had grown to such a degree that just before Chamberlain resigned in April 1877 Hampton reputedly claimed that he would have every tax collector in the state hanged if Chamberlain refused to yield his office. But the final chapter in Republican rule only ended after Hampton visited the newly inaugurated President Rutherford B. Hayes in Washington. There he assured Hayes that he would guarantee political rights and protection to blacks as well as whites, regardless of party, and the president in turn agreed to pull out all remaining federal troops from the state. With federal military protection now gone, Chamberlain had no other recourse but to step down and leave the state.[19]

With Hampton and the Democrats finally undisputed victors, the former cavalry hero continued to claim that he regarded both races as equals before the law and that African Americans should enjoy the same political rights and protections as whites. Perhaps the "redeemer" governor truly believed this, but some, if not most, of his lieutenants did not. Men such as Butler and Gary viewed the election of 1876 in the same stark racial terms as George Tillman had previously characterized the 1868 electoral campaign: "Southern Society . . . will not have these people [that is, blacks] rule over us." Or as another Red Shirt leader and future governor of the state, Ben Tillman, put it when looking back at that pivotal year—it was a battle between white "civilization" and black "barbarism."[20]

Whether Hampton considered racial dominance to be the essence of this political struggle or not, it is obvious that he viewed blacks as second-class citizens who could only participate in politics under white supervision. Old Confederates such as Butler were determined to eradicate black political participation, regardless of who might supervise black voters. Although Butler's extreme goal, namely to remove African Americans both from the State House and from local offices, failed in the early post-Reconstruction era, black political participation was steadily eroded over time. And the process started within months of Hampton assuming undisputed office in spring 1877. In Richland County, Senator Beverly Nash and State Supreme Court Justice Jonathan Wright were forced to resign their offices by the fall of 1877 after trumped-up charges of corruption and drunkenness were brought against them. Even if they were not directly threatened, by the early 1880s most black politicians resigned once they realized how tenuous their own position in the white-dominated government had become. A few African Americans held onto their offices through the 1880s only because they came from predominately black counties. Yet even these few who clung to political office had little but symbolic impact on policy. By the 1890s white supremacy would be complete and remained so for most of the next century.[21]

Hampton's political leadership continued to have an impact through the 1878 election. He worked to improve funding for the budding public education system created by the Republicans, and expenditures per pupil continued to rise for both blacks and whites through the 1880s under subsequent governors. But while Hampton's legacy for equal education appeared genuine, his alleged desire for equality in the political process never did. During the Hampton years constitutional office-holders, that is, the elected heads of state agencies, became all white. The former general's party lieutenants found ways to stuff ballot boxes and restricted minority voters through literacy tests and grandfather clauses, two means that steadily excluded more African American voters from exercising their right to vote. And while Hampton oversaw these new restrictions of voting rights, he also did little to support the few remaining African Americans in local offices, even if they were Democrats. Likewise, the few black legislators did not remain long in office after Hampton left the governorship to become U.S. senator in 1879.[22]

In 1878 Hampton was elected to a second term as governor, but plans were already afoot to send him to Washington where his influence on state politics would be minimized. Although the war hero's prestige as a "redeemer" leader would survive as a symbol of white supremacy over the hated Radical Republican regime, his power on the state political stage was no longer essential to white political dominance. Now over sixty, Hampton's age probably affected his situation, as there were younger leaders poised to take over the reins of real political control. In late 1878, following a serious hunting accident, Hampton's very survival even seemed precarious. Even though the hero and victor of the 1876 election survived his accident and continued his political career in Washington for another decade, Hampton became largely a symbol of the old guard whose influence on state politics was steadily eroded. While respected by most of his colleagues in Congress, Hampton's tenure there had little significance for the state or the nation. He rarely spoke to the Senate and often missed sessions because of illness or infirmity. Although the conservative regime that Hampton had returned to power in 1877 continued to maintain political control in South Carolina through most of the 1880s, its days were clearly numbered as Ben Tillman's star began to rise. By the end of the 1880s even Hampton's symbolic value to the state's Young Turks, led by Tillman, was gone. The State Senate voted him out of office on December 11, 1890.[23]

Hampton lived for another decade and struggled to support his family while attending Confederate reunions inside and outside the state when his health permitted. When he died in April 1902 he was praised for his determination and bravery as a soldier who did all in his power to defend his state and the Confederacy during four years of war. There is no denying that he was one of the last of the old cavaliers who fought ferociously for the cause, but his political leadership during and after Reconstruction is more problematic. After the war Hampton tried, as a member of the old guard, to return the state essentially to some semblance of its prewar days when blacks and most whites had accepted the planter oligarchy without question. Born into this established white planter class, he envisioned a world ordered as he perceived it to have been before secession. Although he verbally opposed violence after Appomattox, he still acquiesced in the Red Shirt campaign of 1876. Even though he continued to claim that he had garnered a significant number of black votes—allegedly sixteen thousand—to win back the governorship in 1876, most of his white supporters in that election subsequently admitted that Hampton was in error. As one of them, Ben Tillman, observed years later, "every active worker in the cause knew that in this he was woefully mistaken."[24]

A noble soldier, Wade Hampton was at best a resolute but reactionary politician, grudgingly willing to concede to blacks a place in the political arena only on white Democrats' terms. Despite his rhetoric to the contrary, Hampton accepted the tactics of intimidation and violence in order to "save" the state from what he and other white Democratic leaders considered chaos under a black-dominated Republican Party. Like most whites, he believed that the best option for all, blacks and whites, was a paternalistic society that controlled the economic and political course of the state. To Hampton, equitable distribution of political power and economic freedom for recently freed slaves were a recipe for disaster. His philosophy and upbringing made his political career one of reaction and retrenchment.[25]

NOTES

1. The author wishes to thank Jennifer Fitzgerald, a colleague at the South Carolina State Museum, for reading this paper and providing valuable comments and suggestions. Walter Brian Cisco, *Wade Hampton: Confederate Warrior, Conservative Statesman* (Washington, D.C.: Brassey's, 2004), 266.

2. Cisco, *Wade Hampton*, 10–12, 17, 23, 29, 31, 46; Hampton to E. Ham, January 1, 1877, Hampton Family Papers, Manuscripts Division, South Caroliniana Library, University of South Carolina–Columbia (here after HFP); N. Louise Bailey, Mary L. Morgan, Carolyn R. Taylor, *Biographical Directory of the South Carolina Senate, 1776–1986* (Columbia: University of South Carolina Press, 1986), vol. 1: 656–59.

3. Cisco, *Wade Hampton*, 51–52.

4. Ibid., 55–163; Charles E. Cauthen, ed., *Family Letters of the Three Wade Hamptons, 1782–1901* (Columbia: University of South Carolina Press, 1953), 113–14; Hampton to E. Ham, January 1, 1877, HFP.

5. Hampton to R. E. Lee, July 21, 1866, HFP.

6. Cauthen, ed., *Letters of the Hamptons*, 126–41. For quotations from this letter see especially 129–31.

7. Hampton to John Connor, April 9, 1868, HFP. For one of the best overviews of the general attitude towards blacks by most whites in the state after 1865 see Stephen Kantrowitz, *Ben Tillman and the Reconstruction of White Supremacy* (Chapel Hill: University of North Carolina Press, 2000), 41, 44.

8. For the failed effort to forestall the election of delegates to the state constitutional convention in November 1867 see Walter Edgar, *South Carolina: A History* (Columbia: University of South Carolina Press, 1998), 385–86. For the division among whites in 1868 and the violent actions led by people like Gary, see Richard Zuczek, *State of Rebellion: Reconstruction in South Carolina* (Columbia: University South Carolina Press, 1996), 51–52.

9. For the support Hampton gave the indicted Klansmen, see Zuczek, *State of Rebellion*, 100; for the violence perpetrated by the organization, see Zuczek, *State of Rebellion*, 94–100, and Cisco, *Wade Hampton*, 204–6. Also see Lou Falkner Williams, *The Great South Carolina Ku Klux Klan Trials, 1871–1872* (Athens: University of Georgia Press, 1996), 53.

10. On the Congressional amnesty for former Confederates see Eric Foner, *Reconstruction: America's Unfinished Revolution, 1863–1877* (New York: Harper and Row, 1988), 504. For Hampton's tragic personal and financial problems in this period, see Cisco, *Wade Hampton*, 198–201, 210–11. And for his acceptance of the Democratic nomination for governor, see the typescript of narration dated July 25, 1876, HFP, and Walter Allen, *Chamberlain's Administration in South Carolina* (New York: G.P. Putnam's Sons, 1888), 400.

11. For details about the Hampton political rallies see the handbill entitled "Celebration in Honor of General Wade Hampton at Winnsboro," October 16, 1876, HFP, and *Yorkville Enquirer*, October 19, 1876; the author wishes to thank Debra Franklin, South Carolina State Museum researcher, for taking extensive notes of the latter for this study.

12. The Loyal League had originally been organized in the North during the war to rally support for the Union; after 1865 many new local chapters sprang up in the South and consisted largely of freedmen.

13. For this and the following see Zuczek, *State of Rebellion*, 174, 176–78.

14. Dewitt Grant Jones, "Wade Hampton and the Rhetoric of Race: A Study of the Speaking of Wade Hampton on the Race Issue in South Carolina, 1865–1878," PhD diss., Louisiana State University, 1988, 144–45.

15. See Edmund L. Drago, *Hurrah for Hampton: Black Red Shirts in South Carolina during Reconstruction* (Fayetteville: University of Arkansas Press, 1998), particularly 16, 22–34.

16. For review of the vote tallies and the stalemate that ensued, see Zuczek, *State of Rebellion*, 193. For black attempts to switch to the Democratic side and how insignificant such occurrences actually were, see Joel Williamson, *After Slavery: The Negro in South Carolina During Reconstruction, 1861–1877* (Chapel Hill: University of North Carolina Press, 1965), 408–12. Nevertheless, Cisco, *Wade Hampton*, 232–34, tries to claim that many blacks did switch to the Democrats. Also see Richard M. Gergel, "Wade Hampton and the Rise of One Party Racial Orthodoxy in South Carolina," *Proceedings of the South Carolina Historical Association* (n.p., 1977), 6–9.

17. For an account of the stalemate in the State House after the election, see Cisco, *Wade Hampton*, 250–52.

18. For an account of Hampton's inaugural address and its contents, see *Charleston News and Courier*, "extra edition," December 14, 1876, HFP, and Cisco, *Wade Hampton*, 256–58. For estimates on the number of black voters that supported Hampton, see Williamson, *After Slavery*, 411.

19. On the threat by Hampton see Cisco, *Wade Hampton,* 267; for the end of Chamberlain's tenure, 266–69.

20. For George Tillman's remark, see Kantrowitz, *Ben Tillman,* 53; for Ben Tillman's characterization, see Zuczek, *State of Rebellion,* 160. Also see William Cooper, *The Conservative Regime: South Carolina, 1877–1890* (Baltimore: Johns Hopkins University Press, 1968).

21. On Wright's removal from office see James Lowell Underwood and W. Lewis Burke Jr., eds., *At Freedom's Door: African American Founding Fathers and Lawyers in Reconstruction South Carolina* (Columbia: University of South Carolina Press, 2000), 64–67. On Beverly Nash's removal see John H. Moore, *Columbia and Richland County: A South Carolina Community, 1740–1990* (Columbia: University of South Carolina Press, 1993), 265–66. For the general campaign used by Hampton and his allies to remove most blacks from office, see Moore, *Columbia and Richland County,* 267. For a comprehensive examination of the removal of blacks from politics in the 1880s, see Cooper, *Conservative Regime,* 90–107.

22. On Hampton's short tenure as governor and his modest success in carrying out his election promises to blacks, see Kantrowitz, *Ben Tillman,* 78–79; Williamson, *After Slavery,* 412–17, and Williams, *Great South Carolina Ku Klux Klan Trials,* 90, 96, 111–12. Also see Gergel, "Wade Hampton and the Rise of One Party Racial Orthodoxy," 9–14.

23. On Hampton's health and waning influence, see Cisco, *Wade Hampton,* 270–324, and Kantrowitz, *Ben Tillman,* 92–94, 185.

24. Kantrowicz, *Ben Tillman,* 78.

25. Kantrowicz, *Ben Tillman,* 78–79, argues persuasively that Hampton's paternalistic view of race was really little different from the violence which Ben Tillman and Matthew Butler advocated in 1876. In the end, both sides believed that the only proper and conceivable order of society was for whites to dominate blacks.

GOVERNOR CHAMBERLAIN AND THE END OF RECONSTRUCTION

(1977)

Robert J. Moore

It was circus day in Columbia, and the parade was the main attraction that morning of April 11, 1877. Hardly anyone noticed a pale, bald, handsome man trudge from the State House for the last time. As Daniel H. Chamberlain climbed into his carriage and slowly made his lonely way down crowded Richardson Street (now Main Street) to his home on Richland Street, there was neither jeering nor cheering to mark his going.[1] He had been the hope of the Republican Party of South Carolina and the dilemma of the national Republican Party in the last few months, but now it was all over. The drama of Reconstruction closed with undramatic compliance by southern Republicans to the nation's loss of will to enforce majority rule in South Carolina.

Thus ended Reconstruction in the Palmetto State. It had been the era of pillage and plunder and imposition of barbarism over civilization—or the era of the noble experiment in biracial democracy replacing a white slaveholding aristocracy. Which of these it was depended on whether one rejoiced with the triumphant Wade Hampton or mourned with the crestfallen Daniel Chamberlain.

Chamberlain did not fit the stereotype of a "Carpetbagger." He was born on a Massachusetts farm, the eighth of nine children. The family had a scholarly bent; three finished college, and the youngest, Leander, became a nationally prominent Presbyterian clergyman. Daniel graduated from Yale in 1862 with high academic and oratorical honors. President Woolsey proclaimed him "a born leader of men." His abolitionist attitudes led him to leave Harvard Law School after only one year to become an officer in a Negro regiment. Though he didn't resume his formal studies, he maintained a lifelong interest in the classics and spiced his high-flown oratory with Latin and Greek phrases. He was a quiet, scholarly intellectual with polished manners who found much that was distasteful in political life. His dignified bearing and personal courage forced grudging admiration from upper-crust South Carolinians.[2] But the circumstances of Reconstruction cast him in the role of leader of the masses rather than the oligarchs and made him untrustworthy in the eyes of the latter. However, the governor's goal of disarming white opposition to the Republican Party enjoyed considerable success for a time. He received numerous commendations for his efforts.[3]

His fiscal conservatism and his leadership against corruption and incompetence within his party, though perhaps motivated less by moral indignation than by ultimate party interest, almost captured the support of a significant portion of white Carolinians. He won the admiration of Francis W. Dawson and his editorial support, for a season, in the influential *News and Courier.* In July of 1876, South Carolina's most widely read newspaper ran a two-week series of lengthy articles spelling out the accomplishments of the Chamberlain administration and urging fellow Democrats to support the reform governor for re-election. Dawson argued that, since Negro voters outnumbered whites by about thirty thousand, the only way a Democratic candidate could win the governor's seat would be through a massive campaign of intimidation and fraud.[4]

This argument became well known. What was not so openly known was that Chamberlain had been working to gain the confidence of major Charleston businessmen. Such an alliance between reform Republicans and business-oriented Democrats would claim a broad middle ground in South Carolina politics that would be hard to beat. The outlines of this discreet movement toward accommodation emerge in the mutually appreciative correspondence between Chamberlain and Dawson.[5] Had the only issues been honesty and competency, the alliance might have worked, with far-reaching effects on southern history. But the ever present issue of race intervened. While Dawson tried to persuade fellow Democrats that Chamberlain was their best bet, racial antagonism boiled over and dissolved his efforts.

First, there were strikes of the rice-field workers in Beaufort and Colleton counties. Chamberlain's even-handed law enforcement and refusal to deal harshly with the strikers reminded planters that the state government was not their tool. Far more dramatic and important in setting Democratic minds on going "Straight-Out" was the Hamburg Massacre. This July clash left six blacks and one white dead, and in its wake Governor Chamberlain put the president on notice that troops might be needed to maintain order. The action was interpreted as antiwhite by most Democrats who had held back from the "Straight-Out," full Democratic campaign advocated by Matthew C. Butler and Martin Gary. How can a white man, they reasoned, be trusted when he doesn't take the side of whites in a racial confrontation? The nomination of Wade Hampton, who returned in 1876 from his second home in Mississippi, was assured, and the "Red Shirt Campaign" geared up. Even Dawson deserted his grand plan and threw the full weight of the *News and Courier* into the bitter and desperate struggle to oust the "carpetbaggers," "scalawags," and "nigras."

The question of who actually won the election of 1876 is unanswerable. There is ample documentation of widespread intimidation and fraud, especially on the part of Democrats, who were absolutely determined to overcome the black majority. Much of the "bulldozing" was admitted both at the time and in subsequent accounts by Democratic participants and observers.[6] The intriguing story is not who should have been elected but how Chamberlain was skillfully maneuvered out of power.

In the months following the election of 1876 South Carolinians were treated to the spectacle of a dual government with all the anxiety, disorder, and danger that suggests. Both Chamberlain and Hampton were sworn in as governor and tried to perform the functions of the office. Two houses of representatives claimed legitimacy, one loyal to "Governor" Hampton, the other to "Governor" Chamberlain, and neither was able to legislate effectively. The situation was extremely dangerous. Republicans were in particular peril because Hampton's Red Shirts held the preponderance of armed strength in the state. Chamberlain's health suffered under the strain of the anxiety, and his wife lived in perpetual fear of his assassination.[7]

Two factors prevented open fighting and the immediate overthrow of the Republican administration. One was Hampton's strategy of force without violence. He restrained his seething supporters from the violence which would have invited large-scale intervention by the federal government. The second factor was the presence of United States troops. There were only a few hundred soldiers in South Carolina, but they were the key to the survival of Chamberlain's government. A detachment took control of the State House on the night before the legislature convened and remained in occupation throughout the four-month period of dual government.

United States troops in the State House brought a storm of protest and controversy. E. L. Godkin, whose journal had turned against Reconstruction long before, characterized the occupation of the State House as unprecedented, unconstitutional, and revolutionary.[8] Chamberlain defended the action as legal, necessary, and proper under the circumstances.[9]

The impact of the dual government on private individuals was striking. Acute anxiety and confusion were the main symptoms. The letters received in Chamberlain's office were filled with expressions of fear and requests for help. Citizens complained of being driven from the land they had rented and farmed for years. Some were physically abused; others were ordered to leave the state. The loss of jobs was the most common complaint. The nearly illiterate letter written by C. S. Belton of Anderson sums up the anguish of many. "We is in a Bade condition" begins the touching letter; then it catalogues the problems—Democrats won't hire you if you voted Republican; doctors make you pay before treatment if you voted Republican; lawyers won't take your case before a trial justice if you voted Republican. He concludes: "som of us sees hard time just because we voted for you."[10] Chamberlain's usual reply expressed his sympathy with their plight and his inability to help. He hoped when the new president was chosen peace and protection might be restored.[11]

Republican local officials suffered some of the same anxiety. There were dual office holding and conflicting allegiances right down to the grassroots local level. In January 1877, Hampton informed Chamberlain's appointees by a printed form letter of removal from office and proceeded to appoint his own officials. In any particular locality there was a question of which officials had authority to enforce the law, make arrests, release prisoners on bond, and collect taxes. Chamberlain received numerous inquiries from officials about how to handle these conflicts. Citizens were also insistent on knowing to which county treasurer they should pay their taxes and to which trial justices they should swear out warrants against offenders. In some instances, Democrats physically took over offices, pushed the Republican claimant out, and established Hampton's man. W. J. Mixson, a trial justice from Barnwell County, informed Chamberlain that whites were breaking into the homes of blacks and beating people, but they would not submit to arrest by a Republican official.[12]

He needed help in law enforcement, but Chamberlain had no help to give. This powerlessness to enforce the law contributed to the Republican's loss of credibility and his downfall. One can sense in the Chamberlain papers and letter books a sweeping away of confidence and a spreading recognition of impending doom.[13] The papers of Wade Hampton evoke an opposite feeling—and for good reason. His star was rising. His policy of force without overt violence was paying off.

Four factors were fundamental to the decline and fall of Daniel H. Chamberlain and Reconstruction in South Carolina. Three were local, and one was national. First among local factors was money. Hampton had the support of the men of property in the state, and he used their financial assistance to oil the gearing up of his administration while the Republican apparatus choked in the dust of empty coffers. On December 21, 1876, the business and professional elite of Charleston, many of whom had sought cooperation with Chamberlain a few months before, met at Hibernian Hall and resolved to pay taxes only to a Hampton government. "Charleston and the sedate Conservatives were finishing loyally with the 'red hots.' Straight-outs and Red Shirts in the middle and up country had begun."[14]

On January 8, 1877, mass meetings were held in at least sixteen counties and endorsed Hampton's request that taxpayers voluntarily submit to his government a portion of their tax liability so that he might have money to operate on.[15] Checks began to arrive directly in Hampton's office within three days, and

$120,000 had poured in by March.[16] Hampton thus was able to pay officials and support state agencies that would recognize the legitimacy of his administration. For example, the Lunatic Asylum ran out of funds and the superintendent, Dr. J. E. Ensor, had the alternatives of releasing the inmates, leaving them interned but unattended, or turning to Hampton for funds. He turned to Hampton.[17]

In contrast, Chamberlain's government had no funds and only a trickle of money coming in. To add insult to penury, the Democrats obtained a Supreme Court injunction in December to prevent any state funds being withdrawn from the banks used as depositories.[18] This was an empty gesture as the bank accounts were also empty.

But this empty gesture was symbolic of the second local factor of major importance—Chamberlain's lack of support from the state courts. After both men won lower court decisions on who had proper authority Hampton won a Supreme Court judgment on his authority to pardon one Tilda Norris. An extraordinary set of circumstances surrounded the case. The court was composed of Franklin J. Moses Sr. and A. J. Willard, both Republicans who had become sympathetic to Hampton, and J. J. Wright, a black Republican. During the proceedings Judge Moses became fatally ill and the deliberations were left to Willard and Wright. Willard's position was known, and powerful pressures were placed on Wright. He first signed the release order after dire warnings from Democrats but later repudiated the act after receiving brotherly advice from Robert Brown Elliott. Finally, on March 2, Judge Willard took the bull by the horns, ordered the release of Tilda Norris, and thus recognized the legitimacy of Wade Hampton as governor.[19]

The courts were making legitimate what the majority of white people in the state were bound and determined to see happen. This absolute determination was a third fundamental factor in the fall of Chamberlain and the triumph of the Democrats. Hampton, himself, showed the way. On the evening after Chamberlain was inaugurated by his friends, Hampton told his cheering admirers: "The people have elected me Governor, and, by the Eternal God, I will be Governor or we shall have a military governor."[20] A Chester County trial justice quoted Judge T. J. Mackey as declaring that "if the Federal Authorities attempt to seat Mr. Chamberlain, Mr. Chamberlain will be destroyed, and I would be the first in that event, to give the word."[21] Hampton reorganized the militia, with the Red Shirt rifle clubs being commissioned as units in the new force."[22] The certainty that thousands of Red Shirts would converge on Columbia if Hampton gave the word was a potent factor in all negotiations."[23] The threat of violence was ever present to chill the ardor of Chamberlain supporters and fire the enthusiasm of Hampton partisans.

At least two writers friendly to Hampton were convinced that he would have led his followers in rebellion against the United States had the dispute not been resolved in his favor. When President Hayes interviewed Hampton in March he asked what South Carolinians would do if Chamberlain were confirmed as governor. Hampton replied "that the first thing would be that every Republican tax collector in the state should be hanged within twenty-four hours."[24] White Carolinians held overt violence to a fairly low level in deference to Hampton's judgment on the proper strategy. They perceived their condition as so desperate under Republican rule that they were ready to do whatever their leader thought necessary to win.

In the face of this dogged determination, backed by armed strength, court decisions, and the propertied interests, the only possible salvation for Chamberlain was active support by an equally determined federal government. But the government at Washington was in only slightly less disarray than the government of South Carolina. Grant was a lame-duck president, and the dispute over the presidential election was not settled until two days before the March 4 inaugural date.

Had Samuel J. Tilden, the Democratic contender, been triumphant, Chamberlain was positive his Republican government would be allowed to perish. However, he nourished some hope that if Rutherford B. Hayes emerged the victor, South Carolina Republicans might be sustained. But Hayes was not inclined to be of any assistance to Chamberlain. His personal temperament, desire for sectional conciliation, reading of northern public opinion, constitutional reservations, and the implied promises employed in winning recognition as president—all militated against Hayes attempting to restore the atrophied Republican administration in South Carolina. Precipitating a head-on test of power and endurance against the iron-willed and fanatically determined majority of white southerners would promote not peace but continued strife. Nor would it be in the long-range interest of the Republican Party in the South, which, in order to survive and flourish, would have to attract white men "of substance." Nor would such a use of federal power be tolerated by northern voters whose enthusiasm for reforming the South and guaranteeing political equality of the races had waned. Thus reasoned President Hayes, who confided to his diary: "Both Houses of Congress and the public opinion of the Country are plainly against the use of the army to uphold either claimant to the State Government in case of a contest."[25]

After his inauguration, Hayes went through the motions of deliberating on the matter, interviewing rival governors and seeking the counsel of his cabinet. But probably the decision was already made, the bargain already struck. In late December, Hayes had been impressed by a visit from Judge T. J. Mackey of Chester, South Carolina, who pressed Hampton's claims and delivered a letter from the would-be governor. Hayes recorded the visit as "The political event of the week. . . . Mackey is a fluent and florid talker. His representations are such as lead me to hope for good results by a wise policy in the South."[26] On the day Hayes was inaugurated, Senator Stanley Matthews, a fellow Ohioan and close confidant of the president, wrote to Chamberlain suggesting that he agree to withdrawal of federal support of his claim "for the sake of the peace of the community" and, he might have added, for the relief of the new president. William M. Evarts, secretary of state–designate, added a postscript to Matthews's letter which seemed to endorse the idea (though he later denied he intended endorsement). The letter, which issued from the spirit of the famous Wormley Hotel agreement, was a crushing blow to any lingering hopes Chamberlain may have retained. As an added insult, the letter was delivered by a special messenger—none other than Colonel A. C. Haskell, chairman of the South Carolina Democratic Committee! Chamberlain found the suggestion that he abdicate "embarrassing beyond endurance." In his reply he contended that there were better means "to conciliate and pacify the South" than "to permit Hampton to reap the fruits of a campaign of murder and fraud."[27]

Although Chamberlain must have realized that the decision had already been made to abandon him, he accepted when the president asked him in late March to come to Washington to confer on how best to end the dispute. He arrived on March 27, and during the next two or three days he had long conversations with the president, cabinet members, and others. Chamberlain told Hayes that removal of the troops would result in the practical resolution of the dispute in favor of the opposition, without regard to legal claims and would leave loyal Republican citizens defenseless against the illegal Democratic military organization.[28]

Hampton, also summoned to Washington, gave the president his promise to "secure to every citizen, the lowest as well as the highest, black as well as white, full and equal protection in the enjoyment of all his rights under the Constitution of the United States."[29] This pledge was justification enough for Hayes and the cabinet. On April 2, 1877, the cabinet unanimously recommended that the troops be withdrawn on grounds that no rioting or civil disturbances existed to justify occupation of a seat of government.[30]

Chamberlain traveled to New York City before making the lonely return to South Carolina.[31] For Hampton the train trip home was a triumphal procession ending with greeting by a huge crowd in Columbia. Music for the occasion was provided by a United States Army band! The rejoicing of the white minority knew no bounds. April 11, the day the governor's office changed hands, was a beautiful spring day. It was an omen for some that Carolina was now to have a new birth. A newspaper advertisement adjacent to the article describing the transition urged people to paint their houses and make them clean and bright in keeping with the brighter times ahead with Hampton.[32]

But the final letters Chamberlain received as governor struck a somber note. A trial justice wrote: If President Hayes abandons you "he leaves the col'd people in the hands of their oppressors without the ability of perpetuating their freedom. And he has taken upon himself a fearful responsibility."[33] A fellow carpetbagger wrote: "A few days ago, a colored man said to me—'To think that Hayes could "go back on us" now, when we had to wade through blood to help place him where he now is.' It was only then, that the full force of our position struck me."[34]

How Americans interpret the Reconstruction is more important than how they interpret most events because that interpretation affects public policy concerning race, role of government, and the relationship of states to the federal government. Daniel H. Chamberlain's own interpretation of Reconstruction and his fall from power went through an evolutionary process and ended up exactly 180 degrees from his defensive statements of 1877. On the day the troops evacuated the State House, Chamberlain declared in his farewell message to the Republicans of South Carolina that "by order of the President whom your votes alone rescued from overwhelming defeat, the Government of the United States abandons you, deliberately withdraws from you its support, with the full knowledge that the lawful Government of the State will be speedily overthrown."[35]

On July 4, 1877, in a lengthy holiday oration at Woodstock, Connecticut, he became much more emphatic in his denunciation of "the cowardice and treachery of President Hayes' Southern policy." It was "unconstitutional and revolutionary, subversive of constitutional guarantees, and false to every dictate of political honor, public justice, and good morals."[36]

Privately, however, Chamberlain admitted to his friend, William Lloyd Garrison, that his ouster was inevitable, given the circumstances. Three factors were most important. First, "the uneducated negro was too weak, no matter what his numbers, to cope with the whites." Second, "We had lost . . . the sympathy of the North, in some large measure, though we never deserved it so certainly as in 1876 in South Carolina." Third, the disputed presidential election caused "the defeated Republicans under Hayes to sell us out."[37]

Nearly two years after his defeat, Chamberlain published in the *North American Review* a resounding defense of Negro suffrage and attacked the Social Darwinist position (though he didn't use the term) that the very overthrow of the Negro-supported governments proves blacks are not capable of self-government and thus do not deserve to participate in government. "Such conclusions are as illogical as they are immoral." The right to vote and exercise political power are "totally independent of the power or wealth or education of the voter."[38]

Nothing seems to illustrate more clearly the rising tide of white-supremacy ideology and Social Darwinism than the fact that by 1890 Governor Chamberlain himself was swept along with it. There were also personal factors that affected the metamorphosis of his public views on race and states' rights and Reconstruction. As a highly successful New York lawyer he had become a political independent in the 1880s and usually supported Democratic candidates for president. In addition, he spent considerable spans of time again in South Carolina, acting as receiver for a bankrupt railroad. (He renewed his friendship and maintained correspondence with Francis W. Dawson.)[39] He circulated in the "best" circles of society and came to a greater appreciation of southern gentlemen.

By the 1890s, about the only portion of his previous interpretation that remained intact was his conviction that Hayes had deserted Southern Republicans "in order to save the Presidency for the Republican Party." In a clever and eloquent speech before a cheering audience in Boston in 1890, he declared that the federal government must let the Negroes alone to work out their own destiny and to protect their own rights. Their constitutional rights are the same as those of whites, and their political freedom will come as they learn how "to use and assert those rights."[40] This is the same argument he had labeled "illogical" and "immoral" in 1879.

In 1901, Chamberlain wrote an article for an important series in *Atlantic Monthly* reassessing Reconstruction. He declared Republican Reconstruction policy to have been a grievous mistake which was motivated largely by blind partisanship and less by misguided philanthropy. He had come to the conclusion that his reform faction could not have brought good honest government to South Carolina even if allowed to continue in office. There had been too much dishonesty, too much ignorance, too much incompetence to overcome. Furthermore, Reconstruction efforts to help Negroes had been harmful to them. They should be allowed to develop on their own to greater proficiency in those simple manual tasks which are their lot as established by decree from a higher being.[41]

Southern whites found great delight and comfort in Chamberlain's conversion to their view. Nothing so confirms conviction as to have the antagonist won over. And the white South's triumph was almost complete by 1901. Scientists had presented evidence that supported popular racial prejudices. The Supreme Court had converted the Fourteenth Amendment into a bulwark of protection for corporations and had placed its stamp of approval on racial segregation. The president and Congress had acquiesced in the disfranchisement and segregation of Negroes in southern states. The nation had accepted what William A. Dunning had approvingly called "The Undoing of Reconstruction." And historians, led by Dunning and John W. Burgess of Columbia University, were joining Daniel H. Chamberlain in accepting the essential southern story of Reconstruction.

NOTES

1. *Charleston News and Courier,* April 12, 1877; F. A. Porcher, "The Last Chapters in the History of Reconstruction in South Carolina," *Southern Historical Society Papers* (n.p.), vol. 13: 83–85.

2. James Green, "Personal Recollections of Hon. Daniel H. Chamberlain, Ex-governor of South Carolina," *Proceedings of the Worcester Society of Antiquity* (1908): 257–69; Walter Allen, *Governor Chamberlain's Administration in South Carolina: A Chapter of Reconstruction of the Southern States* (New York: G. P. Putnam's Sons, 1888), 524–26; *Charleston News and Courier,* June 5, 1876.

3. Governor Daniel H. Chamberlain's Papers, South Carolina Department of Archives and History, Columbia (cited hereafter as Chamberlain Papers).

4. *Charleston News and Courier,* May 30, July 5–18, 1876.

5. Francis Warrington Dawson Papers, David M. Rubenstein Rare Book and Manuscript Library, Duke University, Durham, N.C.

6. See especially Henry T. Thompson, *Ousting the Carpetbagger from South Carolina* (Columbia: R. L. Bryan Co., 1926), 115–16, 129; Alfred B. Williams, *Hampton and His Red Shirts: South Carolina's Deliverance in 1876* (Charleston: Walker, Evans & Cogswell Co., 1935), 365–66; Senator B. R. Tillman, "The Struggles of '76: How S.C. Was Delivered from Carpetbag and Negro Rule at the Red Shirt Reunion at Anderson. Personal Reminiscences and Incidents by Sen. B.R. Tillman" (Anderson, S.C.: n.p., August 25, 1909), 26–39; Chamberlain Papers, August–November 1876; Narcisa Gonzales to Grandmother, August 19, 1876, Elliott-Gonzales Papers, Southern Historical Collection, Wilson Library, University of North Carolina, Chapel Hill.

7. Allen, *Governor Chamberlain's Administration,* 466; Green, "Personal Recollections of Hon. Daniel H. Chamberlain," 264.

8. *The Nation* 23 (December 7, 1876): 337; *The Nation* 24 (January 4, 1877): 4.

9. Allen, *Governor Chamberlain's Administration,* 442–44.

10. February 20, 1877, Chamberlain Papers.

11. General Letters, Governor Daniel H. Chamberlain, South Carolina Department of Archives and History, Columbia (cited hereafter as Chamberlain Letterbooks).

12. January 4, 1877, Chamberlain Papers.

13. In January he exhorted appointees to hold their offices and perform their duties. In March he advised them to wait and see what would happen.

14. Williams, *Hampton and His Red Shirts,* 429; *Charleston News and Courier,* December 22, 1876.

15. *Charleston News and Courier,* January 9, 1877; Williams, *Hampton and His Red Shirts,* 434.

16. Porcher, "Last Chapters in South Carolina Reconstruction," 74.

17. Williams, *Hampton and His Red Shirts,* 426–27.

18. *Charleston News and Courier,* December 9, 1876.

19. *New York Times,* March 2, 1877; Porcher, "Last Chapters in South Carolina Reconstruction," 72–74; T. Harry Williams, *Hayes: Diary of a President, 1875–1881* (New York: David McKay Co., Inc., 1964), 440; Francis Butler Simkins and Robert Hilliard Woody, *South Carolina During Reconstruction* (Chapel Hill: University of North Carolina Press, 1932), 533–34.

20. *Charleston News and Courier,* December 8, 1876.

21. Adam R. Sloan to Chamberlain, February 24, 1877, Chamberlain Papers.

22. Porcher, "Last Chapters in South Carolina Reconstruction," 74.

23. Hampton M. Jarrell, *Wade Hampton and the Negro: The Road Not Taken* (Columbia: University of South Carolina Press, 1949), 105.

24. Williams, *Hampton and His Red Shirts,* 446; Jarrell, *Wade Hampton and the Negro,* 104.

25. Williams, *Hayes: Diary,* 76–77, 85. For discussions of the lack of national will or of Republican Party will to enforce Reconstruction policy in 1877 see Vincent P. DeSantis,

Republicans Face the Southern Question: The New Departure Years, 1877–1897 (Baltimore: Johns Hopkins Press, 1959), 24–65; James McPherson, *The Abolitionist Legacy from Reconstruction to the NAACP* (Princeton, N.J.: Princeton University Press, 1975), 35–52, 81–94; Rayford W. Logan, *The Betrayal of the Negro from Rutherford B. Hayes to Woodrow Wilson* (New York: Collier Books, 1965), 29–30; Eli Ginsberg and Alfred S. Eichner, *The Troublesome Presence: American Democracy and the Negro* (Glencoe, Ill.: Free Press of Glencoe, 1964), 178–88, 232–34; Harry Barnard, *Rutherford B. Hayes and His America* (New York: Bobbs-Merrlll Co. Inc., 1954), 268–69; Kenneth E. Davison, *The Presidency of Rutherford B. Hayes* (Westport, Conn.: Greenwood Press, Inc., 1972), 142–43; Keith Ian Polokoff, *The Politics of Inertia: The Election of 1876 and the End of Reconstruction* (Baton Rouge: Louisiana State University Press, 1973), chapter 7; Stanley P. Hirshon, *Farewell to the Bloody Shirt: Northern Republicans and the Southern Negro, 1877–1893* (Bloomington: Indiana University Press, 1962), 28–33; *New York Times*, April 3, 1877; *The Nation* 23 (December 28, 1876): 376.

26. Williams, *Hayes: Diary*, 61–62.

27. Allen, *Governor Chamberlain's Administration*, 469–71; *New York Times*, March 8, 1877.

28. Allen, *Governor Chamberlain's Administration*, 472–77. *New York Times*, March 28, 29, 30, 31; April 3, 1877.

29. Williams, *Hayes: Diary*, 80–81; *New York Times*, April 4, 1877.

30. *Columbia Daily Register*, April 12, 1877.

31. *New York Times*, April 3, 1877.

32. Williams, *Hayes: Diary*, 444–45.

33. W. J. Mixson to Chamberlain, April 1877, Chamberlain Papers.

34. William T. Rodenbach to Chamberlain, April 8, 1877, Chamberlain Papers.

35. Allen, *Governor Chamberlain's Administration*, 481.

36. Ibid., 519.

37. Chamberlain to William Lloyd Garrison, June 11, 1877, Chamberlain Papers; Allen, *Governor Chamberlain's Administration*, 504–5.

38. *North American Review* 130 (February 1879): 172.

39. Green, "Personal Recollections of Hon. Daniel Chamberlain," 264–65; correspondence in Dawson Papers gives indication that many more letters must have passed between the two.

40. D. H. Chamberlain, "Dependent Pension Bills; and the Race Problem at the South," speech before the Massachusetts Reform Club, February 8, 1890 (n.p.; pamphlet at South Caroliniana Library, University of South Carolina, Columbia).

41. Daniel H. Chamberlain, "Reconstruction in South Carolina," *Atlantic Monthly* 87 (April 1901): 473–84; see also Chamberlain, "Limitations of Freedom," address before Northwestern University at Commencement, June 11, 1896 (pamphlet at South Caroliniana Library); Chamberlain, "Present Phases of Our So-Called Negro Problem," *Charleston News and Courier*, August 1, 1904; Chamberlain to J. C. Hemphill, June 30, 1904, Hemphill Papers, David M. Rubenstein Rare Book and Manuscript Library, Duke University, Durham, N.C.

NO TEARS OF PENITENCE
Religion, Gender, and the Aesthetic of the Lost Cause in the 1876 Hampton Campaign
(2001)

W. Scott Poole

Wade Hampton rode again on October 16, 1876. Flanked by the "rifle clubs" of the South Carolina Democratic Party, Hampton entered the midland town of Sumter. Riding to the center of town, he moved toward the speaker's stand where a black-robed figure, bound in chains, stood solemnly before the crowd of farmers and townspeople. As the gubernatorial hopeful assumed his position on the platform, the dark figure flung off its chains and cast aside its robe of mourning, revealing a beautiful young woman, both white of skin and dressed in gauzy white, a tiara on her head and beribboned with the words "SOUTH CAROLINA." The journalist Alfred Brockenbrough Williams witnessed the crowd erupt at this performance, many of the men weeping openly. Late into the night, frenzied horsemen rode throughout the town crying out "HAMPTON OR HELL!"[1]

The phenomenon of "Hampton Days," in which sleepy town squares became theaters for the performance of social anxieties and political hopes, played a crucial and generally neglected role in the 1876 campaign that led to the state's "Redemption." The historiography of this era has tended to focus on the ways in which conservative whites used fraud and violence to overturn Reconstruction regimes. Whether telling the story of redemption as heroic narrative or as a dream deferred, the emphasis has largely centered on votes—whether bought, coerced, or fraudulently counted.

This paper does not challenge the role of coercion and violence in this and other Redemption contests. Instead, it argues that a close reading of the "Hampton Day" celebrations brings us into a tightly woven network of memory and myth concerned with race, gender, and public representations of cultural ideology. An analysis of these types of discourse moves us beyond traditional

Reconstruction historiography dominated by political and social history. "Hampton Day" celebrations reveal that Carolina conservatives understood how power functioned best within a context of cultural consensus and thus shaped public spectacles that drew on the anxieties and obsessions of white South Carolinians.

Hampton's cavalcade began at Anderson and proceeded on to the mountain towns of Walhalla and Pickens, then to Greenville. Engineering the largest spectacle thus far in the campaign, mounted Rifle Club members greeted Hampton with a torchlight procession, a parade of "citizens afoot and in wagons," and the "Robert E. Lee Fire Company," all dressed in the "Red Shirts" that had come to symbolize devotion to Hampton and support for white conservatism.[2] The Greenville *Enterprise and Mountaineer* noted that "cheer after cheer" greeted Hampton both at the torchlight procession and at the rally the following day on the grounds of Furman University.[3]

The study of such public spectacles opens a window on the much debated, often misused concept of southern conservatism. The attempt to define the conservatism of the South has tended to focus on commitment to the proslavery ideology, the planter's relationship to bourgeois capitalism, or the southern intellectual's European influences. Future attempts at understanding this complex tradition must take into account the private and public rituals of southern conservatism, which, during the years following the Civil War, drew on the aesthetic of the Lost Cause. The Lost Cause aesthetic had as its underpinnings a mythic system, fashioned around the notions of a people fallen under oppression freed by a "holy warrior" and the thematic concerns of evangelical religion. Conjoined with the celebration of Confederate identity, southern conservatism existed as a set of meditative images and symbolic acts, an aesthetic representation of a mythic worldview.

The Lost Cause aesthetic placed at its narrative center the deeds of its heroes. In the eyes of conservative whites, Hampton himself embodied both the ideology of the Lost Cause and the memory of the Lost Eden, the Old South. The response of the crowds as he took the speakers' platform suggests that he became the central vehicle of Lost Cause values for participants in the aptly named "Hampton Days." A contemporary observer described the former cavalryman in language redolent of the medieval chivalric tradition, evangelical fervor, and the cloying magnolia-scent of the southern elite; "Hampton . . . simple unaffected gentleman, dauntless warrior of South Carolina, loving and reverencing his God, his cause and his commonwealth to the last recess of his clean soul."[4] Describing him from a different ideological line of vision, a hostile *Atlantic Monthly* article described Hampton as having "strikingly crystallized all the arrogant old plantation qualities of the South."[5]

The memory of the first struggle against northern domination reverberated throughout Hampton's triumphal march. Reporting on the parade and mass meeting in Laurens on September 20, Greenville's *Enterprise and Mountaineer* suggested that the marches and thunderous cannonades "reminds of the times of 1861 when the boys were starting off for the army."[6] This suggests the notion of "mythic time" that historian Mircea Eliade has used as an interpretive tool across cultures and religious systems—the notion that ritual acts invoke mythic heroes who perform their works over and again in a cycle of eternal repetition. How else can we understand the South's enduring claim that, despite clear empirical evidence, it has "never surrendered?" The unwillingness of the southern mind to accept defeat, to accept the reality of the new world that the Yankee had made, constituted what Eliade calls a "refusal of history."[7]

This mythopoeic interpretation points us towards another area in which the aesthetic of the Lost Cause acquired a representative form; the rhetoric of evangelical religion. Evangelicalism provided much of the necessary ritual for the Hampton celebrations. Prayer and the singing of hymns created a revivalist atmosphere in the mass meetings that occurred along Hampton's route. Moreover the central dogmatic and subjective experience of southern evangelicalism—personal conversion—easily elided into the category of the political. In a particularly evocative phrase Democrats termed the decision—often made under duress—by white Republicans to throw their support to Hampton as "crossing Jordan."[8]

The fashioning of a Lost Cause aesthetic reveals to us much more than the values of Carolina conservatives. Anxieties concerning race and gender also make their appearance in the Hampton campaign. Fears of enslavement by a rapacious federal government fevered the brains of Carolinians during the campaign. The *Enterprise and Mountaineer* editorialized that "marshal law threatened" as a "near probability."[9] Subjugation seemed already a reality to many white South Carolinians. John Leland, imprisoned during the South Carolina Ku Klux Klan trials, wrote that he felt "irresistibly impelled to publish to the world that the grand old State, declared to be free sovereign and independent a hundred years ago is now deposed, gagged and trampled in the dust." [10]

The corruption of the Reconstruction government and the threat it posed to South Carolina's liberty seemed to crystallize in Governor Chamberlain's October 6 decision to ban the Democratic "Rifle Clubs." The fear of social anarchy had steadily increased with armed clashes between blacks and whites in the "Hamburg riot." Perhaps most ominous of all, a riot in Aiken County occurred after ten black men allegedly attacked and robbed "a respectable white woman, in her own home . . . her husband at work in the fields."[11] The deepest anxieties of Carolina conservatives seemed to be occurring even as they sought to reassert political hegemony. The image of "a lawless mob" debauching the wealth and honor of the state in the legislature coalesced with white womanhood being assaulted in the home by emancipated slaves while her husband did the work of the fields that, to the mind of white Carolinians, properly belonged to her attackers.

White conservatives responded to the situation with a gendered language. The grammar of resistance employed by Carolina conservatives tended to construct the state as a woman to be honored while at the same time she represented an honored woman who had been outraged. J. P. Thomas of Charlotte's "Carolina Military Institute," speaking at a Democratic meeting at Edgefield on August 10, 1876, called upon the "sturdy yeoman" take a stand for "Our Mother, South Carolina."[12] John Leland, who dedicated his memoirs "TO THE WOMEN OF SOUTH CAROLINA," used gendered language to describe the allegedly illegitimate Reconstruction government: "Her [South Carolina's] Seat," he wrote, "has been usurped by a brazen-faced strumpet."[13]

The use of gendered images drew both on antebellum constructs of the "Southern Lady" and the increased importance this image had acquired in the mythology of the Lost Cause. Fearing that the Old South had gone down in flames because of moral failure, southern women became the repository of southern virtue.[14] Furthermore Gaines Foster has suggested that southern women averted an extreme anxiety over the loss of southern manhood by welcoming home their Confederate husbands, sons, and brothers with enthusiasm and by declining to use the interstices of war and Reconstruction to challenge the patriarchy of the Old South. The construction of pure Confederate womanhood thus became an essential element of the Lost Cause mythology.[15]

Hampton's cavalcade had passed from acclamation to acclamation in a triumphal tour of the upcountry. The small town of Ninety-Six featured a mounted procession of Confederate veterans two miles long. In town after town "Hampton Days" became a stylized round of mounted torchlight processions, fireworks, cannonade, and speeches by Hampton and lesser Confederate lights calling for resistance and unity among white conservatives. Women played a prominent part in the organization of these campaign stops, but the Republican administration's proscription of the Democratic Rifle Clubs seems to have thrust them into an even more crucial role. Williams wrote the tableaux performed at Sumter on October 7, the incident described at the beginning of this paper, as the "unspoken answer" to the disbanding of the clubs. Williams writes of the sheer emotive power of a chain-enwrapped figure, wearing clothes of mourning transformed into "a radiant young woman in pure white . . . tall and stately, head uplifted and eyes shining like stars." The audience itself was transformed into a congregation of overwrought men and women, whooping rebel yells and willing to do anything to insure the defeat of radicalism.[16]

The most elaborate of the Hampton tableaux occurred at Aiken on October 20. Tensions in this region ran high for several months prior to the campaign. The Hamburg Massacre had occurred in Aiken County in July 1876. Just three days before Hampton's arrival, President Grant issued a proclamation supporting Chamberlain's earlier disbanding of the Democratic Rifle Clubs. White conservative fears coalesced in this region, expressing themselves in rich symbolism.[17] Aiken celebrated southern womanhood by building a platform for the most beautiful young women of the town, decorating it with mottoes such as "Truth," "Virtue," and "Honor." Hampton, welcomed with a legend that read "HAMPTON—WE LOVE, WELCOME AND HONOR HIM," spoke of his "SORROW that the people of Aiken had been subjected to so much undeserved persecution." Seeming to play his assigned role in this unfolding drama, Governor Chamberlain decided to arrest a number of suspected Klan members on the day of Hampton's arrival."[18]

The bodies of white women, displayed as public texts for the celebration of the Lost Cause, combined with a set of racial images to create a powerful ideological construction. Surprisingly, particularly considering the heightened racial tensions in Aiken County, images of emancipated blacks as sexual threats to white southern womanhood played little or no role in the campaign. Hampton's own policy towards South Carolina blacks seems to have been to "fuse" with black Republican leaders by offering them the spoils of patronage.[19] This effort made an appearance in the campaign iconography. The garlanded speaker's platform at Aiken featured what A. B. Williams described as "a large cartoon" that "represented the palmetto [tree] prostrate and white and Negro men working together to lift it and the caption 'Where there's life, there's hope.'"[20] This symbolism suggests a very different southern symbolic world from the one that would emerge in the 1890s. Black men in 1876 are still seen as faithful retainers with a role to play in the southern social order.

The rhetoric of the campaign contrasts the "Southern Lady" sharply with African American female supporters of the Republicans. Constructed by the Democrats as unruly, disorderly, and violent, black women become a symbol of Radical Republicanism in its most horrifying aspects. One of the chief charges leveled against "scalawag" Franklin J. Moses concerned his alleged "dancing with mulatto prostitutes." Williams writes that Moses "flaunting his vice" helped move Carolinians from the "habit of submission" to "burning anger and craving for combat."[21] In this image, black female sexuality served as a trope for the subversion of the political system, a danger to republican liberty.

Images of disorderly South Carolina black women abound in Williams's account of the Hampton campaign. Williams describes a Republican meeting of black South Carolinians on Edisto Island as having a "very ugly mood." Black Republican women seemed "especially maddened and foaming at the mouth."

Williams suggested that the faithfulness of the black male to their former masters faced a twin threat from the "Union Leagues" and the "taunts and abuse of incensed women." African American women greeted the final "Hampton Day" in Charleston with jeers and catcalls described as "frantic."[22]

The image of unruly black women embodying political and sexual disorder literally embodied the forces of social chaos for conservatives. South Carolina matron Florella Meynardie's 1879 novel *Amy Oakley; or The Reign of the Carpetbagger* contains a fictional representation of a Hampton Day celebration in Charleston in which Carolina black women shout "bitter, insulting invectives" at the Red Shirts and are described as "female demons." Significantly the language of religious impurity fills Meynardie's descriptions of the "polluted wretches" who made up the jeering crowd. Moreover they are depicted as destroyers of their households with much of their demonic venom directed at their husbands. In one of Meynardie's scenes an unruly black woman describes how she would rip the Red Shirt off of her "old man, dat varmit Ike" if he chose to don it and "cross Jordan." Thus for Meynardie, and for many South Carolina conservatives, black women came to represent religious miasma. Unruly black women represented *the* destruction of distinction, boundary, balance, and limitation—quite important terms in the grammar of conservatism. Unruly black women rejected the patriarchal prerogative of their husbands—disorderly behavior that seeped into the political realm as they rejected the patriarchal prerogative of Hampton. In this Cathedral of the Lost Cause, jeering, taunting, politically aware African American women became the Gargoyles leering from the shadows.[23]

Hampton's victory seemed to vindicate Confederate memory. "In all the grief and mourning of our stricken state over her 'Lost Cause,'" Leland wrote, "there are found no tears of penitence."[24] South Carolina had not renounced her stand for at least a cultural Confederate nationhood. A sense of Confederate identity continued to play an important role in the southern conservative ethos, informing defiance to interference by the national government. Confederate memory seemed more sacred than ever as conservative Carolinians saw in the Hampton campaign and victory a resurgence and vindication of the southern cause. Post-Reconstruction South Carolina was, Leland asserted, "Re-baptized with the blood of some of her bravest and best."[25]

Recent interpretations of the Lost Cause have seen it as a non-sectional memorial to sacrifice and death and a celebration of white Americanism which, at the beginning of the twentieth century, could "easily enter the mainstream of national memory."[26] The 1876 campaign challenges this interpretation. Hampton's campaign suggests that South Carolinians publicly celebrated the Lost Cause as a direct challenge to the federal and Republican-dominated state governments. In public spectacle Carolina Democrats fashioned the campaign around the aesthetic of the Lost Cause. Fearing domination and the loss of republican liberties, conservatives turned towards a gendered language of resistance. The bodies of southern women became public texts, exhibiting in sometimes elaborate tableaux the anxieties and hopes of Carolina conservatives. The language of the Lost Cause, before it became inscribed on stone monuments, functioned as a grammar of resistance and a vehicle for the southern conservative ethos.

NOTES

1. Alfred Brockenbrough Williams, "Eyewitness Reporter . . . on Events of 1876 in S.C., 8 August 1926–February, 1927," scrapbook of newspaper articles, bound volume, South Caroliniana Library, University of South Carolina.
2. Williams, "Hampton Campaign Opens at Anderson," in "Eyewitness Reporter."
3. "Hurrah for Greenville," Greenville *Enterprise and Mountaineer*, September 13, 1876.
4. Ibid.
5. "The Political Condition of South Carolina," *Atlantic Monthly* 39 (February 1877): 183.
6. *Enterprise and Mountaineer*, September 20, 1876.
7. Mircea Eliade, *The Myth of the Eternal Return, or Cosmos and History* (Princeton, N.J.: Princeton University Press, 1954), 3.
8. Williams, "October '76, Critical for Carolina," in "Eyewitness Reporter."
9. "Marshal Law Threatened," *Enterprise and Mountaineer*, September 26, 1876.
10. John Leland, *A Voice From South Carolina* (Charleston, S.C.: Walker, Evans and Cogswell Press, 1879), 13.
11. Williams, "Ellenton Riots Diffuse Dread and Horror," in "Eyewitness Reporter."
12. "Opening of the Democratic Campaign," *Edgefield Advertiser*, August 10, 1876.
13. Leland, *A Voice from South Carolina*, 13.
14. Charles R. Wilson, *Baptized in Blood: The Religion of the Lost Cause, 1865–1920* (Athens: University of Georgia Press, 1980), 46.
15. Gaines Foster, *Ghosts of the Confederacy* (Oxford, U.K.: Oxford University Press, 1987), 28–29.
16. Williams, "October '76, Critical for Carolina," in "Eyewitness Reporter."
17. Richard Zuczek, *State of Rebellion: Reconstruction in South Carolina* (Columbia, S.C.: University of South Carolina Press, 1997), 178–79.
18. Williams, "October '76 ," in "Eyewitness Reporter."
19. Hampton M. Jarrell, *Wade Hampton and the Negro* (Columbia: University of South Carolina Press, 1949), 123.
20. Williams, "Edgefield Redshirt Shot from Ambush," in "Eyewitness Reporter."
21. Williams, "Straight Out Fight Gets Under Way," in "Eyewitness Reporter."
22. Williams, "Hampton Party Reaches Charleston," in "Eyewitness Reporter."
23. Florella Meynardie, *Amy Oakley; or The Reign of the Carpetbagger* (Charleston, S.C.: Walker, Evans and Cogswell, 1879), 130–31.
24. Leland, *A Voice from South Carolina*, 16.
25. Ibid., 184.
26. Kirk Savage, *Standing Soldiers, Kneeling Slaves* (Princeton, N.J.: Princeton University Press, 1997), 155.

CONTRIBUTORS

PATRICIA DORA BONNIN, One of the few contributions to be derived from an undergraduate paper, Bonnin's honors thesis at the University of Illinois at Urbana-Champaign, "The Loved Ones at Home: The Problem of Relief for the Families of Confederate Soldiers," served as background for a more specific study on the experiences of the families of Confederate veterans in South Carolina.

ORVILLE VERNON BURTON, a professor of history at Clemson University, received his PhD from Princeton University in 1976 and studied under James McPherson. Burton has a prolific publishing record, notably including *In My Father's House Are Many Mansions: Family and Community in Edgefield, South Carolina* (1985) and *The Age of Lincoln* (2007), both nominated for the Pulitzer Prize.

DAN T. CARTER, a Florence, South Carolina, native, received his doctorate from the University of North Carolina, Chapel Hill, in 1967 and is one of his generation's most noted historians. Among his many publications, two of note are his 1985 work, *When the War Was Over: The Failure of Self-Reconstruction in the South, 1865–1867*, and his nationally acclaimed 2000 study, *The Politics of Rage: George Wallace, the Origins of the New Conservatism, and the Transformation of American Politics*.

JOHN B. EDMUNDS JR., professor of history at the University of South Carolina, Upstate, in Spartanburg, focused on South Carolina political history during the Civil War and is best known for *Francis W. Pickens and the Politics of Destruction* (1986). He won the Spartanburg County Commission for Higher Education Distinguished Service Award in 2007.

RICHARD M. GERGEL, a Columbia, South Carolina, native, was a 1979 Duke University Law School graduate who practiced law for many years in Columbia before being appointed to the U.S. District Court for South Carolina in 2010.

FRITZ HAMER earned a doctorate from the University of South Carolina (1998) while serving as curator of history at the South Carolina State Museum. He has written on a variety of topics as well as curating many exhibitions. His published works include, in 2005, *Charleston Reborn: A Southern City, Its Navy Yard, and World War II*.

ROGER P. LEEMHUIS, an Erie, Pennsylvania, native, received his doctorate from the University of Wisconsin in 1970 and spent his academic career at Clemson University. He published his dissertation in 1979 as *James L. Orr and the Sectional Conflict*.

CHRISTOPHER MEKOW, a Citadel graduate student when his article was published, worked for the National Park Service in Charleston and transferred to another park outside of South Carolina.

ROBERT J. MOORE began teaching at Columbia College in the 1960s after receiving his doctorate at Boston University. He has written a variety of articles on southern history and retired from Columbia College.

JAMES WELCH PATTON. Raised in Tennessee, graduated from Vanderbilt University, Patton received a Ph.D. at the University of North Carolina, Chapel Hill. Patton taught at Converse College in Spartanburg, South Carolina, and served as president of the South Carolina Historical Association. From 1942 to 1948, Professor Patton headed the History Department at North Carolina State University in Raleigh. He then returned to Chapel Hill as director of the Southern Historical Collection from 1948 to 1967. Patton was president of the Southern Historical Association in 1956, and among his works are *The Women of the Confederacy* (1936) and *Unionism and Reconstruction in Tennessee, 1860–1869* (1966).

W. SCOTT POOLE, an Anderson County, South Carolina, native, earned his doctorate at the University of Mississippi and has been on the history faculty at the College of Charleston for several years. Among his publications is his 2004 study, *Never Surrender: Confederate Memory and Conservatism in the South Carolina Upcountry*.

LEWIE REECE. With a doctorate from Bowling Green State University (2001), Reece has taught at Anderson University since 2002. His focus of study is on Civil War and Reconstruction history.

LOUIS B. TOWLES, a Charleston native, has a doctorate from the University of South Carolina and has taught at Southern Wesleyan University since the 1970s. His major work to date has been an edited 1996 work, *A World Turned Upside Down: The Palmers of South Santee*.

Contributers

FRANK VANDIVER worked as a staff historian for the U.S. Army in World War II. After the war he earned his doctorate from Tulane and became one of the top Civil War historians of his generation. He published twenty-four books, including *Ploughshares into Swords: Josiah Gorgas and the Confederate Ordnance* (1952).

AUSTIN L. VENABLE, history professor at Winthrop University in Rock Hill, South Carolina, served as chairman of the South Carolina Historical Commission. He specialized in political history and in particular was known for work on the Democratic Party and the secession movement. Venable published *The Public Career of William Lowndes Yancey* (1963), among other scholarly works.

LOWRY P. WARE took a Ph.D. at the University of South Carolina in 1956, and his dissertation, "The Academic Career of William E. Dodd," on America's first ambassador to Nazi Germany, is still cited by scholars. Ware served on the South Carolina Historical Commission and at the South Carolina State Archives. He specialized in local and state history and, in 2011, he received the Distinguished Service Award from Erskine College in Due West, South Carolina.

JOHN HAROLD WOLFE, a Pickens, South Carolina, native, earned his doctorate at the University of North Carolina, Chapel Hill, and taught in several schools, ending his career at Winthrop College. His published works included *Jeffersonian Democracy in South Carolina* (1940).

INDEX

Abbott, Martin, 6; "The Freedmen's Bureau and Its Carolina Critics," 152–60
abolitionism, 14, 54
Advertiser (Edgefield, S.C.), 161, 162, 164, 167
Advertiser (Montgomery, Ala.), 48
Adviser (Mobile, Ala.), 43
African Americans: allied with Democrats, 247; Black Codes, 149, 198, 243; Boyce's attitudes toward, 59; on Charleston police force, 177–79; death rates of, 174; education of, 155–56, 184–92; and equality, 175, 191, 192, 227–28, 250; in Hampton's campaign, 246; Hampton's policies towards, 269; Hampton's views of, 244, 249, 253n25; image of Lincoln among, 22–23; and Insurrection Panic of 1865, 146; and Johnson, 224; and Lincoln, 19, 25; loyalty to Republican Party, 247; in militia, 166; movement away from plantations, 145; political leaders, 1, 6, 161–69, 176–77, 233, 245; political organization of, 165; predictions of extinction of, 147; and representation, 215; soldiers, 162–63, 165, 166–67, 168; testimony by, 214; theological perspective, 15; as Unionists, 18; views of, 142–43; visibility of, 145; whites' support of rights of, 19; women, images of, 269–70. *See also* freedmen; slavery; slaves; vote, African American
The Age of Hate (Milton), 224
"The Age of Lincoln: Then and Now" (Burton), 11–26
Agnew, Samuel, 144
Aiken, S.C., 269
Alabama, Hayne in, 37
alcohol, 38–39
America, meaning of, 16
American Bible Society, 46

American Emigrant Company (AEC), 148
American Missionary Association, 187
American Tract Society, 46
The America Play (Parks), 21–22
amnesty, oath of, 212
Amy Oakley (Meynardie), 270
Anderson, Robert, 30, 31
J. R. Anderson and Company, 99
Andrew Johnson and Reconstruction (McKitrick), 226–27
"Andrew Johnson: The Second Swing 'Round the Circle" (Moore), 221–29
Andrews, Sidney, 142, 211, 214, 215
Anthony, Susan B., 26
Appomattox, 17
arming, of South Carolina, 96–97
armory, 97, 101–2n20
arms, purchase of, 99
arms companies, 97
army, federal, 179, 256
Army of Northern Virginia, 71
Army of Tennessee, 5, 79–88, 92nn29,30
Arnim, Frank, 164
Arrington, Sam L. L., 50
Arsenal Academy, 38
Arthur, B. F., 40
Ashmore, John, 120, 122
associations, 96
Atlanta Campaign, 80
Atlantic Monthly, 266
"Attorney General Isaac W. Hayne and the South Carolina Executive Council of 1862" (Ware), 36–42

Babbitt, Benjamin B., 186, 187
ballot-box stuffing, 204–5, 207n10, 250
Bancroft, George, 223
Bank of Charleston, 96
Barnes, Henry, 164
Barnwell, Robert W., 36, 112n16

Index

Barnwell County, 162
Bartlett v. Strickland, 21
Bate, William, 83, 85, 87, 88, 91n24
Bates, Lewis, 11
Battery Wagner, 71, 72–73, 74
bazaars, 109
Beale, Howard K., 224–25
Beard, Charles, 224
Beard, Mary, 224
Beauregard, P. G. T., 19, 32, 73, 74, 75
Bennet, Lerone, 22
Black, Hugo, 91n25
Black Codes, 149, 198, 243
Black Over White (Holt), 161
Black Reconstruction, 164
Bleckley, Mrs. Sylvester, 111
blockade, 39, 130
blood, 17
Bobo, S., 99
bombardment: of Charleston, 5, 67, 73–76; defined, 68
"The Bombardment of Charleston, 1863–1864: Union General Quincy Gillmore, the Targeting of Civilians, and the Ethics of Modern War" (Mekow), 67–78
Bonham, M. L., 28, 116, 118, 119, 131
Bonnin, Patricia Dora, 6; "The Problem of Relief for the Families of Confederate Soldiers in South Carolina," 126–34
Bonum, John, 162, 164
Booth, John Wilkes, 25
Boston, Joseph D., 189
Boston Advertiser, 213
Bouey, Harrison N., 168
bounties, for deserters, 119
Bower, Claude G., 223–24
Boyce, James P., 212
Boyce, William W., 5, 143; and conduct of Civil War, 57; conservatism of, 56; and desire for social stability, 55; positions on postwar issues, 59–60; in U.S. Congress, 53–54
Boyles, A. J., 121
Bragg, Braxton, 79–80, 81, 82, 84, 86, 119
Breckenridge Democracy, 43
Breckinridge, John, 121
Brewer, Fisk P., 186, 187
Brock, W. R., 228
Brooks, Mack, 166

Brown, Henry, 75
Brown, J. E., 31, 58
Brown, John Calvin, 88
Buchanan, James, 27, 29, 30, 31, 32, 37
Buck, Irving A., 82
Burgess, John W., 262
Burton, Orville Vernon, 3, 4, 6; "The Age of Lincoln: Then and Now," 11–26; "Edgefield Reconstruction: Political Black Leaders" (Burton), 161–72
Butler, Matthew Culbraith, 168, 199, 200, 240, 245, 249, 253n25, 255

Cain, Lawrence, 164, 165, 167, 168
Caldwell, John, 38
Calhoun, John C., 40, 45, 54
California, 60n2
Campbell, John A., 121
Canby, R. H., 175
Cannon, Joseph, 147
capitalism, 13–14, 115
Cardozo, Francis L., 188, 189, 236
Caribbean islands, 142, 143
Carmichael, Stokely, 22
carpetbaggers, 254. *See also* Chamberlain
Carrol, John, 168
Carter, Dan T., 3, 6; "Fateful Legacy: White Southerners and the Dilemma of Emancipation," 137–51
cash crops, 128–29, 141
Cassville, 86
Catholic sisters, 110
Cauthen, Charles Edward, 2
Census (1860), 127–28
Census (1870), 134, 162, 164, 166, 168
Chamberlain, Daniel, 2, 7, 180, 190, 232, 235, 246; accomplishments of, 255; arrest of Klan members, 269; background of, 254–55; banning of Rifle Clubs, 267; and Charleston businessmen, 255; decline and fall of, 257–60; interpretation of Reconstruction, 261, 262; lack of support for, 258, 259–60; meeting with Hayes, 260; on ouster, 261; resignation of, 248, 249, 254; views on race and states' rights, 261–62. *See also* government, dual
Chamberlain, Joshua, 17
Chambers, Pitt, 87

278

Index

Chandler, William, 234
Charleston, S.C.: after Civil War, 174; army in, 179, 256; bombardment of, 5, 67, 73–76; civilians killed in, 78n40; Confederate evacuation of, 75; crime in, 178; mayors of, 175, 176; occupation of, 174; occupation of State House, 256; police force, 6, 174, 175, 177–79, 180, 181n18; politics in, 180; possible burning of, 41; race relations in, 180; refugees from, 116
Charleston Arsenal, 98
Charleston Daily Courier, 40, 96
Charleston Mercury, 31, 67, 73, 74, 182n26
Charleston Zouave Cadets, 96–97
Chattanooga, Tenn., 79
Cheatham, Benjamin, 83, 85, 88
Chesnut, James, 37, 39, 55
Chesnut, Mary Boykin, 27–28, 29, 30, 37
Cheves, Langdon, 110
Chicago Tribune, 21, 213
Chronicle and Sentinel (Augusta, Ga.), 140, 147
chronology, 17
church, 15; and African American political leaders, 169. See also religion
Citadel, 38
citizenship, 137
civilians, bombardment of, 5, 67, 68, 73–76
civil rights, 235, 236–37. *See also* vote, African American; voting rights
Civil Rights Act, 21
civil rights movement, 2, 3–4
Civil War: and contingency, 18–19; hatred in, 17–18; nature of, 17, 70; paying for, 26; purpose of, for Lincoln, 16; separation of Reconstruction from, 16; South Carolina's centrality to, 1
Clark, George W., 177
Clayton, General, 88
Cleburne, Patrick, 80, 83, 85, 87, 88
Clinton, Bill, 12
Clinton, George W., 189, 192
Colbert, Steven, 21
Colbert Report, 21
Columbia, S.C., 75
committees of safety, 96, 101n12
Commonwealth (Marion, Ala.), 44, 49
Compromise of 1850, 53
Compromise of 1877, 200
Confederate Congress, and Sumter, 32

Confederate Ordnance Department, 100
Confederation (Montgomery, Ala.), 44, 47–48
congressional peace party, 57
Connor, James, 244
conscription, 117, 121, 128
conservatism, southern, 266–71
constitution, South Carolina (1790), 214
constitution, South Carolina (1865), 6, 216–17. *See also* Constitutional Convention (1865)
constitution, South Carolina (1868), 198–99, 217, 219n32. *See also* Constitutional Convention (1868)
Constitution, U.S., 12, 223, 226–27
Constitutional Convention (1865), 209–18, 233
Constitutional Convention (1868), 162, 164, 198, 209, 234
Cooper and Pond, 97
cooperationists, 53, 56
Corley, Simeon, 6, 230, 233–35, 237
cotton, 128–29, 140–41
Couch, W. T., 139
Courier (Charleston, S.C.), 153
courts, civil, 175
Cox, John, 227
Cox, LaWanda, 227
crime, in Charleston, 178
The Critical Year (Beale), 224–25
crops, 115, 128–29, 130, 140–41
crop yields, 117, 122
Cuba, 61n10
Culbreath, Luke, 127
Cullen, Joseph, 70
Cummings, Anson W., 186, 187
Cunningham, John, 95, 179
currency, 129, 130
Cushing, Caleb, 29

Dahlgren, John, 72, 75
Daily Intelligencer (Atlanta), 146
Daily News (Charleston, S.C.), 158
Daily Republican, 182n26
Daily Standard (North Carolina), 147
Daily Union Herald, 235
Dallas Gazette, 49
Dalton, Georgia, 80, 81–82, 84, 85, 86
"Dalton and the Rebirth of the Army of Tennessee " (Towles), 79–92
Dart, William M., 189, 190
Davis, Alfred Ward Grayson, 117, 119
Davis, Charles Lewis, 117–18, 121

Index

Davis, Jefferson, 11, 23, 31, 57, 58, 59
Davis, Newton, 83, 84, 86, 90n16, 92n29
Dawson, Francis W., 233, 255–56
Dearing, Spencer, 164
Deas, Edmund, 233
Deas, Elias Henry, 144
Deas, Zachariah, 81, 83
DeBow, J. D. B., 140, 143
Declaration of Independence, 12, 25
defense, of South Carolina, 95–100; and impressment of slaves, 39, 116, 118, 121, 123n13
De Forest, John W., 157
Delaney, Martin R., 167
Delarge, Robert C., 167
democracy: and 1865 constitution, 216–17; and capitalism, 13–14; lack of in South Carolina, 210; under Reconstruction, 230
Democratic Party: and Edgefield Plan, 199–201; expansionist foreign policy, 54; factions of, 55; and League of United Southerners, 47–48; plans to break up, 44, 45, 51; schism in, 205; and *The Tragic Era*, 223
Democrats: African Americans allied with, 247; assumption of power by, 197; in Charleston, 175–76; intimidation and coercion by, 206n6, 207n10, 233 (*See also* elections); persecution of Republicans by, 236
depression (1873), 185
depression (1877), 201
deserters, 114, 118–21, 122, 128, 131
Devens, Charles, 231, 232
Diary of Gideon Wells (Wells), 222
disloyalty, 38
dissatisfaction, 115–16, 122, 131
"Dissatisfaction and Desertion in Greenville District, South Carolina, 1860–1865" (Marrs), 114–25
distillation, 38–39
disunionism, 46, 115. *See also* League of United Southerners; secession
Donald, David, 227
Douglas, Stephen A., 23, 24–25, 55
Drago, Edmund, 247
DuBois, W. E. B., 185, 227
Dunning, William A., 2, 3, 221, 222, 262
Durham, John J., 190

economy: in campaign of 1866, 225; changing, 26; depression (1873), 185; depression (1877), 201; financial instability of South, 129–30; and interpretation of Reconstruction, 224
Edgefield Advertiser, 126
Edgefield District, 6; African American political leaders in, 161–69; relief for families of soldiers in, 126–34
Edgefield Plan, 199–201
"Edgefield Reconstruction: Political Black Leaders" (Burton), 161–72
Edmunds, John Jr., 4; "Francis W. Pickens and the War Begins," 27–35
education, 155–56, 184–92, 250
Eichelberger, Philip A., 165
election laws, 207n13
elections (1860), 28, 43, 56, 95, 242
elections (1864), 57
elections (1867), 244
elections (1868), 60, 234, 244, 245, 249
elections (1872), 167–68
elections (1874), 168
elections (1876), 2, 200, 240, 249, 256, 265; disputed results of, 256; Hampton Days, 265–66, 268, 270; violence and intimidation in, 199–201, 203, 246, 247, 265. *See also* Chamberlain, Daniel; Hampton, Wade III
elections (1878), 202–3, 204–5, 208n20
elections (1880), 234
Eliade, Mircea, 267
Ellenton riots, 247
Elliott, Robert Brown, 162, 164, 235, 258
Emancipation, 6, 12–13, 61n7, 141–47
Enforcement Acts, 232, 245
Enquirer (Georgia), 147
Enquirer (Richmond, Va.), 44, 49
Enterprise and Mountaineer (Greenville, S.C.), 266, 267
equality, 24, 175, 191, 192, 227–28, 230, 237, 250
equipment, supplying of, 104–9
The Era of Reconstruction, 1865–1877 (Stampp), 228
ethics, in war, 67–76
Evarts, William M., 260
Exchange Bank of Columbia, 38, 96
Executive Council, 39–40, 41, 130, 132
extortion, 133. *See also* speculation

Index

fairs, 109
The Farmer, 148
farmers, 147; conscription of, 117; desertion by, 119; desire for freedom from government, 114–15, 117; dissatisfaction of, 122; support for secession, 114; survival of, 116–17
Farrow, John, 212
"Fateful Legacy: White Southerners and the Dilemma of Emancipation" (Carter), 137–51
feminism, and race, 25–26
The Field and Fireside, 140
Fifteenth Amendment, 138, 234
Finney, Charles Grandison, 14
Fischer, David Hackett, 13
Florida, 100
Foner, Eric, 1, 3
Foote, Henry S., 57, 59
Forced Into Glory (Bennet), 23
Ford, Lacy K. Jr., 2, 114
Forrest, Addison, 166
forts, in Charleston Harbor, 29–32. *See also* Moultrie, Fort; Sumter, Fort
Foster, Captain, 119
Foster, Gaines, 268
Foster, William, 69
Fourteenth Amendment, 138
Fox, Henry J., 186, 187, 189
"Francis W. Pickens and the War Begins" (Edmunds), 27–35
fraud, 205
freedmen: and citizenship, 137; conditions of, 146–47; distribution of land to, 153; education for, 155–56, 184–92; Freedmen's Bureau, 152–60, 175, 243; and Insurrection Panic of 1865, 146; Loyalty League, 246, 252n12; movement away from plantations, 145; and northern racial attitudes, 138; views of, 142–43; visibility of, 145; and vote, 156 (See also vote, African American). *See also* African Americans
Freedmen's Bureau, 152–60, 175, 243
freedom, 12, 13
Freehling, William, 2
Fremont, John C., 18
French, Samuel G., 85, 88
Frost, Edward, 215
furloughs, 84

Gaillard, J. H., 119
Gardener, John, 164, 165–66
Garfield, James, 234
Gary, Martin Witherspoon, 199, 202, 240, 245, 249, 255
Gaston, Paul, 140
Gates, Henry Louis Jr., 22
Geddes, C. W., 39
gender, 267–70
Gergel, Richard M., 6; "Wade Hampton and the Rise of One-Party Racial Orthodoxy in South Carolina," 197–208
Gettys, James, 115
Gillmore, Quincy Adams, 69, 71–76
Gist, William H., 37, 39, 56, 95
Godkin, E. L., 256
God's will, 15, 26
Gonzales, A. J., 97
goods: distribution of for relief, 130; impressment of, 116, 117
Gordon, John B., 17
Gorgas, Josiah, 100
government, dual, 256, 257–58
"Governor Chamberlain and the End of Reconstruction" (Moore), 254–64
Graham, David, 168
Graham, William A., 57
Grant, Ulysses S., 69–71, 73, 75, 77n16, 185, 245, 269
Grayson, William, 142
Great Southern Party, 48–49
Greeley, Horace, 44, 167
Greener, Richard T., 186, 187–88, 189, 190, 192
Greenville District: deserters in, 118–21, 122; dissatisfaction in, 115–18, 122; secession in, 114
Greenville Ladies' Association in Aid of the Volunteers of the Confederate Army, 106–7, 109–10
Gregg, Maxcy, 55
guns, 97, 99
Gunter, C. G., 50
Gunter, William A., 50

Hagerman, Edward, 69
Hamburg Massacre, 255, 267, 269
Hamer, Fritz, 6–7; "Wade Hampton: Conflicted Leader of the Conservative Democracy?," 240–53

Index

Hammond, James H., 37, 55
Hampton (family), 241
Hampton, Frank, 242
Hampton, Preston, 242
Hampton, Wade III, 6–7, 188, 232; background of, 241; call for secession, 242; campaign for governor, 246–47; campaign to destroy Republican Party, 202–4; claim of black support, 248; declared governor, 234; descriptions of, 266; and disputed election, 256; and Edgefield Plan, 199–200; efforts to control African American vote, 198; eroding influence of, 250; evaluation of career, 251; finances of, 242–43, 246; hold on state politics, 200–201; inaugurated governor, 248; leadership of, 197, 248, 250; meeting with Hayes, 260; military service of, 242; nomination of, 255; overtures to African Americans, 240–41; and persecution of Republicans, 236, 257; policy toward African Americans, 269; reaction to Republicans, 243–44; reputation of, 206n1; strategy of force without violence, 256; support for, 257, 258; support of Klan violence, 245; use of patronage, 201, 269; views of African Americans, 244, 249, 253n25
Hampton Days, 265–66, 268, 270
Hardee, William J., 85, 88, 91n24, 92n30
Harlee, W. W., 37, 39, 133
Harper's Weekly, 213, 217
Harris, Augustus, 166
Harris, Carey, 166
Harris, David Jr., 166
Harris, David Sr., 164, 165, 166, 167, 168
Haskell, A. C., 260
Haskew, Michael, 70
hatred, in Civil War, 17–18
Hayes, Rutherford B., 7, 200, 208n20, 232, 234, 236, 249, 259–60
Hayne, Isaac W., 5, 31–32, 36–41
Hayne, Robert Y., 37
Hazard Powder Company, 99
Heard, William H., 187, 189, 191
Hendricks, Henry W., 178
heroes, idea of, 23–24
Higginson, Thomas Wentworth, 163
higher law principle, 54

Hindman, Thomas C., 80, 82, 83, 85
Hine, William, 177
history, rewriting, 21
History of the United States (Bancroft), 223
Holden, William, 147
Hollis, Daniel Walker, 184, 185
Holt, Thomas, 3, 161
honor, 15, 16
Hood, John Bell, 18, 83, 85, 86, 87, 88, 91nn24,25, 92nn29,30
hospitals, 108–10, 112n16
Howard, O. O., 156
Howe, Julia Ward, 26
Huger, Alfred, 212
Huiet, G. D., 127
Hunter, David M., 163
Hurtado v. California, 20

Illinois, racism in, 20, 24
immigrants, and vote, 216
immigration craze of 1865, 147–48
impressment: of goods, 116, 117; of slaves, 39, 116, 118, 121, 123n13
industrialism, 140
inflation, 39
Inglis, John A., 212
Insurrection Panic of 1865, 146

Jacksonian Democracy, 175
Jarman, Robert A., 83
Jillson, Justus K., 186
Johnson, Andrew, 6, 11, 59, 138, 139, 153, 210, 211; attitudes toward African Americans, 227–28; criticisms of, 225, 226–27; decline of reputation of, 225; defense of, 222–26; election of, 221; image of, 221–22; position on Constitution, 223, 226–27; reputation of, 228
Johnson, Herschel V., 57
Johnson, John, 72, 77n28
Johnston, Joseph E., 18, 19, 81, 82–85, 86, 87, 88, 91n24, 92nn29,30, 119
joint military committee, 96
Jomini, Antoine, 69
Jones, Jesse, 168
Jones, Walter Raleigh, 190
Jordan, Laylon Wayne, 6; "The New Regime: Race, Politics, and Police in Reconstruction Charleston, 1865–1875" (Jordan), 173–83

282

Index

Kansas Nebraska Act, 54
Keitt, Lawrence, 47, 55, 56
Keller, J. A., 119
Kennedy, John, 202, 203
King, J. Floyd, 148–49
Know-Nothings, 43, 47, 51, 61n11
Ku Klux Klan, 1, 189, 231, 245–46, 267

labor, 140, 142–46, 149, 153–55
LaBorde, Maximillian, 184
The Law of Nations (Vattel), 68
laziness, freedmen accused of, 144
League of United Southerners, 5; attacks on, 45–46; and charges of disunion, 51; constitution of, 43, 47, 50–51; defense of, 46–47; newspapers and, 43–44, 47–50; purpose of, 47; and southern rights party, 48–49
Lee, Robert E., 17, 23, 92n30; on Hood, 19, 87, 88; last words, 22; at Petersburg, 70; response to desertion, 121; surrender of, 71
Lee, Samuel J., 163, 164, 165
Leemhuis, Roger P., 5; "William W. Boyce: A Leader of the Southern Peace Movement," 53–63
Leland, John, 267, 268, 270
Liberia, 187, 191
liberty, 12, 13–14
Liberty and Freedom (Fischer), 13
Lincoln, Abraham, 4, 138; on African Americans, 25; assassination of, 11, 19, 25; debates with Douglas, 24–25; election of, 56, 114, 242; identification with, 22; image of among African Americans, 22–23; inauguration of, 32; interest in, 12; legacy of, 12; on liberty, 13; racism of, 23; and religion, 15; scholarship on, 12; as southerner, 15–16, 17; and Sumter, 32; as theologian, 14; thinking about race, 19; and voting rights, 25
Litwack, Leon, 23
Lochrane, O. A., 141, 149
Lomask, Milton, 225–26
London Illustrated News, 73
Longstreet, James, 19
Looking for Lincoln (documentary), 22
Looney, David, 99
looting, 130

Loring, William W., 85
Lost Cause aesthetic, 266–67, 270–71
loyalty, 38
Loyalty League, 246, 252n12
Lucas and Strohecker, 97
Lynch, John, 188

Mackey, Albert, 232
Mackey, Edmund, 6, 230, 232–33, 248
Mackey, Thomas Jefferson, 232, 258, 259
magistrates, African American, 167
Mahan, Dennis Hart, 69
Mail (Montgomery, Ala.), 47, 50–51
Main, William, 186, 187
Manigault, Arthur, 80–81, 83, 84, 85–86, 88, 89n6
Manigault, Edward, 98
manufacturers, 117
Marrs, Aaron W., 5; "Dissatisfaction and Desertion in Greenville District, South Carolina, 1860–1865," 114–25
Martens, G. F. von, 68, 74
martial law, 38
Matthews, Stanley, 260
McCord, David J., 110
McCord, Louisa Susanna, 110
McGowan, Samuel, 212
McGuire, Captain, 120
McKinlay, Whitefield, 191–92
McKinley, William, 191
McKitrick, Eric, 138, 226–27
McPherson, James, 11, 18, 228
McQueen, John, 55, 56
Meacham, Jon, 12
Mekow, Christopher A., 5; "The Bombardment of Charleston, 1863–1864: Union General Quincy Gillmore, the Targeting of Civilians, and the Ethics of Modern War," 67–78
Melton, C. D., 120, 188, 189
Melton, Samuel, 6, 230, 235–36
Memminger, Christopher G., 36
Methodist Quarterly Review, 186
Meynardie, Florella, 270
Midwest (region), racism in, 20, 24, 25
Miles, William Porcher, 57
military conventions, 67–76
militia, 96, 166
millennialism, 14

Miller, Thomas E., 189, 191, 192, 233
Milton, George Fort, 224
Minutemen, 242
Mishaw, Paul J., 190
Missionary Ridge, 79, 89n6
Mississippi Plan, 199–201
Missouri Compromise, 60n2
Mitchell, J. C. B., 50
Mixson, W. J., 257
"Mobilization for Secession in Greenville District" (Gettys), 115
Mobley, John, 164
moderation, 27, 197, 200
modernization, 140, 147
Montgomery Convention, 31, 32
Moore, Robert J., 6, 7; "Andrew Johnson: The Second Swing 'Round the Circle," 221–29; "Governor Chamberlain and the End of Reconstruction," 254–64
Morgan, George, 168
Morris, John M., 190
Morris Island, 71, 74, 75
Mosby, John, 19
Moses, F. J. Jr., 40, 212, 269
Moses, F. J. Sr., 188, 189, 258
Moultrie, Fort, 30, 33n16
movement, freedom of, 145
munitions, purchase of, 97
Murray, George W., 189, 191

Nash, Beverly, 249
National American (Atlanta), 43
National Association for the Advancement of Colored People (NAACP), 191
National Democrats, 55
navy, Union, 72, 75
Neely, Mark, 23
Neves, Alsey Albert, 117
New Haven Arms Company, 97
"The New Regime: Race, Politics, and Police in Reconstruction Charleston, 1865–1875" (Jordan), 173–83
News and Courier (Charleston, S.C.), 179, 182n26, 232, 255, 256
New South, 140
newspapers: demise of, 182n26; and League of United Southerners, 43–44, 47–50; as representative of popular opinion, 115. *See also individual newspapers*
New York Herald, 68, 71

New York Times, 33, 211, 213
New York Tribune, 210, 211, 213
Norris, Tilda, 258
North (region): racism in, 138, 141, 149; Reconstruction in, 20
North of Slavery (Litwack), 23
Northrop, Lucius, 232, 233
"No Tears of Penitence: Religion, Gender, and the Aesthetic of the Lost Cause in the 1876 Hampton Campaign" (Poole), 265–71
Novick, Peter, 2, 4
Nullification Convention, 37
nuns, 110
nurses, 110

Obama, Barack, 21, 25, 26
opportunism, 237
Ordnance Board, 5, 97–100
Origins of Southern Radicalism (Ford), 114
Orr, James L., 36, 55, 57, 154, 212

Palmer, John S., 80, 82, 84, 86
Parks, Suzan-Lori, 21–22
parties, political: balance of power of, 200, 201–2, 203–4; national parties, 51. *See also* Democratic Party; Democrats; Republican Party; Republicans
paternalism, 131–33, 251
Patriot and Mountaineer (Greenville, S.C.), 115
Patriotic Gore (Wilson), 18
patronage, 201, 269
Patton, James Welch, 5; "The Work of Soldiers' Aid Societies in South Carolina during the Civil War," 104–13
peace, 57–59
Pemberton, John C., 69
Perry, Benjamin F., 59, 114, 115, 211, 212, 213, 216, 219n32
Petersburg, Va., 70–71, 73, 75, 77n16
Phillips, Wendell, 13
Pickens, Francis W., 4–5, 36, 38, 99, 100, 212; blunders by, 29, 30; change in views, 27–28; and Executive Council, 37, 40; and forts in Charleston Harbor, 29–32; powers of, 28; problems faced by, 28–29; return to South Carolina, 27; view of relief, 133

Pierce, Franklin, 55
Pillsbury, Gilbert, 175, 178, 179
plantation system, attacks on, 140
Plessy v. Ferguson, 16
police, night, 38
police force, Charleston, 6, 174, 175, 177–79, 180
Political Textbook for 1860, 44
politicians, African American. *See under* African Americans
politicians, white: effects of on African Americans, 198. *See also individual politicians*
politics: balance of party strength, 200, 201–2, 203–4; oligarchy, 209–10, 214; violence and intimidation in, 199, 203, 204 (*See also* elections (1876)). *See also* Democratic Party; Democrats; Republican Party; Republicans; vote; voting
politics, biracial, 197
Politics, Principle, and Prejudice, 1865–1866 (Cox and Cox), 227
The Politics of Reconstruction (Donald), 227
Polk, Leonidas, 84, 85, 86, 88, 92n30
Poole, W. Scott, 7; "No Tears of Penitence: Religion, Gender, and the Aesthetic of the Lost Cause in the 1876 Hampton Campaign," 265–71
Poppenheim, Mary B., 105
Porcher, John Stoney, 87
Porter, David Dixon, 69
Porter's Rifle, 99
Preston, John, 120, 121
"The Problem of Relief for the Families of Confederate Soldiers in South Carolina" (Bonnin), 126–34
Proceedings of the South Carolina Historical Association, 3
profiteers, 39
prohibition, 38–39
Pryor, Roger, 47
Purcell, Isaac L., 189

Rable, George, 132, 133
race: anxieties about, 267; and feminism, 25–26
race relations, 154, 157, 180, 197, 228
racial equilibrium, 53
racism: in Midwest, 20, 24, 25; in North, 138, 141, 149

Radical Reconstruction, 138
Radicals, 138, 174, 198, 209, 211, 213, 226, 245
railroad stations, wayside homes at, 110–11
Rainey, Joseph H., 1
Randolph, Benjamin, 245
Ravenel, William Henry, 31
Read, John B., 99
"A Reconsideration: The University of South Carolina during Reconstruction (Roper), 184–94
Reconstruction, 3, 138; Chamberlain's interpretation of, 261, 262; and contingency, 19; corruption in, 267; as democracy, 230; doomed by Johnson, 222; Dunning school of, 2, 206n1, 221, 262; economic interpretation of, 224; end of, 16, 254; historiography of, 227; and meaning of America, 16; in North, 20; as part of Civil War, 18; scholarship on, 2–4; separation of from Civil War, 16; in South Carolina, 1; and South's resistance to change, 138–39
Reconstruction, Black, 164
Redeemers/Redemption, 190, 197, 199, 201, 265. *See also* Hampton, Wade, III
Red Shirts, 180, 188, 190, 231, 246, 247, 248, 249, 251, 255, 258
Reece, Lewie, 6; "Righteous Lives: A Comparative Study of the South Carolina Scalawag Leadership during Reconstruction," 230–39
reform movements, 14
relief, 6; and deserters, 128; distribution of goods, 130; lack of guidelines for, 127; left to states, 116; motivations for, 128, 130–31; and paternalism, 131–33; Pickens's view of, 133; practicality of, 128
religion, 14, 15, 26, 110, 270
representation, at 1865 convention, 214–15
Republican Party, 56; in 1878 elections, 203; African Americans' loyalty to, 247; destruction of, 197, 199, 202–3, 205; organization of, 233–34; persecution of, 236; rule in South Carolina, 60; and universal male suffrage, 198. *See also* Republicans
Republicans: after 1876 election, 256–57; in Charleston, 176; purge of, 201–2, 207n10, 249, 257; white Republicans, 164, 230, 232–33 (*See also* scalawags).

Republicans (*continued*)
    See also Radicals
Resaca, 91n24
resources, of Confederacy, 104
retreat, 86
Review, 140
Reynolds, John, 162
Rhett, Robert Barnwell, 28, 31, 43, 55
Rhodes, James Ford, 221, 222
rice-field workers, 255
Rifle Clubs, 182n24, 267, 268, 269
"Righteous Lives: A Comparative Study of the South Carolina Scalawag Leadership during Reconstruction" (Reece), 230–39
rights, southern, 49–50. *See also* League of United Southerners
Ripley, R. S., 101n20, 102n20
Rise of American Civilization (Beard and Beard), 224
Rivers, Prince R., 162–63, 164, 165
Rivers, William J., 188
Roberts, T. N., 186, 187
Rocky Face, 80, 81
Roosevelt, Theodore, 191–92
Root, Truman, 164
Roper, John Herbert, 6; "A Reconsideration: The University of South Carolina during Reconstruction, 184–94
Roper Hospital, 110
Royall, Margaret Shaw, 225
Ruffin, Edmund, 43, 47

salt, 39, 130
Saltus, Thaddeus, 190
Samuels, Henry, 23
Saville, Julie, 3
Saxton, Rufus, 152–53, 156
scalawags, 6, 230–37, 269
Schenck, David, 144
Schirmer, Jacob, 182nn26,27
Schouler, James, 222
Scott, Cornelius C., 189, 190, 192
Scott, Robert K., 156, 158, 245
secession: cooperationists, 53, 56; in Greenville District, 114; and plans to break up Democratic Party, 44; preparation for, 95; right of, 45; separate secession, 53, 56

Secession Convention, 29–30, 36, 40
secessionists, election of, 149
Sellmer, Charles, 72
Sentinel (Raleigh, N.C.), 140
Serrell, Edward, 72
Settle, Thomas, 141
Seward, William, 11, 211
sexuality, black female, 269
Shakespeare, William, 12
Sherman, William T., 19, 69, 75, 76, 85, 86, 87, 91n24
Shinall, James, 165–66
shortages, 39, 115, 116, 117, 129, 130
Shrewsbury, George, 178
Sickles, Daniel, 174–75
siege: defined, 67–68; of Petersburg, 70–71, 73, 75; of Vicksburg, 69–70, 73
Simkins, Andrew, 168
Simkins, Augustus, 168
Simkins, Francis Butler, 2, 184
Simkins, Paris, 168
Simmons, Limus, 168
Simms, William Gilmore, 178
Sinclair, William, 187, 191, 192
Sinha, Manisha, 2
Sisters of Our Lady of Mercy, 110
Slaughter, James S., 43, 44–45, 51
slave insurrections, 38
slavery: at 1865 convention, 213–14; Boyce on, 54; and millennialism, 14
slaves: beliefs about, 144; impressment of, 39, 116, 118, 121, 123n13. *See also* African Americans; freedmen
Smalls, Robert, 1, 19, 233, 236
Smith, A. M., 99
Smith, Owen L. W., 186, 187, 189, 191
Smith, Robert L., 189
Smythe, Mrs. Augustine T., 105
snowball fights, 83–84, 90n16
Social Darwinism, 261
social history, 2, 3–4
soldiers, African American, 162–63, 165, 166–67, 168
soldiers, Confederate: aid societies, 5, 90n12, 104–11, 112n16; relief for families of, 126–34
South (region): divisions in, 139; immigration craze of 1865, 147–48; intellectual changes in, 139–41; Lincoln's understanding of, 16; treatment of, 138

Index

South (Richmond, Va.), 47
South Carolina: attitude toward outcome of Civil War, 210–11; centrality to Civil War, 1; defense of, 39, 95–100, 116, 118, 121, 123n13; distrust of, 210–11; scholarship on, 2; self-interest of, 36
South Carolina, University of. *See* South Carolina College
South Carolina Arsenal, 98
South Carolina College, 39; alumni, 190; closure of, 188; curriculum, 185, 186; faculty, 186–89; finances, 185; graduates, 189–90, 191; Law School, 188; library, 188; publicists, 186–87; scholars, 186, 187; scholarship program, 185–86; student behavior, 185, 188; students, 189–90; vandalism at, 188, 189
"The South Carolina Constitution of 1865 as a Democratic Document" (Wolfe), 209–20
South Carolina During Reconstruction (Simkins and Woody), 184
South Carolina Historical Association (SCHA), 3, 7
South Carolina Ordnance Board, 5, 97–100
"The South Carolina Ordnance Board, 1860–1861" (Vandiver), 95–103
South Carolina Railroad, 38
Southern Cultivator, 143, 147
Southern Enterprise (Greenville, S.C.), 115, 116, 119
southerners, white: attachment to Union, 48; attitudes towards Freedmen's Bureau agents, 157–58; Lincoln, 15–16, 17; reaction to black militiamen, 167; as Unionists, 18; worthiness of citizenship, 137
Southern Historical Association, 3
Southern Rights Democrats, 55
southern rights party, 48, 51
Southern Times (Columbia, S.C.), 37
speculation, 39, 116, 129, 130
Stampp, Kenneth M., 228
Standard (Raleigh, N.C.), 139
Stanton, Edwin, 11
Stanton, Elizabeth Cady, 26
Star of the West, 30
Stephens, Alexander, 58
Stevens, Thaddeus, 227

Stevenson, Carter, 82, 83, 84, 85, 91n24
Stewart, Alexander, 83, 85, 87, 88, 91n24, 92n30
Stewart, Pickens, 166
Stewart, T. McCants, 187, 190, 191, 192
Stone, Lucy, 26
Stoneman's raiders, 106
Stowe, Harriet Beecher, 13
strikes, 255
Strohecker, H. F., 97
Stryker, Lloyd Paul, 223, 225
suffrage: at 1865 convention, 212–13; restrictions on, 202. *See also* vote, African American; voting rights
suffrage, universal male, 198
suffrage, white manhood, 216
Summary of the Law of Nations (Martens), 68
Sumter, Fort, 19, 29, 30, 31, 37, 74; attack on, 32–33; guns in, 77n28; operations against, 71; surrender of, 36
supplies, obtaining, 117–18, 122
supply lines, in siege of Petersburg, 70–71

Tappan, George L., 225
Taveau, Augustin, 144
tax assessment, 216
taxes, and dual government, 257–58
Taylor, Mrs. Thomas, 105, 111
Taylor, Thomas, 86, 88
Tennant, Ned, 164, 168
terrorism, 18, 26, 200, 205
testimony, by African Americans, 214
thievery, freedmen accused of, 144–45
Thirteenth Amendment, 137
Thomas, J. P., 268
Tilden, Samuel J., 259
Tillman, Ben, 249, 250, 251, 253n25
Tillman, George D., 215, 249
Timrod, Henry, 42n49
Toombs, Robert, 31, 32
Topdog/Underdog (Parks), 22
total war, 5
Towles, Louis P., 5; "Dalton and the Rebirth of the Army of Tennessee," 79–92
town, trips to, 145
Townsend, Alonzo G., 189, 190
The Tragic Era (Bower), 223–24
transportation, public, 175

Index

trench warfare, 86
Trescot, William, 29, 30, 156
Tucker, William F., 81
Twenty-Fourth Alabama, 80–81

Uncle Tom's Cabin (Stowe), 13
Urquhart, Kenneth, 69

Vandiver, Frank, 3, 5; "The South Carolina Ordnance Board, 1860–1861," 95–103
Vattel, Emmerich de, 68, 70, 71
Vaughan, Alfred J., 83
Venable, Austin L., 5; "William L. Yancey and the League of United Southerners," 43–52
Vicksburg, Mississippi, 69–70, 73
Vietnam war, 23
villains, 23–24
violence, racial, 182n23
Vizetelli, Frank, 73
volunteer companies, 96
vote, African American, 156, 215, 233; at 1865 convention, 214; control of, 198, 199–201, 203, 244 (*See also* elections (1876)); neutralization of, 197, 202, 204–5; Perry on, 219n32; restrictions on, 202, 250
vote, and immigrants, 216
vote, meaningful, 12–13
voting: ballot-box stuffing, 204–5, 207n10, 250; supervision of, 202, 204, 234–35
voting rights, 25, 213, 232, 234, 236. *See also* suffrage; vote, African American
Voting Rights Act, 21

Waccamaw Light Artillery, 96
"Wade Hampton and the Rise of One-Party Racial Orthodoxy in South Carolina" (Gergel), 197–208
"Wade Hampton: Conflicted Leader of the Conservative Democracy?" (Hamer), 240–53
Wagener, John, 176, 177
Walker, Irvine, 84, 88
Walker, William H. T., 83, 84, 85, 88
Wallace, Alexander, 6, 230, 231–32
Wallace, R. M., 233
Wallace, William H., 248
Walthall, Edward, 83, 84, 85, 88
war, rules of, 67–76

war, total, 5, 76
Wardlaw, D. L., 212
Ware, Lowry P., 5; "Attorney General Isaac W. Hayne and the South Carolina Executive Council of 1862," 36–42
war weariness, 5
Washington, Booker T., 191
Washington States, 44
Watson, John, 57
wayside homes, 110–11
wealth, disparity in, 13
weapons, obtaining, 97–100
Weldon, Archie, 168
Wells, Gideon, 222
West Point, 69
Wheeler, Joseph, 84
Whipper, William J., 180
whites, southern. *See* southerners, white
white supremacy, 261
will, God's, 15, 26
Willard, A. J., 258
"William L. Yancey and the League of United Southerners" (Venable), 43–52
Williams, Alfred Brockenbrough, 265, 269–70
Williams, George, 231
Williams, Lou Falkner, 3
"William W. Boyce: A Leader of the Southern Peace Movement" (Leemhuis), 53–63
Wilson, Barentine, 166
Wilson, Edmund, 18
Wilson, Woodrow, 192
Winston, Robert Watson, 223
Winyah Association of 1860, 96
Wise, Henry, 19
Wolfe, John Harold, 6; "The South Carolina Constitution of 1865 as a Democratic Document," 209–20
women, southern, 5; African American women, images of, 269–70; and anxiety about gender, 267–70; appeals to government, 132; bread riots, 130; government's attitude toward, 132–33; in Hampton Days, 268–69; and paternalism, 132; and soldiers' aid societies, 90n12, 105–11, 112n16; Southern Lady construct, 268, 269; work in hospitals, 109–10
Woody, Robert Hilliard, 2, 184

Wooley, John, 164, 167
"The Work of Soldiers' Aid Societies in South Carolina during the Civil War" (Patton), 104–13
World (New York), 146
Wright, J. J., 258
Wright, Jonathan, 249

Yancey, William Lowndes, 5; abandonment of League of United Southerners, 50; at Bethel Church, 43, 44, 45; charged as disunionist, 43–44, 51; defense of League of United Southerners, 46–47; letter to Slaughter, 43, 44–45; philosophy of, 45; speech at Benton, 45; speech at Montgomery, 46
Yeadon, Richard, 40
yeoman. *See* farmers
York County, 231
Young Ladies' Hospital Association, 110–11

Zuczek, Richard, 3